PASSION AND ACT

HMV: 964-8160
868-9696
Cmbridge
Tower: 876-3377
247-5900

Passion and Action

THE EMOTIONS
IN SEVENTEENTH-CENTURY PHILOSOPHY

SUSAN JAMES

CLARENDON PRESS · OXFORD

OXFORD

UNIVERSITY PRESS

Great Clarendon Street, Oxford OX2 6DP

Oxford University Press is a department of the University of Oxford.
It furthers the University's objective of excellence in research, scholarship,
and education by publishing worldwide in

Oxford New York

Athens Auckland Bangkok Bogotá Buenos Aires Calcutta
Cape Town Chennai Dar es Salaam Delhi Florence Hong Kong Istanbul
Karachi Kuala Lumpur Madrid Melbourne Mexico City Mumbai
Nairobi Paris São Paulo Singapore Taipei Tokyo Toronto Warsaw

with associated companies in Berlin Ibadan

Oxford is a registered trade mark of Oxford University Press
in the UK and in certain other countries

Published in the United States
by Oxford University Press Inc., New York

British Library Cataloguing in Publication Data

Data available

Library of Congress Cataloging in Publication Data

James, Susan.
Passion and action : the emotions in seventeenth-century
philosophy / Susan James.
Includes bibliographical references.
1. Emotions (Philosophy)   2. Philosophy, Modern—17th century.
I. Title.
B815.J36   1997   128'37'09032—dc21   97–11501
ISBN 0–19–823674–3
ISBN 0–19–825013–4 (Pbk.)

Printed in Great Britain
on acid-free paper by
Biddles Ltd.
Guildford and King's Lynn

Acknowledgements

Much of this book was written during the academic year 1994–5, when I held a British Academy/Leverhulme Trust Senior Research Fellowship. I was only able to take up this award because Girton College and the Faculty of Philosophy at the University of Cambridge generously granted me leave from teaching, and I am deeply grateful to all four of these institutions for the incomparable gift of time. I am also indebted to the Humanities Research Centre and the Research School of Social Sciences of the Australian National University for a Fellowship which I held during the summer of 1994. Their thoughtful hospitality, wide-ranging seminar programmes, and beautiful campus created a memorable working environment, and gave me an opportunity to concentrate uninterruptedly on the relations between passion and action in seventeenth-century philosophy. Among the people in Canberra who were kind enough to discuss aspects of my research, I would especially like to thank Moira Gatens, who helped me to see how Spinoza's ideas apply to us, and Philip Pettit, whose zest for philosophy is infectious.

Several parts of this book were given as seminar papers and I have received a wealth of comments from a variety of audiences, some of them outstandingly helpful. Members of the Open University Seventeenth-Century Seminar and the Cambridge Philosophy Faculty Seminar were characteristically constructive about the material in Chapter 7. Sections of Part IV were shaped by incisive questions from the Cambridge University Social and Political Theory Seminar, the Philosophy Department Seminar at the University of Essex, and the contributors to a conference on early-modern theories of the passions organized by Stephen Gaukroger at the University of Sydney. In addition, several people generously made time to read the penultimate draft of the book, and I have benefited from points raised by Stephen Gaukroger (on Part III), Joel Kupperman, Tom Sorell, and the anonymous reader for the Oxford University Press. I am deeply indebted to James Tully, whose many learned and imaginative suggestions I have done my best to incorporate. Most of all, however, I am grateful to Quentin Skinner who provided references, read two successive drafts with great care, and discussed them with sustaining optimism along the way.

My colleagues in the Philosophy Faculty at Cambridge, and the Fellows of Girton College, have been an unfailing support, and I hope they know how much I appreciate their solidarity. Individual friends and colleagues have helped me in more ways than I can say, but I would particularly like to thank Michael Ayers and Daniel Garber, who unwittingly gave me the idea of this book when they commissioned me to write an essay about the passions, and Martin Hollis, who aided the project in its early stages. Betsy Brown, Desmond Clarke, John Cottingham, Sarah Hutton, Neil Kenny, and Michael Moriarty have all shared with me their knowledge of seventeenth-century philosophy and culture, and it has been a pleasure to learn from them. And for conversations about the passions, encouragement, and friendship, my thanks and gratitude go to Teresa Brennan, Raymond Geuss, Ross Harrison, Marilyn Strathern, and Sylvana Tomaselli. Straying further across the indistinct boundary between professional and private life, I want finally to thank my children, Olivia Skinner and Marcus Skinner, for their tact and cheerfulness, and also for keeping me half-way sane.

On a more practical note, my life has been enormously eased by Norberto de Sousa, who checked the references to primary texts and prepared the primary bibliography, by Tizzy Nannini, the Administrative Secretary of the Cambridge Philosophy Faculty, by the staff of the Rare Books Room of Cambridge University Library, and by Tarba Gill, who helped to make domestic life run more smoothly. I also wish to thank the Cambridge University Library for permission to reproduce Plate 1, the Musée du Louvre for allowing me to reproduce Plates 2 and 3, and the Warburg Institute, who generously granted me permission to reproduce Plate 4.

Rowena Anketell brought her enviable meticulousness to bear on the typescript of this book which was much improved by her copy-editing, and at a slightly later stage, Philip Riley cast his eagle eye over the proofs. My thanks to them both. At the Oxford University Press I have had the benefit of Robert Ritter's patient editorial advice. It is, however, a particular pleasure to thank Peter Momtchiloff, whose calm and constructive suggestions have been a consistent source of encouragement.

S. J.

Contents

List of Plates

Note on the Text

As far as possible, I have referred to modern editions and translations of seventeenth-century texts that are comparatively easily available. For example, rather than citing the *Œuvres complètes* of Descartes edited by Adam and Tannery, I have generally quoted the English translations in *The Philosophical Writings of Descartes*, edited by Cottingham, Stoothoff, Murdoch, and Kenny. Occasionally I have departed from this practice. In writing about Malebranche I have sometimes used my own, rather literal renderings of *De la recherche de la vérité*, though in making them I have consulted the English translation by Lennon and Olscamp. This work, and the French edition in the *Œuvres complètes* edited by Robinet, are cited in the notes. Where there is no modern edition of a text I have referred either to the original edition, or to a subsequent seventeenth-century one. A few of the French works I discuss appeared in English shortly after they were published, and in one or two cases I have cited these contemporary translations.

In quoting from early-modern authors I have modernized spelling, punctuation, and capitalization.

I

Introduction: The Passions and Philosophy

In 1649 the Earl of Monmouth published an English translation of a popular French work by Jean François Senault entitled *The Use of the Passions*. Monmouth's Letter to the Reader includes a story about the Count of Gondomar, who, we are told, was wont to say, 'If you make a small inconsiderable present to any great man of the court, or to your mistress, you may do well to steer it in with some preamble, whereby to excuse the meanness, and make the fancy or workmanship thereof plead acceptance; marry, if you will present him or her with a thing of real value, as (for that it was he instanced in) with a bag of gold amounting to some three or four thousand pound, you need not use any circumlocutions, but bring it in, lay it down, and say, "Take it, there it is."' The thing itself will purchase its welcome.'[1] Nowadays, the place and analysis of the passions in seventeenth-century philosophy needs, perhaps, to be steered in with some preamble, since its value, unlike that of a bag of gold, has darkened with time and grown opaque. We tend to forget that philosophers of this era worked within an intellectual milieu in which the passions were regarded as an overbearing and inescapable element of human nature, liable to disrupt any civilized order, philosophy included, unless they were tamed, outwitted, overruled, or seduced.

The power and capriciousness of the emotions made them the subject of an array of testing problems that spread through the various branches of philosophy and could not be ignored. As Thomas Wright explained in *The Passions of the Mind in General*, first published in 1604, natural philosophy deals with 'the actions and operations of the passions'.[2] His view is confirmed by Edward Reynolds, the Bishop of Norwich whose 1640 *Treatise of the Passions and Faculties of the Soul of Man* was dedicated to the Princess Elizabeth of Bohemia with whom, a few years later, Descartes corresponded on the same subject. Natural philosophy, according to Reynolds, investigates the 'essential properties' of the passions, their 'ebbs and flows, springings and decays, the manner of their several impressions, the physical effects which are wrought by them, and the

---

[1] *Use of the Passions*, trans. Henry Earl of Monmouth (London, 1649), sig. A 3ᵛ–4ʳ. On Senault see A. Levi, *French Moralists: The Theory of the Passions 1585 to 1649* (Oxford, 1964), 213–24; P. Parker, 'Définir la passion: Corrélation et dynamique', *Seventeenth-Century French Studies*, 18 (1996), 49–58.
[2] (2nd edn., 1604), ed. W. W. Newbold (New York, 1986), 90.

like',[3] whereas the task of moral philosophy is to explain how these inordinate appetites can and must be bridled,[4] and how 'the indifference of them is altered into good or evil by virtue of the domination of right reason, or the violence of their own motions; what their ministry is in virtuous, and what their power and independence in irregular, actions; how they are raised, suppressed, slackened and governed according to the particular natures of those things which require their motion'.[5] Finally, according to some accounts, civil philosophy revealed 'how they may be wrought upon and impressed, and how, and on what occasion, it is fit to gather and fortify, and to slack and remit them; how to discover, or suppress, or nourish, or alter, or mix them, as may be most advantageous; what use may be made of each man's particular age, nature or propension; how to advance our just ends, upon the observance and the character of these, whom we are to deal withal'.[6] Though distinct, natural and moral philosophy are mutually supportive within this scheme, each enabling the other. It is moral philosophy that 'makes philosophers, and purifying their understanding, makes them capable of considering the wonders of nature'.[7] But a grasp of the passions as natural phenomena contributes to the ability to control and direct them, and this is in turn a prerequisite of fruitful reflection on moral and political questions. The substance of philosophy here encompasses the philosopher, whose own practice becomes a subject of reflection and enquiry.

The interest in the emotions that so pervades seventeenth-century philosophy is itself part of a broader preoccupation in early-modern European culture with the relations between knowledge and control, whether of the self or others.[8] The contribution of the passions to this theme is starkly portrayed in some of the advice books to princes written in this period,[9] and in a closely related genre of works which offer to teach 'the art to know men',[10] construed as

---

[3] *Treatise of the Passions and Faculties of the Soul of Man* (London, 1640), 41.

[4] Wright, *Passions of the Mind*, 90.   [5] Reynolds, *Treatise of the Passions*, 41.

[6] Ibid. 43. Reynolds cites Aristotle's *Politics* as his source for this division of the study of the passions. On changing strategies for dealing with the passions see A. O. Hirschman, *The Passions and the Interests: Political Arguments for Capitalism before its Triumph* (Princeton, 1977), esp. 12–35.

[7] Senault, *Use of the Passions*, sig. C 1ᵛ.

[8] Influential exponents of the view that the New Philosophy embodies a novel aspiration to control the natural world include C. Merchant, *The Death of Nature: Women, Ecology and the Scientific Revolution* (San Francisco, 1980); G. Lloyd, *The Man of Reason: 'Male' and 'Female' in Western Philosophy* (London, 1984), 10–17; E. Fox Keller, *Reflections on Gender and Science* (New Haven, 1985), 33–66; C. Taylor, *Sources of the Self* (Cambridge, 1989), 143–58. For a parallel concern with self-control see S. Greenblatt, *Renaissance Self-Fashioning from More to Shakespeare* (Chicago, 1980); M. Meyer, *Le Philosophe et les passions* (Paris, 1991).

[9] See e.g. François La Mothe le Vayer, *De l'instruction de Monseigneur le Dauphin*, in *Œuvres*, 2 vols. (2nd edn., Paris, 1656), i; Pierre Nicole, *De l'éducation d'un prince* (Paris, 1670).

[10] 'L'art de connaître les hommes'. Marin Cureau de la Chambre, *Les Caractères des passions* (Paris, 1648), Advis necessaire au lecteur; trans. J. Holden as *The Characters of the Passions* (London, 1650), sig. a 2ʳ. On Cureau de la Chambre see A. Darmon, *Le Corps immatériels: Esprits et images dans l'œuvre de Marin Cureau de la Chambre* (Paris, 1985).

including the art to know oneself. To rule successfully, a prince must be able to control his own passions so that he does not, for example, forfeit his subjects' loyalty by doing something unjust while he is in a rage. Equally, he must be able to read and manipulate the passions of those around him, to detect and play on the ambition, envy, fear, or esteem of courtiers, counsellors, and citizens. The extreme vulnerability of a prince makes these kinds of knowledge vital to his survival; but he also symbolizes the qualities needed in any figure of authority, and draws attention to the social relevance of the branch of moral philosophy that teaches the control of the passions. According to Senault, who was the General of the Oratory in Paris, ''Tis she that instructeth politicians and teacheth them by governing their passions to govern their kingdoms; 'tis she that makes fathers of families, and who managing their inclinations teacheth them to bring up their children and command their servants; so that she is to Philosophy the same as foundations are to buildings'.[11]

This wider concern with the importance of directing the passions is reflected in works aimed not specifically at rulers, but at a broader and predominantly male élite who occupy, or will occupy, positions of power.[12] Taking over an ancient tradition, these treatises tend to identify the acquisition of self-knowledge with the ability to master and manipulate passion, and to associate both with a process of cure. Therapy, self-control, and power over others are blended to produce an image of healthy dominion, the elements of which are clearly, if crudely, assembled and displayed by Senault's translator. In his Epistle Dedicatory, Senault himself emphasizes his therapeutic aspirations, praying that his book will help to make men virtuous by showing 'how passions are raised in them, how they rebel against reason, how they seduce the understanding and what sleights they use to enslave the will. . . . When I have known the malady, teach me the remedy that I may cure it.' Monmouth, however, combines this ideal with the will to power by adding an introductory verse:

> If to command and rule o're others be
> The thing desired above all worldly pelf,[13]
> How great a prince, how great a monarch's he
> Who govern can, who can command himself.
> If you unto so great a power aspire
> This book will teach how you may it acquire.[14]

Since the control of the emotions is held to be so transformative, and to unlock such potential, enquiry into this domain is not confined to philosophers.

---

[11] *Use of the Passions*, sig. C 1ᵛ.
[12] The works already cited by Wright, Senault, and Cureau de la Chambre are good examples of this genre.
[13] i.e. wealth or possessions.   [14] *Use of the Passions*, sig. B 6ʳ.

On the contrary, the passions are approached and analysed from many angles: by divines who explicate their place in God's creation and in the history of humankind; by Christian orators who work to arouse them in their congregations; by devout Christians who bridle them to attain quietness of mind; by magistrates who seek to understand their subjects; and by civil gentlemen who must avoid being 'so appassionate in affections that their company [is] to most men intolerable'.[15] Extending Thomas Wright's list, we could add poets, musicians, painters, playwrights, doctors, lawyers, and teachers, all of whom take a professional interest in the arousing and calming of the emotions and investigate them against a background of common assumptions and overlapping legacies. To appreciate the philosophical discussions of the passions that are the subject of this book, we therefore need first to be aware of some of the shared understandings that mould early-modern conceptions of what the passions are, and of the key questions to which they give rise. Immediately, and still more as we go on, we shall find that even the most deeply entrenched positions are contested; but they are nevertheless the comparatively still points around which debate turns and evolves.

Passions, then, are generally understood to be thoughts or states of the soul which represent things as good or evil for us, and are therefore seen as objects of inclination or aversion. When Eurydice sees the snake gliding towards her, she recognizes it as venomous and feels the passion of fear; when she meets Orpheus in the Underworld, she feels (perhaps among several emotions) the passion of love. Like other animals, humans are subject to passions because we are naturally disposed to assess our surroundings and our own states as advantageous or harmful, and because the evaluations we make are not merely a matter of realizing that things have certain properties, such as being dangerous or attractive, but are emotions which move us and guide our actions. Passions, it is agreed, have intrinsic physical manifestations which bridge emotion and action and are written on the body in facial expressions, blushings, trembling, and postures. Eurydice does not merely perceive the life-threatening snake, but is afraid, pales, and tries to avoid it; nor does she simply register that Orpheus has arrived, but yearns to be close to him. Most of our everyday experience is suffused with passions, which are a fundamental aspect of our nature, one of the basic ways in which we interpret the world around us. But while this rough characterization is generally agreed, the repertoire of the passions is a subject of greater controversy. Seventeenth-century thinkers inherit and elaborate a long and palimpsestic tradition of attempts to provide a comprehensive classification of key emotions in terms of which all variants can be analysed; and while they do not arrive at any final consensus, they work with and

---

[15] Wright, *Passions of the Mind*, 92.

sustain the view that certain passions are central. Love and fear, for example, are understood to be of this type, as are their opposites, hatred and hope.

why is it pervasive controversial?

The sense that these passions are of particular importance, so that no classification would be complete without them, derives in part from an informal understanding of the emotional responses that predominate. But this understanding is in turn shaped by various more-or-less articulated conceptions of what the passions are and how they operate, which are themselves expressed in different systems of classification. To opt for a classification is, to some extent, to opt for a broader theory of the passions, and any theory will be measured against existing typologies to see how well it deals with particular cases and configurations. One influential source in this dialectical process is the comparatively informal lists of passions compiled by Aristotle. In his *Rhetoric,* for example, Aristotle cites as passions anger and mildness, love and hatred, fear and confidence, shame and esteem, kindness and unkindness, pity and indignation, envy and emulation;[16] in *The Nicomachean Ethics* he picks out appetite, anger, fear, confidence, envy, joy, love, hatred, longing, emulation, pity, 'and in general the feelings that are accompanied by pleasure and pain'.[17] Some seventeenth-century authors continue to use and build on these enumerations;[18] but others, drawn by their philosophical ambitions to a more structured approach, are impressed by Cicero's claim (itself borrowed from the Greek Stoics) that there are only four fundamental passions: distress and pleasure (*aegritudo* and *laetitia*), and fear and desire (*metus* and *libido*).[19] Continuing the ancient habit of subjecting these cardinal passions to diverse interpretations, some authors held to Cicero's own view that each of these passions is a separate state with its own object.[20] *Laetitia* is a kind of delight at something believed to be a present good, *libido* is a desire for a supposed good. *Metus* is a feeling of fear at what is believed to be a threatening evil, *aegritudo* is distress at a present thing held to be evil. Other theorists, however, gave priority to desire and fear and interpreted joy and distress as states of mind resulting from them. For example, when we fail to get what we want, or are confronted by things we fear, we experience distress, whereas when we attain the objects of our desires, or avoid the things we are afraid of, we are delighted. In this latter and more economical interpretation, the objects of our desires are characterized

Aristotle's passions

Isn't the idea of threat implied in fear? what's to fear?

---

[16] In *The Complete Works of Aristotle*, ed. J. Barnes (Princeton, 1984), vol. ii, 1378ª31–1388ᵇ31. See also *On the Soul*, in *Complete Works*, ed. Barnes, vol. i, 403ª16–18.

[17] In *Complete Works*, ed. Barnes, vol. ii, 1105ᵇ21–3.

[18] See e.g. Thomas Hobbes, *The Elements of Law*, ed. F. Tönnies (2nd edn., London, 1969), 36–48. On the relation between Hobbes's classifications and those of Aristotle see G. B. Herbert, *Thomas Hobbes: The Unity of Science and Moral Wisdom* (Vancouver, 1989), 92 f.

[19] Cicero, *Tusculan Disputations*, trans. J. E. King (Harvard, Mass., 1927), iii. 24–5.

[20] e.g. Antoine Le Grand, *Man without Passions: Or the Wise Stoic according to the Sentiments of Seneca*, trans. G.R. (London, 1675), 77.

in a particular way, as bringing us delight or removing distress. Desire itself is thus seen as directed toward *laetitia* and away from *aegritudo*, as a disposition to seek out one state and avoid the other.[21]

Jostling up against the spare lines of this antique typology was a flamboyant Christian reworking of it—Augustine's Neoplatonic reinterpretation of the passions as species of love. In *The City of God* Augustine adhered to Cicero's view that there are four basic passions,[22] but he analysed each of them in terms of a single overarching prototype. '[A] love which strains after the possession of the loved object is desire; and the love which possesses and enjoys that object is joy. The love that shuns what opposes it is fear, while the love that feels that opposition when it happens is grief.'[23] By unifying the passions, Augustinianism answered, as we shall see, to a strong synthesizing urge within seventeenth-century philosophy, and exerted a decisive influence on thinking about the epistemological implications of the passions. In addition, the reduction it advocated acquired a place in theological disputes, as Senault indicates when he compares the failure of philosophers to appreciate the unity of the passions to the failure of pagans to recognize the unity of God. 'But as amongst the infidels every perfection of God hath passed for a several deity, so among the philosophers the different qualities of love have been taken for different passions.'[24] Augustine's position had to compete, however, with the more elaborate and compartmentalized typologies worked out within the Scholastic Aristotelian tradition, particularly with that of Thomas Aquinas, who identified no fewer than eleven basic passions. Aquinas's classification continued to be used in the seventeenth century, and provided the organizing categories for numerous treatises[25] which identify as the central passions love and hatred (*amor* and *odium*), desire and aversion (*desiderium* and *fuga*), sadness and joy (*dolor* and *delectatio*), hope and despair (*spes* and *desperatio*), fear and daring (*timor* and *audacia*), and finally anger (*ira*), the only passion that has no contrary.[26]

These overlapping maps of emotional possibility furnish an understanding of the range of the passions, distinguish central from marginal cases, and offer

---

[21] This interpretation derives from Stobaeus. See A. A. Long and D. N. Sedley, *The Hellenistic Philosophers* (Cambridge, 1987), 411. Seventeenth-cent. authors tended to condense his interpretation still further by combining *libido* and *metus* into one passion—desire—which is understood to include aversion. See Ch. 11, below.

[22] Ed. D. Knowles (Harmondsworth, 1972), 14. 6.   [23] Ibid. 14. 7.

[24] *Use of the Passions*, 26.

[25] See e.g. Nicolas Coeffeteau, *Tableau des passions humaines, de leurs causes et leurs effets* (Paris, 1630), 17 f; Jean Pierre Camus, *Traité des passions de l'âme*, in *Diversitez* (Paris, 1609–14), viii. 96 f; La Mothe le Vayer, *Morale du Prince*, 850; Cureau de la Chambre, *Characters of the Passions*, sig. a 5ʳ⁻ᵛ; Henry More, *An Account of Virtue or Dr. More's Abridgment of Morals put into English*, trans. E. Southwell (London, 1690), 850. On Coeffeteau, Camus, La Mothe le Vayer, and Cureau de la Chambre, see A. Levi, *French Moralists: The Theory of the Passions 1585–1649* (Oxford, 1964). On Henry More see Ch. 10, below.

[26] Aquinas, *Summa Theologiae*, ed. and trans. by the Dominican Fathers (London, 1964–80), 1a. 2ae. 23.

ways to get a grip on the infinite variety of particular emotions that people experience. At the same time, they delineate a central set of oppositions. Our affective life is portrayed as for the most part a susceptibility to pairs of positive and negative emotions, which are variously characterized in terms of inclination and aversion, and of unity and separation. It is worth noting at the outset that these typologies include, alongside states that are nowadays classed as emotions, the passion of desire. For early-modern writers, desire—and feelings such as love, anger, or sadness—are all states of a single kind, and all answer to the rough definition of passion outlined above. In holding this view, seventeenth-century theorists differ sharply from contemporary philosophers, who tend to distinguish desires and emotions.[27] Although early-modern writers recognize that the role played by desire in reasoning and action differs in certain ways from that played, for example, by fear, they regard the similarities between these states as more significant than the differences. Consequently, their category of passions does not coincide with modern interpretations of the category of emotion, from which desire is excluded. Some early-modern writers use the terms 'passion' and 'emotion' synonymously.[28] But in following their practice, we need to remember that their sense of these terms diverges from common contemporary usage.

The classificatory schemes just sketched are designed, in part, to specify key passions to which everyone is prone. But this attempt to grasp the range of human emotions is counterbalanced by a lively awareness of the vast variety and diversity of passions to be found in different individuals, sexes, classes, nationalities, professions, and so forth. At an individual level, our passionate dispositions begin to be moulded at the moment of conception, as Pierre Charron explained in some detail in his popular work *La Sagesse*, which first appeared in 1601 and was frequently reprinted during the first half of the century. Urging prospective fathers to take care that their seed is of the right temperature to engender children of a good physical and psychological temper, Charron offers them some practical advice. To beget male children that are sound, wise, and judicious, a man must not couple with a woman of vile, base, or dissolute condition, or of a naughty or vicious composition of body; he must abstain from copulation for seven or eight days; during this time he must nourish himself with wholesome victuals, more hot and dry than otherwise, and must use more than moderate exercise. When the great day arrives, he must apply himself

---

[27] The dominance of this view is reflected in textbooks—e.g. S. Guttenplan (ed.), *A Companion to the Philosophy of Mind* (Oxford, 1994)—and is particularly evident in contemporary discussions of agency, where desires, along with beliefs, are habitually singled out as the antecedents of action. E.g. see P. Pettit, *The Common Mind* (Oxford, 1993), 10–24; M. Hollis, *Models of Man* (Cambridge, 1977), 137–41; F. Jackson, 'Mental Causation', *Mind*, 105 (1996), 377–409. This assumption also underlies the theory of rational choice. See J. Elster (ed.), *Rational Choice* (Oxford, 1986), 12–16.

[28] See e.g. René Descartes, *The Passions of the Soul*, in *The Philosophical Writings of René Descartes*, ed. J. Cottingham *et al.* (Cambridge, 1984–91), i. 27–8, For further discussion of his view see Ch. 5, below.

passions can be imprinted

to his encounter on an empty stomach, and not near the monthly term of the woman but six or seven days before or as much afterward.[29] This regime, however, is only a beginning, for the passions continue to develop in the womb, where we share our mothers' griefs and joys, some of which may become indelibly imprinted on our characters.[30] Once we are born, our emotions develop with our nurse's milk, our first education, and with a host of individual experiences. Traumas leave their mark, so that 'this man sweats at the presence of a cat; that falls into an agony by casting his eye upon a frog or a toad; another man can never be reconciled to oysters'.[31] Vivid sights and sounds, chance associations, and idle conversations all shape our passions,[32] which continue to be formed and altered by the whole range of our experience.

While differences in people's lives account for the diversity of passions in any human population, biological and environmental factors explain patterns of distribution. In the first place, 'divers complexions are inclined to divers passions', a truth borne out, Thomas Wright tells us, by an old Italian proverb:

> If little men were patient
> And great men were valiant
> And red men were loyal,
> All the world would be equal.[33]

Another rhyme quoted by Wright affirms that this variability is as much a feature of women as of men;[34] but belief in the correlation between physical type and emotional temperament is more generally associated with the conviction that the bodily differences between the sexes are systematically reflected in their passions. Women are held to be more impressionable than men because their brains are softer, to resemble children in the inconstancy of their feelings, and to be susceptible to different passions,[35] and, according to Charron, are particularly liable to the effeminate emotions of vengefulness and sadness.[36] In addition, the changing conceptions that women and men have of their own bodies affect their sense of power, so that passions alter with age. For example,

---

[29] Charron, *Of Wisdome*, trans. S. Lennard (London, 1608), 7; see also 438 f. On Charron see M. Adam, *Études sur Pierre Charron* (Bordeaux, 1991) and 'L'Horizon philosophique de Pierre Charron', *Revue philosophique de la France et de l'Étranger*, 181 (1991), 273–93.

[30] See Ch. 10, below.

[31] Walter Charleton, *A Natural History of the Passions* (London, 1674), 75–6.

[32] On these aspects of our vulnerability see esp. P. Nicole, 'Discours où l'on fait voir combien les entretiens des hommes sont dangereux', in *Essais de Morale* (Paris, 1672), ii. 241–64. On Nicole see E. D. James, *Pierre Nicole, Jansenist and Humanist: A Study of his Thought* (The Hague, 1972).

[33] *Passions of the Mind*, 121.

[34] 'Faire and foolish, little and lowde | Long and lazy, black and prowde | Fatte and merrie, leane and sadde | Pale and pettish, redde and bad.' Ibid. 120.

[35] Nicolas Malebranche, *De la Recherche de la Vérité* (2nd edn.), ed. G. Rodis Lewis in *Œuvres complètes*, ed. A. Robinet (Paris, 1972), i. 266. For an Eng. trans. see *The Search after Truth*, trans. T. M. Lennon and P. J. Olscamp (Columbus, O., 1980), 130–1.

[36] *Of Wisdome*, 85–6, 90.

while the physical strength of young men makes them proud, the weakness of old men and women makes them covetous.[37]

Complementing and cross-cutting these divisions are a number of environmental factors, many of which are widely held to contribute to our characters. Climate, first of all, determines our internal heat, and this in turn produces spiritual differences.

climate matters as much as age + sex.

For the southerners, by reason of their cold temperature, are melancholic and therefore staid, contemplative, ingenious, religious, wise . . . From the melancholy temperature it likewise cometh that the southerners are unchaste, by reason of their frothy, fretting, tickling melancholy, as we commonly see in hares; and cruel, because this fretting sharp melancholy do violently press the passions and revenge. The northerners are of a phlegmatic and sanguine temperature quite contrary to the southern, and therefore have contrary qualities save that they agree in this one, that they are likewise cruel and inhumane, but by another reason, that is, for want of judgement, whereby like beasts they know not how to contain and govern themselves.[38]

Education, too, forms our dispositions, as Wright attests in his pathetic picture of the results of English discipline.

Our English youths are brought up with too much fear and terror. . . . The Italians and Spaniards, contrariwise, by bringing up their children with more liberty, enlarge their hearts with boldness and audacity in such sort, as usually you shall see them at sixteen or seventeen years of age, as bold and audacious as ours of thirty; and contrariwise, ours at sixteen or seventeen, drooping with fear and timidity, as if they were so many chickens drawn out of a well.[39]

Finally, then as now, European writers delight in sensational national stereotypes. Wright, for example, assures his readers that, 'I have seen by experience, there is no nation in Europe that hath not some extraordinary affection, either in pride, anger, lust, incontinence, gluttony, drunkenness, sloth or such like passion.'[40]

As assessments of the benefit or harm that things may cause us, the passions are vital to our life. Without them we would lack both the dispositional wariness that alerts us to danger, and anything beyond a basic, instinctive urge to improve our condition, and would be infinitely more helpless and vulnerable than we already are. 'No mortal man', Burton declares in *The Anatomy of Melancholy*, 'is free from these perturbations; or if he be so, sure he is either a god or a block.'[41] Since divine invulnerability is not an option, the alternative to

---

[37] Wright, *Passions of the Mind*, 117.   [38] Charron, *Of Wisdome*, 156–7.

[39] *Passions of the Mind*, 83–4.

[40] Ibid. 92. On national character as a topos in early-modern Europe see L. Van Delft, *Littérature et anthropologie: Nature humaine et caractère à l'âge classique* (Paris, 1993), 87–104.

[41] Ed. T. C. Faulkner *et al.* (Oxford, 1989–94), i. *Text*, 249. On Burton see B. C. Lyons, *Voices of Melancholy: Studies in Literary Treatments of Melancholy in Renaissance England* (London, 1971), 113–48; E. P. Vicari, *The View from Minerva's Tower: Learning and Imagination in The Anatomy of Melancholy* (Toronto, 1989).

the passions seems to be blockhood, a prospect that puts their functional traits in perspective. Whatever their limitations—and there are many—the passions are a prerequisite of everyday human existence. Explanations of their functional character interpret them simultaneously as a natural adaptation of species to environment and as evidence of God's beneficence. According to the first view, the passions promote our well-being as embodied creatures; according to the second, this goal dovetails neatly with our spiritual well-being so that, sometimes in spite of appearances, all passions are for our good. Senault, an enthusiastic promoter of this latter view, credits God with a homoeopathic talent for distilling antidotes out of poisons.

Thou employest fear to take off a covetous man from those perishable riches which possess him; thou makest a holy use of despair to withdraw from the world a courtier, whose youth had been mis-employed in the service of some prince; thou makest an admirable use of disdain to extinguish therewith a lover's flames, who is enslaved by a proud beauty. . . . In fine, thou makest claims of all our passions to unite our wills to thine.[42]

Even among less sanguine writers we encounter the view that, since God has equipped us with passions, and since he is benevolent, there must be something to be said for them. And in exploring what this might be, most authors fix on their role in promoting our well-being, where this is conceived not simply as a matter of survival and basic comfort, but more ambitiously in terms of a complex intermingling of pleasures and pains which give texture to our lives. Our passions do more than incite us to avoid danger; they also create our attachments and aspirations. They are the stuff of our responses to the course of events, so that it is hard (though not impossible) to imagine life without them. This point is forcefully made by the Dominican bishop Nicolas Coeffeteau in his *Tableau des passions humaines* of 1630. 'Would not a mother be inhuman', he asks rhetorically, 'if she were to see her child in the grip of wild beasts . . . or only seized by a violent illness, without feeling her heart filled with sadness?'[43]

Natural and theological defences of the functional character of the passions are therefore central to their interpretation. But these are not nearly so strident as the litany of complaint and lamentation about the imperfection of human nature that runs through the literature, creating the impression that the passions are an unmitigated burden. In the Epistle Prefatory to the *Natural History of the Passions*, for example, Walter Charleton mourns the fact that, 'Our inordinate affections be the bitter fountain whence . . . our practical errors, and by consequence most of the evils we suffer, flow.'[44] An initial sense of uneasiness and trouble is reflected in the rich vocabulary used to describe the passions. In *The*

---

[42] *Use of the Passions*, sig. B 2^{r-v}.   [43] p. 133.   [44] (1674), sig. A 4^r.

City of God, Augustine had noted that there are various Latin translations of the Greek term *pathe*, of which he favours the literal *passiones*, the term eventually taken over in French and English. Like the related deponent verb *patior*, this combines the idea of passivity with that of suffering, a sense nowhere more vividly conveyed than in the story of Christ's Passion. But two other translations listed by Augustine have more volatile connotations. *Pathe* is also rendered, he reminds us, as *perturbationes* (notably by Cicero) and as *affectiones* or *affectus*.[45] The view that these terms are all roughly synonymous quickly became fixed, and Augustine's discussion continued to be widely invoked and reiterated. Aquinas cites it,[46] and a range of English and French authors of the seventeenth century either replicate Augustine's list or unselfconsciously employ the range of terms it contains. Wright, for instance, remarks that the passions are also called affections or perturbations of the mind, as well as motions and affects.[47]

The passivity of passions and the stirrings of perturbations may initially seem at odds with one another: the one at rest, the other in motion; the one inactive, the other driving. But these two descriptions are brought together in an understanding of the passions as forces that are at once extremely powerful and actually or potentially beyond our control. They perturb the economy of soul and body in ways that we are sometimes unable to prevent, and in the most extreme cases can overwhelm a person so completely that they die. The Cambridge Platonist Henry More, for instance, regards it as 'a known and granted truth that passion has so much power over the vital temper of the body as to make it an unfit mansion for the soul' and attributes the deaths of both Sophocles and Dionysius the Sicilian tyrant to the sudden news of a tragic victory.[48] These characteristics are captured in a sequence of long-standing and ubiquitous metaphors. The passions are rebels who rise up against reason and understanding, make secessions, raise mutinies,[49] 'brawl with one another and so cause riots and tumults'.[50] Charmed by the sensible realm, they often prove deaf to the voice of reason, and, casting off their yoke of allegiance, 'aspire to unbounded licence and dominion'.[51] As opponents they are cunning, resilient, and insatiable; 'they are Hydras which thrust up as many heads as are cut off, they are so many Antaeuses who gather strength from their weakness and who rise up stronger after they have been beaten down; all the advantage one can expect from such subjects is to clap irons upon their hands and feet, and leave them no more power than is requisite for the service of reason'.[52] To be

[45] *City of God*, 9. 4.   [46] *Summa*, 1a. 2ae 22.   [47] *Passions of the Mind*, 94.
[48] *The Immortality of the Soul*, ed. A. Jacob (Dordrecht, 1987), 168. The same claim is made by Reynolds, *Treatise on the Passions*, 73, and Wright, *Passions of the Mind*, 136.
[49] Francis Bacon, *The Advancement of Learning*, ed. G. W. Kitchin (London, 1973), 147.
[50] Wright, *Passions of the Mind*, 141.   [51] Charleton, *Natural History of the Passions*, 58.
[52] Senault, *Use of the Passions*, 90. Antaeus was a giant killed by Hercules.

PLATE I. Frontispiece to J. F. Senault, *The Use of the Passions*, trans. Henry Earl of Monmouth (1649)

subject to such tyrants is, moreover, a peculiarly terrible fate, since one cannot escape servitude by running away. The passions are part of us, and we are condemned to drag our chains along, carrying our masters with us.[53] The same image is also used, moreover, to portray the aspiration to reverse this state of affairs by bringing down our despotic emotions and enslaving them in their turn. On the frontispiece of the English translation of Senault's book, Aquinas's eleven principal passions form a chain-gang. With the exception of Love, who is held by both wrists to prevent him firing his bow, each is manacled at the ankle and attached to the wrist of Reason. Sitting on her throne, she controls them by loosening and tightening the chain, assisted by Grace, who offers her advice, and also by a small dog which stands by, ready to round up any strays (see Pl. 1).

Images of civil strife within the soul are matched by a view of the passions as natural disorders—as storms, torrents, tempests. They are winds that put the mind in tumult, sweeping us along like ships in a gale,[54] and as storms disturb the harmony of nature, passions are discordant and jangling. In these metaphors passion is understood as motion, an interpretation which spreads into a wider range of descriptions. The passions are turbulent, they are furious reboundings, they are violent and rash sallies, they are accessions and recessions of folly.[55] As such, they are often portrayed in addition as diseases, pathological states to which we easily succumb and of which we need to be cured, since to neglect these illnesses would be little short of suicidal, 'as if a blind man who hath not the power of directing his own feet should be permitted to run head-long, without wit or moderation, having no guide to direct him'.[56]

The passions, then, 'trouble wonderfully the soul'.[57] They induce blindness of understanding, perversion of the will, alteration of the humours, and by these means maladies and disquietness.[58] In early-modern writing, our constitutional inability to govern our emotions is often attributed to the Fall; as punishment for Adam's sin, God removed from us the capacity to control, moderate, and direct them, creating the inward chaos that is the lot of all but a very few exceptional people. But even writers who do not agree with, or do not emphasize, this Christian interpretation of our distress, nevertheless share with their Christian counterparts an understanding of its painful consequences. Our passions, they concede, make us false, foolish, inconstant, and uncertain.[59] They are the flaws that trip us up and the stuff of which tragedy is made. When Lodovico asks wonderingly about Othello,

---

[53] Ibid. 96.
[54] Bacon, *Advancement of Learning*, 171; Baruch Spinoza, *Ethics*, in *The Collected Works of Spinoza* ed. E. Curley (Princeton, 1985), vol. i, III. 59 s; Charleton, *Natural History of the Passions*, 69.
[55] Charron, *Of Wisdome*, 213.   [56] Reynolds, *Treatise of the Passions*, 45.
[57] Wright, *Passions of the Mind*, 94.   [58] Ibid. 125.   [59] Charron, *Of Wisdome*, 215–16.

> Is this the nature
> Whom passion could not shake, whose solid virtue
> The shot of accident nor dart of chance
> Could neither graze nor pierce?[60]

he registers a common amazement at the capacity of affect to defeat a mature
and settled character and destroy social order. Because passion eats into us,
making us wayward and obsessed, it renders us intensely vulnerable. At the
same time, it has the destructive habit of feeding its own restlessness by setting us off on courses of action that fail to satisfy us and further damage our
well-being. Shakespeare knows this, too, of course, and allows the Player King
to lay out the problem before the troubled Claudius.

> What to ourselves in passion we propose,
> The passions ending, doth the purpose lose,
> The violence of either grief or joy
> Their own enactures with themselves destroy.
> Where joy most revels, grief doth most lament;
> Grief joys, joy grieves, on slender accident.[61]

These elements combine to produce a common understanding of what
the passions are, and why they are important, which spans the culture of
seventeenth-century Europe and creates a frame within which more specialized debates are conducted. But perhaps the most striking fact about the images
outlined here is their equivocality: on the one hand the passions are functional
characteristics essential to our survival and flourishing; on the other hand they
are painful and destructive impulses which drive us to pursue the very ends
liable to do us harm. God's benevolence in fitting us for our environment is
tempered by his penalty for our first disobedience, so that our passions, which
are among the most intense forces shaping our lives, condemn us to misery and
error. This ambivalence poses problems that preoccupy and inspire writers of
many kinds. Prominent among them are those philosophers who rise, unwisely
perhaps, to the challenge of devising theories capable of reconciling these conflicting tendencies, and of situating the passions within systematic analyses
of the mind and body, the moral community, the polity, and the history of
humankind. Aspects of this project are undertaken by many writers who now
belong to the established canon of seventeenth-century philosophers: Hobbes,
Descartes, Locke, Pascal, Malebranche, and Spinoza are all, in different ways,
profoundly interested in the passions, which play a major part in shaping both
the philosophical problems they address and the solutions they propose.

---

[60] William Shakespeare, *Othello*, in *The Complete Works*, ed. S. Wells and G. Taylor (Oxford, 1988),
IV. i. 844.
[61] William Shakespeare, *Hamlet*, in *Complete Works*, ed. Wells and Taylor, III. ii. 672.

Precisely because the passions are so central, and bear on such a wide range of issues, my discussion of them in this book will necessarily be selective. I shall not, on the whole, discuss particular passions, or the typologies in which they are embedded. Nor shall I focus directly on the ethical character of our affections or the part they play in a virtuous life.[62] My aim is rather to explore the place of the passions in seventeenth-century interpretations of the body and mind, and to understand the roles they play in reasoning and action. Since the investigation of these neglected themes bears most directly on problems usually allocated to metaphysics, the philosophy of mind, and epistemology, these areas of philosophy will figure largely in this book. Many of the views I shall discuss point invitingly to early-modern ethics, politics, and aesthetics, and many discoveries remain to be made about the connections between these fields. Meanwhile, however, an appreciation of the centrality of the passions to seventeenth-century conceptions of our grasp of ourselves and the world is significant for at least three reasons, one of them bearing specifically on the history of early-modern philosophy, the other two raising questions about contemporary philosophical practice.

Philosophers have tended in the first place to neglect the fact that their early-modern ancestors wrote about the passions.[63] This may partly be due to the influence of Hume and other Enlightenment thinkers, who represented the seventeenth century as an era dominated by dogmatic, religious values in which a proper appreciation of sentiment was suppressed. But the neglect also stems in the twentieth century from a preoccupation with philosophy as a scientific and secular form of enquiry distinct from psychology, a conception which has shaped our understanding of historical texts and led us to read them as mainly addressing the metaphysical, scientific and epistemological issues that now tend to be seen as the core of the subject. While not necessarily mistaken, the resulting interpretations are partial in several ways: they skip over topics, such as the passions, that are perceived as marginal or irrelevant to a particular interpretation of what philosophy is; they focus on philosophers whose work most easily answers to the preconceptions created by this interpretation; they select from the works of favoured philosophers those which strike them as most relevant and coherent; and having thus shaped the subject, they string philosophers together into schools and traditions. This process yields maps of the past which are, from the perspective of certain contemporary issues and problems, highly informative. But for travellers of a more historical bent, it is as

---

[62] For a survey of these issues see S. James, 'Ethics as the Control of the Passions', in M. Ayers and D. Garber (eds.), *The Cambridge History of Seventeenth-Century Philosophy* (Cambridge, 1997), vii. 5.

[63] Among important exceptions to this generalization see Levi, *French Moralists*; Meyer, *Le Philosophe et les passions*; M. Nussbaum, *The Therapy of Desire: Theory and Practice in Hellenistic Ethics* (Princeton, 1994); A. O. Rorty, 'From Passions to Emotions and Sentiments', *Philosophy*, 57 (1982), 159–72; J. Cottingham, 'Cartesian Ethics: Reason and the Passions', *Revue internationale de philosophie*, 50 (1996), 193–216; D. Kambouchner, *L'Homme des passions: Commentaires sur Descartes* (Paris, 1996).

though the contour lines were missing. The landscape is flattened, stripped of many of the vistas and surprises that enliven a journey, and deprived of the singularity and complexity that makes a region distinctive. Such a map is not only misleading but—to many people, at least—less enticing than it might be, for although flat lands have their charm, they are also monotonous.

The fact that cartographies of early-modern philosophy have tended to leave out the passions of the soul is, I believe, a significant loss. As well as obliterating a deeply fascinating set of configurations, this practice has impoverished our awareness of the territory as a whole. The passions are not, for seventeenth-century philosophers, embellishments to be tacked on to the back of a treatise once the real work is done, or added to a map when the surveying and measuring are completed. They are integral to the landscape, vital to a philosophical grasp of our own nature and our power to comprehend and negotiate the natural and social environments in which we live. Unless we realize this, we are liable to read over the connections that seventeenth-century philosophers draw between the passions and other problems or arguments that strike us more forcibly, and are also prone to construct anachronistic links of our own. On a map without contours, two communities cut off from one another by an impassable mountain may appear as close neighbours; comparable misunderstandings can arise from a map without passions.

I aim to show that misunderstandings of this type have actually arisen, and that the study of the passions can in consequence substantially revise our views about the character and achievements of philosophy in the seventeenth century. In Part II, I shall argue that a conception of passions as states that straddle body and mind enabled philosophers of this period to confront with subtlety and insight questions about the interconnections between thoughts and bodily states, questions about the development of individual identity and questions about the significance of the bodily expression of passions. An appreciation of their work in these areas undermines the stereotypical image of early-modern philosophy as gripped by a thoroughgoing dualism between body and mind, and strengthens the revisionist historiography that has begun to replace it.[64] It also sets in a more variegated light the view—often presented as a novelty of this period—that the mind is transparent to itself. Building on this discussion, Part III turns to epistemology, and argues that, by neglecting the role of the passions both as obstacles to and prerequisites of knowledge, commentators have tended to misidentify the epistemological issues that exercised philosophers in the seventeenth century and the character of the knower, the subject capable of acquiring knowledge. By sharply splitting off reason

---

[64] Unsurprisingly, the initial focus of these reinterpretations has been on Descartes's dualism. See A. O. Rorty, 'Cartesian Passions and the Union of Mind and Body', in *Essays on Descartes' 'Meditations'* (Berkeley and Los Angeles, 1986); A. Baier, 'Cartesian Persons', in *Postures of the Mind* (London, 1985), 74–92; G. Rodis Lewis, 'La Domaine propre de l'homme chez les cartésiens', in *L'Anthropologie cartésienne* (Paris, 1990), 39–83.

from passion, they have generated a parodic interpretation of the processes by which knowledge is attained, and have obscured from view a fruitful conception of the emotional character of learning and the role of the passions in rational thought and action. Part IV addresses the relation between passion and action. It fills in some contours, so to speak, by showing how different accounts of the passions yield different analyses of decision-making and indecision, and also draws attention to a largely neglected analysis of the place of desires among the antecedents of action. Recognition of this view allows us to trace the emergence of the claim that actions result from beliefs and desires, and to appreciate some of the intellectual pressures to which it was a response.

The cumulative effect of investigating the passions in these various contexts serves, I believe, not merely to vindicate their importance within early-modern philosophy but to revise some currently influential conceptions of this area and its relation to the philosophical positions that we associate with the Enlightenment. However, some of the assumptions and standpoints that it encourages us to give up have had an impact beyond the confines of avowedly historical enquiry, and form part of a picture of the history of philosophy that shapes all kinds of current work. The view, for example, that Descartes made an absolute distinction between states of the body and states of the soul and allowed nothing to cross it, has long been a mainstay of the philosophy of mind;[65] but it is a mainstay that will not stand up once the Cartesian account of the passions is taken into account. More recently, the claim that Descartes divided reason from emotion, and banished the latter to the body, has gained currency among a wide range of philosophers concerned to reassess the relation between thinking and feeling; but this too fails to take account of an important Cartesian distinction between passions and so-called intellectual emotions. On a larger scale, the seventeenth century continues to be portrayed as the dawn of modernity, the cradle of a culture in which man becomes set over against nature and nature takes on a purely instrumental significance, and in which a range of emotional responses to the natural world give way to dispassionate calculations of utility.[66] This interpretation rests, it seems to me, on an oversimplification both of the tensions between function and dysfunction within

[65] This interpretation seems to have solidified in the 19th cent., alongside a conception of Descartes as an epistemologist. See B. Kuklick, 'Seven Thinkers and How They Grew' in R. Rorty *et al.* (eds.), *Philosophy in History* (Cambridge, 1984), 130; S. Gaukroger, *Descartes: An Intellectual Biography* (Oxford, 1996), 2–7. Its influence on the 20th-cent. analytical tradition owes much to G. Ryle, *The Concept of Mind* (London, 1949) and it remains prominent in histories of philosophy—e.g. R. Scruton, *From Descartes to Wittgenstein* (London, 1981)—and in surveys of the philosophy of mind—e.g. P. Smith and O. R. Jones, *The Philosophy of Mind: An Introduction* (Cambridge, 1986); G. McCulloch, *The Mind and its World* (London, 1995).

[66] For this type of analysis of modernity see Lloyd, *Man of Reason*, esp. 10–18; Taylor, *Sources of the Self*, 143–58; P. A. Schouls, *Descartes and the Enlightenment* (Montreal, 1989); S. Toulmin, *Cosmopolis: The Hidden Agenda of Modernity* (New York, 1990); R. B. Pippin, *Modernity as a Philosophical Problem: On the Dissatisfactions of European High Culture* (Oxford, 1991), 16–45. For a measured interpretation see H. Blumenberg, *The Legitimacy of the Modern Age*, trans. R. M. Wallace (Cambridge, Mass., 1983), esp. ii.

the passions, and of a sequence of debates about how this is to be resolved, as well as underestimating the complexity of early-modern debates about the self.[67]

If none of these interpretations can be sustained without a great deal of qualification, it becomes interesting to ask why they are so widely accepted and reiterated. In part, they serve as a backdrop against which contemporary positions are shown off and displayed, and hence as a reassuring sign of philosophical progress. By demonizing aspects of our own philosophical past, we are able to bask in our own purportedly dispassionate originality and insight. By branding our most celebrated predecessors as incompetent, we release ourselves from the obligation to look as sensitively and creatively as we can at their philosophies, and fend off the possibility of having to acknowledge that sometimes they were there before us. This strategy will clearly not go away. It is part of an Oedipal struggle between philosophy and its past without which the subject would come to a standstill, and is a stage in a longer dialectical pattern of rejection and recovery. But it is nevertheless a strategy about which it is helpful to be self-conscious. A second reason for studying what early-modern philosophy has to say about the passions is therefore that it provides both an exemplification of, and a commentary on, this approach, and offers us an opportunity to consider some of the ways in which it has most recently been used.

This line of enquiry is particularly relevant in relation to feminist philosophy, one of the most innovative areas in contemporary philosophical research. During the last few years, a group of exceptionally original authors have shown how deeply embedded interpretations of the differences between men and women are reflected in some of the most central of our philosophical categories. In certain ways, oppositions such as those between reason and passion, or mind and body, carry connotations of male and female, and mirror the power-relations of a patriarchal society in which women are dominated by men. Taking up the widespread view that modern philosophy begins with Descartes, some feminist writers have also argued, or assumed, that the patriarchal character of philosophy was clinched and consolidated in the seventeenth century: the emergence of a clear division between body and mind served to attach women more firmly to the physical world, and a comparable split between reason and passion condemned them to the realm of affect.[68]

---

[67] See S. James, 'Internal and External in the Work of Descartes', in J. Tully (ed.), *Philosophy in an Age of Pluralism* (Cambridge, 1994), 7–19.

[68] See Lloyd, *The Man of Reason*; S. Bordo, *The Flight to Objectivity: Essays on Cartesianism and Culture* (Albany, NY, 1987) and 'The Cartesian Masculinisation of Thought', in S. Harding and J. O'Barr (eds.), *Sex and Scientific Enquiry* (Chicago, 1987), 247–64; N. Scheman, 'Though this be method yet there is madness in it: Paranoia and Liberal Epistemology', in L. M. Anthony and C. Witt (eds.), *A Mind of One's Own: Feminist Essays on Reason and Objectivity* (Boulder, Colo., 1993), 145–70; N. Tuana, *The Less Noble Sex: Scientific, Religious and Philosophical Conceptions of Women's Nature* (Bloomington, Ind., 1993), 60–4. The view that it was Descartes who succeeded in separating mind from body and passion from reason is taken for granted by a wide range of feminist writers. See e.g. E. Fox Keller, 'From Secrets of Life to Secrets of Death', in *Secrets of Life: Essays on Language, Gender and Science* (London,

These interpretations belong, on the one hand, to a not-yet-completed stage in which the patriarchal face of philosophy as it has traditionally been practised has been boldly, if sometimes crudely, outlined. In breaking with the past, exponents of these views have relied on the familiar technique of discrediting its key figures, and have achieved the intended effect of enabling people to see them differently. The fact that many of these interpretations are partial in the ways I have mentioned is therefore not altogether a criticism. But feminist research has now reached a point at which the insights yielded by the demonizing approach have been absorbed, and it is safe—and indeed necessary—to muddy the picture by looking more critically at the strategy of vilification. By condemning our forebears as empiricist, rationalist, Christian, or patriarchal, we generate the access of enthusiasm and hope that comes from starting afresh. But at the same time we enact one of the passionate strategies that philosophers such as Hobbes, Malebranche, or Spinoza identify as a flaw in self-knowledge and an obstacle to understanding.

To cast the luminaries of the early-modern canon as villains is to mimic the treatment that many seventeenth-century philosophers meted out to the ancients. For example, when Descartes and Spinoza assured their readers that no one before them had written anything to rival their own analyses of the passions,[69] they joined a chorus of condemnation of classical and Scholastic philosophy in which a break with the past was artfully constructed. While almost all philosophers were anxious to distance themselves from at least some aspects of their history and were not too intellectually fussy about how they did it, there was at the same time a sophisticated awareness of the dangers inherent in the use of this device. Reflection on its character and limitations was not usually applied directly to the practice itself; but the two existed side by side, so that the connection between them was there to be made. One interpretation of our disposition to condemn other people and erase our debts, as Hobbes runs down Aristotle or some feminist philosophers run down Descartes, was attributed to a concern with grandeur that is deeply etched into human nature. Our craving for esteem, and the enviousness and anxiety that this breeds, shapes our intellectual life and makes us prone to the demonizing strategy, which, by diminishing others, serves to augment our sense of our own value. In addition, as Hobbes explains, our undirected passions tend to fix on particular objects,

1992), 39; J. Flax, 'Political Philosophy and the Patriarchal Unconscious: A Psychoanalytic Perspective on Epistemology and Metaphysics', in N. Tuana and R. Tong (eds.), *Feminism and Philosophy* (Boulder, Colo., 1995), 227–9; E. Grosz, *Volatile Bodies* (Bloomington, Ind., 1994), 6–10; S. Benhabib, *Situating the Self: Gender, Community and Postmodernism in Contemporary Ethics* (Cambridge, 1992), 207.

[69] See Descartes, *Passions of the Soul*, 68 (though compare the more concessive view in his letter to Princess Elizabeth, 21 July 1645, in *Philosophical Writings*, ed. Cottingham, et al., iii. *Correspondence* 256); Spinoza, *Ethics*, pref. to prt. III, 491. On ancients and moderns see S. Gaukroger (ed.), *The Uses of Antiquity* (Dordrecht, 1991); B. P. Copenhaver and C. B. Schmitt, *Renaissance Philosophy* (Oxford, 1992), 285–328; T. Sorell (ed.), *The Rise of Modern Philosophy* (Oxford, 1993).

so that antipathy or frustration can focus on a philosopher or a tradition. This process may be driven more by a desire to order and legitimate our emotions than by careful judgement, and may yield states in which belief merges with pacifying fantasy. But once this has occurred, it becomes more difficult to reconsider the evaluations we have reached, and to ask ourselves whether a position is really as obtuse as we have made out.

This self-reflective strand within seventeenth-century philosophy—discussed in Part III of this book—has been obscured by the contention that the mind came to be regarded, during this period, as transparent to itself. Recovering this line of thought gives us an opportunity both to reassess this interpretation and to reflect on the way we ourselves have used it. At the moment, this change of stance is particularly germane to feminist philosophy, where a history organized around rigid oppositions is in the process of giving way to finer grained studies of the cross-cutting conceptions of masculinity and femininity that run through early-modern debate.[70] But because the demonizing strategy is so common, it is also of wider relevance.

A third reason for studying seventeenth-century treatments of the passions relates more directly to current philosophical work, much of which is designed to overcome the rather narrow approaches to the topic which became entrenched around the middle of the present century. In its heyday, analytical philosophy tended to place the emotions in an unduly cramped and restrictive frame, so that the questions asked about them, and the range of answers discussed, now seem to have missed an awful lot out. This was partly because the compartmentalization of philosophy, psychology, and some of the other social sciences meant that questions previously considered philosophical came to be seen as lying outside the boundaries of the subject. For instance, the variation in emotions from place to place and group to group which fascinated seventeenth-century writers came to be regarded as psychological or anthropological. The constriction also occurred because analytical philosophy was itself dominated by theories of knowledge and action—and also to a great extent by ethical and political theories—in which emotion played at best a marginal role, and whose hold over the subject made it difficult to see that the emotions raise important and central philosophical problems. For example, an emphasis within epistemology on criteria for knowledge left little room for discussion of the role of emotion in the processes by which we come to know things;[71]

---

[70] Outstanding examples of a more fruitful approach to 17th-cent. philosophy include M. Atherton, 'Cartesian Reason and Gendered Reason', in Antony and Witt (eds.). *A Mind of One's Own*, 19–34, and G. Lloyd, 'Maleness, Metaphor and the "Crisis" of Reason', Antony and Witt (eds.), *A Mind of One's Own*, 69–83.

[71] Though on this issue see M. Stocker, 'Intellectual Desire, Emotion and Action', in A. O. Rorty (ed.), *Explaining Emotions* (Berkeley and Los Angeles, 1980), 323–38; A. Jagger, 'Love and Knowledge: Emotion in Feminist Epistemology', in A. Garry and M. Pearsall (eds.), *Women, Knowledge and Reality* (Boston, 1989), 129–56; J. Benjamin, *The Bonds of Love* (London, 1990); T. Brennan, *History after Lacan* (London, 1993).

an emphasis on meta-ethical issues left little room to explore the emotional dimensions of virtue.[72] Finally, analytical philosophy's rather narrow approach to the emotions stemmed not just from the character of its interests, but also from its adherence to a set of standards and distinctions which made it hard to incorporate the emotions into a broader account of our experience. Among the conditions that proved problematic was the requirement that a satisfactory analysis of emotions should be applicable to all central cases. Not an unreasonable demand, to be sure, but one that proved difficult to meet and led in some cases to stipulative conclusions.[73] Another debate, shaped by a powerful distinction between cognitive and non-cognitive mental states, concerned the cognitive status of the emotions. William James's view that these are our experience of bodily changes caused by perceptions[74] was rejected by a series of philosophers who interpreted our passions as more or less rational judgements.[75] While their analyses reflected a wish to maintain a clear distinction between the cognitive and non-cognitive, they also imposed a conception of the passions which obscured some of their distinctive characteristics and helped to keep them on the fringe of the mental phenomena studied by philosophers.[76] Only gradually has it become possible to acknowledge the complexity and diversity of the emotions, and to use this insight to reconsider their part in our mental life and behaviour.[77]

As a result of these and comparable developments, there is now an established sense among the inheritors of the analytical tradition that the study of the emotions provides a fruitful standpoint from which to question the terms in which mental states are analysed and, independently, that the emotions are a richer topic than had been allowed. This shift has been particularly marked and successful in ethics. In other areas it remains more hesitant, as though, while agreeing that our philosophical predilections have been too tightly laced for our own good, we remain tempted to maintain the outline of old-fashioned respectability and elegance. Nevertheless a change is under way, and this puts us in a stronger position to integrate the passions into areas of philosophy in which they have had little or no place.

This book is intended as a contribution to the reinstatement of the emotions within philosophy, to the gathering tide of opinion that we need to take account of our emotional life if we are to understand, among other topics,

[72] This position has recently changed. See the surveys by J. R. Wallach, 'Contemporary Aristotelianism', *Political Theory*, 20 (1992), 613–41, and J. Oakley, 'Varieties of Virtue Ethics', *Ratio*, 9 (1996), 128–52.

[73] See e.g. R. C. Roberts, 'What an Emotion Is: A Sketch', *Philosophical Review*, 97 (1988), 184–5. Roberts acknowledges that his analysis will not cover various states which other philosophers regard as emotions, but does not regard this as an objection to his view.

[74] *The Principles of Psychology* (Cambridge, Mass., 1983), 1,065.

[75] See e.g. R. C. Solomon, *The Passions* (Notre Dame, Ind., 1983).

[76] On this debate see P. Greenspan, *Emotions and Reasons: An Inquiry into Emotional Justification* (London, 1988), 3–36; C. Armon Jones, *Varieties of Affect* (London, 1991).

[77] See Jones, *Varieties of Affect*; J. Oakley, *Morality and the Emotions* (London, 1992), 6–37.

moral motivation and growth, the springs of action (rational and otherwise), and the nature of reasoning. The philosophy of the seventeenth century remains a crucial moment from which we trace our own origins, and an appreciation of the significance accorded to the passions during this period can serve us as a model and a source. It can help us to see how problems related to the passions pervade many areas of philosophy. They are not merely ethical or merely psychological, but spread through the whole subject. It can also enable us to find in the history of philosophy itself insights and perspectives to inspire us; for it is not only in the ecological domain that recycling, and the transformations that go with it, are vital to our well-being.

Many of the most celebrated innovations introduced by seventeenth-century philosophers were provoked by the conviction that Scholastic Aristotelianism suffered from terminal deficiencies and needed to be replaced. While the initial dissatisfactions prompting this change were concerned mainly with physics and the metaphysics underpinning it, the failures of Aristotelianism that attracted most attention also bore on Scholastic interpretations of the passions. These interpretations are accordingly introduced in Part I of this book. Writers who aspired to produce systematic philosophies free from the taint of Aristotelianism were therefore committed to articulating uncontaminated analyses of the passions, and this motivation partly accounts for a series of original and sometimes piercing treatments of the subject, notably those of Hobbes and Descartes. However, as in other areas of philosophy, any suggestion that there is a clean break between Aristotelianism and the New Philosophy needs to be handled with care. The break is real enough, but it is offset by several sorts of continuity, both in the works of writers dedicated to leaving Scholasticism behind, and in the philosophical culture at large.[78]

First and most obviously, Aristotelianism did not collapse all at once, and throughout the seventeenth century many writers continued to adhere to one or other of its numerous variants. In the case of the passions, Aquinas's analysis of the states of the tripartite soul (among which the passions are included) remained particularly influential, and the transition to a post-Scholastic philosophical psychology was extremely protracted. This was partly because the planks of the vast and cumbersome Aristotelian ship could not all be replaced simultaneously. But the urge to scrap it was also tempered by the eclecticism of many philosophers, who were content to salvage a doctrine here or a principle there and incorporate them into purportedly more seaworthy vessels. While some of the resulting craft appear extraordinary to our eyes, the disposition to save and modify arose in many cases from the belief—inherited from Renaissance humanism and expressed in the use of the dialogue—that

---

[78] For this continuity in interpretations of the passions see Levi, *French Moralists*, 329–38; Van Delft, *Moraliste classique*, 129–37.

all the philosophical schools had arrived at truths which could be amalgamated into a single complete and correct system.[79] This approach was widespread, but is particularly well exemplified by the Cambridge Platonists. While such writers as Cudworth and More accord priority to the divine Plato, they also appeal to a much wider and more varied range of authorities. In his posthumously published *Treatise concerning Eternal and Immutable Morality*, Cudworth imaginatively welds together a sequence of pagan and Christian traditions and legitimates the mechanical philosophy by tracing it back to the dawn of the historical record.

If we may believe Posidonius the Stoic, who, as Strabo tells us, affirmed this mechanical philosophy to have been ancienter than the times of the Trojan War, and was first invented and delivered by one Moschus a Sidonian, or rather a Phoenician . . . Now what can be more probable than that this Moschus the Phoenician, that Posidonius speaks of, is the very same person with that Moschus the physiologer that Jamblichus mentions in the Life of Pythagoras, where he affirms that Pythagoras, living some time at Sidon in Phoenicia, conversed with the prophets that were the successors of Mochus physiologer, and was instructed by them . . . And what can be more certain than that both Mochus and Moschus the Phoenician and philosopher was no other than Moses, the Jewish lawgiver, as Arcerius rightly guesses[80]

Less extravagantly, but eclectically none the less, More's *Enchyridion Ethicum*, first published in 1667, which contains his most sustained discussion of the passions, appeals to numerous sources: to Plato and Plotinus, to Cicero and Marcus Aurelius, to Aristotle and Aquinas, to Epictetus and sundry Pythagoreans.[81] In these texts, and in others like them, Aristotle appears as one philosopher among others, an authority who had some useful and some not-so-useful ideas, rather than as The Philosopher who must be either revered or rejected.[82]

A second kind of continuity is created by the rejection of Aristotelianism itself. Searching for something to replace it with, philosophers of a systematic bent were drawn to reconsider alternative classical traditions, to see whether, or how, they could be adapted and used. Gassendi, for example, embarked on a wholehearted revival and modification of Epicurean atomism, which had a considerable impact on natural philosophy.[83] And although Epicureanism was not much favoured by seventeenth-century theorists of the passions, they were

[79] For syncretists who held this view see C. B. Schmitt and Q. Skinner (eds.), *The Cambridge History of Renaissance Philosophy* (Cambridge, 1988): on Vernia, 494; on Pico, 494, 578; on Ficino, 675.

[80] *A Treatise concerning Eternal and Immutable Morality With A Treatise of Freewill*, ed. S. Hutton (Cambridge, 1996), 38–9.

[81] Trans. and abridged as *An Account of Virtue or Dr. Henry More's Abridgment of Morals* (London, 1690).

[82] On Renaissance antecedents of this approach see B. Copenhaver and C. Schmitt, *Renaissance Philosophy*, 75–126.

[83] See L. S. Joy, *Gassendi the Atomist* (Cambridge, 1987); M. J. Osler (ed.), *Atoms, Pneuma and Tranquillity: Epicurean and Stoic Themes in European Thought* (Cambridge, 1991).

strongly influenced by the revival of Stoicism which had been undertaken in the same wholehearted spirit by Lipsius.[84] It would be a drastic oversimplification, however, to interpret interest in the Stoics as fuelled simply by the need to find an alternative to Scholastic orthodoxy. While the study of natural philosophy had been effectively dominated by Aristotelianism, so that its demise threatened to create a gulf in this region of philosophy, the situation facing theorists of the passions was less desperate. Enquiry in this field had for a long while been spread between a Scholastic Aristotelian tradition and a Roman one, both of which had a place in standard educational curricula. As well as reading commentaries on Aristotle and Aquinas, students learned about the place of the passions in rhetoric, as discussed by Aristotle, Cicero, and Quintilian, and about their moral and political significance, as discussed by Cicero and Seneca among others.[85] This training made certain strands of Stoicism available; and these had in turn been taken up by writers, including Lipsius, who were dedicated to reviving a Christianized version of its ethical doctrine, a fortitude and tranquillity deriving from a recognition of the futility of worldly existence and the greatness of the life to come. Stoicism therefore formed part of the intellectual background of seventeenth-century philosophers writing on the passions, and was correspondingly widely discussed and criticized. As Aristotelianism declined, it seemed to some philosophers to offer solutions to certain outstanding problems: Hobbes and Spinoza, for example, draw on its metaphysical doctrines to develop their accounts of the passions.

Running alongside these pagan philosophies are a number of strands of Christian thought, each with its own continuities and discontinuities, of which two are, perhaps, particularly important to our concerns. On the one hand, Aquinas's immense and continuing influence is partly due to the fact that he embeds the passions in a familiar and orthodox world-view, and explains them as a function of the position of humanity within this all-encompassing scheme. On the other hand, the figure of Augustine towers over philosophers of various denominations. His conception of the passions as modifications of a will that may be rightly or wrongly directed remains central to Catholic doctrine and

---

[84] On aspects of early-modern Stoicism see L. Xanta, *La Renaissance du Stoïcisme au XVIe siècle* (Paris, 1914); C. Chesnau, 'Le Stoïcisme en France dans la première moitié du XVIIe siècle: Les Origines', *Études franciscaines*, 2 (1951), 384–410; J. L. Saunders, *Justus Lipsius: The Philosophy of Renaissance Stoicism* (New York, 1955), 492–519; Levi, *French Moralists*; on Du Vair, M. Fumaroli, *L'Âge d'éloquence* (Geneva, 1980); G. Oestreich, *Neostoicism and the Early-Modern State* (Cambridge, 1982); G. Monsarrat, *Light from the Porch: Stoicism and English Renaissance Literature* (Paris, 1984); A. Chew, *Stoicism in Renaissance English Literature* (New York, 1988); Osler, *Atoms, Pneuma and Tranquillity*; M. Morford, *Stoics and Neo-Stoics: Rubens and the Circle of Lipsius* (Princeton, 1991).

[85] On changing curricula in the English universities see J. Gascoigne, *Cambridge in the Age of the Enlightenment: Science and Religion from the Restoration to the French Revolution* (Cambridge, 1989); on English grammar schools see Q. Skinner, *Reason and Rhetoric in the Philosophy of Hobbes* (Cambridge, 1996), 19–40; on France see L. W. B. Brockliss, *French Higher Education in the Seventeenth and Eighteenth Centuries* (Oxford, 1987); on the Jesuit curriculum see F. de Dainville, *L'Éducation des Jésuites* (Paris, 1978).

is, for example, never far from the mind of authors such as Malebranche or Senault. His impact on Luther ensures that this view is taken up within Protestantism, where it is reflected in the emphasis placed by Puritan writers on the need for self-abasement and the constructive role of passions such as self-hatred and despair. In addition, Augustine's influence on Jansen, who entitled his *magnum opus Augustinus*, in turn shapes the work of authors such as Pascal and Nicole.

In this book, I focus on a period in which philosophers appeal to a variety of traditions in order to challenge and displace the understanding of the passions embedded in Scholastic Aristotelianism. Although there is no determinate point at which this process begins, and no moment at which one can say that Aristotelianism is finally left behind, I argue that the need to replace it preoccupies philosophers throughout the seventeenth century, and that during this time they not only formulate a post-Aristotelian conception of the passions and their place in the mind, but also begin to come to terms with its implications. For all its complexity and equivocality, the urge to transcend the perceived limitations of Aristotelianism remains a central philosophical motivation. Rather than trying to assess the contribution of traditions such as Stoicism or Platonism to an altered understanding of the passions, I approach this theme through the work of individual philosophers. Some of them are nowadays obscure figures, and my aim in discussing them is to illustrate the place of the passions in the broader philosophical culture of the period. On the whole, however, I concentrate on the seventeenth-century philosophers whose names are most familiar. This is not because of any profound attachment to the established canon. However, by exploring the work of acknowledged giants, I aim to show that the study of the passions is a central topic even within the accepted heartland of early-modern philosophy.

PART I

2

Passion and Action in Aristotle

When seventeenth-century philosophers describe states such as sadness, ambition, or fear that are nowadays identified as emotions and desires, they usually call them passions or affections.[1] In doing so, they allude to two sprawling and connected distinctions between passion and action, and cause and effect, and situate the emotions within a broader philosophical framework.[2] To classify a state as a passion or affect is to say something about its metaphysical and causal status, and something about its epistemological credentials; at the same time, it is to place it in a hierarchical structure of human thoughts and feelings and a broader topography of the mind and body, each replete with moral significance. So when Descartes names his treatise *Les Passions de l'âme*, or when Spinoza offers general definitions of the affects (*Affectuum Definitiones*),[3] the terms they use carry with them a web of implications as to what the emotions are and how they work. Before we can appreciate the power and subtlety of early-modern treatments of the passions, we need to familiarize ourselves with these various dimensions of activity and passivity. In a metaphor beloved by many of the writers to be discussed, we have to learn to hear the metaphysical harmonies that join with the melodic line. These are taken to be the very stuff of argument, to be employed, contested, elaborated, or derided. Reverberating, they provide the setting within which interpretations of the passions gain their identity, and against which they are judged.

This chapter and the one that follows will be concerned with the categories of action and passion as these are inherited and put to use. While there is no single theory in whose shadow philosophers pursue their work, some available interpretations have more influence than others, and one tradition in particular functions for many writers as a point of reference that any analysis of the passions must acknowledge. Aristotelianism, in its various guises, continues to set

---

[1] English: 'passion'; French: *la passion*; Latin: *passio*. English: 'affect' or 'affection'; French: *l'affection*; Latin: *affectus*.

[2] For contemporary treatments of these distinctions see R. M. Gordon, 'The Passivity of the Emotions', *Philosophical Review*, 95 (1986), 371–92; R. C. Roberts, 'What an Emotion Is: A Sketch', *Philosophical Review*, 97 (1988), 183–209; M. Wetzel, 'Action et passion', *Revue internationale de philosophie*, 48 (1994), 303–26.

[3] Spinoza, *Ethics*, in E. Curley (ed.) *The Collected Works of Spinoza* (Princeton, 1985), vol. i, III, Definition of the Affects, p. 531.

the terms of a wide range of debates, and to constitute the starting-point from which novel conceptions of passivity and activity develop. Because its grip is only slowly relinquished, philosophers continue to react to it throughout the century, and their analyses of the affections are shaped by this experience. To understand them, we need to be aware of the Aristotelian environment they inhabit, and Part I accordingly offers an outline of the main themes and distinctions on which they draw.[4] In this chapter I sketch the conceptions of activity and passivity that seventeenth-century writers find in Aristotle himself in just enough detail to enable us to see how they are used later on.[5] These interpretations were subsequently taken up by generations of commentators who spun out of them a vast web of divergent positions. However, the Scholastic interpreter who exerted the greatest influence on early-modern theorists of the passions was undoubtedly Thomas Aquinas. His analyses of the differences between activity and passivity, alongside his description and classification of the passions of the soul, were reiterated and discussed throughout the seventeenth century, and may well have been more widely read than Aristotle's own texts. They are therefore set out in Chapter 3 which aims, once again, to provide a context for the more detailed analyses contained in the subsequent parts of the book.

Activity and Passivity in Aristotle's Metaphysics

Aristotle ties the ideas of activity and passivity to a fundamental metaphysical distinction between form and matter, which he uses to elucidate the notion of being. The existence of individual things depends, according to this view, on the inherence of form in matter; for instance, in order for a cherry seed to exist, the stuff of which it is made—matter—must somehow contain its form—the power to grow into a tree of a particular kind. Aristotle applies this analysis to natural objects, and also to artefacts; a stone statue, to take one of his own examples, has matter (the marble of which it is made) and form (its shape). But in both types of case he has to deal with the fact that the matter in question already has distinctive qualities, and can therefore be further analysed into a combination of form and some more elementary matter. The statue, for example, is carved out of a particular kind of stone, and it is by virtue of a form inhering in matter that it is marble rather than, say, pumice. The question therefore arises: where does this regress end? Aristotle replies by postulating

---

[4] As indicated in Ch. 1, above, Aristotelianism melds in the 17th cent. with several other traditions. In relation to theories of the passions, Stoicism and Augustinianism are particularly influential, and I shall discuss them where they are most relevant.

[5] All too obviously, I do not aim to do justice to the complexity of Aristotle's philosophy, and merely excerpt a set of influential doctrines about action and passion.

what he calls prime matter, a sort of substrate that does not itself have any qualities but in which any form can inhere. Because it lacks properties, prime matter cannot be described; but it is nevertheless the basis of all being.

It is immediately obvious that Aristotle's notion of form is extremely capacious. Each thing, by virtue of its form, has the properties and dispositions that make it what it is, and these include relatively static properties like the shape of a statue, as well as capacities to change, such as the power of a cherry seed to grow into a mature tree. Moreover, Aristotle connects the idea that a form makes a thing what it is with the idea that a form is the end for the sake of which that thing exists. This link is easiest to understand when we conceive of forms as powers to do or become something, such as the power of the cherry seed to grow. The form of the seed can perhaps be conceived as its capacity to develop into a mature tree, and becoming a mature tree is the end of this process. It is less easy to grasp when we think of forms as static properties, such as the shape of a statue or the sphericality of a bronze sphere, because here the idea that these properties are the *end* for the sake of which the statue or sphere exist is more opaque. However, drawing on intuitively accessible cases, we can make sense of the claim that it is by virtue of its form that a thing behaves in certain characteristic ways, and that by behaving in these ways it expresses its end. The end of cherry trees is to reach maturity, the end of a builder is to build, the end of an axe is to chop, and so on.[6]

Aristotle strengthens the connection between the form of a thing and its pattern of normal behaviour by analysing form in terms of activity. First, he argues that when a thing behaves in the manner characteristic of it, its end becomes actual. When the cherry seed grows, and even when it remains dormant, its end is being actualized.[7] Secondly, this actualized end is conceived as activity. What it is for the seed to actualize its end is for it to act in a particular way, for instance to remain dormant, to germinate, or to produce leaves.[8] So the actualization of the end specified by the form of a thing consists in a particular pattern of action, where action has to be construed generously to include what might normally be considered kinds of inaction; the dormant cherry seed, for example, is acting in the relevant sense. The implication that actualization consists in action is underlined by the remark that 'even the word "actuality" is derived from "action" '.[9] Aristotle's most general account of what makes a thing what it is therefore relies on a conception of activity.

This interpretation of what it is for a form to be actualized is set within the context of Aristotle's broader claim that form is actuality and matter

---

[6] Aristotle, *Metaphysics*, in *The Complete Works of Aristotle*, ed. J. Barnes (Princeton, 1984), vol. ii, 1050ᵃ4–14.

[7] Ibid. 1050ᵃ7–9. 'For that for the sake of which a thing is, is its principle, and the becoming is for the sake of this end; and the actuality is the end.'

[8] Ibid. 1050ᵃ22–4. 'For the action is the end, and the actuality is the action.'   [9] Ibid. 1050ᵃ22.

potentiality.[10] Starting at the most ontologically basic level, prime matter on its own has no qualities and no characteristic patterns of action. To put the point differently, it is not actually anything. However, it does have the potential to receive any form, and once combined, matter and form together constitute a thing of a particular kind. Since it can combine with any form, prime matter is potentially anything. But by itself it is all potentiality and no actuality.[11] This analysis helps to shape the complementary claim that form is actuality. When form inheres in matter, an actual thing of a particular kind is constituted. Pure potentiality (matter) is transformed into something actual (a thing of a particular kind which behaves or acts in a characteristic manner). And the actuality is contributed by form.

Existence is therefore analysed in terms of potentiality and actuality; the process by which a thing comes into being is a transition from one to the other. As long as we are talking about prime matter, these terms also carry connotations of passivity, and activity. On the one hand, since prime matter lacks all actuality, it cannot do anything or prevent anything; and the only thing that can happen to it is that it can 'receive' any form whatsoever. So there is a sense (which will become progressively more familiar) in which it is entirely passive: while something can happen to it, it cannot act. On the other hand, forms, as we have already seen, contribute the characteristic patterns of action that make things what they are, and in this sense things may be said to act.

In this originary scenario we find a comparatively sharp division between form, actuality, and activity, and matter, passivity, and potentiality. But when, instead of focusing on the transition from non-being to being, Aristotle shifts to consider how one kind of thing can become another kind of thing—how a block of marble can become a statue, or a seed a cherry tree—the connection between potentiality and passivity is greatly weakened. The statue is a form inhering in matter. But the matter in which it inheres, in this case the marble, is not pure potentiality. On the contrary, it is a chunk of a particular kind of stone with qualities and dispositions which limit what it can become. Whereas prime matter is potentially anything, the potential of the marble is to some extent fixed. It is potentially a statue, but not a blanket; potentially a bench, but not a cherry seed. Unlike prime matter, it can act in certain ways; and unlike prime matter, there are some forms that it cannot receive. In short, it is not completely passive.

Cases like this call for a fuller analysis of potentiality. Starting from the claim that 'the actuality of any given thing can only be realised in what is already potentially that thing',[12] Aristotle distinguishes various ways in which

---

[10] *On the Soul*, in *Complete Works*, ed. Barnes, vol. i, 412ª9.

[11] *Metaphysics*, 1041ª26: 'by matter I mean that which, not being a "this" actually, is potentially a "this"'.

[12] *On the Soul*, 414ª26.

a thing can be potentially something else by virtue of the fact that it possesses potentialities to act and be acted on. In the first place, a thing can have a potentiality to be changed. For example, a sharp axe has the potentiality to be blunted by pieces of hard wood. Aristotle attributes the potentiality to be acted on to 'the principle in the very thing acted on, which makes it capable of being changed and acted on by another thing, or by itself regarded as other',[13] and elsewhere describes it as a potentiality to suffer.[14] So this kind of potentiality is attributed to a feature of the object in question, which Aristotle calls a principle. But it is described in language which carries strong connotations of passivity. It is a potential to suffer, to have something done to one, to be acted on.

How extensive is potentiality of this kind? On the face of it, it seems that any thing has the potentiality to be changed into a vast number of other things. And yet we have been taking it for granted that there are some limits to this mutability—that a block of marble is potentially a statue but not potentially a blanket. How, then, do we identify the potentialities of a thing? Aristotle warns that we cannot rely on language to solve this problem and must guard against taking passive grammatical constructions as a mark of the true potentialities of things.[15] We need to take into account that we sometimes describe an object as having a potentiality when we are talking about its capacity to suffer changes for better or worse, and sometimes use the term in a more restricted sense to describe cases where a thing is changed for the better, as when a sick person becomes healthy. So a potentiality to be acted on can be a capacity to be changed; or it can be a capacity to be changed in a way that is characterized as an improvement.[16] This latter usage obviously drastically limits the range of a thing's potentialities. At the same time it links the potentiality of a thing to its end. According to Aristotle, changes that count as changes for the better are those that enable a thing to attain the end specified by its form. This seems to leave us with two views. Starting with the more inclusive one, things are passive in so far as they have the potentiality to be changed by other things for better or worse, and in all cases this potentiality is both made possible and limited by what Aristotle calls the principle of the thing in question. A cherry seed has the potential to be changed for the worse by being ground up, because this will destroy its capacity to germinate and grow; it does not have the potential to be changed for the worse by being made into an apple seed (genetic engineering apart) because it simply does not contain the relevant ingredients. Equally, it has the potential to be changed for the better, for example by being placed in ideal germinating conditions; but once again, its potential is limited by what it is. Aristotle's exclusive interpretation of the potentialities of a thing focuses on this last pair of cases. The seed possesses a potential to germinate,

---

[13] *Metaphysics*, 1046ᵃ12.   [14] Ibid. 1019ᵃ20.
[15] *Sophistical Refutations*, in *Complete Works*, ed. J. Barnes, vol. i, 178ᵃ11.
[16] *Metaphysics*, 1046ᵃ17.

and is thus in a sense passive; it cannot germinate by itself but must be acted on by other things. But the potential in question is not simply a potential to have something done to it; rather, it is a potential to do something, to act in a way that expresses and conforms to the set of powers that constitute its form. What is from one perspective a potential to be acted on can be viewed from another angle as a potential to act.

A second dimension of this problem bears directly on the question of what is potentially what. Aristotle argues that we say one thing is potentially another when it is not impossible that it should actually become that thing.[17] So we must ask ourselves: is it impossible that a particular quantity of earth should become bronze, or not? And is it impossible that it should become a statue, or not? How, though, are we to answer these questions? According to Aristotle, we must take account of the stages by which one thing can be transformed into another, and limit a thing's potentialities to comparatively immediate alterations. It is not impossible, he claims, that this earth should become bronze; and it is not impossible that this bronze should become a statue; but it is impossible that this earth should become a statue.[18] To put it another way, earth has the potentiality to become bronze, and bronze has the potentiality to become a statue. But earth lacks the potentiality to become a statue. Summing up, things have potentiality in so far as they have the potentiality to be changed by being acted on. But only some of the ways in which they are capable of being changed count as potentialities. First to be excluded are capacities to be changed in ways which would require the intervention of a series of agents, such as the capacity of earth to become a bronze statue. And among the remaining capacities, we sometimes exclude capacities to be changed which would not be improvements, such as the capacity of a person to become ill.

The potentiality to be acted on, which we have so far considered, is complemented in Aristotle's works by a discussion of two further types of case: the potentiality to resist being acted on and the potentiality to act. The first of these cases is limited to 'a state of insusceptibility to change for the worse and to destruction by another thing or by the thing itself qua other'.[19] So only capacities to resist being altered for the worse count as potentialities to resist change. Moreover, Aristotle seems to think of these as potentialities to act, perhaps because he conceives of the capacity to resist change as the exertion of a kind of power, and thus as the contrary of the capacity to be changed or acted on. The second kind of potentiality—the potentiality to act—is characterized by Aristotle as 'in the agent', as opposed to the patient.[20] For example, 'heat and the art of building are present, one in that which can produce heat and the other in that which can build'.[21] The central idea here seems to be

---

[17] Ibid. 1047ᵃ24.   [18] Ibid. 1049ᵃ15.   [19] Ibid. 1046ᵃ14.   [20] Ibid. 1046ᵃ27.
[21] Ibid.

that a thing can have the potentiality to exercise causal powers. A stove, for example, has the potentiality to become hot, and its heat can then act on other things. In our earlier discussion of the potentiality to be acted on, we analysed capacities such as that of the stove to become hot as a potentiality to be changed by something else. But Aristotle is now asking us to move forward a stage in the chain of causes and effects. Once the stove's potentiality to become hot has been actualized and it is in fact hot, it has the potentiality to act on other things by heating them, as when it warms someone's hands. And even before it becomes hot, we can say that the stove has the potentiality to heat other things, presumably because heating is one of its characteristic actions. In the case of the stove, we are considering an object with a potentiality to act which can only become actual if something else acts on it. The stove has the potentiality to become hot, but it can only become hot if, say, someone lights it. However, Aristotle contrasts this sort of case with that of a man who knows grammar, but is not at the moment exercising his knowledge. The man's knowledge is potential or inactive. But to make it active or actual he need not be acted on by something outside him. He can start to reflect whenever he wants to, if nothing external prevents him.[22]

We are now in a position to see how potentialities to act and be acted on dovetail with one another. In natural objects, each potentiality to be acted on, once actualized, consists in a potentiality to act, which can in turn be actualized only in an object which has the corresponding potentiality to be acted on. For example, the stove has the potentiality to become hot which, once actualized, consists in a potentiality to heat which can in turn be actualized only in objects like my hand which have the potentiality to be heated. And so on. So if an object A is to change an object B, A's potentiality to act must be matched by B's potentiality to be acted on. The stove can only warm my hand if my hand has the potentiality to be warmed, or as Aristotle puts it, 'The active and passive imply an active and a passive capacity and the actualisation of these capacities, e.g. that which is capable of heating is related to that which is capable of being heated, because it *can* heat it.'[23]

The examples Aristotle uses suggest that this analysis of change is intended to apply to two kinds of cases: to those where one thing is transformed into another, that is, where one form is destroyed and another created, as when a block of marble is carved into a statue; and to those where a thing undergoes a change in its affections or accidental properties but retains its form, as when my hand becomes warm but remains my hand. In all such cases, change consists in a transition from potentiality to actuality; and this transition can only be brought about by something actual. So in this sense, among others, actuality is prior to potentiality.[24] In addition, the notion of action employed

---

[22] *On the Soul*, 417ᵃ27.   [23] *Metaphysics*, 1021ᵃ15.   [24] Ibid. 1049ᵇ24.

in this account is designed to capture various different processes of change. To say that a thing acts can be a way of talking about motion, and Aristotle does in fact conceive of physical changes as motion, requiring contact between bodies. But it can also be a way of talking about thinking (as when a man who exercises his knowledge of grammar is said to act) and about processes which seem to involve both thought and motion, such as the action of a doctor in healing a patient.

So far, we have traced in the *Metaphysics* and *On the Soul* two contrasts between activity and passivity. First, there is a sense in which matter is passive and form active, which is clearest in the case of prime matter. Prime matter is passive in that it can only receive forms, and forms are active because it is only when they inhere in matter that particular things begin to exist. A residual version of this distinction applies when the matter in question is not prime; matter still receives form, as when a block of marble receives the shape of the statue. Suppose that this captures one of the senses in which Aristotle uses the opposition between activity and passivity. He then goes on to identify form with actuality and matter with potentiality. So we might expect that actuality would be interpreted as active and potentiality as passive. Is this supposition borne out? To some extent it is, for, as we have seen, Aristotle is explicit about the connection between actuality and act. But to some extent it is not. For, as we have also seen, his account of potentiality encompasses both potentialities to be acted on and potentialities to act. Potentialities can be either active or passive.

This seems to leave us with two senses of passivity. One encourages us to conceive of matter as passive. The other offers us an account of potentiality as sometimes passive and sometimes active. But the two have a great deal in common. First, both present passivity as potentiality. The passivity of prime matter consists in its potential to become anything, and a passive potentiality is already what it says—a potentiality. Passivity is thus a capacity to become or be changed. Secondly, both accounts present passivity as a capacity to be changed by something else, by an agent of some sort. How it is that forms inhere in matter to become particular things is obscure, to say the least. But it seems clear that Aristotle thinks of forms as in some way acting on matter, and holds that matter is changed in the process. Equally, it is central to his account of potentialities that they are actualized by the intervention of an agent.

Action and passion are therefore among the most fundamental concepts of Aristotelian metaphysics, in which they are used to explicate the notion of being and the related issue of change. These ideas—together with those of form and matter, and of actuality and potentiality, with which they are most closely associated—remained central, so that a broadly Aristotelian understanding of activity and passivity continued to inform metaphysical enquiry, and contributed to analyses of the causal relations between natural things. Because of their striking longevity, these ideas were still being recycled in commentaries on Aristotle written in the seventeenth century. By then, moreover, they had become so much a part of philosophy that they provided the material from which philosophers of all persuasions fashioned their positions and arguments. Within the philosophical community, understandings of action and passion were predominantly shaped by this Aristotelian view.

Activity and Passivity in the Aristotelian Soul

As well as using his two interpretations of activity and passivity to account for being and change, Aristotle employs them to explain the soul and characterize its powers. The association of form with activity provides the basis for an analysis of the special qualities distinguishing the soul from other kinds of things; and the distinction between active and passive potentialities contributes to an analysis of the soul's various states and capacities, including its passions. Together, these are built into an immensely influential framework within which affections and desires are explored.

When Aristotle turns to the soul, he allows one exception to his claim that everything is composed of form and matter. The soul, he argues, is not a composite. Rather, it is a form which combines with a body to make a living thing.[25] We can grasp this relationship by analogy if we imagine the eye as an animal. The matter of such an animal would be the eyeball, retina, and so on; but unless it also had the power to see, these physical organs would not really be an eye. The power to see would be what made them into an eye, and what made them into that particular kind of thing, and this would therefore be its form. Similarly, the soul is the power a body must have if it is to be a living thing. It is a bundle of capacities that makes a body into a particular type of animal, whether a clam or a human being.[26]

As a form, the soul is actual, though Aristotle is careful to specify the particular sense in which this is so. There are, he says, two senses of actuality, two senses in which the soul exists and operates. Returning to the example of the eye, this is actual in one sense when it is exercising its power of sight. But it is actual in another sense by virtue of the fact that it possesses the power of sight, regardless of whether this power is actually being exercised. The actuality of the soul is of this latter sort. The soul consists in a bundle of powers which endure even when they are not being exercised. For example, when we are asleep our power to think does not vanish, even if we are not thinking. To put the point differently, our power to think remains actual. And the same goes for all the powers that make us into the kind of living things we are.[27]

---

[25] *On the Soul*, 413ᵃ2. 'The soul *plus* the body constitutes the animal.'
[26] Ibid. 412ᵇ10–24. See J. L. Ackrill, 'Aristotle's Definition of psûche', in J. Barnes *et al.* (eds.), *Articles on Aristotle*, iv. *Psychology and Aesthetics* (London, 1979), 65–8.
[27] *On the Soul*, 412ᵃ22 f.

There may still be a temptation to think of the powers that constitute the actuality of the soul as both potential and actual. For example, a person who has the power to move, but is not exercising it because she is asleep, might be thought to have that power only potentially, and to have it actually when she wakes and gets up. But this misses Aristotle's point. His claim is that the *power* to move, the *power* to think, and so on, are always actual. They are always there. What comes and goes from actuality to potentiality is their exercise. But the exercise of these powers is achieved by the soul–body composite rather than the soul alone. To keep this view in focus, it is helpful to refer back to the notion of form discussed in the previous section. A form, we found, can be understood as the set of powers to behave in certain characteristic ways that make a thing what it is. The cherry seed, for example, has the capacity to germinate and grow even when it is dormant; and even when it is dormant these powers are actual. This claim loses its straightforwardness, however, when we remember that actuality is in turn linked to activity. While it seems reasonable enough to say that the powers of the cherry seed or the soul are actual when they are not being exercised (meaning that they are still there), it is harder to see what it means to say that they are active. At this point we need to recall that the active quality of forms does not consist in the exercise of a set of powers. As Aristotle sees it, the form of a cherry seed acts so long as it differentiates the matter in which it inheres, bringing it about that the cherry seed exists. It is active in the sense that it makes that particular thing exist. The same goes for the soul. The soul contributes to the soul-body composite the powers that characterize a living thing of a particular kind, and in doing so both acts and makes these powers actual.

To complement this analysis of the soul as actual, Aristotle offers an interpretation of the body as potential. 'The soul', he tells us, 'is actuality in the sense corresponding to sight . . . the body corresponds to what is in potentiality.'[28] The soul-body composite that makes up a living thing is therefore conceptually divided into an active or actual part and a passive or potential one. But the properties of a living thing are always in fact the properties of a composite, and this blurs the boundary between the passive body and the active soul. As Aristotle is the first to tell us, the powers of the soul can be actual or potential in the soul-body composite; for example, when a man starts to analyse the grammatical structure of a sentence, his knowledge of grammar undergoes a change from potentiality to actuality. We see Aristotle moving here from one sense of actuality to another. The powers of the soul, considered alone, are actual and active, in so far as they make a living thing what it is. But the powers of the soul–body composite are actual and active when they are being exercised, and it is for this reason that they can be either actual or potential.

---

[28] Ibid. 412^{b}28.

In Aristotle's account of the specific powers of the soul, the properties of the soul–body composite are uppermost. It is possible to give a list of the powers manifested in living things; but whether a particular power is manifested in a specific kind of animal depends on the matter in which the soul inheres. Aristotle ranks living things according to the number of powers they manifest, putting humans at the top and simpler organisms such as clams at the bottom; but this is a ranking of types of soul-body composite, rather than of bodies or souls alone. Equally, in accordance with the mixture of actuality and potentiality found in composites, their powers are characterized as variously active and passive. The resulting account of the powers or capacities possessed by living things, together with their classification into these two categories, not only creates a picture of the mind that is enormously influential; in addition, the analysis of certain powers as passive draws on and elaborates a conception of passivity that shapes subsequent understandings of the passions of the soul.

Concentrating on Aristotle's characterization of powers as active or passive, we find that the nutritive power, which is possessed by all living things and is responsible for nutrition and generation, is active.[29] This characterization stems from the view that the capacities of a living thing to nourish itself and reproduce are abilities to transform one kind of thing into another by acting. Food, for example, does not nourish unless an organism acts on it and breaks it down into its components. As Aristotle expresses it, nutrition is the power of a creature with a nutritive soul to act on food, thereby changing it into the matter of which the body is constructed.[30] Sensation, Aristotle's next power, is classified as passive on the grounds that our senses only become active when they are stimulated by sensory objects. 'What is sensitive', Aristotle explains, 'is so only potentially, not actually. The power of sense is parallel to what is combustible, for that never ignites itself spontaneously, but requires an agent which has the power of starting ignition.'[31] Passivity is here interpreted as an inability to exercise a power unaided. Sensation is passive because we cannot sense unless there is something *for* us to sense which stimulates our sensory organs in the appropriate fashion. Our senses are excited by individual things in the world,[32] and it is only when an individual is present that we are able to receive its sensory form. While this account is intuitively accessible, it already suggests that it is going to be difficult to establish a boundary between active and passive powers. Why, after all, should we not follow this lead and say that nutrition is passive because living things can only exercise their power to transform food if there is something for them to eat? This question reveals a further dimension of the distinction between activity and passivity which does not concern the circumstances in which powers are exercised but has to do with the nature of the powers themselves. Sensation, according to Aristotle, is

---

[29] Ibid. 416ᵃ19.   [30] Ibid. 416ᵃ21–ᵇ2.   [31] Ibid. 417ᵃ6.   [32] Ibid. 417ᵇ21.

a process of receiving sensory forms and in this respect is 'like bare asserting or thinking'.[33] When we sense, we receive the sensory forms of things, as wax receives the impression of a signet-ring,[34] but we do not alter or transform them. By contrast, nutrition and generation transform one kind of matter into another. When Aristotle classifies the nutritive power as active and the sensitive power as passive, this conception of the difference between action and passion seems to be carrying most of the weight.

As well as the power of sensation, the sensitive soul has the ability to perceive whether an object is pleasant or painful, and to make a corresponding judgement which Aristotle describes as 'a kind of affirmation or negation', and as appetite or aversion. Appetite is also characterized as a desire for things that appear pleasurable and an aversion for what appears painful which in turn gives rise to movement.[35] But because appetite is an aspect of sense,[36] and always occurs together with sensation,[37] it too is classified as passive.

Before we can probe the claim that appetite is passive, we need to get a clearer idea of what it is. At one point, Aristotle characterizes appetite as the desire for pleasure,[38] which is in turn analysed as 'consciousness, through the senses, of a certain kind of emotion'.[39] So we have the idea that appetite is a desire for a certain kind of emotion, namely pleasure. This generic account does not imply, however, that humans and other animals are ruled by a single desire for a single emotion, and Aristotle argues that two complicating factors need to be considered. First, our desires are sensitive to our perceptions. We recognize sensory objects as certain sorts of things which, by virtue of their properties, have the capacity to provide particular sorts of pleasure or to inflict distinctive sorts of pain, and react to them accordingly. Rather than consisting simply of desire and aversion, appetite consists in varieties of desire and varieties of aversion. Secondly, the satisfaction of sensory appetite does not produce the bare emotion of pleasure any more than the failure to satisfy it produces unmodified pain. Rather, it results in particular kinds of pleasure such as revenge or love, which are matched by specific kinds of pain such as hatred or pity.

Appetite is therefore intimately connected to the passions which, according to Aristotle, are found in the souls of humans and animals. But the precise character of the connection is harder to work out. At one point in *The Nicomachean Ethics* Aristotle describes passions as 'feelings accompanied by pleasure or pain'.[40] Allied to his definition of appetite as desire for pleasure, this may seem to suggest that passions are the feelings we experience when our desires are satisfied or thwarted, as distinct from our desires themselves.

---

[33] Ibid. 431ᵃ8.   [34] Ibid. 424ᵃ18.   [35] Ibid. 433ᵃ9.   [36] Ibid. 431ᵃ13.
[37] Ibid. 414ᵇ3.   [38] *Rhetoric*, in *Complete Works*, Barnes, vol. ii, 1370ᵃ17.   [39] Ibid. 1370ᵃ27.
[40] In *Complete Works*, Barnes, vol. ii, 1105ᵇ21. Aristotle lists the following as passions: appetite, anger, fear, confidence, envy, joy, love, hatred, longing, emulation, pity.

Elsewhere, however, passions are identified with desires: Aristotle not only lists appetite as a passion, but also defines anger as 'a desire accompanied by pain for a conspicuous revenge for a conspicuous slight at the hands of men who have no call to slight oneself or one's friends'.[41] So it now looks as though the desires and aversions that constitute the appetite are themselves passions. Two further features of Aristotle's account support this interpretation. One is his description of anger as a desire accompanied by pain. Anger therefore satisfies the definition of passions as 'feelings accompanied by pleasure or pain'. Rather than conceiving of appetite as containing desires *for* states that are pleasurable and aversions to states that are painful, we do better to think of it as consisting of desires and aversions that are *already* pleasurable or painful, which give rise to actions that in turn produce further kinds of pain and pleasure. For example, anger is painful. The angry man desires revenge—that is, he desires to act to bring about a different state of affairs. And his desire to achieve this is at the same time a desire to replace his pain with a kind of pleasure.

Further evidence for this interpretation is supplied by Aristotle's account of a passion as a state of mind, directed at a certain object, on certain grounds.[42] To pursue the same example, my anger is a desire for revenge, directed at a particular person, on the grounds that he has insulted me. This account moves away from the suggestion that passions are simply feelings to the idea that they are rather more like judgements. They are feelings with grounds and objects. In fact, Aristotle presents our desires for sensory objects as answering to this analysis. They are desires for particular things, grounded on the fact that these things have properties which enable them to provide us with certain sorts of pleasure. I desire apricots, for example, because I believe that their taste will be delicious and their scent evocative of summer. Moreover, the states of pleasure we achieve as the result of pursuing our desires also seem to satisfy the more elaborate analysis. For example, what gives pleasure to our angry man is having revenged himself on his enemy, on the grounds that the villain had behaved outrageously. It therefore seems that all the states of the sensory appetite are passions, although the objects and grounds of these states will be diverse, and of varying degrees of sophistication.

Why, to return to our present theme, does Aristotle hold that passions are passive? One argument in favour of this judgement is his view that our ability to feel passions is not an ability to transform one kind of thing into another; rather, as with sensory perceptions, it is a capacity to be affected by the world around us. The argument for counting passions as passive is thus the same as the one for classifying sensory perceptions in this way. Against this, one might claim that we do not simply 'receive' passions as Aristotle holds that we receive sensory forms; instead, they result from complex interpretations and evaluations

---

[41] *Rhetoric*, 1378ᵃ31.   [42] Ibid. 1378ᵃ21.

that are themselves a species of action. Whatever the truth of this last claim, however, the fact that Aristotle does not take it up suggests that he does indeed view passions as similar to sensory perceptions, as responses that have to be provoked in us by external things and as states that we suffer. We do not have the power to experience passions unaided, but must wait on circumstances to excite them.

So far we have been talking about passions as states of the soul. But Aristotle views them as properties of the soul–body composite, and thus as having what we would call physical as well as psychological effects. Turning to these bodily manifestations, he goes on to introduce a further dimension of passivity. When people become angry, for example, they become hot around the heart, and while this heat is not identical with the experience of anger, it always accompanies it. Similarly, when people are afraid, the interiors of their bodies become cold. These interior bodily events in turn cause and explain the visible effects of passions. Because angry people are hot around the heart, and because in anger this heat moves upwards, they become 'red in the face and full of breath'. With characteristic sensitivity to the physical language used in ancient Greek to describe the emotions, Aristotle remarks that this is why expressions about anger boiling up, rising, and being stirred up are appropriate. They are not simply metaphors but describe a physical process.[43] In addition, this process explains why anger is hard to overcome. Once the bodily motions that go with it are excited, they are not under our direct control and are difficult to stop.[44] Even when an angry person sets up counter-motions, the passions continue to move them on in the same direction as at first. Aristotle's discussion implies that this problem afflicts us both when we set up counter-motions to a particular fit of anger, for example by calming down, and when we set up counter-motions to habitual anger by trying to become less irascible. In the latter case, he says, we are like people who resolve not to hum a tune that has got fixed in their heads but find themselves doing so none the less.[45] Running through these reflections is the idea that neither passions nor their physical symptoms are entirely under our control. We cannot help ourselves going red in the face when we are angry, and, yet more seriously, we often cannot prevent ourselves from getting angry. So the passive character of passions does not just lie in the fact that they are responses to the world which only occur when circumstances excite us; it also lies in the fact that we often cannot control the way we respond to a situation. Faced with a cherry tree in full leaf, it is not in my power to perceive it as orange rather than green. Similarly, Aristotle seems to be saying, when someone insults me it may not be in my power to feel forgiving rather than angry.

---

[43] *Problems*, in *Complete Works*, J. Barnes, vol. ii, 947^{b}23. (The authenticity of this work has been seriously doubted.)

[44] *On Memory*, in *Complete Works*, ed. Barnes, vol. i, 453^{a}26.   [45] Ibid.

The passive powers of the sensitive soul are more or less elaborated in animals of varying degrees of complexity. In the first place, because animals possess more than one sense, the process of perceiving is complicated by the fact that the information contributed by different senses has to be integrated into perceptions of objects with more than one type of sensory property. We have distinct senses of smell and touch, but perceive a baby's head, for example, as simultaneously soft and scented. In addition, Aristotle argues that many animals (though not, for instance, ants, bees, or grubs) are capable of imagination,[46] a complex notion which he applies to dreams;[47] to waking fantasies such as that of a man who every time he glimpses a boy on the street imagines that it is his lover;[48] to events that we are inclined to take as paradigmatic cases of imagination, such as our ability to call up a picture;[49] to sensory judgements about which we are uncertain, as when we say that a distant shape looks like a horse;[50] and to perceptions that we know to be misleading, such as the perception of the sun as a foot in diameter.[51] Imagination is closely related to sensory perception—Aristotle describes it as a movement resulting from the actual power of the senses.[52] But it diverges from perception in two ways. Imagination, unlike perception, is in our power;[53] and while perceptions are generally true, imaginings are not.

These two differences are in turn important for Aristotle's account of passivity, although the first works better for some cases than for others. Perhaps it is in your power to imagine yourself discussing imagination with Aristotle; but dreams, and the fantasies fuelled by our emotions, are usually not under our control. Aristotle's spread of cases suggests that imaginings are sometimes active and sometimes passive. When we imagine at will, and can control what we imagine, imagination satisfies two of Aristotle's criteria for active powers. But when fantasies come upon us, and seem to take their own course regardless of our attempts to direct them, they answer to his characterization of passivity. The second difference—that imaginings are usually erroneous—points to a further feature of imagination, namely that when we imagine something we make a kind of judgement to the effect that this may not be how things really are. We can see, Aristotle claims, that we do not treat our everyday imaginings as a reliable account of the world from the fact that we do not respond emotionally to them, so that imagining a frightening situation, for example, does not make us afraid.[54] Similarly, when we try to discern objects in poor conditions we come out with claims such as 'It *appears* to be a horse'; and when we acknowledge that the sun looks about a foot in diameter, we know perfectly well that this is not the case. Once again, not all kinds of imagining

---

[46] *On the Soul*, 428ª10.   [47] Ibid. 428ª7.
[48] *On Dreams*, in *Complete Works*, ed. Barnes, vol. i, 460ᵇ3 f.   [49] *On the Soul*, 427ᵇ19.
[50] Ibid. 428ª12.   [51] *On Dreams*, 460ᵇ18; *On the Soul*, 428ᵇ2.   [52] *On the Soul*, 429ª2.
[53] Ibid. 427ᵇ16.   [54] Ibid. 427ᵇ21.

answer to this description. For instance, when we dream, we do not usually know that we are dreaming and adopt a sceptical stance, although, when we are awake, we distinguish dreams from veridical experiences. Putting this point aside, however, Aristotle seems to imply that this difference between sensory perception and imagination does not undermine the fact that they are both passive powers.

In addition to their powers to perceive, to experience passions, and to imagine, some animals possess the further capacity to think—to arrive at judgements that are true or false. According to Aristotle, this ability depends partly on perceptions which provide us with information about sensible objects, and partly on deliberative imagination, a capacity he distinguishes from the sensitive imagination possessed by all animals.[55] Thus provided for, the soul is able to exercise its power of thinking: it can acquire speculative knowledge by coming to know the forms of things; and it can acquire practical knowledge of good and bad. The capacity to think in these ways lies within the control of the soul itself, so that when it speculates and calculates about means and ends, it acts.[56] It activates its own capacities rather than being pushed into action by anything else, and these capacities are active powers—capacities to act rather than to be acted on.[57]

These links between thinking and activity are important and influential, in part because they contribute to Aristotle's account of the causal antecedents of action. As we have already seen, Aristotle connects appetite with sensation, and regards animals as drawn to or repelled by objects they perceive as pleasant or painful. The perceptions of the sensitive soul excite passions and desires which explain the actions of animals, and some human action as well. However, humans are also able to reflect actively on their own good; '[S]ometimes by reason of the images or thoughts that are within the soul, just as if it were seeing, [the soul] calculates and deliberates what is to come by reference to what is present; and when it makes a pronouncement, as in the case of sensation it pronounces the object to be pleasant or painful, in this case it avoids or pursues. And so generally in cases of action.'[58] Calculative reasoning can therefore contribute to action; but it is not sufficient to bring it about because, in Aristotle's view, thought cannot move us to action without appetite.[59] Taking account of this claim, Aristotle concludes that we are moved by appetite alone.[60] Appetite is a single faculty of the soul, sharply distinguished from reasoning in that it has no deliberative element.[61] But appetite is not always sensitive. While the sensitive appetite contains desires and passions, the calculations of the thinking part of the soul excite rational appetites—wishes—which move people to rational action.[62] Moreover, when rational and irrational appetites

[55] Ibid. 434ᵃ6.   [56] Ibid. 431ᵇ1; 432ᵇ26.   [57] Ibid. 430ᵃ18.   [58] Ibid. 431ᵇ6.
[59] Ibid. 432ᵇ25.   [60] Ibid. 433ᵃ21.   [61] Ibid. 434ᵃ12.   [62] Ibid. 414ᵇ2; 432ᵇ5.

conflict, desires can overrule wishes, and wishes subdue desires.[63] The faculty of appetite therefore has two aspects, one active, the other passive, and consequently can both move and be moved. In so far as it desires, it is moved by the objects of its desire; in so far as it responds to desires, passions, and wishes it *is* a kind of movement, expressed in bodily motion.[64]

In the first section of this chapter, we saw that many things have capacities to act and to be acted on by each other reciprocally.[65] But a process of change must start somewhere; it must originate, Aristotle seems to say, in an agent capable of acting without being acted on.[66] In the inanimate world, this role is allotted to the outermost heaven, which moves continually and effortlessly in an eternal, circular motion. Of all natural things it is the most active, because it has no potentiality, no capacity to be changed by any other natural object.[67] In the economy of the soul this role is played by thought, which is in its essential nature activity.[68] This interpretation of thinking draws on several conceptions of what it is to be active that have already been discussed. First, Aristotle seems to claim that, although the capacity of the soul to think about particular truths and falsehoods depends on sensory experience, so that people cannot think about things they have never heard of, the capacity to start thinking and direct one's thoughts belongs to the soul itself. In this respect thinking contrasts with sensory perception and passion, and while they are passive, it is active. Secondly, thinking of this kind cannot be captured in the passive language of receiving and imprinting used by Aristotle in connection with perception. It is more like nutrition in that it creates new conclusions that were not there before, and is therefore active in this second sense. Thirdly, Aristotle seems sometimes to suggest that thinking is the soul's end and the greatest of its powers. Plants possess nutritive and generative powers, and animals add to these the powers of sense, sensitive appetite, and imagination. But only humans possess the intellectual powers, so that it is only in humans that all the powers of the soul are manifested and the soul is able to operate to its fullest extent. Moreover, since the soul is 'in its essential nature activity'[69] this scale of increasing powers is at the same time a scale of levels of activity; it is by virtue of their souls that human beings are more active than onions. Finally, by virtue of their capacity to act by initiating their own thoughts, humans approach the divine. Like the movement of the outermost heaven, divine activity is ungenerated and eternal. Since nothing acts upon it, either to set it going or alter it, it has no potentiality but is always actual, perfectly realizing its own end.

[63] Ibid. 434ᵃ12.   [64] Ibid. 433ᵇ16.

[65] Aristotle, *On Generation and Corruption*, in *Complete Works*, ed. Barnes, vol. i, 323ᵃ25; 328ᵃ19.

[66] Ibid. 324ᵃ32.

[67] *On the Heavens*, in *Complete Works*, ed. Barnes, vol. i, 270ᵇ7; 284ᵃ12; 286ᵃ9; *On Generation and Corruption*, 336ᵇ27–34; *On the Universe*, 397ᵇ9–401ᵇ30.

[68] *On the Soul*, 430ᵃ18.   [69] Ibid.

Intellectual thought carries with it this possibility, and is therefore both the activity and perfection of the soul.

So far, I have tried to show how the notions of activity and passivity play important parts in Aristotle's most general account of being and change, and are also central to his conception of living things. Like a painter outlining a vast mural, Aristotle offers us a grand design. Viewing it from the opposite side of the room, we see that particular things are composed of active form and passive matter, and that as composites they have both actuality and potentiality. Moving a little nearer, we discern that their potentiality is of two kinds, active and passive. Coming closer still to get a good look at one section of the composition, we find that living things are composites of passive body and active soul. Finally, peering at the wall now, we see that some of the powers in which the soul consists are active, while others are passive capacities to be changed by external things. This picture is repeatedly copied by Aristotle's Scholastic commentators. Some meticulously reproduce much of the original as they perceive it, while others make subtle alterations and additions; but the composition remains largely unchanged for many centuries and continues to provide a design for philosophical thinking as well as a stock of more detailed motifs. Among the subjects to which this applies is the study of the soul; for although their precise characterizations alter and proliferate, the hierarchy of nutritive, sensitive, and intellectual powers explicated by Aristotle proved extremely enduring. For our purposes, the work of Aquinas—which will be discussed in the next chapter—is of unparalleled importance. His analysis of the passions extends and alters the picture painted by Aristotle and exerts a tremendous influence, both on later Scholastic philosophical psychology up to and throughout the seventeenth century, and on the opponents of Scholasticism. It becomes, in short, a second Aristotelian orthodoxy, part of the legacy on which early-modern theorists of the passions depend.

3

Passion and Action in Aquinas

To leap from Aristotle to Aquinas, from the work of a pagan Greek living in the fourth century BC to that of a Christian monk of the thirteenth century AD, may at first sight appear unhistorical, but the shift can readily be justified. In his *Summa Theologiae* Aquinas takes over Aristotle's philosophy as he understands it and incorporates it into a systematic account of the place of humanity in God's creation. He not only draws on and elaborates the Aristotelian notions of activity and passivity discussed in Chapter 2, but employs these in a treatise of great range and complexity on the passions of the soul.[1] For Catholic audiences, this work became a philosophical staple as well as a benchmark of religious orthodoxy, an established and accepted synthesis of Aristotelian and Christian doctrine whose influence was not significantly diminished by the resurgence of interest in the ancient world during the Renaissance. The recovery of the Greek language in Western Europe, and the wider availability of classical texts, made it easier to read Aristotle either in the original or in Latin translation; but Aquinas's interpretation of his work remained orthodox and formative.

A number of the seventeenth-century philosophers who will be discussed in this book viewed Aquinas as eminently worth taking seriously and worth arguing with. Whether they defended or rejected him, he remained an imposing presence, an icon of the Scholastic tradition with which many of them were deeply concerned. His influence exerted a particularly strong hold on authors writing about the passions, who continued to rely on his outstandingly detailed and systematic treatment of this theme, and to refer back to the metaphysical framework in which it was set.[2]

Writing in Latin, Aquinas pursues the connotations of *energeia* and *entelechia*—Aristotle's principal terms for activity, actualization, fulfilment, and realization—and of *dunamis*—meaning potentiality, capacity, possibility, potency, and power. The first of these sets of ideas is captured by *actus* in which the Greek etymological link between act and actuality remarked on by Aristotle is retained, and also by the terms *opus* and *operatio*. The affinities among all these

---

[1] *Summa Theologiae*, ed. and trans. by the Dominican Fathers, 30 vols. (London, 1964–80), 1a. 2ae. 22–48.

[2] For a discussion of the authors to whom Aquinas is indebted in his work on the passions see *Summa*, vol. xxi, app. 3.

words are extremely close and the differences between them often vanish in translation; for example, Aquinas speaks of the *operatio* of the soul, meaning its characteristic operations or activities, and of understanding as one of the soul's *opera* or acts.[3] Another meaning of *energeia*—fulfilment or realization—is often expressed in Aquinas's work by the term *finis*, meaning fulfilment or end, but this too is associated with *actus, opus,* and *operatio.* Turning to the terms for potentiality, two senses of *dunamis*, namely potentiality and power, remain yoked together in the Latin *potentia.* Active and passive power, for example, are *potentia activa* and *potentia passiva.* But in discussing the Aristotelian notion of power Aquinas also uses two terms with active connotations, namely *vis,* meaning force, and *virtus,* the word for virtue or strength, but also for value, merit, or worth. The active and passive aspects of potentiality are reflected in this range. Coming now to passivity itself, Aquinas generally captures this idea with the deponent verb *patior*, meaning to suffer, and its cognates. Among these is the term *passiones* (the Latin title of his treatise is *De Passionibus Animae*) although, as he remarks in a comment on Augustine's discussion of the trans-lations of *pathe*, *passiones* are identical with *affectiones* or affections.[4]

Activity and Passivity in Thomist Metaphysics

Aquinas faithfully retains the load-bearing planks of Aristotle's metaphysics, and preserves most of the conceptions of activity and passivity discussed in the previous chapter, leaving in place the claim that things are made up of form and matter and the connected interpretation of form as active and actual, and of matter as potential and passive. Broadly speaking, these are used in the ways examined in Chapter 2: to explicate existence, to explain how it is possible for the accidents of things to alter while their essences remain the same, and to give an account of change. But Aquinas also introduces far-reaching modi-fications into Aristotle's scheme, prompted by his conviction that God created the world in the fashion described in the Old Testament, and his belief that natural things are to be understood as a hierarchy culminating in God him-self. The need to accommodate Aristotle's metaphysics to these Christian tenets, alongside a desire to improve it by tidying up some of its most philosophically puzzling corners, is reflected in a number of significant alterations which bear on the interpretation of activity and passivity.

For Aristotle, the order of nature is a progression ranging from pure passiv-ity or prime matter at one extreme to pure activity or the divine at the other. While Aquinas is deeply committed to an overarching and hierarchical scheme encompassing both lower and higher things, he is not satisfied by Aristotle's

---

[3] *Summa*, 1a. 76. 4.   [4] Ibid. 1a. 2ae. 22.

accounts of the poles of this order and therefore constructs fresh interpretations of these two points of closure. Starting at the passive end, Aquinas confronts a tension in Aristotle's work between the claim that all existing things are composed of matter and form and the claim that prime matter, lacking form, is pure potentiality. The first of these implies that, if prime matter has no form, it cannot exist. By taking this implication seriously, Aquinas arrives at the conclusion that there is no prime matter. The formless stuff that Aristotle posits as the ground of all being does not exist. Instead, prime matter is to be conceived as a conceptual limit, an idea of pure passivity that both extends and closes off the spectrum of existing things. This reinterpretation gets rid of an anomaly in Aristotle's metaphysics, and at the same time reinforces the assumption that all existing natural things are subject to a single kind of analysis in that they are composed of matter and form. Aquinas's revision spells the demise of prime matter as capable only of being acted on, and carries with it the implication that natural things, without exception, possess both actuality and potentiality. To put the point differently, they are all without exception capable of acting in certain characteristic ways, and capable of being acted on or changed.

When Aquinas turns his attention to the other end of the spectrum, and thus to pure activity, he already has in mind the series of Aristotelian links discussed in Chapter 2 between activity and form, and between the form of a thing and its end. But whereas Aristotle had analysed the ends of things in a variety of ways, for example as their proper functions or patterns of growth, Aquinas subsumes these interpretations under a single, all-inclusive end—the God of Christianity. God is the purpose or end for the sake of which all things exist, and particular things act for ends which contribute to the all-inclusive divine plan. To understand the purposes the world is created to fulfil, we must therefore look not just to nature, but also to theology;[5] and to understand nature, we must recognize it as God's creation. In working out this scheme Aquinas draws on Aristotle's view that eternal or unchanging things are all actuality and no potentiality, describing God as 'pure and boundless act'. God possesses no potential, no capacity to be changed by the forms or accidents of other things. He is the apotheosis of activity, continually exercising all his powers.[6]

The order of creation is to be seen, then, as a sequence of increasingly active kinds of things, divided into the inanimate realm, plants, animals, human beings, angels, and finally God. A Christian conception of the creation here replaces an Aristotelian understanding of nature as the focus of metaphysical enquiry, but both are held to be hierarchically organized in terms of levels of activity, which Aquinas in turn analyses in terms of potentiality and actuality. Like Aristotle, he treats these as the ingredients of a general analysis of change,

---

[5] The structure of the *Summa* makes this clear.   [6] Ibid. 1a. 75. 6; 1a. 79. 2.

intended to cover various types of causes and effects, including motions, thoughts, and human actions. Like Aristotle, he further believes that there are two basic kinds of potentiality—potentiality to act and potentiality to be acted on; or, as he more often puts it, active and passive potentialities or potencies. These potentialities are distinguished by their objects. The object of a passive potency is its source or cause (*principium*), as colour is the object which moves sight. By contrast, the object of an active potency is the end (the *terminus* or *finis*) towards which it moves, as the power of growth moves towards growth of a certain shape and size.[7] In these examples we find two connected notions of activity and passivity, both of them familiar. From the first, we get the idea that a passive potentiality is a power to be moved or, more generally, acted on; from the second, the idea that an active potentiality is the power of a thing to behave or develop in the way proper to it and according to its end.

Along with this Aristotelian analysis, Aquinas inherits certain difficulties. To what extent can the active powers of things to act on other things be construed as cases of the former things realizing their ends? For instance, when the fire acts on my hand by warming it, is the fire moving to its end? When I act on a vase by knocking it over, am I moving to my end? Aquinas answers yes to the first question, but denies that the second is a case of an active potency at all. Active potencies, in his view, pertain to the essences of things, and while it belongs to the essence of fire to heat, it does not belong to the essence of humans to knock over vases. This move allows him to save the connection between active potencies and ends and ensures that active powers can be interpreted teleologically.[8] To exercise an active power, a thing must act in a manner relevant to, and expressive of, its end.[9]

A further difficulty is that one might wonder whether every case of being acted on corresponds to a passive power. Here Aquinas has more to say and moves somewhat beyond Aristotle's view of the matter. Strictly speaking, he tells us, we say that a thing is passive when something that belongs to it, or to which it inclines, is taken away from it, as when a man becomes sick or sad. In this sense, a passive potentiality is a capacity to be changed for the worse, where better and worse changes are in turn referred back to the forms of things. This is not, however, the only sense in which we describe things as passive. Less strictly, a thing is passive when something either congenial or uncongenial is taken away from it, as when a man becomes sick or becomes healthy, becomes joyful or becomes sad. This reading classifies a far wider range of powers as passive, though they remain related to form. The passive powers of a thing are its capacities to be changed in ways which either help or hinder

---

[7] Ibid. 1a. 77. 3.   [8] Ibid. 1a. 77. 3.

[9] For the Thomist doctrine of potency see H. P. Kainz, *Active and Passive in Thomist Angelology* (The Hague, 1972), 30–5.

it from fulfilling its end. For example, when a sick man becomes healthy he is changed for the better by the removal of his sickness; and when he becomes ill he is changed for the worse by the removal of his health; and normal people possess both these capacities non-accidentally. Finally, we say a thing is passive in the most general sense whenever it passes from any state of potentiality to actuality without anything being taken away in the process, and even if the transition fulfils or perfects it.[10] For example, the man whose knowledge of grammar is potential in the sense that he is not using it, and who then actualizes his knowledge by beginning to think about a grammatical problem, is in this sense passive. Here Aquinas takes issue with Aristotle, who had remarked in *On the Soul* that it is strange, and in fact wrong, to speak of a wise man as being 'altered' when he uses his wisdom; we should say instead that he develops into his true self or actuality.[11] But Aquinas disagrees, claiming that there is an intelligible sense in which any change in a thing presupposes a passive potentiality to be changed in that way, whatever the character of the change itself.

The tensions between these divergent senses of passivity pervade various aspects of Aquinas's work. On the one hand, things are passive when they are changed for the worse, away from their natural dispositions; and to have passive potentialities is to be capable of being changed for the worse. On the other hand, things are passive when they are changed for better or worse, and passive potentialities are capacities to be helped or harmed. Both senses are evaluative. But, as Aquinas acknowledges, the difference between them can be significant. According to the first, for example, Adam was impassible[12] before he sinned—he was incapable of being changed for the worse because he could curb his passions and avoid death by refraining from sin. But according to the second he was passive, because he was capable of being perfected in both body and soul.[13] In the *Summa* no attempt is made to reconcile these senses; Aquinas simply registers the differences between them and appeals sometimes to one, sometimes to the other. In this he preserves a polysemy noted by Aristotle, which lived to haunt early-modern debates.

Since all created things have active potentialities determined by their forms as well as passive potentialities to be diminished or changed, it remains to see how Aquinas explicates his claim that some are more active than others. Here we find him appealing to criteria that are not obviously Aristotelian. Higher powers, Aquinas tells us, are distinguished by the scope of their activity.[14] The nutritive powers of the soul have as their object the body with which the soul is

---

[10] *Summa*, 1a. 79. 2; 1a. 97. 2.

[11] *On the Soul*, in *The Complete Works of Aristotle*, ed. J. Barnes (Princeton, 1984), vol. i, 417^{b}5.

[12] The Latin term here is *impassibilitas*, the trans. of the Greek *apatheia*. See Augustine, *City of God*, ed. D. Knowles (Harmondsworth, 1972), 14. 9.

[13] *Summa*, 1a. 97. 2.   [14] Ibid. 1a. 77. 3.

united; the object of the sensitive powers extends beyond the body to external, sensible things; and the object of the intellectual powers extends beyond the sensible world to all being.[15] This progression is at the same time conceived as a tipping of the balance away from matter and towards form. The lowest level of activity belonging to the soul—nutrition, growth, and generation—takes place through physical organs and by virtue of physical qualities. The next level—the activity of the sensitive soul—takes place through physical organs but is not itself physical. And finally, the activity of the rational soul is not even exercised through a physical organ. Disembodied beings can understand and will, and of the human powers, only these intellectual ones are immortal.

In this progression we find two criteria for distinguishing levels of activity, both of which are worked out in the context of the powers of the soul. Aristotle's view that an active power is a power to transform one thing into a thing of another kind is not prominent; but his view that the active power of thinking can be exercised at will is perhaps echoed in Aquinas's claim that the intellectual powers of the soul do not depend on bodily organs. When we think, we do not have to wait for certain bodily events over which we have only partial control to occur, but can simply begin. Equally, the suggestion that the activity of a power reflects its scope carries traces of the connection between activity and control that we found in Aristotle. A power is more active when its possessor can exercise it over a greater range. Finally, as we would expect, both these Thomist criteria are designed to ensure that God is supremely active. Since God is immaterial, his powers do not depend on any physical body; and since he is omnipotent, they extend over all creation.

Aquinas's treatment of the metaphysical categories of activity and passivity reinforces to some extent the diverse senses of these terms found in Aristotle, and at the same time extends the list of interpretations by glossing and modifying them. His revisions of Aristotle's accounts of being and change subordinate these firmly to the demands of Christianity so that activity comes to be exemplified by God, and degrees of action and passion are measured by their distance from this fountainhead. At the same time, Aquinas's interest in these ideas focuses more narrowly than Aristotle's on their application to the soul. As we have seen, certain general metaphysical issues need to be tidied up; but it is in the portrayal of fallen humanity, balanced between the divine and the mundane, and between animals and angels, that they really come into their own.

Activity and Passivity in the Thomist Soul

Aquinas appeals to the active and passive potentialities of things to construct an intricate account of sensation and appetite which continued to impress

[15] Ibid. 1a. 78. 1.

early-modern philosophers and to influence their understanding of the mind. Sections of the foundations of this structure are familiar from Aristotle; for example, Aquinas retains the view that the soul is the form of the body, and possesses an assortment of powers that are themselves patterns of activity. But in order to reconcile these claims with the demands of Christianity, and to distinguish the finite human soul from the infinite activity of God, he also takes a stand on a number of hotly debated theological issues, one of the most important of which concerns the so-called 'real distinction' between the soul and its powers. According to Aquinas, the powers of the soul are distinct both from each other and from the soul itself; for example, the capacity to see is distinct both from the soul, and from other powers such as hearing or imagining, and has the eye as its particular seat.[16] Part of the motivation for this view is that it offers a way of separating the actuality of God from the potentiality of human beings. God, as we have seen, is pure actuality. But the human soul contains potentialities that are not actualized, such as the potential of a man to acquire knowledge that he does not yet possess, or the potential ability of a person who is asleep to see. Powers such as these, which can be either potential or actual, cannot constitute the essence of the soul. For the soul, Aquinas believes, is of its essence actual and, as the form of the soul–body composite, is acting all the time to make an individual person what he or she is. If powers such as sight or appetite *did* constitute the essence of the soul, they would be actual, in which case humans would be like God, continually in act. But, as is all too obvious, they are not. So there must be a distinction between the powers of the soul and whatever it is that constitutes its essence.[17]

Turning to these powers themselves, Aquinas follows Aristotle in classifying those of the nutritive or vegetative soul as active, and those of the sensitive soul as passive.[18] In addition, he retains an Aristotelian view of the sensitive soul as divided between apprehension and appetition. The precise operations of the sensitive soul are, however, of great interest to Aquinas, and he develops a novel and influential account of them. Part of the inspiration for this investigation derives from the commonplace observation that, although non-human animals have no intellectual powers of reasoning and understanding, they are nevertheless capable of purposive action. This aspect of their behaviour must therefore be due to the powers of their sensitive souls, and the challenge Aquinas faces is to show how this can be so. In dealing with this problem he arrives at a distinctive view of the sensitive powers of animals. But these are, of course, powers that animals share with human beings, and by reflecting on them Aquinas is led to articulate important differences between the passions and actions of

---

[16] See K. Park, 'The Organic Soul', in C. B. Schmitt and Q. Skinner (eds.), *The Cambridge History of Renaissance Philosophy* (Cambridge, 1988), 477–8; N. Kretzmann, 'Philosophy of Mind', in id. and E. Stump (eds.), *The Cambridge Companion to Aquinas* (Cambridge, 1993), 128–60.

[17] *Summa*, 1a. 77. 1.   [18] Ibid. 1a. 77. 3.

humans and of other animals. From animal beginnings, he thus arrives at a full interpretation of the sensitive appetite in humans and the principal passions it contains.

The sensitive soul is what enables humans and animals to perceive the sensory properties of external objects and, on the basis of these properties, to perceive objects as pleasant or painful and pursue or avoid them accordingly. Taking the example of a sheep fleeing from a wolf, Aquinas analyses this complex process which begins when the sheep receives the sensible form of the wolf by using its common sense to integrate information provided by each of its five particular senses. From an assortment of sounds, smells, sights, and so on, it assembles a sensible form which it retains in its imagination. Before it can flee, however, the sheep must not only apprehend an object of a certain shape, size, and smell, but must apprehend the wolf, in Aquinas's words, 'as its natural enemy'. But since enmity is not a sensible quality,[19] it remains to ask how this can be done. According to Aquinas, the sheep possesses an estimative power which enables it to perceive an intention—itself some sort of idea of the wolf as enemy—stored in its memory. And it is the perception of the intention that causes it to flee.

While this process is conscious in animals, it works simply by a power that Aquinas labels *aestimatio naturalis*. The sheep has no control over the intentions accompanying its sensory perceptions or its responses to them. When it sees a wolf, it merely recollects an intention of it as a natural enemy and runs away. Humans are somewhat different. In place of the estimative power found in animals, they possess a cogitative power of the sensible soul, sometimes called the particular reason, which allows them to compare the intentions stored in their memories. Before settling on an evaluation of a wolf, they are able to make a quasi-syllogistic search through their stock of intentions. Rather than automatically perceiving it as an enemy, they can embark on a process of critical comparison before arriving at something resembling a judgement about its properties and the appropriate way to respond to it.[20]

Aquinas follows Aristotle in classifying sensory apprehension and sensitive appetite as powers of the sensitive soul and thus as passive. But it is clear from his accounts of them that they answer to this characterization in rather different ways. The power of perceiving or apprehending is the power by which we come to know about the sensory and evaluative properties of external things, and according to Aquinas it resembles rest. By contrast, the appetitive power by which we incline to the objects of our appetite resembles motion.[21] Starting with apprehension, we find the connection charted in Chapter 2 between being passive and being acted on. For example, a person who apprehends a wolf receives its sensible species, where 'receiving' is a way of being acted on. It is

[19] Ibid. 1a. 78. 4.   [20] Ibid. 1a. 78. 4.   [21] Ibid. 1a. 81. 1.

worth noticing that this case does not trade on Aquinas's narrowest conception of passivity as being changed for the worse, since when we perceive we make use of powers that belong to us as soul–body composites. So all that is implied here is that we are passive in the broad sense of being acted on or changed. Coming now to appetite, this is an inclination towards, or away from, an external object, which Aquinas describes as a kind of motion.[22] But in what sense is it passive? The answer becomes clear once we realize that our appetites are responses to things that attract or repel us, and that these act on us by moving us, as Aquinas indicates by using the verbs *inclinare* and *trahere*. Appetite not only inclines us, but draws or drags us to objects which we perceive as good or evil.[23] Once again, we may be changed for the worse by being drawn to objects that are bad for us, or for the better by being drawn to the good. The connotations of passivity lie not in the *way* we are changed, but in the conceiving of appetite as a power to be acted on by external things.

Both apprehension and appetite, then, are passive in the sense that they are powers to be affected or acted on by external objects; and it consequently seems that both should be regarded as giving rise to passions. There seems no reason why we should not say that an apprehension of a wolf, as much as an aversion to it, is a passion. This proposal would not strike Aquinas as strange or unnatural since, in the sense we have just explored, both perceptions and appetites *are* passions and, as we shall see, this affinity between them remains extremely important in early-modern philosophy. However, Aquinas claims that, although both are passive powers, there are further reasons for regarding appetites as still more passive than apprehensions.

Returning to a point already touched on, he first claims that we are more passive when we are drawn to other things than when we are simply affected by them.[24] The image at work here seems to be spatial: if something affects me but fails to move me, I am less passive than I am when it draws or moves me to another place. Aquinas puts this idea to more extensive use in his discussion of particular inclinations, which he construes as stages of movement: love, for example, initiates a motion; desire is the motion itself; joy is the rest that follows its completion. Viewed as parts of a single process, all these inclinations constitute a motion and are thus all passive; but viewed singly, it is possible to see those that Aquinas identifies as motions as more passive than the states of rest that precede and follow them. Secondly, in the grand order which represents perfection as activity, passion pertains to defect.[25] Animals and humans experience apprehensions and appetites because, and in so far as, they are embodied, which is itself a kind of imperfection. Thirdly, appetites are more closely associated than apprehensions with bodily change. When

---

[22] Ibid. 1a. 2ae. 23. Aquinas notes here that Aristotle makes this claim.   [23] Ibid. 1a. 22. 1.
[24] Ibid. 1a. 2ae. 22.   [25] Ibid.

the sensible soul apprehends, it receives sensible species, and any other bodily changes that occur are incidental. But its appetites are accompanied by physical alterations that are essential to them. Anger, for example, *is* a boiling of blood around the heart. Because appetites have these bodily aspects, they are more intimately connected than apprehensions with matter, and this connection gives them stronger connotations of passivity.[26] As before, none of these explications relies on the claim that passions are changes for the worse. But they are all compatible with it, and Aquinas does indeed allow that appetites which are changes for the worse are more passive than those which are changes for the better. Sadness, he tells us, is more properly a passion than joy.[27]

Aquinas's most general account of the sensitive appetite therefore revolves around the claim that it is a passive power of the soul which brings it about that humans and animals are continually drawn to, or repelled by, objects and states of affairs they regard as beneficial or harmful. But he also examines the particular inclinations (which, because they are passive on several counts, are also known as passions) and identifies a repertoire of types of response to good and evil. Classifying the passions was, of course, nothing new. But Aquinas's typology is distinctive not only in the passions it selects but also in what it attempts to do with them. Rather than simply compiling a list, Aquinas aims to incorporate in his scheme of particular passions the basis for an explanatory account of action and emotional conflict.

Central to this enterprise is a division of the sensitive appetite into two powers. Taking up a division of the sensible soul made by Aristotle[28] (who was in turn drawing on a distinction made by Plato) Aquinas distinguishes the concupiscible appetite, which responds to sensible good and evil, from the irascible appetite, which responds to good or evil that appears difficult to obtain or avoid.[29] He claims, rather confusingly, that these powers are distinguished by their objects.[30] In fact, however, they are differentiated not by the kind of objects that they are appetites for or aversions to, but rather by the relation that an agent has to an object as easy or hard to obtain. For example, a hungry girl who finds herself standing next to a laden apple tree which happens, conveniently, to be growing on common land, will experience the concupiscible appetite of desire for an apple. But if she glimpses the tree through a tall fence topped with spikes, and hears guard dogs howling, she may hope to reach the fruit, and hope is an irascible appetite.

---

[26] Ibid. 1a. 2ae. 22.   [27] Ibid. 1a. 2ae. 22.

[28] Aquinas's terms *appetitus concupiscibilis* and *appetitus irascibilis* are taken from William of Moerbeke's Latin trans. of Aristotle's *On the Soul*. In pt. III Aristotle divides the powers of the soul into the rational and non-rational (*logistikon* and *orexis*) and then within the non-rational subdivides the sensory appetite (*aisthetike*) into *epithumetike* and *thumike*. Moerbeke sometimes translates *thumike* as *irascibilis* and *epithumike* as *concupiscibilis*. Aquinas takes over these terms and uses them consistently. See E. D'Arcy, 'Introduction' to *Summa*, vol. xix, p. xxv.

[29] *Summa*, 1a. 81. 1.   [30] Ibid. 1a. 2ae. 23.

To appreciate this rather obscure distinction, it is helpful to ask what Aquinas uses it to achieve. Part of the answer lies in the fact that it is designed to reinforce an understanding of the passions as extremely sensitive to an agent's perceptions of the world. To love Eurydice, for instance, Orpheus must at least perceive her as good for him. But this rather generalized inclination will be modified as he arrives at a fuller perception of his relationship to her. When he first sees her, he hopes; when their love seems secure, he desires; when they are united, he is joyful; and when he embarks on the apparently impossible task of rescuing her from the Underworld, he is determined to succeed. Aquinas takes the view that passions modulate around one main kind of perception, namely whether the object of a passion is easy or difficult to fend off or attain. He therefore defines his two appetites along these lines, and allocates certain passions to each of them. In the concupiscible appetite there are six passions that we feel when our inclinations to good and away from evil are not attended by any sense of doubt or difficulty. Our appetite for things we perceive as good originates in love (*amor*), which gives rise to a movement of the soul towards the object in question, which is desire (*desiderium*). When we get what we want, we feel a kind of pleasure, namely joy (*gaudium*). This progression is matched by the passions that accompany our responses to things that we perceive as evil. An initial aversion—hatred (*odium*)—is followed by a motion away from the evil object—avoidance (*fuga* or *abominatio*)—which, when it fails, comes to rest in a kind of pain, namely sorrow (*tristitia*).[31]

The concupiscible appetite therefore contains a set of relatively straightforward passions directed to things we do and do not like. But these inclinations are complicated by the superimposition of the irascible appetite, which accounts for our ability to strive for difficult ends and resist things that stand in our way. These kinds of action depend on a further five passions. To incline towards a good that appears difficult to attain is hope (*spes*), while to be repelled by such a good is despair (*desperatio*). The inclination of the appetite towards a threatening evil is audacity (*audacia*), and an aversion to it is fear (*timor*). Lastly, the inclination to resist a present evil is anger or *ira*.

Aquinas therefore identifies eleven basic passions, six concupiscible and five irascible. To appreciate the explanatory tasks he intends them to perform, it helps to recognize that the final irascible passion of *ira* only overlaps and does not correspond with modern colloquial understandings of anger, or even with Aristotle's definition of anger as a response to insult. For Aquinas, *ira* has a much broader sense, sometimes translated as aggressiveness or resolution: it is the passion we experience whenever the sensitive appetite is faced with obstacles to what we perceive as our present good and starts to resist them.[32] These obstacles may literally be things that stand in the way of our inclinations,

---

[31] Ibid. 1a. 2ae. 23.   [32] Ibid. 1a. 2ae. 23.

as when someone who wants to enter a room finds that the door is locked and becomes still more determined to go in. But they can also be states of other people's souls (as when Iago resolves to destroy Othello's love for Desdemona) or indeed our own passions.

Aristotle clearly regarded anger as an important passion to which men are naturally prone. He conjures up a picture of touchy Athenian citizens who rise to the slightest hint of an insult and are ever anxious to defend themselves. Aquinas transforms this image of anger into a more pervasive power not only to defend oneself but also to persevere, not only to challenge insults but to pursue whatever one perceives as the good and resist whatever one perceives as evil. Its objects are therefore not so much insults as threats, in the face of which we exhibit some degree of tenacity and obstinacy.

As well as introducing a certain toughness into the passions, the division between the concupiscible and irascible appetites aims to create space to deal with conflict in the soul. It is, of course, possible to be torn between concupiscible passions when an object seems to have both desirable and undesirable qualities. A painting, for example, may strike a viewer as both beautiful and repellent, or a student may both want and not want to go on working. Equally, concupiscible and irascible passions can be opposed, as when a ruler excites both love and fear. Besides allowing for such clashes, Aquinas aims to account for some of our capacities to cope with them, in particular our ability to struggle against our passions and act in the face of our desires. These dispositions can be explained, in his view, by appealing to the division between the concupiscible and irascible appetites, since this alone creates the capacity of the sensitive appetite to assess and criticize its own inclinations. When, for example, a student wants to stop working but knows she ought to continue, her concupiscible desire to stop may be resisted by her irascible appetite to the point where *ira*, strengthening her desire to continue, keeps her at her desk.[33] So as well as modifying passions directed at outward things, for example by turning aversion into fear, the irascible appetite can deploy its capacities to resist and succumb on the soul itself. Where passions conflict, it can strengthen or undermine one at the expense of another. While it is not clear exactly how the irascible appetite performs these tasks, the general significance of Aquinas's position is plain. Rather than trying to explain all mental struggle in terms of conflict and cooperation between the sensitive and rational souls, he follows Aristotle in locating psychological struggle within the sensitive soul itself. Our passions are neither simple nor unified, and they include inclinations to resist or succumb which may be more or less powerful.

In practice, Aquinas tells us, passions occur in sequences, beginning with love and hatred, the presence or absence of an aptitude or inclination of one

<hr />

[33] Ibid. 1a. 81. 2.

thing for another.[34] These give rise to desire, a movement of the appetite towards the loved object, and aversion; but having reached this point, a sequence can develop in many ways, depending on what else the sensitive soul perceives about the object of its passion. Suppose, for example, a woman wants a future good which may or may not be within her reach. In this case desire will be succeeded by hope. Or suppose she wants a present good which is surrounded by obstacles. Then desire will become *ira*. Aquinas is clear, however, that these inclinations must at some point come to rest in the two last passions of the concupiscible appetite,[35] terminating either in joy, the union of the soul with an object, or in sadness, a retraction of the appetite which impedes the vital motion of the body and is therefore detrimental to it.[36]

As well as breaking new ground in these ways, Aquinas's analysis of the passions is explicitly designed to incorporate and supersede the accounts given by his most illustrious predecessors, whose views are examined with varying degrees of assiduousness in the relevant sections of the *Summa*. Most prominent is Aristotle, whose works are often invoked, and whose insights are regularly accommodated. Aquinas will start off, for example, with a definition taken from the *Rhetoric*, and spin from it an analysis fractured by subdivisions, distinctions, and qualifications;[37] but although the outcome appears foreign to Aristotle's text, it is presented as a natural development of it, as a conscientious gloss rather than a departure. This basically respectful attitude is extended to other authorities, though not always to quite the same degree. In his discussion of Augustine's view that there is only one passion, that of love, Aquinas disposes of it briskly by explaining what Augustine really meant. He was not saying that fear, desire, and so forth are *essentially* the same as love, but that they and the other passions are causally related to love which, Aquinas agrees, is the first passion in the sequences of appetites.[38] When he turns to the Ciceronian view that there are four principal passions—joy and sadness, hope and fear[39]—Aquinas again considers it in order to reject it. He notes that it is customary to distinguish these passions by tense, so that hope and fear are directed to future good and evil, whereas joy and sadness are the passions that people feel when good or evil are present,[40] and he allows that this is an intelligible interpretation. But his own position implies that, while it is possible to classify the passions on this basis, it is more fruitful to analyse them in terms of the concupiscible and irascible appetites, within which tense is included. The salient point about hope and fear is not just that they are directed to the future, but that their futurity introduces an element of uncertainty as to whether an end will be achieved or avoided which is itself a kind of obstacle or difficulty. Equally, the significant feature of joy and sorrow is not that they

---

[34] Ibid. 1a. 2ae. 25.   [35] Ibid.   [36] Ibid. 1a. 2ae. 37.
[37] See e.g. ibid. 1a. 2ae. 30 on *concupiscentia*.   [38] Ibid. 1a. 2ae. 26.
[39] Aquinas attributes this view to Boethius, ibid. 1a. 2ae. 25.   [40] Ibid.

relate to present objects but that, because their objects are present, these passions do not involve any struggle.

Aquinas's analysis of the passions is far more thorough and meticulous than those of his predecessors, and is worked out with a fervent attention to detail to which none of them aspired. Rather than simply listing the principal passions, each one is examined and anatomized in best Scholastic style. In this way, the relevant sections of the *Summa* set a standard for later discussions of the subject, and established a format that endured into the seventeenth century. Long after philosophers ceased to organize their works into *quaestiones*, treatises on the passions still opened with a section on the passions in general, and followed this up with elaborate chapters on individual passions, in which interpretation is mixed with assessments of various authorities, summaries of other writers, and instructive anecdotes. Both as to form and content, the influence of Aquinas was, therefore, enormous. But it was by no means confined to his treatment of the sensitive soul, and in order to appreciate its full range it is important to stand back and see how the intricate operations so far considered contribute to a broader account of human thought and action.

In some cases, humans act on the apprehensions and appetites of their sensitive souls—in short, they act on their passions. But because these states are also perceived by the intellectual soul, our actions are often the outcome of more complex processes involving the interaction of these two sets of powers. While many objects present themselves to us as good or bad, we are not compelled to take these presentations at face value. It is possible for our passions to be modified by the powers of the intellectual soul which, like those of its sensitive counterpart, are twofold: an apprehensive power (the intellect) and an appetitive power (the will).

Aquinas follows Aristotle in claiming that the principal difference between sensitive and intellectual apprehension is that, whereas the sensible soul can only apprehend the particular things that are presented to the senses, the intellect apprehends universals. The truths it grasps are not available to sense, yet it is able both to understand them and to reason from one to another. We have already seen that the sensitive soul contains interlocking active and passive potentialities, although it is classified overall as passive. We find the same sort of situation when we turn to the apprehension of intellectual species. Overall, and by comparison with the sensitive soul, the intellect is active. But this general characterization is compatible with the existence of a sense in which it is passive, namely that, unlike God, the human intellect has a potentiality to understand which is not always actual. This power, which Aquinas calls the possible intellect, is a power to be moved from potentiality to actuality.[41] But since a potentiality can only be made actual by something already actual, the

---

[41] Ibid. 1a. 79. 3.

question remains: what actualizes it? The problem Aquinas faces here is to explain how the intellect is able to derive knowledge of forms or universals from the particulars presented to it by the sensitive soul. Siding with Aristotle against Plato, he holds that particulars are not directly intelligible by the intellect. But this brings him face to face with the problem of how particulars are transformed into objects capable of being apprehended by the intellectual soul, a difficulty he resolves by positing an *agent intellect*, a power to abstract intelligible forms from sensible particulars. The agent intellect acts on sensible species, and in doing so creates objects the intellect can apprehend. The possible intellect is then moved by these objects, which it receives and retains.[42]

Allied to this kind of apprehension is the intellectual appetite or will, an inclination to pursue good and avoid evil which encompasses both the power to will (to incline to or from an object for its own sake) and the power to choose (to seek something for the sake of something else).[43] Intellect and will work together in the same way as the sensitive powers: the intellect apprehends truths and the will then moves towards or away from them. But whereas the powers of the sensitive soul respond to sensible good and evil, and thus to the objects particular agents regard as good or bad, these intellectual powers are directed to the ultimate ends of truth and goodness. Moreover, although intellectual apprehension is directed to truth and intellectual appetite to goodness, there is no strict division of labour between them. Goodness is among the truths available to the intellect and truth is among the goods pursued by the will.

As powers of the soul alone, volitions have no bodily effects and are in this respect quite different from passions.[44] Nevertheless, there are similarities between the two kinds of appetite. Volitions are inclinations,[45] and are experienced as what Aquinas calls affects[46] which resemble passions except that they are somewhat calmer. Aquinas often lists emotions such as desire, sadness, and joy as affects.[47] But in his more detailed discussions he marks the differences between affects and passions by the use of distinct terms. For example, *amor*, the passion of love, is contrasted with *dilectio*, its intellectual equivalent;[48] *concupiscentia* is contrasted with *desiderium* or intellectual desire;[49] and so on. The fact that intellectual affects are not directed to the same objects as passions, together with the fact that they cause no perturbations in the body, serves to transmute them into related but distinct emotions. There is some sense in

---

[42] Ibid. 1a. 79. 3. See A. Levi, *French Moralists: The Theory of the Passions 1585–1649* (Oxford, 1964), 31–6.

[43] *Summa*, 1a. 81. 4. See D. Gallagher, 'Thomas Aquinas on the Will as Rational Appetite', *Journal of the History of Philosophy*, 29 (1991), 559–84.

[44] Aquinas draws attention to the bodily connotations of the names of some particular passions. *Laetitia*, he claims, derives from *dilitatione cordis*, and *exultatio*, which is literally inward joy breaking its bounds, refers to the external signs of inward delight. *Summa*, 1a. 2ae 31.

[45] Ibid. 1a. 82. 3.   [46] Ibid. 1a. 82. 5.   [47] Ibid. 1a. 77. 8.

[48] Aquinas points to the etymological connections between *dilectio* and *electio* (choice); ibid. 1a. 2ae. 26.

[49] Ibid. 1a. 2ae. 31.

which intellectual love, for example, *feels* different from passionate love; but because the first will often be accompanied by the second, the phenomenological difference between them may easily evade us.

The powers of the sensitive and intellectual souls are, therefore, distinct. But in humans they are not disjoined. On the one hand, the cogitative power which collates the individual intentions of the sensitive soul is responsive to the rational understanding, so that reasoning can both calm and arouse our passions. On the other hand, our passions respond to our volitions so that we, unlike sheep, do not always respond to wolves with fear, let alone always run away.[50] Moreover, the fact that the connections between sense and reason go in both directions means that we can act both rationally and irrationally. Sometimes the existence of a passion can immobilize reason and induce the will to move in accordance with the sensitive appetite. Sometimes the apprehension of intellectual truths gives rise not only to emotions of the intellectual soul but also to passions and thence to actions.[51] And sometimes the will is torn between reason and passion.

One of the most puzzling features of this analysis is its depiction of states of the soul as motions. The characterization of volitions and some of the passions as movements draws these phenomena into an explanatory scheme designed to cover both the soul and the material world, in which two sets of metaphors are used to blend the physical with the psychological. On the one hand, Aquinas applies ideas now considered psychological to physical things; for example, he describes the disposition of heavy objects to fall towards the centre of the earth as an expression of natural love.[52] On the other hand, he also employs the reverse strategy, describing the soul in terms whose most transparent applications are to the physical world. Desire, for instance, is a *movement* towards a loved object. When these metaphors are run together, motions are variously conceived as pushes and pulls, attractions and repulsions, loves, and hatreds; and repulsions, loves, and so forth are in turn explicated as motions. Motion is therefore invoked in a wide range of contexts. But while Aquinas indulges in this apparently rather cavalier mode of explanation, he also acknowledges its limitations when he distinguishes the properties of physical movement from those of its angelic counterpart. In his discussion of disembodied intellectual beings or angels, Aquinas specifies that the movement of a body consists, as Aristotle pointed out, in its continuous motion through the successive parts of a continuum.[53] Moreover a body is contained by its place—by the space it occupies. Angels, however, obey different rules. It makes no sense to think of an angel as being contained by a place, since he has no body and occupies no space. Instead, he is in contact with a place simply by virtue of

    [50] Ibid. 1a. 81. 3.   [51] Ibid. 1a. 2ae. 10.   [52] Ibid. 1a. 2ae. 26.
    [53] Aristotle, *Physics*, in *Complete Works*, ed. Barnes. vol. i, 219^{a}12; Aquinas, *Summa*, 1a. 53. 2.

exercising his power there. And whereas the places occupied by a moving body must be spatially continuous, the movement of an angel from place to place need be nothing but a series of distinct contacts.[54]

Does the fact that angelic motion is unlike the bodily variety, and is governed by different principles, tell us anything about the motions of the human soul? While human souls differ substantially from those of angels, Aquinas suggests that they have a certain amount in common,[55] for example when he points out that we can think of France and then of Syria without thinking of Italy.[56] Like angels, memory and imagination can move from place to place without traversing all the territory in-between. At least some motions of the soul therefore differ from those of physical bodies in that they are not constrained by the spatial relations between their objects. For example, I can desire to be in Damascus without desiring to cover the territory that separates me from it. However, it remains unclear how this claim is supposed to apply to thoughts which are not about spatially located things. A desire, for example, is a movement of the sensitive appetite; but the claim that there are types of motion which are not continuous does not seem to help much when we try to grasp a sense in which a desire for wisdom, or lilies, can be construed as a motion. Taking the first example, wisdom is not spatially locatable; and taking the second, it is surely possible to desire lilies without having any spatially located lilies in mind. To make sense of these cases, it looks as though we need a conception of motion which is not explicated in terms of place.

The angelic analogy is therefore of limited use, the more so since humanity is wedged between angels and animals in the Great Chain of Being and shares in the properties of both. For instance, while a disembodied angel can occupy a place by exercising his powers there, humans, like other physical things, can only exercise their powers in the place occupied by their bodies. They can think *about* Syria, but as long as their bodies are in Italy cannot think *in* Syria. Combining as they do the corporeal and the divine, humans move in two ways. To explain them, as Aquinas's seventeenth-century successors were quick to point out, we therefore need to understand not only how the motions of bodies and souls differ, but also how they interconnect.

Aquinas's profoundly influential account of the passions conceives them, as we have seen, in Aristotelian terms as effects, as instances of being acted on, as powers that may or may not be exercised, and as rooted in matter. Passions are consequently those states of mind that are understood as the effects of sensible objects, which are also closely connected to the human body. However, the notion of a passion or passive power also has much broader

---

[54] *Summa*, 1a. 53. 2.

[55] e.g. ibid. See J. J. MacIntosh, 'St. Thomas on Angelic Time and Motion', *Thomist*, 59 (1995), 547–76.

[56] *Summa*, 1a. 53. 2.

connotations. It can be properly applied to other states of the soul, particularly perceptions. And it can be applied to purely material bodies which are passive in their capacity to suffer change. In all these contexts it is presented as the counterpart of action, actuality, and form. The works of Aristotle and Aquinas display, better than any, the philosophical subtlety and dialectical ingenuity with which this set of interconnected ideas can be woven together to a point where it becomes difficult to think about potentiality without actuality or actuality without motion. Nevertheless, the web of Scholastic Aristotelianism was not so fine that it defied alteration. While some scholars have claimed that the most innovative of the early-modern philosophers rejected Aristotelianism,[57] a study of the passions suggests—so I shall argue—that this is an exaggeration. Writing about philosophical psychology, even the great revolutionaries of the New Philosophy did not reject their Scholastic heritage outright. While they abandoned some aspects of it, they retained many others, creating theories at once critical of the analyses so far discussed and continuous with them. This balancing act between continuity and change is, of course, achieved in more than one way: Descartes, for instance, retains aspects of the Scholastic framework that Hobbes rejects. Neither is it completely lacking in uniformity: some Scholastic doctrines and assumptions are generally agreed to be obsolete while others survive largely unscathed. Among the features of Aristotelianism that endure is the centrality and scope of the opposition between action and passion, which, in most cases, continues to underpin physical and psychological explanations, and to span the workings of the body, senses, and intellect. It is within this framework, as I shall show in the following parts of this book, that the New Philosophy of the seventeenth century addresses the passions.

---

[57] For this interpretation of the New Science in general see J. Losee, *A Historical Introduction to the Philosophy of Science* (Oxford, 1980); M. Boas, *The Scientific Renaissance 1450–1630* (London, 1962), 81, 185, 201; M. Osler, *Divine Will and the Mechanical Philosophy* (Cambridge, 1994), 2–4; on Hobbes as an anti-Aristotelian see T. Sorell, *Hobbes* (London, 1986), 2–3, 5; T. A. Spragens Jnr., *The Politics of Motion: The World of Thomas Hobbes* (London, 1973), 187–93; on Locke see J. Gibson, *Locke's Theory of Knowledge* (Cambridge, 1917), 182–6; M. Mandelbaum, *Philosophy, Science and Sense Perception* (Baltimore, 1964), 32, 43–4; on Descartes, see P. Schouls, *Descartes and the Enlightenment* (Montreal, 1989); J. Cottingham, *Descartes* (Oxford, 1986), 4–7; on Gassendi see B. Brundell, *Pierre Gassendi: From Aristotelianism to a New Natural Philosophy* (Dordrecht, 1987).

4

Post-Aristotelian Passion and Action

The interpretation of the passions as powers of the sensitive soul secured, for Aristotelian philosophers, two significant implications. It defined a sense in which the passions are passive by placing them in the receptive part of the soul, the part capable of perception and appetite that connects the self to others. At the same time, it ensured that our passions are states of the soul–body composite. They consist of the feelings we identify as love, envy, hope, and so on, and of bodily changes to which these are essentially related. By positioning them at this point, Aristotelian philosophy deals deftly with a feature of the passions that early-modern philosophers continue to regard as extremely important. As properties of the sensitive soul, the passions just are—to force a distinction—simultaneously physical and psychological. Bodily motions are shot through with feeling, and feeling is expressed in a vast range of bodily manifestations. Some of these we register in our language, as when we speak of the pallor of fear or the lethargy of sadness, while others we can barely articulate.

These strengths of the Aristotelian view help to account for its continued popularity throughout the seventeenth century. (A great many writers continue, for example, to reiterate Aquinas's account of the central features of the passions and to reproduce his classification.)[1] These strengths are, however, not completely unalloyed, since they presuppose doctrines that, by the seventeenth century, were widely regarded with suspicion. The objections to Aristotelianism that rapidly became standard during this period were not primarily directed at Scholastic theories of the passions, but they had grave implications for them which exercised philosophers of a systematic bent. A discontent with the deep-dyed habits of the Schoolmen first surfaced in natural philosophy, where it stimulated the development of novel accounts of bodies and thus of the relations between bodies and minds. This change in turn generated a revival of metaphysical interest in the passions, and a need to reconsider at the most basic level what they are. What sort of states of the soul are the passions? What sort of states of the body are they? And if they are both, how are these two components related? Attempts to answer these questions were in many cases shaped by the need to avoid Aristotelian doctrines that had become unacceptable.

---

[1] See Ch. 1 n. 25.

But this is only part of the story. Even some of the most innovative theorists of the passions continued to draw more or less directly on aspects of this older tradition, so that novelty is tempered by continuity in their work. In addition, the project of extending the New Philosophy to the passions sometimes ran into problems which cast doubt on the metaphysical and physical positions around which this philosophical system was organized. For some writers, the passions therefore proved subversive, a troublesome afterthought that, true to their character, threatened the order and purity of systematic philosophy.

In this chapter I shall show how certain criticisms regularly levelled at Aristotelianism by some of the most original and well-known philosophers of the seventeenth century served to undermine the interpretations of activity and passivity discussed in Chapters 2 and 3. The rejection of substantial forms, the repudiation of the tripartite soul with its sets of separate powers, and a conviction that the language of Scholastic philosophy concealed a host of errors, all indicated that the established Aristotelian readings of action and passion could not be right, thereby creating space for an alternative. Debate about these points duly produced revised conceptions of the active and passive which had an impact on many areas of philosophy. Brought to bear on the passions of the soul, they gave rise to new conceptions of the causal role of the passions, new conceptions of the relations between the passions and the soul's other powers, and new accounts of the connections between the passions' psychological and physical manifestations.

Rejecting the Aristotelian Analysis of the Passions

Seventeenth-century critics of the Aristotelian theory of the passions base their opposition on a set of interconnected, stock objections, all of which question its ability to provide satisfactory explanations, and all of which bear on the way in which notions of activity and passivity are interpreted.[2] One of these unsettles Aristotelianism's most fundamental metaphysical principles by challenging the idea of form which, as we saw in Part I, plays a central role in the explanation of both being and change. It is the forms of particular things that differentiate matter and make them what they are, so that the form of

---

[2] 'Aristotelianism' is a general label for a wide variety of interpretations of Aristotle's philosophy. On the development of its early-modern forms see C. B. Schmitt, *Aristotle and the Renaissance* (Cambridge, Mass., 1983); J. Kraye, 'The Philosophy of the Italian Renaissance', in G. Parkinson (ed.), *The Routledge History of Philosophy, iv. The Renaissance and Seventeenth-Century Rationalism* (London, 1993), 16–69; E. Kessler, 'The Transformation of Aristotelianism during the Renaissance', in S. Hutton and J. Henry (eds.), *New Perspectives on Renaissance Thought: Essays in the History of Science, Education and Philosophy; In Memory of Charles B. Schmitt* (London, 1990), 137–47; B. P. Copenhaver and C. B. Schmitt, *Renaissance Philosophy* (Oxford, 1992), 60–126; R. Ariew, 'Descartes and Scholasticism: The Intellectual Background to Descartes' Thought' in J. Cottingham (ed.), *The Cambridge Companion to Descartes* (Cambridge, 1992), 58–90; C. Mercer, 'The Vitality and Importance of Early-Modern Aristotelianism', in T. Sorell (ed.), *The Rise of Modern Philosophy* (Oxford, 1993), 33–67.

marble, for example, is what makes it hard and white, and that of bronze accounts for its dark colour, weight, and texture. Equally, it is the form of a thing that guarantees its existence through time, and it is only when things are 'transformed' that their identity changes, as when earth becomes bronze. To criticize this idea is therefore to criticize a foundational category. But opponents of Aristotelianism nevertheless speak dismissively both of the notion of form and of the way it is used. A related complaint, regularly made about theories of the soul, is mainly directed at Scholastic philosophers who were held to abuse the resources of Aristotelianism by positing a plethora of substantial forms, adding new ones on an *ad hoc* basis whenever they ran into explanatory difficulties. In practice, the form of a thing is expressed as a list of powers, and the Schoolmen were accused of simply adding to this whenever it proved convenient. Parodically, the discovery that a metal is magnetic might be 'explained' by positing an attractive power as an aspect of its form. The problem runs deeper than this suggests, however, and centres on the charge that appeals to form are never satisfactory because forms themselves are occult. An Aristotelian would of course agree that forms are occult in the literal sense of concealed, meaning that they are not available to sense. But this concession fails to meet the criticism, which is not primarily directed against the fact that forms are unobservable. The problem is rather that it is not clear what sort of entities they are. For while the opposition of form and matter seems to indicate that they are spiritual phenomena, some of their traits suggest that they must be physical. As well as being concealed, forms are therefore occult in the more derogatory sense of mysterious.[3] When philosophers appeal to them, it is not at all clear what they are talking about.

The view that forms had become a scientific panacea which, though widely applied, failed to explain anything, was common among philosophers. Descartes, for example, expressed it when he wrote in a letter to Regius in January 1642 that substantial forms

were introduced by philosophers solely to account for the proper actions of natural things, of which they were supposed to be the principles and bases . . . But no natural action at all can be explained by these substantial forms, since their defenders admit that they are occult, and that they do not understand them themselves. If they say that some action proceeds from a substantial form, it is as if they say that it proceeds from something they do not understand; which explains nothing.[4]

---

[3] On explanatory appeals to occult entities see A. G. Debus, *The English Paracelsians* (London, 1965); B. Vickers (ed.), *Occult and Scientific Mentalities in the Renaissance* (Cambridge, 1984); G. Macdonald Ross, 'Occultism and Philosophy in the Seventeenth Century', in A. J. Holland (ed.), *Philosophy, its History and Historiography* (Dordrecht, 1983), 95–115; S. Schaffer, 'Occultism and Reason', in Holland (ed.), *Philosophy*, 117–43; K. Hutchison, 'What Happened to Occult Qualities in the Scientific Revolution?', *Isis*, 73 (1982), 233–53; D. M. Clarke, *Occult Powers and Hypotheses: Cartesian Natural Philosophy under Louis XIV* (Oxford, 1989), 70–4.

[4] In *The Philosophical Writings of Descartes*, ed. J. Cottingham, *et al.* (Cambridge, 1985–91), iii. *Correspondence*, 208.

However, as well as casting doubt on a favoured mode of explanation, this attack on substantial forms damaged a central interpretation of the notion of activity. As we have seen, the basic opposition between matter and form was aligned, for Aristotelians, with that between passivity and activity. It was because things were composed of form as well as matter that they could be described as active; and the activity of a thing was in turn identified both as the characteristic pattern of behaviour that it displayed and as its end. Form thus accounted for activity and imposed on this activity a teleological interpretation. The rejection of form consequently removed the basis upon which things were normally described as active. What it meant to describe a thing as active, how one identified the activities of a thing, and what explained this activity, once again became open questions.

By raising these problems, the critics of Aristotelianism simultaneously cast into confusion existing conceptions of passivity. If form was suspect, so was the division between form and matter, and with it the parallel opposition between the active and passive. Moreover, in so far as this opposition had provided the basis for distinguishing active and passive powers, they too now rested on sand. We saw in Chapter 2 that the line between form and matter was to some extent independent of that between passive and active powers: both kinds of power could, it seemed, belong to the form of a thing, and it could consequently possess both characteristic powers to change the world by acting on it and characteristic powers to be changed. So the differences between these types of powers were not inextricably intertwined with the differences between form and matter. The gap between the two in fact offered a way to reconceptualize the notions of active and passive, maintaining many of their Aristotelian connotations but purging them of any offending connection with form. This proved, as we shall see, an attractive way to solve the problem, but it remained to be worked through.

The explanatory deficiencies of forms therefore had wide-ranging implications which were voiced by natural philosophers anxious to devise a more unified explanatory account of the physical world. They also extended, however, to the philosophical study of the soul, where the metaphysical status of the soul's powers proved deeply contentious. According to their critics, Aristotelian philosophers offered to account for the workings of the mind by appealing to the soul's powers or faculties; but their efforts were often futile, because what they presented as explanations were merely redescriptions. Locke is one of many philosophers to make this point, and he labours it in the *Essay*, as though to leave no room for doubt.

But the fault has been, that faculties have been spoken of, and represented, as so many distinctive agents. For it being asked, what it was that digested the meat in our stomachs? It was a ready, and very satisfactory answer to say, that it was the digestive faculty. What was it that made anything come out of the body? The expulsive faculty.

What moved? The motive faculty: and so on in the mind, the intellectual faculty, or the understanding, understood; and the elective faculty, or the will, willed and commanded, which is in short to say, that the ability to digest digested; and that the ability to move, moved; and the ability to understand, understood . . . And in truth it would be very strange if it were otherwise.[5]

An initial problem, then, is to give an account of how a power works which is more than the bare assertion that it performs a given task. But there is also a further problem: to explain how the various powers or faculties of the soul communicate with one another. Here, too, as Hobbes loves to point out, there is a danger of taking refuge in familiar but obfuscatory verbs.

Some say the senses receive the species of things and deliver them to the common sense; and the common sense delivers them over to the fancy, and the fancy to the memory, and the memory to the judgement, like handing of things from one to another, with many words making nothing understood.[6]

The accusation that these descriptions have no explanatory force suggests that the Aristotelian picture of the soul will have to be drastically reworked. Moreover, the criticism calls into question the Aristotelian distinction between active and passive powers. As we saw in Chapters 2 and 3, the passivity of the senses, and to some extent the passions, is explicated by appeal to the claim that, as Hobbes puts it, they 'receive the species of things'. Passivity consists in being acted on, and receiving is an instance of this. But if receiving is just a word, 'making nothing understood', this interpretation of the passive powers fails to explain either how they operate or in what sense, if any, they are passive.

Each of these criticisms of Aristotelian philosophy is implicitly a plea for more unified and integrated explanations. In natural philosophy, the positing of a substantial form to account for each kind of thing leads to a massive proliferation of forms, each of limited explanatory force. And in the case of the soul, the positing of separate faculties, each with its own active and passive powers, promotes a model of the mind which comes to be regarded as little more than a glorified redescription. In both contexts, it is being argued, there is a need for stronger and richer explanatory principles, but the likelihood of formulating these within an Aristotelian framework is held to be slight. The passages quoted above all attribute the weaknesses of Scholastic philosophy to the language in which its theories are expressed, and to its dependence on terms which appear to be meaningful but prove, on close inspection, to

---

[5] *An Essay Concerning Human Understanding* (ed.) P. H. Nidditch (Oxford, 1975), II. xxi. 20. For the same point see Ralph Cudworth, *A Treatise on Free Will*, in *A Treatise Concerning Eternal and Immutable Mortality With A Treatise of Freewill*, ed. S. Hutton (Cambridge, 1996), 170; Antoine Arnauld, *Vraies et fausses idées*, in *Œuvres*, ed. G. du Parc de Bellegards and F. Girbal (Brussels, 1965–7), xxxviii. 291; Robert Boyle, *The Origine of Formes and Qualities according to the Corpuscular Philosophy, Illustrated by Considerations and Experiments* (Oxford, 1666), *passim*.

[6] *Leviathan*, ed. R. Tuck (Cambridge, 1991), 19; for the same point see Locke, *Essay*, II. xxi. 20.

be nonsense. Writers who employ them are not merely advocating theories that are weak, but are guilty of a kind of ignorance and laziness bordering on self-deception. They talk about forms but do not understand them; they utter tautologies without knowing it; they use many words, but make nothing understood.

Underlying these objections is the implication that a fruitful philosophy must cleanse itself of the bemusing web of technical terms favoured by Scholastic Aristotelians and develop a lucid, straightforward language, in which the meanings of words are clear and their explanatory power can be readily examined. Philosophers who pride themselves on being up to date certainly take this view, and continue to rail and scoff at the language of the Schoolmen. But Aristotelianism also had defenders who, needless to say, were not as stupid as their opponents implied, so that the debate between them was by no means instantly resolved. An exchange between Hobbes and John Bramhall, then the bishop of Londonderry, published in 1655, contains a fascinating example of this clash of allegiances. Hobbes's relentless baiting goads Bramhall into a defence of Scholasticism, in terms which initially seem to play into Hobbes's hands.

What, then, must the logicians lay aside their first and second intentions? their abstracts and conceits, their subjects and predicates, their modes and figures, their method synthetic and analytic, their fallacies of division and composition, etc. Must the moral philosopher quit his means and extremes, his principles congenita ad acquisita, his liberty of contradiction and contrariety, his necessity absolute and hypothetical, etc.? Must the philosopher give over his intentional species, his understanding agent and patient, his receptive and eductive power of matter, his qualities infinitae or influxae, symbolae or dissimbolae, his temperament ad pondus and ad iustitiam, his parts homogeneous and heterogeneous, his sympathies and antipathies, his antiperistasis, etc.?[7]

All this is surely grist to the mill of the critics of Aristotelian philosophy, who believe that philosophy must indeed give up this jargon. However, Bramhall offers a further defence of it. These expressions, he claims, deal with a subject-matter which is specialized, and intrinsically obscure. Nothing will be gained by putting it in a 'plain English' which lacks the resources to cope with it. The fact that philosophy is not accessible to the uninitiated is not an objection but a fact of life.

Let him [i.e. Hobbes] put [the obscure expressions] into as plain an English as he can, and they shall be never a whit the better understood by those who want all grounds of learning. Nothing is clearer than mathematical demonstration, yet let one who is altogether ignorant in mathematics hear it and he will hold it to be, as Thomas Hobbes terms these distinctions, plain fustian or jargon. Every art or profession hath its proper

---

[7] Bramhall, *A Defence of True Liberty from Antecedent and Extrinsicall Necessity: Being an answer to a Late Book of Mr Thomas Hobbes of Malmesbury entitled 'A Treatise of Liberty and Necessity'* (London, 1655), 157.

mysteries and expressions which are well known to the sons of art, but not to strangers. ... Let him go on shipboard, and the mariners will not leave their starboard and larboard because they please him not, or because he accounts it gibberish.[8]

While Bramhall's reply does not answer the charge that the language of the Schools is gibberish, it shows a realistic appreciation (surely shared by many philosophers writing today) of the need for specialized, technical vocabularies in various walks of life. The ordinary language of philosophy is not altogether ordinary.[9] It suggests, in addition, that part of the attraction of the vocabulary of Aristotelianism was its exclusiveness, which made it intelligible to the 'sons of art' and incomprehensible to everyone else. Finally, Bramhall raises a deeper philosophical point about language when he dismisses Hobbes's view that philosophy should base itself on clear definitions on the grounds that, because language is always changing, fixed definitions are simply not to be had.[10] This objection to an ideal of philosophical transparency runs against the grain of anti-Aristotelianism and, significantly, is not taken up.

The criticisms of Scholasticism from which we began are, therefore, not only directed at a particular set of theories. They also challenge a style of doing philosophy and the position of an entrenched élite.[11] With their slapstick sallies against caricature Schoolmen, anti-Aristotelian philosophers are making a bid for power as well as for intellectual purity, and are backing an insurgent conception of what philosophy should be like and where authority should lie. Nevertheless, the problems they pose are serious enough; some of the key metaphors that had for centuries sustained Aristotelianism were on the decline, and the days when it was regarded as explanatory to appeal to the receptive powers of the soul were numbered. Radical solutions were called for, among them a reinterpretation of the central categories of activity and passivity, freed from the taint of the Scholastic distinction between form and matter.

Rethinking Passion and Action

Because activity and passivity are such basic categories within Aristotelian philosophy it was neither possible nor desirable for its opponents to get rid of them completely. Their task was rather to cut back their sprawling and invasive growth and confine them within acceptable limits, taking special care to remove the spreading tendrils of the Scholastic notion of form. They went to work by taking advantage of the natural division between those connotations of activity

---

[8] Ibid.   [9] Ibid. 158.

[10] Ibid. 170. 'It is in words as it is in money. Use makes them proper and current. A tyrant at first signified a lawful and just prince; now use hath quite changed the sense of it.'

[11] See S. Shapin, *A Social History of Truth: Civility and Science in Seventeenth Century England* (Chicago, 1994).

and passivity which are most closely connected to form and matter, and those which attach to the powers of individual things. By removing the first, they arrived at a more restricted and manageable interpretation of the second.

As we saw in Part I, a particular thing can have both active powers to act and passive powers to be acted on; and these powers can in turn be either actual or potential. For example, a knife has a passive power to be blunted and an active power to cut, which it possesses whether or not it is at the moment cutting or being blunted. In addition, the degree of activity of a thing is gauged by looking at the way in which its potential powers are actualized. The potential active power of the knife to cut, for instance, can only be actualized if it is acted on by something else, as when someone puts it to use. But the potential active power of a man to think about grammar can be actualized without the intervention of an external agent, since he can actualize it himself. The capacity of the man to actualize his own powers is a further active power—a kind of active metapower—that is held to make him overall a more active kind of a thing than inanimate objects. Focusing on this conception of active and passive powers, a number of seventeenth-century philosophers take up Aristotle's claim that these provide the basis for an account of change, which occurs when active and passive powers interlock. The potential active power of a stove to heat, for example, can only be actualized in the presence of an object such as my hand that has a potential passive power to be heated; and conversely, the passive power of my hand to be heated can only be actualized in the presence of something with a power to heat.

This configuration of ideas is used by a generation of early-modern writers to produce a cut-down analysis of activity and passivity designed to answer to the needs of their natural philosophies. Hobbes offers a representative account of how these terms are to be understood in the English version of his *De Corpore* in 1656.

A body is said to work upon or *act*, that is to say, *do* something to another body, when it either generates or destroys some accident in it; and the body in which an accident is generated or destroyed is said to *suffer*, that is, to have something *done* to it by another body; as when one body by putting forward another generates motion in it, it is called the AGENT; and the body in which the motion is so generated, is called the PATIENT; so fire that warms the hand is the *agent*, and the hand, which is warmed, is the *patient*. That accident, which is generated in the patient, is called the EFFECT.[12]

A comparable point is put with characteristic brevity by Descartes.

In the first place, I note that whatever takes place or occurs is generally called by philosophers a 'passion' with regard to the subject to which it happens and an 'action'

---

[12] *Elements of Philosophy: The First Section Concerning Body*, in *The English Works of Thomas Hobbes*, ed. Sir William Molesworth (London, 1839–45), i. 121. On Hobbes's account of causation see F. Brandt, *Thomas Hobbes' Mechanical Conception of Nature* (London, 1928), 250–92.

with regard to that which makes it happen. Thus, although an agent and a patient are quite often different, an action and a passion must always be a single thing which has two names on account of the different subjects to which it may be related.[13]

In these passages Descartes and Hobbes focus on what an Aristotelian would call actual powers; they are concerned with what goes on when change occurs, as opposed to the standing capacities of things to change. It is also noticeable that they distance themselves from Scholasticism by eschewing talk of powers. This latter precaution was not always taken, however, perhaps because the notion of power came to seem innocuous as it gradually lost its association with form, or perhaps because it was more difficult to avoid it when discussing powers that were, in the Aristotelian sense, potential. Locke, for example, explains in remarkably old-fashioned terms that,

we say Fire has a *power* to melt Gold, i.e. to destroy the consistency of its insensible parts, and consequently its hardness, and to make it fluid; and Gold has a *power* to be melted; that the sun has a *power* to blanch Wax, and Wax a *power* to be blanched by the Sun, whereby the Yellowness is destroyed and Whiteness made to exist in its room . . . *Power* thus considered is twofold, *viz.* as being able to make, or able to receive any change: the one may be called *Active*, and the other *Passive Power*.[14]

As Descartes and Hobbes explain, an event such as a stove warming my hand can be described in two ways: with reference to the agent which acts, in which case the event is called an action; or with reference to the patient acted on, in which case it is called a passion. Neither of them would disagree, however, that an actual event presupposes powers of the kind described by Locke.[15] The agent must possess the power or capacity to change the patient on which it acts, and the patient must have the power to be changed by the relevant agent. Moreover, in their discussions of material things these philosophers also agree that bodies can serve both as agents and patients. Hobbes makes this clear when he explains that actions and passions occur in sequences.

When an agent and patient are contiguous to one another, their action and passion are said to be immediate, otherwise mediate; and when another body, lying betwixt agent and patient, is contiguous to them both, it is then itself both an agent and a patient; an agent in respect of the body next to it, on which it works, and a patient with respect of the body next before it, from which it suffers.[16]

These mechanical philosophers therefore retain the view that bodies have bundles of capacities or powers, some passive and some active; but they do their best to break the connection of power with form. To say that a thing has active

---

[13] *The Passions of the Soul,* in *Philosophical Writings,* ed. Cottingham *et al.,* i. 1.
[14] *Essay,* II. xxi. 1–2.
[15] See Descartes's Letter to Mersenne, 5 Oct. 1637, in *Correspondence,* 74, and Letter to Morin, 13 July 1638, ibid., 109.
[16] *Elements of Philosophy: Concerning Body,* 120–1.

and passive powers, or that it can be both agent and patient, is to say that it has capacities to act and be acted on. But that is all. Powers are no longer held to be expressions of forms which make particular things into distinct substances.[17]

By identifying the accident generated in a patient as an effect, Hobbes makes it clear that the notions of action and passion are here being used to explicate the causal relations between things. But if actions and passions are to be shorn of their connection with form, the causes and effects into which they are analysed must be so too. For Aristotelians, there are four kind of causes—material and formal, efficient and final. The first two of these clearly bear the marks of the divide between form and matter and therefore need to be reinterpreted. We find Hobbes grappling with this difficulty in *De Corpore* where he argues that, in order to explain an event, we have to take account of the relevant properties of both agent and patient. Together, these constitute the total cause. But they can also be divided into two partial causes,[18] in which case the aggregate of relevant accidents in the agent is the efficient cause and constitutes the power of the agent or active power. 'Wherefore, the *power of the agent* and the *efficient cause* are the same thing.'[19] Correspondingly, the aggregate of accidents in the patient is the material cause, and constitutes the power of the patient or passive power.[20] It follows that neither an efficient nor a material cause is sufficient to produce an effect; to put it differently, neither an active nor a passive power can bring about an act by itself, since 'the agent has power if it be applied to a patient; and the patient has power if it be applied to an agent'.[21] The material and efficient causes are, however, jointly sufficient for the act so that, as Hobbes points out, there is no need to appeal to formal or final causes. 'The writers of metaphysics', he reminds his readers,

reckon up two other causes beside the *efficient* and *material*, namely the ESSENCE, which some call the *formal cause*, and the END, or *final cause*, both which are nevertheless efficient causes. For when it is said that the essence of a thing is the cause thereof, *as to be rational is the cause of man*, it is not intelligible; for it is all one, as if it were said, *to be a man is the cause of man*; which is not well said. And yet the knowledge of the *essence* of anything is the cause of the knowledge of the thing itself; for, if I first know that a thing is *rational*, I know from thence, that the same is *man*; but this is no other than an efficient cause. A *final cause* has no place in such things as have sense and will; and this also shall prove hereafter to be an efficient cause.[22]

While the reasons Hobbes gives here are reminiscent of the banter of Shakespeare's fools, it is clear that his aim is to provide a simplified analysis of causation by expanding the category of an efficient cause to encompass formal and final causes, and realigning efficient and material causes with active and

---

[17] See S. Nadler, *Causation in Early-Modern Philosophy* (Pennsylvania, 1993), esp. 1–8.
[18] *Elements of Philosophy: Concerning Body*, 122.   [19] Ibid. 127.   [20] Ibid.
[21] Ibid. 129.   [22] Ibid. 131–2.

passive powers. If there are no formal causes, the notion of a material cause can be set free from the Aristotelian conception of matter; reinterpreted along the lines Hobbes describes, it no longer carries connotations of inert, undifferentiated stuff in search of a form. Moreover, together with the idea of an efficient cause, it provides the materials for an analysis of the necessary and sufficient conditions of events which can be described, depending on the point of view, as either actions or passions.

Although few writers are as cavalier as Hobbes in their treatment of final causes, many are sympathetic to the spirit of his enterprise and make comparable moves to break away from the idea of form. As we have seen, they analyse active and passive powers as interlocking components of causal change; but the success of their approach obviously depends on their ability to explain what these powers are, without falling back on the unacceptable resources of Aristotelianism. Moreover, for most of them, the desire to provide a completely general analysis of actions and passions which can be applied to as wide a range of objects as possible is offset by their continuing belief that certain sorts of things are more active than others. This latter claim suggests that the overall activity or passivity of a thing will be reflected in the kind of powers it possesses, so that there will be more than one answer to the question: what active and passive powers constitute the capacities of things to change and be changed?

In the case of material bodies, the most influential reply is offered by mechanism,[23] various versions of which were developed within the space between an active conception of God and a more or less passive conception of matter.[24] With few exceptions, mechanist philosophers retained the view that God is pure activity. He is active in the sense that he acts without being acted on. Nothing can alter God, who is eternal or unchanging. But he is also active in the sense that he initiates his own motion. Since nothing can act on him, he must be intrinsically active, the source of his own activity. They also share the conventional view that the universe God has created is less active than he is himself, and that material bodies are the most passive of his creations because they lack the power to generate their own activity. The key opposition here is familiar—active things can act by themselves, whereas passive ones can only act by being acted on.

Advocates of the mechanical philosophy construe the actions and passions of bodies as motions. A body acts when it transfers its motion to a second; and the second body is acted on when the direction and force of its motion are changed. Equally, the standing capacities or powers of bodies to move and be moved in particular ways are also explained by their motions, in conjunction

[23] On the general features of the mechanical philosophy see L. Frankel, 'Hows and Whys: Causation Unlocked', *History of Philosophy Quarterly*, 7 (1990), 409–29.
[24] See E. Craig on what he calls the Image of God Doctrine. *The Mind of God and the Works of Man* (Oxford, 1987), 13–68.

with their geometrical properties such as shape and size. Once moving, a body will continue to do so, and will transfer its motion to other bodies. But it lacks the power to start moving by itself, and its motions can only be changed by impact with other bodies. To explain how bodily motion is initiated and conserved, mechanists usually claim that, when God created the world, he created a certain amount of motion distributed in a certain way, and also created the laws that govern bodily interaction. So whereas Scholastic Aristotelians had explained the powers of material bodies by appealing directly to form and indirectly to God, mechanism attributes the motions that constitute bodily action to God alone. It is because physical bodies would be entirely inert unless God initiated and sustained their actions that they are held to be passive.[25]

While this approach to natural philosophy was widely adopted, the precise character of bodily interaction, and thus the precise sense in which bodies were properly to be described as passive, proved difficult to work out. Differences of opinion in this area can sometimes be traced to a methodological debate about the part played by God in explanations of physical phenomena. Those philosophers who believe that the point of science is to reveal God's greatness and quash human pride tend triumphantly to invoke the inscrutable powers of the Godhead, whereas others, more deeply committed to mechanistic explanation, argue that such appeals should be strictly limited. Malebranche, for example, regards nature as an expression of the divine will that cannot be sufficiently admired but can never be fully understood.[26] But others argued that, while natural philosophers should of course allow that God 'started the world up' when he created it, they should be able to explain everything that happened subsequently without further appeal to divine intervention. Writing in 1686, Robert Boyle wryly observed that when a philosopher 'can say little' in answer to questions 'but that it pleased the Author of the Universe to make them so . . . we pretend not to give the particular physical reasons of the things proposed, but do in effect confess we do not know them'.[27]

A more immediate source of disagreement sprang from the need to develop a mechanistic theory capable of dealing with a wide range of physical phenomena, and from the coexistence of several competing hypotheses about how to do this. Among these, attempts to explain the world by appealing solely to God's initial creation of bodily motion and the subsequent impact of one body on

[25] K. Hutchinson, 'Supernaturalism and the Mechanical Philosophy', *History of Science*, 21 (1983), 297–333. On this interpretation see Clarke, *Occult Powers and Hypotheses*, 104–30; D. Garber, 'Descartes and Occasionalism', in S. Nadler (ed.), *Causation in Early-Modern Philosophy* (Pennsylvania, 1993), 9–26; R. A. Watson, 'Malebranche, Models and Causation', in Nadler (ed.), *Causation*, 75–91.

[26] *De la recherche de la vérité*, ed. G. Rodis Lewis, in *Œuvres complètes*, ed. A. Robinet (Paris, 1967–72), ii. 70. For an English trans. see *The Search after Truth*, trans. T. M. Lennon and P. J. Olscamp (Columbus, Oh., 1980), 332.

[27] *A Free Inquiry into the Vulgarly Received Notion of Nature*, in *The Works*, ed. T. Birch, 6 vols. (London, 1772), v.165.

another upheld a conception of bodies as passive. But they encountered formidable obstacles in explaining phenomena such as inertia, resistance, magnetism, and what appeared to be the creation of new motion, for example when gunpowder exploded or people began to dance.[28] Many advocates of mechanism therefore developed more complex interpretations of bodily interaction, some of which suggested that, although bodies are passive in comparison with God, they are not entirely passive in the sense so far outlined. Among exponents of this type of view is Hobbes, whose account of resistance rests on a property of bodies called 'endeavour', a translation of the Latin *conatus*, from *conari*, the verb meaning to try or strive. The lath of a crossbow, Hobbes points out, bends when pressure is exerted on it, but springs back to its original position as soon as the pressure is removed. Its resistance is due to the fact that the force exerted on it does not extinguish the endeavour or motion of its internal parts. So at least some bodies do not passively receive actions, but endeavour to restore themselves to the situation from which they have been forced.[29]

More significantly, perhaps, Descartes takes a comparable line, drawing a distinction between the motion of a body and its *vis* or power.

In this connection we must be careful to note what it is that constitutes the power of a given body to act on, or resist the action of, another body. This power consists simply in the fact that everything tends, so far as it can, to persist in the same state, as laid down by our first law. Thus what is joined to another thing has some power of resisting separation from it; and what is separated has some power of remaining separate. Again, what is at rest has some power of remaining at rest and consequently of resisting anything that may alter the state of rest; and what is in motion has some power of persisting in its motion, i.e. of continuing to move with the same speed and in the same direction.[30]

Descartes seems to say here that bodies have a power to resist change which is different from the motion imparted to them by impact. Like Hobbes, who identifies endeavour with the motion of the internal parts of a body, Descartes is not suggesting that this power of bodies is anything other than motion, and is thus not introducing a radically new or different conception of action. Rather, both philosophers are suggesting that the internal motions of bodies conform

---

[28] On the difficulties encountered by mechanists see A. Gabbey, 'The Mechanical Philosophy and its Problems: Mechanical Explanations, Impenetrability and Perpetual Motion', in J. C. Pitt (ed.), *Change and Progress in Modern Science* (Dordrecht, 1985), 9–84; M. D. Wilson, 'Superadded Properties: The Limits of Mechanism in Locke', *American Philosophical Quarterly*, 16 (1979), 143–50.

[29] *Elements of Philosophy: Concerning Body*, 347. See Brandt, *Hobbes' Mechanical Conception of Nature*, 294 f; G. B. Herbert, *Thomas Hobbes: The Unity of Science and Moral Wisdom* (Vancouver, 1989), 25–54.

[30] *The Principles of Philosophy*, in *Philosophical Writings*, ed. Cottingham, *et al.*, vol. i, II. 43. Throughout this passage 'power' translates 'vis'. See M. Gueroult, 'The Metaphysics and Physics of Force in Descartes', in S. Gaukroger (ed.), *Descartes: Philosophy, Mathematics and Physics* (Sussex, 1980), 169–229; A. Gabbey, 'Force and Inertia in the Seventeenth Century: Descartes and Newton', in S. Gaukroger (ed.), *Descartes*, 230–320.

to comparatively stable patterns which are not necessarily destroyed by impact, so that a body's capacity to resist change survives many of its interactions. As Hobbes explains, in hard bodies

which are compressed or extended, if that which compresseth or extendeth them be taken away, they restore themselves to their former situation, it must need be that this motion or endeavour of the internal parts, by which they were able to recover their former place or situations, was not extinguished when the force by which they were extended or compressed was taken away.[31]

This capacity is a power (for instance, to resist separation) which begins to operate or is actualized when one body acts on another. In order to explain the behaviour of physical bodies, natural philosophy has to recognize it and take it into account. Rather than thinking of bodies as receptacles that receive motions (initially from God and subsequently from other bodies) which they store and pass on, mechanism needs to acknowledge that the character of the interactions between bodies is also determined by their capacity to react against external motions, which Descartes sometimes describes as a force or power (*vis*) and sometimes as an action (*actio*).

Does this mean that bodies are active? It does not imply, obviously, that they have the capacity to initiate their own action, as God does. Their power to resist change presumably originates in God, and only becomes actual when the body in question is acted on by another. It does imply, however, that it is not altogether apt to describe the effect of one body on another as a passion, or to call the latter body the patient. For while it remains true that such a body is acted on when motion is transferred to it, this description conceals the fact that it also resists the transfer of motion. Moreover, because resistance is a causal force independent of the force of impact, it becomes appropriate to classify it, so Descartes seems to suggest, as an action.

Descartes is not alone in believing that bodies are, in a limited sense, active. An Epicurean tradition, stemming from Gassendi and popularized in England by Walter Charleton, held that God 'invigorated' or 'impregnated' atoms at their creation 'with an internal energy or Faculty Motive, which may be conceived the first cause of all natural actions or motions'. Atoms move, not because they are moved but because they have a power to move themselves, and '[t]hat same motive virtue, therefore, wherewith every compound body is naturally endowed, must owe its origin to the innate and co-essential mobility of its component particles'.[32] In addition, a number of separate and ontologically more extravagant conceptions of active matter were canvassed in England before

---

[31] *Elements of Philosophy: Concerning Body*, 347–8.
[32] Charleton, *Physiologia Epicuro-Gassendo-Charltoniana: Or a Fabric of Science Natural upon the Hypothesis of Atoms* (London, 1654), 126, 269.

Newton.[33] In a work published posthumously in 1692, Boyle, for example, acknowledged that there are aereous, ethereal, luminous spirits 'in all mixed bodies' which are 'the only principles of energy, power, force and life in all bodies wherein they are, and the immediate causes through which all alteration comes to the bodies themselves'.[34] And Robert Hooke held that, because vibration is a fundamental property of bodies and their parts, there is no such thing in nature 'as a body whose particles are at rest, or lazy and inactive in the Great Theatre of the World, it being quite contrary to the grand economy of the universe'.[35]

The view that bodies possess active powers contributed greatly to the explanatory range of the new natural philosophy but it also ran certain risks. On the one hand it might be branded as hylozoism, the form of atheism that Cudworth attacks in *The True Intellectual System of the Universe*.[36] On the other hand it might be seen as a tacit reversion to Aristotelian forms. Descartes explicitly fends off this latter accusation, insisting that the power of bodies he has identified is not a substantial form but a mode.

It would certainly be absurd for those who believe in substantial forms to say that these forms are themselves the immediate principles of their actions; but it cannot be absurd to say this if one does not regard such forms as distinct from active qualities. Now we do not deny active qualities, but we say that they should not be regarded as having any degree of reality greater than that of modes; for to regard them so is to conceive of them as substances.[37]

By classifying the power of a body to resist as a mode or quality, Descartes avoids the charge that it is yet another substantial form cluttering up an otherwise orderly ontology. But as Newton's work testifies, the suspicion that forms are being reinvoked proved hard to overcome. In the *Opticks*, he still feels the need to remind his readers that his occult powers, unlike those of the Schools, are methodologically respectable.

To tell us that every Species of Things is endowed with an occult specific quality by which it acts and produces manifest effects, is to tell us nothing. But to derive two or three general principles of motion from phenomena, and afterwards to tell us how the properties and actions of corporeal things follow from those manifest principles,

---

[33] See J. Henry, 'Occult Qualities and the Experimental Philosophy: Active Principles in Pre-Newtonian Matter Theory', *History of Science*, 24 (1986), 335–81; id., 'Medicine and Pneumatology: Henry More, Richard Baxter and Francis Glisson's *Treatise on the Energetic Nature of Substance*', *Medical History*, 31 (1987), 15–40.

[34] *The General History of the Air*, in *Works*, ed. Birch, v., 641. See G. Giglioni, 'Automata Compared: Boyle, Leibniz and the Debate on the Notion of Life and Mind', *British Journal for the History of Philosophy*, 3 (1995), 249–78.

[35] *Micrographia . . . Or some Physiological Descriptions of Minute Bodies made by Magnifying Glasses, with Observations and Enquiries thereupon* (London, 1665), 16.

[36] See J. Yolton, *Thinking Matter: Materialism in Eighteenth-Century Britain* (Oxford, 1983), 3–13.

[37] Letter to Mersenne, Jan. 1642, in *Correspondence*, 208.

would be a very great step in philosophy, though the cause of those principles be not yet discovered.[38]

Advocates of the view that matter possesses active powers sometimes exaggerate the extent of their quarrel with mechanism by arguing that it rests on a conception of passive, inert matter. We have seen that one of the things this caricature fails to take into account is the active power that at least some mechanists attribute to bodies. When they allow that the interactions between bodies involve two sets of active powers—the active power of the agent to transfer its motion to the patient and the active power of the patient to resist being changed—these philosophers acknowledge that it is necessary to posit active powers in the patient to explain what happens to it. To say that it is acted on is not enough. Rather, it has to be conceived as acting in a certain way, as contributing to the production of its own resultant state. This analysis blurs the clean lines distinguishing action from passion in the definitions from which we began, and modifies the view that one can unequivocally identify causal sequences of active agents and passive patients. It concedes that physical bodies are more complex than such an account suggests, and in doing so adapts to physical bodies an insight sometimes reserved for the soul, namely that when the soul senses, it cannot simply passively receive motions, but must have some sort of active capacity to comprehend them. As Ralph Cudworth puts it, 'Neither is this passion of the soul in sensation a mere naked passion or suffering; because it is a cogitation or perception which hath something of active vigour in it . . . [which] must need arise partly from some inward vital energy of the soul itself.'[39] The cogitative power of the soul cannot, in Cudworth's view, be reduced to motion in the way that all the powers of bodies can. But the explanations of bodily interactions and of passive powers of the soul such as perception share a common structure. In both cases, the patient both acts and is acted on.

The interpretations of action and passion traced so far slough off substantial forms, while retaining from Aristotelianism the view that entities of diverse kinds display different degrees of activity. They are designed on the one hand to be philosophically acceptable, and on the other to be incorporated into explanatory theories. Unsurprisingly, matter is placed, as we have seen, at the passive end of the scale: though by no means completely inert, it lacks any active power to initiate its own motion. Equally unsurprisingly, God is cast as quintessentially active. Working in the space between these two ideas, anti-Aristotelian philosophers take up the questions implicit in Cudworth's remark about the inward vital energy of the soul and apply their understandings of action and passion to the explanation of living things, human and otherwise. Once again,

---

[38] *Opticks, Based on the Fourth Edition* (New York, 1979), 401–2.
[39] *A Treatise concerning Eternal and Immutable Morality* in *A Treatise concerning Eternal and Immutable Mortality With A Treatise on Freewill*, ed. S. Hutton (Cambridge, 1996), 51.

they aim to arrive at theories free from empty talk about substantial forms or vacuous appeals to powers. And it is in this context that they approach the passions, challenging and revising the received view that they are to be understood as passive powers of the sensitive soul.

The task of reconceptualizing the soul and its passions is, of course, subject to many pressures, philosophical and theological, but the aspiration to overcome the limitations inherent in the Aristotelian picture remains prominent. As we have seen, the main problem here is to explain in a non-tautological manner what the various powers of the soul are, and how they interrelate; but the complexity of this task is increased by the sheer variety of the powers traditionally attributed to it. The attempt to provide a unified theory is going to be difficult if it has to accommodate, say, the will, the memory, and the power to digest. A desire to provide a more unified analysis of the soul therefore militates in favour of reducing the number of powers attributed to it, an aspiration which also gains support from developments in medicine and from the growing consensus that some bodily functions can be explained mechanically. If so, powers previously attributed to the soul, such as reproduction or nutrition, might be reinterpreted in physical terms as powers of complex bodies. These anti-Aristotelian suggestions are, however, approached from several angles by philosophers with varying commitments to, and animosities towards, particular doctrines. While there is agreement about the need to shake off what are regarded as the most pernicious features of Aristotelianism, there are several ways of trying to realize this goal, each with its own gains and losses. The existence of different orders of philosophical priorities is particularly evident in the range of innovative analyses of the passions developed in the seventeenth century, each of which hits on a different solution to the problem of how to conceptualize the passions as states of both body and soul. The rest of Part II will be devoted to considering how the four most substantial and influential attempts to deal with this question—those of Descartes, Malebranche, Hobbes, and Spinoza—arrive at novel interpretations of the passions of the soul, each resting on a broader understanding of the difference between, and significance of, passion and action.

PART II

5

Negotiating the Divide: Descartes and Malebranche

Like their predecessors, early-modern theorists of the passions are close observers of the manifestations of emotion, and watch attentively as lovers blush, the envious grow pale, and the enraged grimace and tremble. The bodily symptoms of feeling interest them deeply both as diagnostic tools and as a means of manipulation since, as Senault remarks in his book *The Use of the Passions*, 'an ambitious man hath no fence against one who discovers his passions'.[1] But more metaphysically inclined writers are also concerned to explain how such revealing bodily states relate to our experience of passion, to the desires, sadnesses, and joys that others may or may not detect. Their approach to this problem is shaped by their belief that the passions are both in the body and in the mind, and thus by the conviction that any satisfactory analysis must do justice to this insight: it must explain the muscular spasms, gestures, and changes of colour that characterize different affections; it must explain what our feelings of emotion are; and it must explain how the two are connected. In short, it must interpret the passions by placing them within a wider account of the soul and its relation to the body. The need for such an ambitious theory is widely recognized in the seventeenth century, as is the difficulty of providing one. Not many philosophers undertake to articulate this kind of systematic account of the passions, but those who do so use the opportunity to think through some of the most fundamental problems in the philosophy of mind.

This chapter and the one following are devoted to four divergent analyses, each of which takes up the daunting challenge of positioning the passions within the body and the soul and explaining how they are manifested in both. The interpretations offered by Descartes and Malebranche are set within an account of body and mind as separate substances, and share a view of the physical aspects of the passions. They disagree, however, about the character of the thoughts that are our passions, and this difference bears on their more general conceptions of action and passion in the soul. Chapter 6 explores two theories which do not allocate the physical and psychological features of the passions to distinct substances. Hobbes's materialism, and to an even greater extent

---

[1] *The Use of the Passions*, trans. Henry Earl of Monmouth (London, 1649), 99.

Spinoza's dual-aspect theory of body and mind, give rise to interpretations of the emotions which have far-reaching implications, and largely undermine the Aristotelian constructions of action and passion considered in Part I. The disparities between these four accounts are symptomatic of the liveliness and innovativeness of debates about the passions in early-modern philosophy, where many insights call out for attention and many ways of accommodating them are proposed. These variations, however, are written on recurrent themes which sound throughout the philosophy of this period. To understand what is going on, we need to pick them out, and then try to follow the many transformations to which they gave rise.

A first preoccupation concerns the transgressive quality of the passions, which cross two boundaries—that between soul and body, and that between the body and the physical space around it. The philosophers discussed here are all typical in believing that the passions turn up on both sides of the first division, however that is delineated, and they regard emotion as simultaneously a kind of thinking and a physical event. Once they are in the body, however, passions pass from one person to another, and the expression of feeling provokes in other people emotions over which they often have little control. The experience of passion is a kind of involuntary thinking that goes on in and between the bodies of individuals, binding them together or forcing them apart, drawing them to respond enviously or compassionately, haughtily or subserviently, to creatures they recognize as like themselves.

The need to give an account of the physical sensitivities that form part of our emotional life is not confined to the analysis of the passions as bodily states. It also sounds through discussions of their position in the soul. If our bodies can pick up other people's emotions, then the passions must, it seems, be thoughts of, or about, the body, a record of our physical states and the changes to which they are subjected. The process of breaking with Aristotelianism makes this problem urgent and difficult, and the philosophers we shall consider all resolve it by analysing the passions as secondary qualities. They are viewed, that is, as thoughts which, like colours, tastes, or smells, are not independent properties of things around us but result from our interaction with the world. At the same time, however, this interpretation sits uneasily with the awareness that passions are highly inflected responses which take into account our experience and circumstances. What we feel about a situation depends on how we interpret it, and to this extent passions seem to be complex judgements. The problem of balancing and reconciling what seem to be the relatively instinctive with the more reflective aspects of the emotions echoes through this period, and we shall trace it in the struggles of our four philosophers to identify the thoughts that are passions and to characterize their function.

Because this difficulty does not crop up in isolation, attempts to deal with it have to harmonize with another post-Aristotelian theme: the need to unify the powers of the soul, which was examined in Chapter 4. The powers posited by Aristotelian philosophers, along with centuries of dispute about their relation to the soul itself, had come to be regarded as obsolete. There were to be no more digestive powers to digest or sensory powers to sense, and no more mysterious messages passed between them. The task of transcending this way of thinking was, however, neither unequivocal nor straightforward; it carried with it some conceptual losses, and required philosophers to reconcile the view that there are different kinds of thoughts—memories, passions, and sensory perceptions, for example—with the view that the capacity to think thoughts of these kinds does not require separate powers. As will become clear, such a position only develops gradually, and on the way to it there are many back-slidings and fresh starts. Nevertheless, these themes form an important part of the philosophical context within which the theories proposed by Descartes and Malebranche, Hobbes and Spinoza, are written, and provide a key to the significance of the positions at which they arrive. We shall see how each author takes them into account, and how they shape a series of ambitious conceptions of the passions, conceived as states at once of the body and of the mind.

The Cartesian Soul

One of the boldest and most celebrated attempts to deal with the problems associated with the Aristotelian soul is that of Descartes, who departs radically from the view that the possession of a soul is what makes a thing alive. Whilst Aristotle and his successors had held that any animate thing capable of nutrition and reproduction must have a soul of sorts, Descartes opts for a narrower definition, arguing that the division between creatures with and without souls lies along the line between those that can and cannot think. Thinking, according to this view, is the essence of the soul. It is not an attribute that may be present or absent; rather it is the power that constitutes the soul. It follows that, so long as the soul exists, it is always thinking.[2] The question therefore arises: what counts as thinking? It would not have been inconceivable for Descartes to classify digesting, for example, as a kind of thought. But in fact he takes the view that our thoughts are limited to states of which we are conscious. Although the processes involved in nutrition and reproduction often go on without our being aware of them, we cannot, so Descartes claims, sense, perceive, imagine, remember, doubt, will, understand, or feel passions without being conscious that we are doing so. These, then, are kinds of thought. And only creatures that think in these ways have souls.

[2] Letter to Arnauld, 4 June 1648 in *The Philosophical Writings of Descartes*, ed. J. Cottingham *et al.* (Cambridge, 1984–91), iii. *Correspondence*, 355.

Support for this view came from changes in medical theories, which had begun increasingly to suggest that the powers traditionally allotted to the nutritive or vegetative soul could be explained mechanically in purely physical terms. As Descartes puts it in the preface to his *Description of the Human Body*, functions 'which some people attribute to the soul, such as moving the heart and arteries, digesting food in the stomach and so on, do not involve any thought and are simply bodily movements'.[3] These powers are therefore reallocated to the body, a shift which implies that plants, for example, do not possess souls at all. Rather than merely denying souls to vegetables and attributing them to animals, however, Descartes argues that many powers which are accompanied by thinking in humans are in animals purely mechanical. When a dog welcomes its owner, or a horse finds its way home, no thinking occurs.[4] These actions are due entirely to the motions of the body, of which neither animal has any consciousness. Only humans, then, are capable of thinking, and only humans possess souls.[5]

This reorganization of the spiritual and material has far-reaching implications. One of them concerns dying, for whereas death had previously been held to occur when, and because, the soul departs from the body, it was now held to consist fundamentally in bodily decay. Both humans and animals die when their bodies, like clocks, or automata, wear out and become incapable of producing heat or moving.[6] Related to this is a further implication concerning immortality. The Scholastic followers of Aristotle had had some difficulty in upholding the orthodox Catholic view that the human body is corruptible and the soul immortal, and that when the body dies the soul departs from it, since their claim that all living things were ensouled suggested that onions or cockroaches, as much as humans, must be immortal. To block this conclusion, it was possible to argue that only the intellectual soul survives death, while the vegetative and sensitive powers die with the body. But this was not altogether tidy, since it raised a number of taxing questions about the nature of the soul's powers in the afterlife and also compromised its unity. One of the potential strengths of the Cartesian view was that it offered a way out of both these difficulties. The soul survives complete with all its powers—it continues to be able to think. Moreover, since only humans possess souls, only humans are immortal.[7]

---

[3] In *Philosophical Writings*, ed. Cottingham *et al.*, i. 314.

[4] On Descartes's view of animals see P. Harrison, 'Descartes on Animals', *Philosophical Quarterly*, 42 (1992), 219–27; S. Gaukroger, *Descartes: An Intellectual Biography* (Oxford, 1995), 278–90. For a broader discussion of this topic see P. Harrison, 'Animal Souls, Metempsychosis and Theodicy in Seventeenth-Century English Thought', *Journal of the History of Philosophy*, 31 (1993), 519–44.

[5] On Descartes's rejection of the tripartite soul see Letter to Regius, May 1641, in *Correspondence*, 182.

[6] Descartes, *The Passions of the Soul*, in *Philosophical Writings*, ed. Cottingham *et al.*, i. 5 and 6.

[7] See L. E. Loeb, *From Descartes to Hume: Continental Metaphysics and the Development of Modern Philosophy* (Ithaca, NY, 1981), 114–26; M. Rozemond, 'The Role of the Intellect in Descartes' Case for the Incorporeity of the Mind', in S. Voss (ed.), *Essays in the Philosophy and Science of René Descartes* (Oxford, 1993), 97–114; E. and F. S. Michael, 'Two Early-Modern Concepts of Mind: Reflecting Substance and Thinking Substance', *Journal of the History of Philosophy*, 27 (1989), 29–48.

It is also vital to Descartes's attempt to overcome the limitations of Aristotelianism that he regards body and soul as ontologically distinct. The human body, which belongs to the extended world, is composed of matter and obeys the laws that govern all physical things. But the soul, being spiritual, is not extended and therefore has no spatial properties. This view circumvents the need to engage with a series of enduring and tortuous debates about the location of the soul's powers in the body. For example, while Aquinas had held that the power to see is located in the eye,[8] many advocates of the *via moderna* had claimed that it is present in every part of the body.[9] For Descartes, however, it makes no sense to say that the powers of the soul are distributed around the body, because they are not the sort of thing that can 'be' anywhere. And yet there remains some non-extensional sense in which 'the soul is really joined to the whole body' so that 'we cannot properly say that it exists in any one part of the body to the exclusion of others'.[10] The task of explaining how the powers of the soul operate is thus transformed, though not removed. First, there is only the power of thinking to contend with. Secondly, there is no question of allocating this power to any particular bodily part. Instead, Descartes faces the task of explaining how a purely mechanical body and a purely spiritual soul can interact at all, and how they can do so, as he claims they can, at the pineal gland in the centre of the brain.[11]

As well as addressing the question of where the soul's powers are located, Descartes aspires to overcome the division of powers within the soul, and the error involved in 'identifying the different functions of the soul with persons who play different, usually mutually opposed roles'.[12] Since 'there is within us but one soul, and this soul has within it no diversity of parts',[13] it cannot be divided into intellectual, sensitive, and nutritive souls. Furthermore, the soul does not possess diverse powers; it possesses a single power of thinking. The point of this initial unifying move is to overcome the need to explain how powers interact. If there is only one power, this problem does not arise. But what about the fact that there are various kinds of thinking? These, Descartes

---

[8] *Summa Theologiae*, ed. and trans. the Dominican Fathers (London, 1964–80), 1a. 77. 1.

[9] The movement known as the *via moderna* was the last major school of Scholastic philosophy, a self-conscious reaction against the *via antiqua* of the Thomists. Its most influential exponent was William of Ockham. See Ch. 3 n. 16, above; B. C. Copenhaver and C. B. Schmitt, *Renaissance Philosophy* (Oxford, 1992), 39–43.

[10] On the long-standing debate about the ontological status of the soul–body composite see M. Gueroult, *Descartes' Philosophy Interpreted according to the Order of Reasons*, trans. R. Ariew (Minneapolis, 1985), 97–124. For an informative recent contribution see L. Alanen, 'Reconsidering Descartes' Notion of the Mind–Body Union', *Synthese*, 106 (1996), 3–20.

[11] On the interaction of mind and body see R. C. Richardson, 'The "Scandal" of Cartesian Interactionism', *Mind*, 91 (1982), 20–37; J. Cottingham, 'Cartesian Dualism: Theological, Metaphysical and Scientific', in id. (ed.), *The Cambridge Companion to Descartes* (Cambridge, 1992), 236–57; P. McLaughlin, 'Descartes on Mind–Body Interaction and the Conservation of Motion', *Philosophical Review*, 102 (1993), 155–82; L. E. Loeb, *From Descartes to Hume*, 134–49; N. Jolley, 'Descartes and the Action of Body on Mind', *Studia Leibnitiana*, 19 (1987), 41–53; E. O'Neill, 'Mind–Body Interactionism and Metaphysical Consistency: A Defence of Descartes', *Journal of the History of Philosophy*, 25 (1987), 227–45.

[12] Descartes, *Passions of the Soul*, 47.   [13] Ibid.

tells us, are all operations of the one power of the soul which, according to its different functions, 'is called either pure intellect, or imagination, or memory, or sense perception'.[14] '[W]hen applying itself along with imagination to the "common sense", it is said to see touch, etc.; when addressing itself to the imagination alone in order to form new figures, it is said to imagine or conceive and . . . when it acts on its own, it is said to understand'.[15] The brunt of Descartes's argument here seems to rest on his view that, by defining all states of the soul as kinds of thinking, he overcomes the problem of explaining how they 'communicate'—how, for example, we are able to alter our memories in the light of our perceptions or use our imagination to enhance our understanding. The divisions within the Aristotelian soul purportedly made it impossible to understand how states of the sensitive soul can be available to the intellectual soul and vice versa, and how, for example, appetites of the sensitive soul can be available to the will. But once the soul is unified so that it is 'at once sensitive and rational too, and all its appetites are volitions',[16] this difficulty vanishes. All the soul's thoughts are mutually accessible; and as we think, we are able to take our other thoughts into account.

The plausibility of this line of argument depends on two connected claims. First, it trades to some extent on the view that things of the same kind can be related and explained by a single set of principles. This assumption underlies Aristotelian interpretations of the relation between body and soul, since it is because disparate capacities such as movement and volition are all powers of the soul, and thus of one kind, that they can affect one another. It also underlies one of the problems to which Descartes's work gives rise: we can explain how thoughts connect with other thoughts, and how bodies are causally related to other bodies; but we cannot grasp how bodily motions relate to thoughts, and vice versa. Secondly, the claim that things of one kind can interact needs to be grounded, in Descartes's view, on an account of how this is possible, and it is at this point that Aristotelianism falls down, since it contains no coherent account of how the powers of the soul relate to one another. The mutual accessibility of Cartesian thoughts is, however, guaranteed by the fact that they are conscious. If I cannot have a thought without being aware of it, I can always bring this thought to bear on other thoughts of which I am similarly aware.[17] By limiting the power of the soul to thinking, and claiming that all thoughts are conscious, Descartes is able to provide a novel account of the unity of the soul which answers the old question: how do its powers communicate?[18]

---

[14] *Rules for the Direction of the Mind*, in *Philosophical Writings*, ed. Cottingham *et al.*, i. rule 12.
[15] Ibid.   [16] Ibid.
[17] Descartes makes this point in relation to volitions in *Passions of the Soul*, 19.
[18] The success of this solution was, of course, contested; e.g. Malebranche objected that the Cartesian account of thinking relies on a conception of faculties as obscure as the Aristotelian one, and gives no satisfactory analysis of the mind's capacity to think. 'Éclaircissemens', in *De la recherche de la vérité*, in *Œuvres complètes*, ed. G. Rodis Lewis (2nd edn, Paris, 1972), iii. 144; trans. T. M. Lennon and P. J. Olscamp as *The Search after Truth* (Columbus, Oh., 1980), 622.

These departures mark off the Cartesian account from the Scholastic model of the soul and introduce a revolutionary analysis of the activity of thinking. And yet there are ways in which the two models are strongly continuous.[19] Although Descartes's claim—that thinking comprises not only willing and understanding, but also sensing, remembering, imagining, and the experience of passions—seems at first sight to obliterate the division between the intellectual and sensitive souls, some traces of it survive. Following his Aristotelian predecessors, he ties the erstwhile sensible powers more tightly to the body than their intellectual counterparts when he claims that, although willing and understanding occur in the soul alone, sensory perceptions, passions, some memories, and some fantasies depend on the interaction of soul and body. A disembodied soul, for example, cannot see or taste. He also adheres to some extent to the familiar distinctions between the active and passive powers of the soul, for although what had been sensible powers are merged with those of the intellect in the overarching category of thought, some of the old connotations of activity and passivity remain. Descartes emphasizes the view discussed in Chapter 4, that 'one and the same thing is called an activity in relation to a terminus *a quo* and a passivity in relation to a terminus *ad quem* or *in quo*'.[20] This is as true of the relations between thoughts as of the material world, though whereas in the latter case both actions and passions are local motions, in immaterial contexts the term 'action' refers to whatever plays the role of a moving force, and 'passion' refers to whatever plays the role of something moved.[21] The mutual accessibility of thoughts ensures that any thought can act on any other and can function either as an action or a passion so that, for example, 'the intellect can be either stimulated by the imagination or act on it. Likewise the imagination can act upon the senses . . . while the senses in their turn can act on the imagination.'[22] Actions and passions are here identified with causes and effects. But, in a manner that should not surprise us, Descartes also allows a sense in which the powers of the soul display varying degrees of activity. Our thoughts

are of two principal kinds, some being actions of the soul and others its passions. Those I call its actions are all our volitions, for we experience them as proceeding directly from the soul and as seeming to depend on it alone. On the other hand, the various perceptions or modes of knowledge present in us may be called passions in a general sense, for it is often not our soul which makes them such as they are, and the soul always receives them from the things that are represented by them.[23]

Volitions are actions of the soul because they seem to depend on it alone or, to put it another way, because the soul possesses the power not just to experience

---

[19] See Rozemond, 'Role of the Intellect', 97–114; A. Maurer, 'Descartes and Aquinas on the Unity of a Human Being: Revisited', *American Catholic Philosophical Quarterly*, 67 (1993), 497–511.

[20] Descartes, Letter to Hyperaspistes, Aug. 1641, in *Correspondence*, 193.

[21] Id., Letter to Regius, Dec. 1641, ibid, 199.   [22] Id., *Rules*, rule 12.

[23] *Passions of the Soul*, 17; see also 13.

volitions but to initiate them. According to this account, we are capable of starting to will whenever we want. By contrast, some other thoughts are passions because they have to be caused in the soul by something else. For example, I cannot see a beech tree unless there is a beech tree within my visual field.

Which sorts of thought are which? When Descartes discusses the passions or perceptions of the soul, he distinguishes five kinds. First come 'perceptions that we refer to things outside us, namely to the objects of our senses'.[24] We perceive external objects when motions in the environment cause motions at the surface of the body which in turn excite motions of the animal spirits—the finest and fastest-moving parts of matter—in the nerves. Because the nerves are like taut threads connecting the brain to various parts of the body, a motion at any point of a nerve is immediately transferred to the brain.[25] Motions from the various sensory organs converge on the common sense (the part of the brain where sights, smells, sounds, and so forth are integrated) and finally move the animal spirits in those cavities of the brain in which the pineal gland is suspended. This causes a movement of the gland, which in turn causes a sensory perception in the soul. Our sensory perceptions are definitely in the soul rather than the body, 'for when the soul is distracted by an ecstasy or deep contemplation, we see that the whole body remains without sensation, even though it has various objects touching it'.[26] But they are nevertheless caused by the body, and proximately by the brain.[27]

Sensory perceptions in turn give rise to a second kind of passion—our memories and fantasies. The motions of the common sense are transferred by the spirits and stamped on the part of the brain called the phantasy, which is large enough to change shape, and receives the imprint of motions as wax receives the imprint of a seal. In this way sensory perceptions are stored[28] and are available to be experienced by the soul as memories, or as dreams and reveries. Imaginings of these kinds occur, Descartes seems to say, when the motions correlated with images of things that are not actually present are imprinted on the pineal gland.[29] Although his discussions of both memory and imagination are complex and somewhat equivocal, he clearly believes that thoughts of these kinds are at least sometimes passions.[30] At other points, however, he follows Aristotle in allowing a distinction between memories and imaginings that come to us unbidden and those we actively set ourselves to construct or recall. When we try to imagine something non-existent, such as a chimera, or apply our

---

[24] Ibid. 23; see also *Rules*, rule 12.

[25] *Principles of Philosophy*, in *Philosophical Writings*, ed. Cottingham *et al.*, vol. i, IV. 189. See also *Optics*, in *Philosophical Writings*, Cottingham, *et al.*, i. 166.

[26] *Optics*, 164.   [27] Ibid.   [28] *Rules*, rule 12.

[29] Conversation with Burman, in *Correspondence*, 344.

[30] Letter to Mersenne, 11 June 1640, ibid. 148. See V. M. Foti, 'The Cartesian Imagination', *Philosophy and Phenomenological Research*, 46 (1986), 631–42; D. L. Sepper, 'Descartes and the Eclipse of Imagination', *Journal of the History of Philosophy*, 32 (1994), 573–603.

minds to objects that are purely intelligible, such as geometrical figures, we cause ourselves to have thoughts 'which depend chiefly on the volition which makes the soul aware of them'. And these are usually regarded as actions rather than passions.[31] Moreover, in a letter about his own fantasy life, Descartes characteristically takes control of it.

Here I sleep for ten hours every night, and with never a care to wake me. Once sleep has let my mind wander at length among groves, gardens and enchanted palaces, where I sample all the pleasures that are dreamt of in fables, I gradually intermingle my day-dreams with my night dreams; and when it dawns on me that I am awake, it is only to make my contentment more perfect and to enable my senses to share it—for I am not so austere as to deny them anything a philosopher could grant without doing violence to his conscience.[32]

The mechanism that accounts for our sensory perceptions also gives rise to perceptions of two other kinds. On the one hand, the perceptions that we refer to the body, such as appetites of hunger and thirst, and sensations such as heat, pain, or dampness, occur either when external objects cause motions in the nerves that are transferred to the pineal gland and then experienced in the soul, or when the internal motions of the body itself are so transferred. On the other hand, bodily motions caused by the body itself, but more commonly caused by external things, give rise to feelings of joy, anger, and so on that are called passions in the narrow sense. While sensory perceptions are referred to things outside us and sensations are referred to the body, our passions are perceptions 'whose effects we feel as being in the soul itself, and for which we do not usually know any proximate cause to which we can refer them'.[33] They are 'perceptions, sensations or emotions of the soul which we refer particularly to it, and which are caused, maintained and strengthened by some movement of the spirits'.[34] And they 'dispose the soul to want the things that nature deems useful to us'.[35]

Like his Scholastic predecessors, therefore, Descartes groups together a set of states of the soul that depend, in his view, on the capacity of the body to affect the soul; and also like them, he locates the passivity of all these states in the fact that they are caused by external events. Just as Aquinas, for example, had classified as passive our powers to receive representations in the soul, Descartes continues to emphasize that the soul's capacity to receive ideas is a passivity.[36] However, he interprets this as meaning that the motions of the nerves are literally imprinted on the brain, altering its shape.[37] The pineal gland is acted on by motions in the body, and the changes that occur in the gland in turn act on the soul. In addition, where Aquinas had argued that sensory

---

[31] *Passions of the Soul*, 20.   [32] Letter to Balzac, 15 Apr. 1631, in *Correspondence*, 30.
[33] *Passions of the Soul*, 25.   [34] Ibid. 27.   [35] Ibid. 52.
[36] Letter to Princess Elizabeth, 6 Oct. 1645, in *Correspondence*, 170–2.   [37] *Rules*, rule 12.

perception, sensible imagination, memory, and passion are powers of the sensible soul which can only be exercised in the soul–body composite, Descartes
describes these states in strikingly similar terms. We experience within ourselves, he argues,

certain other things which must not be referred either to the mind alone, or to the
body alone. These arise . . . from the close and intimate union of our mind with our
body. This list includes, first, appetites like hunger and thirst; secondly, the emotions
or passions of the mind which do not consist of thought alone, such as the emotions of
anger, joy, sadness and love; and finally all the sensations, such as pain and pleasure,
light, colours, sounds, smells, tastes, heat, hardness and other tactile qualities.[38]

So far, this account suggests that Descartes identifies as passions exactly
those kinds of thoughts that Aristotelians had described as powers of the
sensible soul. But this is not the case, since he also discusses a fifth kind of
perception—understanding—which occupies a slightly uneasy place in his
account of the varieties of thought. Strictly speaking, he explains in a letter to
Regius, understanding is the passivity of the mind, a perception like the rest,[39]
and willing is the mind's activity. The soul can only understand when in some
sense it receives ideas. In practice, however, perceptions of this kind are hard
to distinguish from active volitions. '[B]ecause we cannot will anything without
understanding what we will, and we scarcely ever understand anything without at the same time willing something, we do not easily distinguish in this
matter activity from passivity'.[40] Understanding also differs significantly from
the kinds of perception we have so far discussed, for whereas they depend on
the motions of the body, the soul is capable of understanding by itself. It does
not have the power to initiate its own understanding, as it has the power to
will. But ideas that are innate in the mind, or are derived from the interaction of the soul with the body, can be understood by the soul, which has the
capacity to identify some of their relations. Descartes's category of passions or
perceptions therefore crosses the old boundary between the sensible and intellectual souls, and also crosses his new boundary between thoughts arising from
the close and intimate union of soul and body, and thoughts that can occur in
the soul alone. To qualify as passive, a kind of thought must presuppose that the
soul is acted on in a certain way, either by the body or by the soul itself.

Cartesian Passions

The passions of the soul, then, are for the most part passive perceptions of
bodily motions. This general characterization allows Descartes to fit them into
an overall picture of thinking substance; but he also provides a more sustained

---

[38] *Principles*, I. 48.   [39] Ibid. I. 32.
[40] Letter to Regius, May 1641, in *Correspondence*, 182. See also *Passions of the Soul*, 19.

account which aspires to explain their content and function, to differentiate them more closely from the other kinds of perceptions we have discussed, and to outline their role in thought and action. In *The Passions of the Soul* he approaches this topic, 'not as an orator or a moral philosopher, but simply as a natural philosopher',[41] though as a natural philosopher much concerned with the unity of the soul. This interest emerges particularly in an attack on Aquinas's discussion of the passions, with which Descartes would have been familiar both from the summary provided by Eustache St Paul in the manual used in the moral philosophy course at La Flèche, where Descartes was educated,[42] and from the *Summa* itself.[43] The force of Descartes's criticism of Thomism is directed against the distinction between the concupiscible and irascible appetites, which, he points out, amounts to claiming that the soul has two powers, one of desire, the other of anger. 'But since the soul has in the same way the powers of wonder, love, hope and anxiety, and hence the power to receive in itself every other passion . . . I do not see why they have chosen to refer them all to desire and anger.'[44]

Elaborating his own definition of the passions, Descartes asserts that they can properly be described as perceptions (*les perceptions*), as sensations (*les sentiments*), or as emotions (*les émotions*). By calling them perceptions we draw attention to the fact that they are not actions of the soul, that is to say, they are not volitions. By describing them as sensations we indicate that they 'are received into the soul in the same way as the objects of the external senses, and are not known by the soul any differently'. But, Descartes goes on, it is even better to call them emotions, not only because this term can be applied to all kinds of thought, 'but more particularly because, of all the kinds of thought which the soul may have, there are none that agitate and disturb it so strongly as the passions'.[45] Of these characterizations, the first pair reinforce the point that the passions of the soul, like sensory perceptions, are passive. But the third adds the further, though familiar, idea that the passions can be exceptionally powerful and unsettling. Although Descartes does not by any means regard the passions as pathological, he allows that their presence in the soul ensures that it is liable to be troubled, and that the course of life is in consequence unlikely to run smooth.

As well as containing this warning note, Descartes's definition of the passions aims to pin them down by contrasting them more sharply with other kinds of

---

[41] 'Mon dessein n'a pas été d'expliquer les passions en orateur, ni même en philosophe moral, mais seulement en physicien.' *Les Passions de l'âme*, ed. G. Rodis Lewis (Paris, 1988), 63.

[42] Ibid. 'Introduction', 21. On Descartes's education see Gaukroger, *Descartes*, 38–61.

[43] In a letter to Mersenne of 25 Dec. 1639 (in *Correspondence*, 142), Descartes reassures him that he is not short of things to read and has a copy of the *Summa*.

[44] *Passions of the Soul*, 68.

[45] Ibid. 28. On Descartes's definition, see J. Deprun, 'Qu'est ce qu'une passion de l'âme?', *Revue philosophique de la France et de l'Étranger*, 178 (1988), 407–13.

thought. While our sensory perceptions are experiences of things outside us, such as distant bells or nearby shouting, and while we experience sensations, such as a pain in the foot, as located in the body, we experience our passions as being in the soul. When we joyfully greet a returning friend, for instance, our joy has an external object and may have bodily effects. But the feeling of joy itself is not in the outside world or in the body—it is in the soul. This account relies on two sets of criteria, one phenomenological, the other causal, to characterize and situate the passions. As far as their causal origins go, they are 'caused, maintained and strengthened by some movement of the spirits';[46] but phenomenologically they resemble volitions in being 'in the soul'. Since the soul has, in Descartes's view, 'no relation to extension',[47] this spatial description is evidently metaphorical. To claim that our passions are in the soul is not so much to point to a place where they are as to indicate the absence of a spatial component to this class of feelings. Where is this joy? Spatially, nowhere; it's in the soul. Yet, taken as a whole, the definition presents the passions as lying between two categories, sharing some of the features of each without answering completely to either. Once we take account of their phenomenological as well as causal character, the passions, like nomads, traverse the border between perceptions and volitions, between passions and actions of the soul, between states that are, and are not, directly dependent on the body. Disorderly yet fascinating, they turn up on both sides of the line.

Descartes in fact has more to say about how the passions are caused than about what it is like to experience them, and this second theme is best explored in the light of his treatment of the first. As we have seen, there is a close resemblance between the opening of the causal sequences in which the passions are embedded and the sequences issuing in sensory perceptions.[48] In both cases, animal spirits move along the nerves from the sense-organs to the brain and move the animal spirits in the cerebral cavities. At this point one of two things can happen. Motions in the cerebral cavities may push the spirits along other nerves, causing bodily events such as a rush of blood to the area around the heart, or contractions of the muscles in the limbs. This purely physical mechanism explains all the behaviour of animals (a sheep therefore flees the wolf without feeling fear);[49] involuntary responses such as breathing and digesting which, according to Descartes, have solely physical causes in both humans and animals;[50] and reflex actions such as putting up a hand to shade one's face when one suddenly glimpses something coming towards it. These types of behaviour occur 'in the same way as the movement of a watch is produced merely by the strength of its spring and the configuration of its wheels'.[51] In humans,

---

[46] *Passions of the Soul*, 25, 29.   [47] Ibid. 30.
[48] See G. Hatfield, 'Descartes' Physiology and its Relation to his Psychology', in Cottingham (ed.), *Cambridge Companion to Descartes*, 335–70.
[49] *Discourse*, 134, 139–40, *Passions of the Soul*, 38.   [50] *Passions of the Soul*, 13, 16.   [51] Ibid.

however, there is a second possibility: motions in the cerebral cavities may move the pineal gland, thereby causing perceptions in the soul which may be sensory representations or passions, depending on the exact composition of the motion in question.[52] Where passions are concerned, these two effects usually occur together. The movement of the gland that causes a passion in the soul also causes further movements in the body, so that emotions frequently have typical physical manifestations[53] which Descartes itemizes at length. Shame is accompanied by blushing, fear by trembling, grief by pallor, and so on.

Extending this mechanical analysis, Descartes indicates that the passions, unlike other kinds of perceptions, have several types of cause. In many cases passions originate, like sensory perceptions, in motions of the sense-organs caused by external objects: in the presence of a snake, for example, I not only see it but also feel afraid.[54] Sometimes they originate in internal motions of the body. 'For example, when the blood has the right consistency so that it expands in the heart more readily than usual, it relaxes the nerves scattered around the openings and sets up a movement which leads to a subsequent movement in the brain producing a natural feeling of joy in the mind.'[55] In both these cases the causal sequence follows the direction we have already traced, from the body to the pineal gland and from there to the soul. This sequence is reversed, however, when passions are caused by other thoughts. Just as the flow of the animal spirits shifts the pineal gland and causes passions, so our thoughts move the gland, thereby redirecting the animal spirits in the brain. The mechanism here is convoluted even by Descartes's standards, as the following example makes clear. 'If we imagine ourselves enjoying some good, the act of imagination does not itself contain the feeling of joy, but it causes the spirits to travel from the brain to the muscles in which these nerves [i.e. the nerves around the heart] are embedded. This causes the openings of the heart to expand, and this in turn produces the movements in the tiny nerves of the heart which must result in the feeling of joy.'[56] So we have a three-stage transaction from soul to body to soul: the initial act of imagination moves the pineal gland; the gland pushes the animal spirits to the nerves around the heart; this motion in turn pushes the animal spirits to the brain where they move the gland. Finally, the movement of the gland causes the passion of joy. Taking these various sequences together, we can see that Descartes regards passions as a particularly pervasive kind of thought, caused both by bodily motions and by other types of perceptions. We feel emotions as we perceive, but also as we imagine and remember. Moreover, since Descartes believes that even our more abstract thought processes usually give rise to passions, it follows that our thinking is in general passionate.

Descartes works hard to explain in mechanical terms not only how passions occur, but also how they vary and change. There are, he suggests, certain

---

[52] Ibid. 31–4.   [53] Ibid. 46.   [54] Ibid. 51.   [55] *Principles*, IV. 190.   [56] Ibid.

regular connections 'ordained by nature' between bodily motions and passions, which account for however much emotional uniformity there is in humans.[57] Some of these may date from the very beginning of our existence as individuals, from the time when the soul was first joined to the body. At this point, Descartes speculates, the first passions of the soul

> must have arisen on some occasion when the blood, or some other juice entering the heart, was a more suitable fuel than usual for maintaining the heat which is the principle of life.[58] This caused the soul to join itself willingly to that fuel, i.e. to love it; and at the same time the spirits flowed from the brain to the muscles capable of agitating the parts of the body from which the fuel had come to the heart, so as to make them send more of it. These parts were the stomach and intestines, whose agitation increases the appetite, or else the liver and lungs, which the muscles of the diaphragm can press. That is why the same movement of the spirits has ever after been accompanied by love.[59]

However, the passions an individual experiences also depend on a number of other factors. They depend, first, on the shape and texture of a person's brain: the very same movement of the gland which in some excites fear may excite courage and boldness in others.[60] They also depend on the body—on the concentration of bile and other humours in the blood, for instance, which affect its temperature and mobility. Even more important, though, is the fact that an individual's proneness to certain passions is continually being altered by their experience. Each time a motion in the brain that correlates with a passion occurs, the animal spirits move through the brain, carving out an ever-changing configuration of channels into which the spirits then flow.[61] This process begins *in utero*, where a mother's bodily motions are transferred to the foetus, and can have a marked effect on its soft and delicate brain. For example, a pregnant woman who has a craving for a certain kind of fruit can transfer this desire to her child,[62] altering its brain in such a way that when, later in life, it encounters the fruit in question, it desires it. The same process continues with experience and habituation. If a child enjoys playing with a cat, the motions caused in its brain by representations of cats will be correlated with feelings of love; and the more it enjoys cats, the more will these motions enlarge a channel in the brain, thereby increasing the likelihood that the spirits will flow through it and strengthen the intensity of the love that cats provoke. Equally, if a friendly cat turns into a scratching fury, the child's animal spirits will start to move along

---

[57] Id., *Passions of the Soul*, 94.

[58] See A. Bitbol-Hespériès, 'Le Principe de vie dans *Les Passions de l'âme*', *Revue philosophique de la France et de l'Étranger*, 178 (1988), 416–31.

[59] *Passions of the Soul*, 107.   [60] Ibid. 39.   [61] Ibid. 39, 72.

[62] Letter to Mersenne, 30 July 1640, in *Correspondence*, 148; Letter to Meysonnier, 29 Jan. 1640, ibid. 144.

another course, one that connects cats with fear, and will be diverted from the channel linking cats to love.

As well as providing a mechanical explanation of the way in which our passions are continually altered by our experience, Descartes aims to account for the fact that some are stronger, and some are longer-lasting than others. Their strength and resilience varies both with the depth of the channels in the brain along which the animal spirits flow—so that, as we still say, some feelings are deeply ingrained—and with the force of the animal spirits themselves. While much of our experience excites comparatively mild passions to which we pay little attention, others are sudden and powerful, and their intensity and duration correlate with the force of the motions that give rise to them. 'We see this, for example, in those who have taken some medicine with great aversion when they are ill, and cannot afterward eat or drink anything approaching it in taste without immediately feeling the same aversion.'[63] The same mechanism explains the effects of traumas suffered in childhood. '[T]he smell of roses may have caused a severe headache in a child when he was still in the cradle, or a cat may have terrified him without anyone noticing and without any memory of it remaining afterwards; and yet the idea of the aversion he then felt for the roses or for the cat will remain imprinted on his brain till the end of his life'.[64]

Descartes's view that all the soul's thoughts are conscious has a dramatic impact on his account of the emotional effects of past experience. Where we might now appeal to unconscious memories to explain the manifestations of childhood traumas, Descartes holds that there can be no such things and resorts instead to the physical configuration of the brain. As he explicitly points out, no memory of the terrifying cat now exists. All that remains is a cerebral fold, like that in a piece of paper,[65] which ensures that any motions of the nerves caused by cats give rise to the movement of the pineal gland that produces terror in the soul.[66] Much of the weight of memory and experience in explaining our passions is here translated entirely into physical shapes and motions capable of carrying information about the past passions by which our personalities have been shaped. When Descartes infers from someone's behaviour that they must once have been frightened by a cat, he is not attempting to recover lost memories or speculating about the contents of the unconscious. Rather, he is postulating the existence of an event whose only remaining trace is in the body. Passions are therefore shaped by two sorts of conditioning.

---

[63] *Passions of the Soul*, 107.   [64] Ibid. 136.

[65] Id., Letter to Meysonnier, 29 Jan. 1640, in *Correspondence*, 143; Letter to Mersenne, 11 June 1640, ibid. 148; Letter to Mesland, 2 May 1644, ibid. 233.

[66] *Passions of the Soul*, 136. For further discussion see G. Rodis Lewis, *Le Problème de l'inconscient et le cartésianisme* (Paris, 1950), 38–103.

On the one hand, the repetition of bodily motion alters the brain, reinforcing the association of events and emotions. On the other hand, such associations can be created by recollection in the soul. Dispositions of both soul and body therefore contribute to the pattern of our emotional lives, and the fact that we are in these ways so responsive makes it easy to explain why people differ from one another emotionally, and how their passionate tempers can be always on the move. As we go about the world, our passions are forever being changed, although for every individual person it is 'ordained by nature' that at a given moment a particular movement of the pineal gland will produce a specific passion in the soul.[67] A person who confronts a wild animal for the first time may perceive it as a strange and remarkable object and simultaneously feel a passion that Descartes calls wonder and defines as surprise at the unfamiliar. By contrast, a person who has come across this type of animal before, and whose experience has led them to regard it as dangerous, will suffer the passion of anxiety.

As well as having physical antecedents, the passions have physical consequences, and in discussing these Descartes shifts to a functional mode of explanation. The objects that move the senses do not excite passions in us by virtue of the differences between them ('à raison de toutes les diversités qui sont en eux'). Rather we respond passionately to things because of the various ways in which they can harm or benefit us, 'or in general have importance'. 'The function of the passions consists solely in this, that they dispose the soul to want the things which nature deems useful to us, and to persist in this volition; and the same agitation of the spirits which normally causes the passions also disposes the body to make movements which help us to attain these things.'[68] Several features of this account are familiar. There is the assumption that certain things are naturally good or bad for us and that our passions are adjusted so that we pursue the first and avoid the second. Descartes follows this line while admitting that it is in some ways counter-intuitive. In so far as the movements of the pineal gland have been joined to certain thoughts by nature,[69] which is itself the creation of a benevolent God, our passions must be potentially beneficial to us. True, our experience may alter the dispositions with which we are endowed. But before they are overlaid, possibly for the worse, these must be designed to promote our well-being. It is, however, difficult to see how this doctrine applies to certain cases. 'Although I cannot believe that nature has given to mankind any passion which is always vicious and has no good or praiseworthy function, I still find it very difficult to guess what function [timidity and the fear or terror that is opposed to boldness] might serve.'[70] But with the odd exception, our passions clearly promote our good as natural

⁶⁷ *Passions of the Soul*, 36.   ⁶⁸ Ibid. 52.
⁶⁹ Ibid. 44; id., *The Treatise on Man*, in *Philosophical Writings*, ed. Cottingham *et al.*, i. 102.
⁷⁰ *Passions of the Soul*, 174, 175. The passions in question here are *la lâcheté* and *la peur ou l'épouvante*.

beings, by arousing emotions about things that are, to take Descartes's most general formulation, important to us. Within this category are things that can help or harm us; but it also includes those more broadly in our interest. For example, we are likely to benefit from paying special attention to the unfamiliar, and this is why, according to Descartes, we are susceptible to the passion of *l'admiration* or wonder.[71] Finally, we find a further familiar configuration of ideas in the reiteration of the Scholastic distinction between sensory perception and sensitive appetite which underlies Descartes's claim that the passions move us to action. Of the movements produced by the animal spirits, he tells us, we can distinguish two kinds. The first 'represent to the soul the objects which stimulate the senses, or the impressions occurring in the brain; and these have no influence on the will'. The second sort, 'which do have an influence on the will, cause the passions or the bodily movements which accompany the passions'.[72] So on the one hand we have perceptions which, Descartes goes on to tell us, do not conflict with the actions of the soul, since they have no immediate impact on the will and cannot directly oppose it, and on the other hand we have passions which can influence the will.[73] Moreover, this is what the passions are for. '[It] must be observed that [love, hatred, desire, joy and sadness] are all ordained by nature to relate to the body, and to belong to the soul only in so far as it is joined with the body. Hence, their natural function is to move the soul to consent and contribute to actions which may serve to preserve the body or to render it in some way more perfect.'[74] On the one hand, this passage offers a narrower specification of the sort of well-being that at least some of our principal passions are designed to secure—the preservation and perfection of the body. On the other hand, Descartes implies that this criterion should not be interpreted too strictly. It is true that we only experience passions because we are embodied. But our well-being as embodied souls extends far beyond the preservation and perfection of the body itself. And it is this wider well-being that our passions help us to secure.[75]

To some extent, as we have seen, the causal connections between the bodily motions that initiate passions, the passions themselves, and the bodily motions to which they give rise, are ordained by nature. In animals, after all, the connection between input and output is purely mechanical, so that when a sheep sees a wolf the motions in its sense-organs cause it to run away without the intervention of any thought at all. In the human case a passion is inserted into this process, but it need not always make a tremendous difference to the outcome. A soldier exposed to gunfire, for example, may feel terror as he turns to run away; but he runs away none the less, and at the limit his action may

[71] See Ch. 7.   [72] Descartes, *Passions of the Soul*, 47.   [73] Ibid.   [74] Ibid. 137.
[75] e.g. the function of pride and shame is to move us to virtue. Ibid. 206. On self-preservation see A. O. Rorty, 'Descartes on Thinking with the Body', in Cottingham (ed.), *Cambridge Companion to Descartes*, 371–92.

have an automatic quality which makes it not altogether unlike the response
of the sheep. Human actions of this sort are, however, comparatively rare, and
in general, Descartes suggests, our passions play a more subtle causal role in
shaping our behaviour. The question therefore arises: how do they do this?
What sort of thoughts do they have to be to prompt us to avoid bodily harm
and seek out bodily health and perfection? As a first requirement, we can note
that passions seem better able to fulfil their function when they have reasonably determinate objects, as when the object of Orpheus' love is Eurydice and
that of her fear is a snake. However, Descartes does not rule out the possibility of passions whose objects are vague, even to the point where it is difficult
to make sense of the claim that they have objects at all. An unfocused joy
caused by the motions of the blood, or a melancholy brought on by an excess
of bile, can still, in a minimal sense, dispose us to pursue things that are beneficial
to us. Someone who does not know what they are melancholy about may still
experience their condition as unpleasant, and this may be enough to prompt
them to try to get rid of it. Equally, undirected joy will be experienced as pleasurable, and thus as something to be maintained. The difficulty with these
passions is that they tell an agent very little about how to pursue health or
avoid harm, whereas passions that are directed to specific objects give us much
more to go on. However, the functioning of a passion does not depend on its
having an identifiable object, nor do all passions possess them.

Pursuing the problem in hand, we still need to know how it is possible to
perceive that something is harmful or beneficial. How do we discriminate between
things that are lovable, desirable, enviable, insulting, and so forth? Descartes's
treatment of this question pivots on an analogy between sensory perceptions
and passions which appears, at the outset, vastly unpromising. Taking an everyday point of view it seems that, while physical objects possess properties to
which our sensory organs are attuned, so that we are able to perceive their
colours, textures, or smells, they do not possess any comparable evaluative properties. We cannot simply perceive that a snake is frightening as we perceive
that it is green and smooth. Descartes up-ends this position in two stages, by
disagreeing with the account of sensory perception that it presupposes and
by subsequently re-evaluating the analogy between sensory perception and passion. The first of these steps is taken in his well-known argument that sensible
properties such as colours, tastes, smells, sounds, and textures are secondary
qualities. They are not monadic properties of objects but are relational qualities, explicable by the physical properties of external and human bodies and
by the properties of human minds. The greenness of grass, for example, depends
on our interaction with grass, and not on the grass alone. However, because
these properties appear to us to be in external things, this fact escapes our
ordinary understanding. The property 'looks green to humans' masquerades
as the property 'is green', and it takes philosophical ingenuity to unmask it.

In his *Principles of Philosophy*, Descartes's account of how to avoid this kind of error is headed 'How sensations, emotions and appetites may be clearly known, despite the fact that we are frequently wrong in our judgements concerning them'.[76] In the case of sensible properties such as colours we must be careful not to infer from our perception of green grass that the grass itself is green; and in the case of sensations, we must be equally careful not to infer from a pain in the foot that the pain exists anywhere outside the mind.[77] What, now, about the third class of perceptions—the affections or passions? Descartes does not take up this question, though the inclusion of affections and appetites in his title suggests that he intends them to be interpreted in the same way, and our earlier discussions of what it is to be acted on suggest that this is what perceptions normally involve. Thoughts classed as perceptions occur, as we have seen, when the mind is acted on by bodily motions. But it does not receive these motions completely passively; after all, there must be something about the mind which enables it to experience some motions as sensations, others as passions, and so on. So there must be some sense in which the mind interacts with bodily motions, in which case passions, like other perceptions, must be relational properties explicable by the motions of external and human bodies, interacting with the mind. Pursuing the analogy with sensory perceptions, then, external objects are not in themselves lovable, frightening, desirable, and so on, but appear lovable and frightening to humans. Moreover, it is easier for us to understand this fact about passions than about sensory perceptions, since we do not experience passions as properties of external objects, but experience them in the soul itself.

The evaluations of good and harm contained in passions directed to objects outside the mind are therefore not in the world, waiting to be read. But this would not by itself imply that things and events do not possess moral properties; there might be primary evaluative qualities, just as there are primary physical properties such as shape and size. It does imply, however, that human beings do not, in their everyday lives, perceive and respond to these qualities. Instead they perceive the evaluations that they experience as passions which, like their perceptual counterparts, enable them to function reasonably well in their environment. Colours, textures, smells, etc. provide us with an understanding of the natural world which allows us to make discriminations necessary to our survival and well-being. Similarly, the discriminations we make between desires, loves, hates, sorrows, and so forth provide us with a repertoire of distinctions that are useful in exactly the same way. To be sure, this analogy has its limits; whereas our perceptions are relatively stable so that, for example, grass continues to look green and flutes can be relied on to make a high-pitched sound,

---

[76] Descartes, *Principles*, I. 66. 'Quomodo sensus, affectus et appetitus, clare cognoscantur, quamvis saepe de iis male judicemus'.

[77] Ibid. I. 67.

our passions are much more malleable, and change over time. Moreover, they vary from person to person to a far greater degree than do perceptions. Nevertheless, the two sets of qualities have in common the fact that, although neither tells us what the world in itself is like, both enable us to function in it.

This analysis of passions as secondary qualities clarifies their ontological status. But it does not throw much light on the question of how we perceive these relational, evaluative properties. An initial difficulty here is that whereas there are, according to Descartes, regular configurations of material particles underpinning our perceptions of colours or tastes, there seems to be nothing comparable in the case of the passions. We can offer a general answer to the question 'What is it about this snake which causes us to see it as green?', but cannot provide a comparable analysis of what causes us to find it frightening. Descartes might respond that this disanalogy is due to differences between the movements of particles we experience as colours, say, and those we experience as passions. The fact that people mainly agree about the colours of objects, and agree about the extent to which colours do and do not change, is evidence for the claim that our perception of them depends on our ability to respond in a relatively constant way to regular patterns of motion. You and I can agree that a snake is green, for example, because the motions transmitted to your eye resemble those transmitted to mine, and because these motions are not much altered as they pass through our bodies. Equally, the fact that each of us continues to perceive the snake as green, from moment to moment or month to month, implies that the correlation between the movements transmitted to our brains and the perceptions in our souls does not alter significantly.

We already know, however, that the motions we experience as passions are not transmitted in such a regular fashion. The paths taken by the animal spirits and the resulting motions of the pineal gland can change over time, as can the passions they cause. But this poses no great problem, and certainly does not force Descartes to posit distinct physical configurations which, when transmitted, are experienced as passion. Rather, the same motions that underpin our experience of perceptual properties such as colours also underpin our emotional responses. Just as they may cause us to see a snake as green, so they may cause us to feel wonder at it, not because it possesses some mysterious, wonder-causing property, but simply because we perceive a long green object which is also unfamiliar. However, whereas healthy human bodies do not usually change much in ways that alter colour perception, they can and do change in ways that alter our passions. A green snake may first arouse wonder, and later excite fear.

The clue to our problem seems to lie, then, in bodily motion. How far can we get in attempting to analyse affections in these terms? The fact that passions rest on complex interpretations (for example, in order to wonder at a snake I must realize that I have never seen anything like it before, whereas to fear it I must believe that it is a threat) suggests that they are the fruit of judgements and inferences occurring in the soul rather than flows of animal spirits, and casts a shadow over Descartes's project. He, however, is nothing daunted.

For Descartes, the evaluative perceptions that constitute our passions are just as basic and as natural as our sensory perceptions and sensations. We are designed to experience the world as beneficial or harmful to us as much as we are designed to experience colours or sounds; and we are designed to experience some of our bodily states as beneficial or harmful as much as we are designed to experience them as itches or pains. Moreover, our capacity to discriminate between, say, situations that are angering and those that are frightening is marked on the body. Layers of experience are recorded, so to speak, in the connections between the movements of the pineal gland and the passions of the soul, so that we do not need to make a judgement in order to feel that a situation is frightening; we simply experience it as frightening. An obvious difficulty is that it is hard to see how the interconnections between bodily motions and thoughts can account for the articulated character of our passions. Our emotions depend on a host of factors, including the context in which a particular event occurs, and it is not obvious how such complex and situated interpretations can be explained in the way that Descartes suggests. If this problem does not appear to worry him, it is partly because, in his view, passions usually occur in conjunction with judgements, which in turn modify them. Suppose, for example, that the sight of Charon guarding the entrance to the Underworld fills Orpheus with fear. This initial passion may be modified once he reflects that his music will persuade Charon to let him in. The fact that passions are continually being transmuted in this way makes it hard to see exactly what their phenomenological content is, and how fine-grained they are.[78] But Descartes's classification certainly suggests that they are quite fine-grained— that they discriminate envy from ambition, for example. And this in turn implies that quite a lot of information is carried by the bodily motions that cause passions in the soul. Some passions, Descartes suggests, have objects while others do not. Some are grounded on complex interpretations while others—like the fear of cats in Descartes's example—have no grounds of which we are aware. Phenomenologically, some passions are comparatively 'raw' feelings—waves of sexual desire, clouds of depression—while there are others that it is almost impossible to avoid conceiving of as judgements. In virtually all of these, passions caused by the motions deriving from external things or from the body are mixed with passions that are causally dependent on the will. But while we know that both these components are involved, it will often be impossible to say which aspects of the resulting feelings are attributable to which.

[78] For this reason it is unhelpful to take Neuberg's approach of applying the contemporary distinction between cognitive and physiological analyses of the emotions to Descartes. See M. Neuberg, 'Le Traité des passions de l'âme de Descartes et les théories modernes de l'émotion', *Archives de philosophie*, 53 (1990), 479–508.

As in the seventeenth century, so in recent discussions of Cartesianism there has been a tendency to focus on what are in fact aspects of its rejection of Aristotelianism: on its reorganization of the tripartite soul and its introduction of a dualistic division between the soul and the body. Emphasis has been laid on Descartes's claim that the soul and body are distinct substances, and on its implication that the properties of human beings must be analysed either as physical motions of the body or as thoughts of the non-extended soul.[79] What has tended to get neglected is the extent to which Descartes remains sympathetic to some features of Aristotelian psychology, among them the claim that sensory perception and passion are powers expressed in the soul–body composite. Descartes strives to combine his metaphysical division between body and soul with the view that there are states which 'cannot be referred to the body alone or to the soul alone'. And among these he includes, in best Aristotelian style, both sensory perceptions and passions. While passions are thoughts, and are therefore allocated to the soul, their dependence on the body pulls them across the boundary so that, in order to understand what they are and how they work, one has to take account, as Descartes implies, of their bodily causes. To this extent, they straddle the very divide Descartes has created; and in doing so they place a question mark against his doctrine that body and soul engage in different sorts of activity: matter moves and soul thinks. As we have seen, Descartes goes to great lengths to defend this view and explain how bodily motions relate to spiritual thoughts. In doing so, however, he also emphasizes that the passions are completely dependent on the body, so that the whole process of feeling an emotion contains both physical and mental components. In addition, he argues that habits of feeling are, so to speak, stored in the body, in the particular folds and configurations of the brain. Putting these points together, it is not hard to imagine that a less metaphysically rigorous defender of the Cartesian view of the soul might conclude that the body thinks, and that among its thoughts are the passions.

By treating the *Meditations on First Philosophy* as Descartes's philosophical testament, scholars have created a one-sided interpretation of Cartesianism in which the division between body and soul is overemphasized and sometimes misunderstood.[80] The same approach has also stressed Descartes's interest in our non-evaluative perceptions at the expense of his interest in our emotions.

[79] Among authors who have resisted the temptation to oversimplify the implications of Descartes's dualism see A. O. Rorty, 'Cartesian Passions and the Union of Mind and Body', in *Essays on Descartes' 'Meditations'* (Berkeley and Los Angeles, 1986), 513–34; A. Baier, 'Cartesian Persons', in *Postures of the Mind* (London, 1985), 74–92; G. Rodis Lewis, 'La Domaine propre de l'homme chez les cartésiens', in *L'Anthropologie cartésienne* (Paris, 1990), 39–83; J. Cottingham, 'Cartesian Ethics: Reason and the Passions', *Revue internationale de philosophie*, 50 (1996), 193–216.

[80] See e.g. M. D. Wilson, *Descartes* (London, 1978); H. Frankfurt, *Demons, Dreamers and Madmen* (Indianapolis, 1970); T. Sorell, *Descartes* (Oxford, 1987); G. Dicker, *Descartes: An Analytical and Historical Introduction* (Oxford, 1993). These scholars go against the advice given by Descartes himself in his *Conversation with Burman*. See D. M. Clarke, *Descartes' Philosophy of Science* (Manchester, 1982), 3–7.

As we have seen, the thoughts we have as embodied creatures represent the world in two ways: as containing objects with certain physical properties, and as containing objects beneficial or harmful to us. These two modes of representation—sensory perception and passion—are equally fundamental and equally pervasive, so that we experience our own bodies and the world beyond them as an ever-changing kaleidoscope of linked perceptual states and feelings which we are continually sifting, assessing, responding to, and modifying. For while our perceptions and passions are the conscious register of our bodily states—a flow of information designed to maintain and preserve us, above all, as the embodied creatures that we are—our passions are also responsive to our thoughts. Sensory perceptions come 'from outside', and our thoughts about them do not issue in further sensory perceptions. But with passions this is not the case. External stimuli produce passions in us; but so does the process of imagining which is part and parcel of much of our thinking. Not only our experience of the world, but also our thinking about that experience, is shot through with passions like a piece of silk. This understanding of human behaviour as affective, and of the affections as suffused through body and soul, remains as important to Descartes as to his predecessors. Indeed, it is one of the aspects of Scholastic philosophy that he takes over, reorganizes and refines. It is perhaps particularly important to grasp that, according to Descartes, our experience of affect is not a background pattern of emotional light and shade upon which thought is superimposed, but is rather an integral part of our thinking. Nor is it an obviously 'irrational' sort of thinking; as we have seen, many of our passions are finely tuned perceptions of our own interests. While Descartes does distinguish specialized and comparatively abstract modes of reasoning which aim to disengage themselves from the influence of the passions, these need to be seen in the context of his analysis of 'normal' passionate thought. The thorough-going interconnection between body and soul therefore ensures that both changes in our bodily states and the patterns of our own thoughts give rise to passion. Throughout our lives, we are subject to delicately inflected and ever-changing emotions which direct and redirect our actions and are a central feature of our experience.[81]

The capacity of the passions to stream across the line between body and soul is matched by their capacity to cross the boundary around the body. By virtue of our passions, our thoughts are enormously sensitive to the states of our bodies, which have their own economies of normal and abnormal motions. Physical disease is accompanied by emotional disturbance, and a multitude of transitions in the temperature and pace of the blood coming from the various bodily organs cause a succession of passions, like clouds.[82] Furthermore, we

---

[81] On the disparity between Descartes's account of the passions and the doctrines generally attributed to him see also Cottingham, 'Cartesian Ethics', 193–216.
[82] *Passions of the Soul*, 15.

are continually affected by the world around us and respond emotionally to other people, their gestures, conversations, the books we read, the weather, music, the buildings we inhabit, and a thousand things besides. The fact that so many emotions pass through our porous outer skins ensures that our emotional life is constant and various, often more so than we realize. It serves not only to protect us from harm, but also to connect us to the material realm beyond our bodies. This theme, already present in Descartes, is taken up and greatly elaborated by Malebranche, whose partly continuous and partly contrasting analysis of these issues we next need to investigate.

Malebranche's Relocation of the Passions

Descartes's enormously influential analysis of the passions was adapted and developed not only by his disciples,[83] but also by a number of less faithful followers who produced a brilliant if bemusing family of descendants, some with the Cartesian curl of the lip, others with the troubled eyes. Among these successors, one of the most important was Nicolas Malebranche. Forty or so years younger than Descartes, Malebranche spent his life as a member of the Oratory in Paris where he produced a series of works, the most celebrated being his *De la recherche de la vérité*, originally published in two volumes in 1674 and 1675. While Malebranche adheres faithfully to Descartes's division of the body and soul and also reproduces his account of the bodily motions that accompany the passions, his Cartesianism is cross-pressured by a series of other commitments, philosophical and religious, which he aims to integrate into a distinctive philosophical system. First and most famously, he is unpersuaded by Descartes's account of the interconnection between body and soul at the pineal gland, a rejection which affects his analysis of the passions by blocking off the possibility that they are states of the soul caused by bodily motions. Malebranche is also impressed by the need to maintain aspects of the Aristotelian distinction between the perceptions and the appetites of the tripartite soul. Whereas Descartes had reduced the active, appetitive states of the soul to volitions, Malebranche upholds a version of the Scholastic view that there are sensible appetites, directed at sensible things, and also intellectual appetites, directed at universal ideas. This distinction, too, bears directly on his understanding of the passions. Finally, Malebranche's work is informed by a view of what philosophy is for. A scientific understanding of the natural world is not, as it is for Descartes, a significant and fascinating aspect of the quest for *sagesse*. On the contrary, a fashionable obsession with nature distracts us from the truly philosophical task of understanding ourselves as the most favoured and yet most unhappy part of God's creation, whose overriding goal

---

[83] e.g. Louis De La Forge, *Traité de l'esprit de l'homme* in *Œuvres philosophiques*, ed. P. Clair (Paris, 1974), 69–349.

is the search for forgiveness and salvation. *De la recherche de la vérité*, perhaps Malebranche's greatest work, is therefore above all an investigation of human nature, of the truths about ourselves that we need to understand in order to offset the consequences of the Fall and prepare ourselves, as far as possible, for redemption. This orientation affects the whole of Malebranche's philosophy, and is reflected in an Augustinian analysis of the passions as the disorderly impulses of souls burdened by sin. The wish to reconcile these strands of thought in a modern yet redemptive philosophy is evident in Malebranche's account of the soul, and in his more specific interpretation of its passions.

The best-known divergence between Descartes and Malebranche concerns their account of the relation between soul and body.[84] Whereas Descartes argues that these interact at the pineal gland, Malebranche dismisses this hypothesis as wildly implausible.

For I cannot understand how certain people imagine that there is an absolutely necessary relation between the movements of the blood and spirits and the emotions of the soul. A few tiny particles of bile are rather violently stirred up in the brain. Therefore the soul must be excited by some passion, and the passion must be anger rather than love. What connection can be conceived between the idea of an enemy's faults, or a passion of contempt or hatred, and between the corporeal movement of the parts of the blood, striking against certain parts of the brain? How can they persuade themselves that one depends on the other, and that the union or connection of two things so remote and incompatible as spirit and matter could be caused and maintained in any other way than by the continuous and all powerful will of the author of nature?[85]

As this passage indicates, Malebranche solves his own problem by adopting the occasionalist view that God has created a universe in which he maintains a great many constant correlations between types of physical events and types of thought. For example, whenever my retina is stimulated in a particular way, I have an idea of a beech tree. But this is not because the first event causes the second. It is because God has so ordered the world that this correlation always holds. The principal cause of my idea is therefore God's will, expressed in the laws he has made. The stimulation of my retina, by contrast, is merely the occasional cause of the perception, the event which activates, so to speak, the correlation established by God. And in the same way, our experiences of passions are correlated with movements of the animal spirits, this movement with love, that one with anger, and so on.[86]

---

[84] See T. M. Schmaltz, 'Descartes and Malebranche on Mind–Body Union', *Philosophical Review*, 101 (1992), 281–325.

[85] *De la recherche de la vérité*, ii. 79; trans. Lennon and Olscamp, 338–9.

[86] On Malebranche's occasionalism see T. M. Lennon, 'Occasionalism and the Cartesian Metaphysic of Motion', *Canadian Journal of Philosophy*, suppl. vol. 1 (1974), 29–40; Loeb, *From Descartes to Hume*, 191–228. On the views of the mind–body relation Malebranche rejects, see S. Nadler, 'Malebranche and the Vision in God: A Note on *The Search after Truth* III. 2. iii', *Journal of the History of Ideas*, 52 (1991), 304–14.

Occasionalism offers a way to retain the view that the passions straddle the division between body and soul, and a way to retain the Cartesian claim that tiny variations in bodily motion account, in a sense, for the differences between passions. But it also offers a way to bypass Descartes's speculations about what goes on in the pineal gland. In place of causal interaction, this view appeals to properties of God which are beyond our power to comprehend in more than broad outline. We know that there are laws governing body, soul, and the correlations between them; but we cannot expect to understand exactly what all these laws are, let alone how God maintains them. 'There is nothing more admirable than the natural connections found between the inclinations in men's souls, between the motions of their bodies, and between these inclinations and motions. This whole hidden interconnection [*enchainement*] is a marvel that cannot be sufficiently admired and can never be understood.'[87]

Although occasionalism severs any direct causal relation between body and soul, it allows Malebranche to retain much of the Cartesian analysis of what lies on either side of this divide. The motions of the body work, in his view, along the lines explained by Descartes, as does the soul, which possesses a single power to think.[88] This is expressed, however, in the capacities to understand and to will, each of which is manifested in various kinds of thoughts. Taking the first, Malebranche argues that the mind has a passive power to understand by perceiving (a power, that is, to receive ideas of objects) which is comparable to the capacity of bodies to receive figure[89] and can be exercised in three ways.[90] First, present, sensible objects make an impression on the sense-organs, which is in turn communicated to the brain, so that the soul perceives *sentiments ou sensations*. Secondly, the soul imagines when it represents absent, sensible objects to itself, a process which involves the formation of images in the brain. Finally, the soul is capable of pure perception when it perceives non-material objects by representing them to itself directly, without forming any corporeal image. (Sensory perceptions and imaginings are correlated with corporeal events. But this is not the case with pure perception, a mode of understanding that humans share with immaterial beings.) Images perceived in these ways are in turn of three kinds. At the simplest level they can be isolated representations, as when I start visualizing a picture I have recently seen. At a somewhat more complex level they can be perceptions of the connections between two or more things. At their most complex they can be inferences (*raisonnements*)—perceptions of the connections of the connections between things or to put it more simply, perceptions of the connections between judgements.[91]

---

[87] Malebranche, *De la recherche*, II. 70; trans. Lennon and Olscamp, 332.
[88] On Malebranche's analysis of the soul see the excellent essay by Rodis Lewis, 'Domaine propre de l'homme', in *Anthropologie cartésienne*, 39–99.
[89] *De la recherche*, i. 43; trans. Lennon and Olscamp, 3.
[90] Ibid. 66; trans. Lennon and Olscamp, 16.   [91] Ibid. 49–50; trans. Lennon and Olscamp, 7–8.

Perception is therefore a term for a whole class of thoughts which Malebranche goes on to contrast with volitions. Somewhat as matter is capable of 'receiving' motions, so the will 'receives' from God a constant inclination towards the good in general. But whereas matter is *toute sans action* and has no force to arrest its own motions or alter their directions, the will is, in a sense, active (*agissante*). For the soul has the power to determine its inclination to the good in general by turning it towards objects that please it and ensuring that it terminates in objects of certain kinds.[92] Moreover, just as there are types of perception, so there are two types of inclination: the natural inclination towards the good in general that God continually impresses on us; and our passions, our inclination to love our body and all that is useful in its preservation.

To get a clearer idea of these two classes of thoughts, we need to look more closely at the senses in which they are held to be active and passive. Malebranche's interpretation of passivity is perhaps the more familiar, since the passivity of perception lies in the fact that the soul receives ideas. It is changed by them, but has no power to alter them and can only re-present them. The active character of the will's capacity to direct its impulse to the good is, however, more elusive. In *De la recherche*, Malebranche first portrays the will in traditional style as a blind power which must order the understanding to represent ideas to it. It can respond in various ways to particular representations, but does not itself contain any representations on which it can get to work. As his contemporary critics pointed out, however, the pathetic image of the will as a blind commander reverts to the unacceptable language of faculties of the soul which order, obey, listen, or move towards one another. Responding to this objection in a series of 'Éclaircissemens' published with the third edition of the *Recherche* in 1677–8, Malebranche seems to shift his ground. The claim that the will orders the understanding is not, he replies, to be taken *au pied de la lettre*, but is a quaint and evocative way of saying that, as long as there is a given idea in the soul, the will can think about it simply by wanting to. Following out another of Malebranche's formulations, the will can realize its desires simply by desiring, and is active by virtue of the fact that it can initiate its own inclinations.

So far, then, we have the following picture. The soul perceives—it receives representations which provide it with a stock of ideas—and the will is able to call up particular ideas from this stock. Its function, however, is not merely to contemplate perceptions but to respond to them, and its responses depend, according to Malebranche, on its ability to discriminate between judgements of two kinds. In the face of judgements or inferences about what is true, the will gives or withholds its assent. But when it attends to judgements about

<hr />

[92] Ibid. 46; trans. Lennon and Olscamp, 5. See T. Schmaltz, 'Human Freedom and Divine Creation in Malebranche, Descartes and the Cartesians', *British Journal for the History of Philosophy*, 2 (1994), 35–42.

what is good, it both assents and moves towards the good object, a capacity resting on the ability of human agents to perceive whether or not things agree with them or are good for them, and giving rise to a *rapport de convenance* between them and the object in question.

Malebranche's account of how the will relates to these two classes of perceptions goes beyond the view of the will's activity outlined in the 'Éclaircissemens'. It is true that all the soul's perceptions are available to the will, so that it can focus on any it chooses. But the direction it takes as it ranges over them, and the interest it shows in particular judgements, are determined by the fact that it is itself an impulse towards the good in general. Rather than flipping idly through its stock of ideas, the will is searching for perceptions that will satisfy its inherent craving for the good. To judgements about the truth—about what the relations between things are like—it acquiesces or consents, but is not itself touched, for as Malebranche explains, '[L]a vérité ne nous touche pas'.[93] Judgements about the good, however, do touch it and prompt it to act in two ways. It acquiesces to the judgement in question. And it loves, or moves towards, the object of the judgement.[94]

Our concern for our own well-being therefore belongs to the will. It is the nature of the will's impulse towards the good which explains our selective interest in the world, our overriding focus on whether things are good or bad for us. God has equipped human souls with natural inclinations to love him and all his works, which are not a matter of choice. The first of these is the will itself, an inclination to the good in general. In addition, we possess two other natural inclinations towards particular goods: our *amour propre*, or inclination toward things which aid our preservation and well-being; and an inclination to other creatures which are useful to us, or to those which we love.[95] These three impulses are inclinations of the soul which we share with disembodied intelligences such as angels. Properly understood, they are inclinations to love God and his creation without regard for our physical existence, which remain with us when our souls leave our bodies at death. In addition, however, God has given us an inclination to preserve our bodies, the various manifestations of which are our passions. Our passions are 'emotions that naturally affect the soul on the occasion of some extraordinary motion in the animal spirits and blood'[96] and function to promote the preservation and well-being of the body. Malebranche makes much of this claim in itemizing the errors to which we are prone. Ideally, our passions should function to preserve our bodily well-being while remaining subservient to the good of the soul, but in our fallen state we pay an excessive amount of attention to them. Rather than being guided by our natural inclinations, we are enslaved to our bodies and their strident

[93] *De la recherche*, i. 52; trans. Lennon and Olscamp, 9.
[94] Ibid. 53; trans. Lennon and Olscamp, 9.   [95] Ibid. ii. 4; trans. Lennon and Olscamp, 268.
[96] Ibid. 78; trans. Lennon and Olscamp, 337.

demands. Adapting the Scholastic distinction between the appetites of the sensible and intellectual souls, Malebranche aligns these with our natural inclinations and passions. The natural inclinations are directed towards our true good, namely the good of our immaterial souls; but the passions are directed towards the good of our clamorous and unruly bodies. In virtuous people, attention to the body is firmly subordinated to that of the soul, but most of us are ruled by passionate impulses directed to our corporeal well-being. To speak about the passions is therefore already to speak about impulses that are the mark of a human sensibility distorted by an excessive concern with the body.[97]

Passion and Volition

Experiencing a passion is, for Malebranche, a complicated, seven-stage process made up of scrupulously correlated thoughts and motions.[98] Its intricacy stems partly from Malebranche's occasionalism and rests to some extent on his retention of a distinction between the sensible and intellectual operations of the soul, but it is also shaped by his theory of the will. The fact that Malebranche cannot explain passions as Descartes does, by appealing to the movements of our bodies, leads him to search for a more acceptable account of their natural causes, and prompts him to argue that a passion originates in a judgement of the mind about the relation between an object (which may be present or imagined) and the perceiving subject. For example, a man may imagine himself suffering a grievous insult, or may meet an old lover on the street. By itself, however, this perception will not excite his passions. It is only when his will, searching as ever after the good, directs its impulse towards the perception, that he experiences a *sentiment* such as anger or joy, a modification of the mind intimately connected to the movement of the will with which it is associated. Thus far, such a sequence could occur in a disembodied being;[99] but in humans it is accompanied by further changes. The movement of the will is correlated with motions of the animal spirits, which give rise to the physical symptoms of passion and also cause us to act. (An angry man, for instance, may flush, and move to strike the person who has insulted him.) Furthermore, these motions are accompanied by alterations in the soul, since the forcefulness of the flow of animal spirits is matched by an intensification of the soul's impulse towards the good, and of the sensation accompanying it. The workings of our 'machine', as Malebranche calls it, strengthen our passions, and in doing so heighten our consciousness of harmful or pleasurable states of affairs.

---

[97] Ibid. 78–9; trans. Lennon and Olscamp, 338–9.
[98] Ibid. 87–99; trans. Lennon and Olscamp, 347–56.
[99] Ibid. 91; trans. Lennon and Olscamp, 350.

Malebranche's account emphasizes, if anything even more strongly than that of Descartes, that passions are features of the soul–body composite, constituted of both motions and thoughts. But whereas Descartes classifies passions as perceptions, and thus as passive states, Malebranche analyses them into what are traditionally passive and active components by incorporating into them the movements of the will. Feelings such as anger and love are tied, about as tightly as can be, both to bodily movements and volitions, so that passionate sensations are not only matched, Cartesian style, with motions, but are the natural consequences of impulses of the will. 'The movements of the will are the natural causes of the mind's *sentiments*, and these *sentiments* of the mind in turn support the determination of the will's movements.' So in the case of the man who believes he has been insulted, the sensation of hatred 'is a natural consequence of the movement of his will, which is excited by the perception of evil, and this movement is then supported by the *sentiment* of which it is the cause'.[100]

This positioning of the will reflects Malebranche's debt to Augustine,[101] whose inspiration can be traced in his account of what the passions are, and in his conception of the human condition. Discussing the first of these topics in the *City of God*, Augustine argues that, with the exception of pains and pleasures caused by the body,[102] emotions have their source in the soul itself and are essentially acts of will. The actual course of events may conform to our will or diverge from it, or as Augustine puts it, the two may agree or disagree. But such agreements and disagreements are not merely facts that we register; rather, we experience them as passions.

We use the term desire when this agreement takes the form of pursuit of what we wish for, while joy describes our satisfaction in the attainment. In the same way, when we disagree with something we do not wish to happen, such an act of will is fear; but when we disagree with something that happens against our will, that act of will is grief. And in general, as a man's will is repelled or attracted in accordance with the varied character of different objects which are pursued or shunned, so it changes and turns into feelings of various kinds.[103]

The essentially emotional character of these volitions is also brought out by Augustine's description of them as aspects of love. 'A love which strains after the possession of the loved object is desire; and the love which possesses and enjoys that object is joy. The love which shuns and opposes it is fear, while the love that feels that opposition when it happens is grief.'[104] In the first of these pairs, the connections are relatively transparent. Desire and love are, if you like,

---

[100] Ibid.

[101] See G. Rodis Lewis, 'Augustinisme et cartésianisme', in *L'Anthropologie cartésienne*, 101–25. See also ead., *Problème de l'inconscient*, 25–33. On Augustine's influence on 17th-cent. philosophy see J.-F. Nourrisson, *La Philosophie de St. Augustin* (Paris, 1865), ii. 186–281.

[102] Ed. D. Knowles (Harmondsworth, 1972), 14. 15.   [103] Ibid. 14. 6.   [104] Ibid. 14. 7.

modes of love; they are volitions we experience about things we agree with, which prompt us to act towards them in certain ways—to seek them out, try to retain them, and so on. The claim that fear and grief are kinds of love is a little less straightforward. To fear something is to disagree with it, to conceive it as a threat to what you love which is to be avoided or vanquished. To fear something is therefore to will to avoid it—in fact, this volition is what fear is. But this volition is at the same time an expression of love for whatever it is that the feared object threatens. If we had no loves and desires, we would have no reason to avoid anything. So there is a sense in which fear is an aspect of love—it presupposes it, is a manifestation of it, and in this way part of it. The same goes for grief. It is an aspect of loving something that we grieve when it is harmed.[105]

Needless to say, Malebranche modifies this Augustinian interpretation of passions as acts of volition, since in his view the will must have an object to evaluate. It needs perceptions to respond to. Moreover, Augustine's identification of emotion with volition blurs the line between thoughts depending on the soul alone and thoughts depending on both soul and body, which plays such a central part in Cartesian philosophy. Malebranche, as we have seen, views this with caution, not only separating volitions from *sentiments*, but distinguishing sensations of the soul from the strengthened passions experienced by embodied humans. In spite of these differences, however, he is indebted to the Augustinian view that volitions are not just acts of assent but vivid and potentially powerful emotions, and uses it to provide a theoretical account of the forcefulness of the passions. Whereas Descartes adds, almost as an afterthought, that the passions are more agitating than other perceptions, and also move the will,[106] there is nothing in his account of the passions themselves to explain why this should be so, other than the claim that they monitor our bodily well-being. Malebranche, by contrast, builds these aspects of the passions into his analysis. Our capacity to respond to good and evil lies, in his view, in the will, which is engaged in a continuous and restless search for good. It is by bringing our will to bear on our perceptions that we arrive at evaluations of them, and it is because the will is an outstandingly active capacity of the mind that we act on the basis of these evaluations.[107] Since the passions

[105] On Augustine's discussion of the passions and the will see Nourrisson, *Philosophie de St. Augustin*, ii. 28–42; É. Gilson, *Introduction à l'étude de St. Augustin* (Paris, 1929), 162–76; A. Dihle, *The Theory of the Will in Classical Antiquity* (Berkeley and Los Angeles, 1982), 123–44; Gerard O'Daly, *Augustine's Philosophy of Mind* (Berkeley and Los Angeles, 1987), esp. 40–60; Charles Kahn, 'The Discovery of the Will: From Aristotle to Augustine', in J. M. Dillon and A. A. Long (eds.), *The Question of Eclecticism* (Berkeley and Los Angeles, 1989), 234–59; E. J. Hundert, 'Augustine and the Divided Self', *Political Theory*, 20 (1992), 86–103.
[106] *Passions of the Soul*, 28.
[107] On Malebranche's conception of volition see P. Riley, 'Divine and Human Will in the Philosophy of Malebranche', in S. Brown (ed.), *Nicolas Malebranche: His Philosophical Critics and Successors* (Assen, 1991), 49–80.

are themselves evaluations of bodily good and evil, they must involve volition. Rather than moving the will, the sentiments we experience are the natural consequences of volitions, which they in turn support. On this account, it would be amazing if the passions did not issue in action, since movements of the will are, according to Malebranche, correlated with movements of the animal spirits. Volitions just are, among other things, the mental counterparts of actions.

The qualities of the will also serve to explain, after a fashion, the vivacity of our *sentiments*. As the natural consequences of volitions, they inherit some of the properties of the will and reflect the single-minded absorption of its quest for the good. Malebranche explains that, as soon as the mind perceives a new object, the general movement of the will is immediately directed to it,[108] and the attentiveness of its scrutiny is mirrored in the forcefulness of our passions. The working of the will is itself phenomenologically powerful, and is intensified by the motions of the animal spirits as they course around our body. As we have seen, Malebranche expresses these ideas through a sequence of spatial metaphors. Our passionate responses to perceptions are not distant or remote. Rather, they occur when a perception comes right up to us and touches us in a manner that is impossible to ignore. The effect of physical contact is here transferred from the corporeal to the spiritual realm, allowing the touch of benefits and harms to excite both will and passion.

Malebranche's analysis of the soul also reflects the deeply influential Augustinian conviction that our passions, construed as volitions, are fundamental to our salvation. The passions are morally right when we will to act in the right way towards the right things, when we love or fear what is truly lovable or frightening. But they are wrong when our dispositions to act do not reflect the value that things actually have, as when we lust for revenge, money, or victory but are indifferent to God.[109] People whose wills are good or rightly directed are described by Augustine as citizens of the City of God; while they feel the whole range of emotions—for example they fear eternal punishment, desire salvation, and rejoice in good works—their volitions are directed with the right degree of strength to the right things. By contrast, people who dwell in the City of Flesh err, in that their wills are misdirected. They love wrongly, and therefore respond to things in morally inappropriate ways.[110] Still following Augustine, Malebranche holds that one of the crucial consequences of sin is the disorder of the human will. Before they ate the fruit of the tree of knowledge, Adam and Eve had rightly directed wills and emotions, but since their transgression humankind has willed badly. Rather than pursuing its natural inclinations, and paying just as much attention to the body as is needed to ensure its well-being, the will now has the wrong order of priorities. It is unduly

---

[108] *De la recherche*, ii. 88; trans. Lennon and Olscamp, 347.
[109] Augustine, *City of God*, 14. 15.   [110] Ibid. 14. 9.

responsive to perceptions of the body and other sensible things and turns to them in its search for the good, with the result that our most forceful emotions are about our embodied existence. Our sinfulness is manifested in the quality of our wills and passions, and without the intervention of divine grace we are incapable of escaping from our flawed impulses and becoming virtuous.

By interpreting passions as the effects of volitions, Malebranche combines in them elements of both activity and passivity. In so far as they are sensations, they carry connotations of passivity; but in so far as they are the motions of the will they are actions, manifestations of the search for the good that is the will's essence. Depending on how one reads this, one can construe Malebranche as making the will more passive or as making the passions more active. However, the more familiar, passive aspect of our emotions is uppermost in Malebranche's bold analysis of the functions they serve. We saw earlier in the chapter that Descartes takes the usual view that passions are expressed in bodily changes. The motions that follow on from them are primarily designed, in so far as they are functional at all, to advantage the person in whose body they occur—for example, when someone feels desire, the heart sends a great quantity of spirits to the brain, putting their body in a state of readiness to obtain the object they crave.[111] The fact that these internal motions of the blood and spirits also affect the surfaces of the body and its whole configuration—so that we blush or grow pale, smile or frown, shrink away or relax our limbs—makes it possible for other people to recognize our passions, and for teachers, priests, doctors, or natural philosophers to study them. But this is not itself accorded any functional significance. That our passions can be read by others does not contribute to their capacity to direct us to the things that nature deems useful to us.

According to Malebranche, however, the manifestations of our passions have an extremely important function that extends beyond the survival and well-being of an individual body. One cannot overemphasize, he tells us, that all the passions mechanically excited in us by the sight of external things spread fitting expressions over our countenances.[112] If I am overcome by fear, my emotion will be involuntarily reflected in my face, and indeed in my whole body. Still more significantly, other people who see me will be mechanically disposed to experience passions that are useful for the good of society, and will move accordingly. For example, when you observe the expression of terror on my face, you too may begin to feel afraid. The intensity of your response will be proportional to the strength of my original passion, and this, Malebranche asserts, is as it should be. When great good or evil is at hand, we need to pay attention and unite with others to flee evil or pursue good. More moderate

---

[111] Descartes, *Passions of the Soul*, 106.
[112] *De la recherche*, ii. 121–2; trans. Lennon and Olscamp, 377.

passions do not have such marked bodily manifestations, because they are not expressions of particularly urgent concerns, and it is not appropriate that they should impress themselves upon the imaginations of other people or distract them from their occupations.[113]

It is therefore partly through their bodily expressions that the passions are able to fulfil their allotted task. Because other people read and respond to them, we are able to engage in collective acts of preservation which not only benefit us as individuals but also benefit the societies to which we belong. In Malebranche's view, this economy of our passions, as he calls it,[114] has elaborate social consequences. In some cases, as in the example given above, the effects of our passions are mimetic: my fear makes you afraid, my wonder makes you feel wonder too. But in other situations a person's passions produce complementary feelings in those who read their bodies. A man of high rank who thinks a lot of himself will reveal his self-esteem and contempt for others in his bearing, his walk, his tone of voice and the tilt of his chin. Upon seeing this *grandeur*, a lesser man will feel and express the passions of esteem or veneration. And quite right too, according to Malebranche.

It is necessary . . . to be humble and timid, and even to make a show of one's inward disposition by displaying a modest countenance and a respectful or fearful air, when one is in the presence of a person of high rank, or of a proud and powerful man. For it is almost always advantageous to the body's welfare if the imagination submits in the face of sensible *grandeur*, and shows it the exterior marks of its submission and of its interior veneration. But this happens naturally and mechanically, without any action on the part of the will, and often in spite of its resistance.[115]

The designer of these interactions has clearly opted for *realpolitik* and constructed us in such a way that we engage others in our causes when we can succeed or have no alternative, but otherwise bow to the imperious demands of status and power in the name of our bodily welfare. However, the dynamics surrounding certain other passions suggest a more merciful divine artificer. At the prospect of losing a great good,

a face naturally takes on expressions of rage and despair so lively and unexpected that they disarm and immobilise even the most impassioned. This terrible and sudden view of death, painted by the hand of nature on an unhappy countenance, stops those motions of the enemy's spirits and blood which are sweeping him towards vengeance, as though he has been struck. At this moment, when the opponent is accessible and favourably disposed, nature traces a humble and submissive air on the face of the unhappy man (who begins to hope when he sees his enemy's stillness and changed expression) and the opponent receives in his spirits and blood an impression that he was incapable of

---

[113] *De la recherche*, trans. Lennon and Olscamp, 377.

[114] Ibid. 122; trans. Lennon and Olscamp, 377.

[115] Ibid. 121; cf. Pascal, *Pensées*, trans. A. J. Krailsheimer (Harmondsworth, 1966), 25.

receiving before. He begins mechanically to experience the motions accompanying compassion, which naturally incline his soul to charity and pity.[116]

Setting aside the particular emotional exchanges that Malebranche regards as conducive to survival, it remains a striking feature of this account that it presents the passions as a social phenomenon. Like his predecessors, Malebranche takes it that we respond passionately to anything we perceive as beneficial or harmful. He allies this to another traditional view, that while God has given us a natural inclination to love all his works, our strongest inclination is to love other human beings. As humans, we are exceptionally responsive to each other's emotions, a sensitivity made possible by the natural bodily manifestations of our passions. Much of the time we express emotion involuntarily. And much of the time, whether we like it or not, we read and respond to the passions of others. 'For God, in his infinite wisdom, has placed in [our bodies] all the springs or principles of action needed for our preservation'; and 'although the soul necessarily witnesses the operation of its machine, and although it is moved by its machine as a result of the laws concerning its union with the body, it has no part at all in its various movements, of which it is in no way the true cause'.[117] The passions are therefore forces of a kind that pass continually between us, binding us together in a sympathetic web of feeling which works to our individual and collective advantage. The boundary of the body is, for them, no boundary at all, and they pass through space between one person and another.

Malebranche's occasionalism ensures that the forces that are passions have both corporeal and psychological components. But the process by which they are communicated from one person to another is nevertheless corporeal or, as Malebranche puts it, mechanical. One person's passion is correlated with motions in the interior of their body, which then spread to its surface, changing its shape. When this is perceived by someone else, motions in their sense-organs are transferred to their animal spirits and thence to their brain. When this movement of the brain occurs, they experience a particular passion. In describing the communication of passions as mechanical, Malebranche is drawing attention to the character of this process. He is not implying that we all read and respond to, say, a particular facial expression in the same way. On the contrary, he stresses that our passions vary with our bodily constitutions and change as our bodies change, and also points out that a single object will make a different impression on people of diverse occupations and ways of life.[118] So, as in Descartes's account, our 'mechanical' responses are conceived as subtle and highly articulated. Characteristically, Malebranche imposes a relentlessly optimistic interpretation on this aspect of human nature: if our bodily preservation

---

[116] *De la recherche*, ii. 92–3; trans. Lennon and Olscamp, 351.
[117] Ibid. 93; trans. Lennon and Olscamp, 351.
[118] Ibid. 117; trans. Lennon and Olscamp, 373. See also ibid. i. 148–9; trans. Lennon and Olscamp, 64.

depended on our care and vigilance we should not last a minute, but God has so designed us that our bodies contain in themselves mechanisms (*ressorts*) and principles of action for promoting their own survival. Some of his contemporaries were less sanguine, however, and saw the transferability of the passions as a threat. We are intensely vulnerable to the passions of others, which impinge on us from all directions and, whether we like it or not, we are continually responding to passions, and having our own altered in the process, as patterns of association are reinforced or changed. We are so affected by body-language, facial expression, and speech that purity of spirit cannot, it is feared, survive the encounters of an ordinary social life. Pierre Nicole, one of the authors of the Port Royal Logic and a celebrated moralist, is eloquent on this theme: the young are particularly susceptible to unwanted associations which may remain with them all their lives;[119] the souls of theatre-goers are corrupted by the love, choler, revenge, and ambition that actors communicate;[120] and even ordinary conversation can reinforce unwelcome associations and feelings that sully the character. Fixing on words as the primary culprit, Nicole advocates silence as the ideal solution to the problem—only a life of taciturn retreat can adequately protect the soul from the dangers of sociability.[121] In the absence of such a drastic strategy, people who value their own moral worth must treat the world with suspicion and take account of the fact that the passions conform to dynamic laws of their own which can both expose and protect us.

In dwelling on this aspect of the passions, Malebranche takes up a common theme which interested a wide range of writers and artists. For orators, the expression and communication of emotion was a vital part of the art of persuasion; for poets and playwrights, the power of language to excite passion was a stock in trade; and for painters, the question of how to represent the emotions presented challenging aesthetic and technical problems which were widely discussed. A celebrated, and in many ways representative, analysis of these is contained in a *conférence* given to the French Académie de Peinture by Charles le Brun, an enormously popular and prolific artist appointed by Louis XIV to design fireplaces, tapestries, and furniture for his palaces and to decorate the Grands Appartements at Versailles. As a master of narrative scenes, Le Brun was familiar with the difficulties of representing emotions on a large scale, and accompanied his lecture with a series of drawings of the manifestations of passion and an analysis of the movements of particular parts of the body—such as the eyebrows—that accompany wonder, sadness, fright, and so on. (See Pl. 2.) While the introductory section of his text draws in a rather sporadic fashion on Descartes's account of the bodily motions that give rise to passions, the lecture is mainly designed as a manual for painters.

---

[119] *De l'éducation d'un prince* (Paris, 1670), 28.
[120] 'De la comédie', in *Essais de morale* (Paris, 1672), iii. 211.
[121] 'Discours où l'on fait combien les entretiens des hommes sont dangereux', ibid. ii. 261.

Wonder   Hatred or Jealousy

PLATE 2. Drawings from Charles le Brun, *Conférence sur l'expression
générale et particulière* (1688)

If one wishes to represent desire, this can be done by showing the eyebrows pushed
forward over the eyes, which are more than usually open; the pupil will be situated in
the middle of the eye, and full of fire, and the nostrils more pinched than usual, and
slightly drawn up towards the eyes; the mouth is also more open than in the preceding
action [simple love], the corners drawn further back, and the tongue may appear on
the edge of the lips; the complexion is more enflamed than in love. All these movements show the agitation of the soul, caused by the spirits which dispose it to want
what is represented as beneficial to itself.[122]

Observations like these disassemble the facial expressions on which
Malebranche's account of the communication of passion depends, and analyse
bodily motions that are held to be natural and involuntary. It is certain,
Malebranche claims, 'that the soul cannot often prevent the operation of its
machine, however it resists, and that it cannot make it work in any other way
except when it has the power vividly to imagine some other object, the open
traces of which may redirect the animal spirits'.[123] While this interpretation
captures the idea that some of our passions are beyond our control, having
been designed that way by a loving God concerned for our survival and well-
being, it is not obvious that it is consistent with Malebranche's view that the
processes he identifies as passions include movements of the will. If they include
acts of will they surely do not occur involuntarily, as Malebranche claims.

---

[122] *Conférence sur l'expression générale et particulière*, in *The Expression of the Passions*, ed. J. Montagu
(New Haven, 1994), 135.
[123] *De la recherche*, ii. 93; trans. Lennon and Olscamp, 351.

This difficulty is one of a number of ambiguities in Malebranche's treatment of the will that made his work the target of contemporary criticism and drew him into convoluted and inconclusive exchanges. By incorporating an active element into his analysis of the passions, Malebranche captures their forcefulness and their close connection with action; but this interpretation makes it hard for him to model the experience of being taken over by emotion or responding involuntarily in an emotional fashion. While another philosopher might have saved the position by dismissing the putatively unstoppable character of strong passions as mere self-indulgence, a phenomenon dreamt up by the weakwilled, Malebranche cannot take this way out. In his view, the involuntary aspects of emotions are essential to their proper functioning and create bonds of passion rather than interest which weld us into communities. The problem is therefore held in place by Malebranche's unwillingness to relinquish a conception of humanity made vulnerable by its passions. Without these forces, individuals would not be emotionally and morally shaped by their experience, nor would they be sensitive and susceptible to emotions written on the countenance, which pierce our indifference to one another. Because some emotional relations between people are not a matter of choice, but constitute a natural sympathy which engages everyone, they cannot be attributed to the will. And yet it is the searching of the will itself that excites our passions.

Malebranche here seems to interpret the disorder of the human will as a limit on its power, and in doing so offers a more pessimistic picture than the Cartesian one of our capacity to control our passions. Although Descartes is not exactly sanguine about our prospects, he cautiously inclines to the view that there is a sense in which all our passions lie within our power; we can gradually learn how to modify them so that they are in line with our considered understanding of ourselves and our situation, to the point where we only become righteously angry, only desire things that are worth desiring, and so on. To achieve this level of autonomy, we have to counteract the will's natural tendency to assent too readily to our passions, and must go about this indirectly, by thinking through the consequences of a course of action, reconsidering the interpretations embodied in a passion, and so on. The active will works with the passive understanding so that, as Descartes says, their operations cannot really be separated, gradually reinforcing and altering our emotional constitutions. While Malebranche agrees that we can indeed change some passions in this way, he is alive to the limits of the technique. On the one hand, he regards it as fortunate that we cannot tamper with a range of emotional responses set up by a benign God to improve our chances of survival. On the other hand, he believes we are powerless to prevent our wills from directing their search to the sensible realm, despite the fact that this is not where our true good lies. Because we are sinful, even our most rigorous attempts to redirect our passions will not be enough to make us virtuous.

The control of the passions thus possesses profoundly important moral and theological implications which are reflected in Malebranche's discussion of their functioning; as he reminds us, 'all these things are involuntary . . . [S]ince the Fall they are in us, even in spite of ourselves'.[124] At the same time, his detailed analysis of the components of an emotion draws attention to some of the more puzzling aspects of the tidy Cartesian division between passive perceptions and the active will. Descartes claims that 'the will is by its nature so free that it can never be constrained';[125] and yet this pronouncement does not prevent him from allowing that the actions to which our passions give rise are sometimes involuntary, or that we are sometimes unwillingly gripped by emotions that are at odds with our judgement. Malebranche's account of the passions stresses these limitations of the will's power, emphasizing both the extent to which it works in an integrated way with the other capacities of the soul, and the extent to which its very responsiveness undercuts its ability to move itself, which is the fount of its activity. In this he broaches a series of problems in the philosophy of action which will be further discussed in Part IV.

---

[124] *De la recherche*, 990; trans. Lennon and Olscamp, 349.   [125] *Passions of the Soul*, 41.

6

Mental and Bodily Passions Identified: Hobbes and Spinoza

Despite their diverging philosophical allegiances, we have seen that Descartes and Malebranche approach the task of explaining what the passions are from certain common premisses. They share a commitment to a sharp ontological division between body and soul, so that in analysing the passions they are bound to divide them into corporeal and spiritual components, and to posit some sort of relation between the two. In addition, they both retain the Aristotelian conviction that there are in the soul two kinds of thoughts—active volitions and passive perceptions—in terms of which passions must be interpreted. This ontological stance was profoundly influential, and provided a framework for thinking about the mind and the place of the passions within it; but it also generated difficulties that called into question the assumptions on which the framework was based.

Diverse as their opinions were, philosophers of the early-modern period were able to agree that any systematic analysis of the passions would have to be situated within a more general account of the body and the soul, taken singly and together. This problem could not be pushed aside, and the strengths and weaknesses of existing attempts to solve it therefore demanded attention. If body and mind are separate substances, and if motions and thoughts are categorically distinct, it must somehow be possible to explain what appear to be interconnections between them; yet none of the accounts that had emerged with the New Science met with general approval. While many philosophers agreed with Malebranche that the Cartesian account of interaction at the pineal gland was wildly implausible, just as many were unpersuaded by occasionalism. The sheer mysteriousness of the process by which God matches up thoughts with corporeal events, although regarded by many occasionalists as a strength of their position, struck its opponents as a weakness. Theories that made a virtue of unintelligibility were, in their view, defective, if only because they offended against the deep assumption that an understanding of the world lies within our reach. To give up this ideal was, amongst other things, a sort of theologically inspired laziness which often went with self-deception about how much had been achieved, as Spinoza points out in connection with philosophers who argue that corporeal substance was created by God. 'But by what divine power could it have been created?', he asks. 'They are completely ignorant of that. And this shows clearly that they do not understand what they themselves say.'[1] Occasionalists, like believers in a God who created the world, are in danger of not understanding what they themselves say, in which case the problem of how states of the soul are connected with states of corporeal substance still awaits a solution.

Analyses of the soul itself, organized around the division between perceptions and volitions, were also problematic. Although Descartes and Malebranche continue to distinguish these Scholastic categories, they insist, as we have seen, that understanding and will are not separate powers of the soul but are mutually accessible modes of thinking. There is therefore no question of their having to communicate with one another, and a serious limitation of Aristotelianism is purportedly overcome. However, each of these philosophers is content to adapt existing interpretations of what these two kinds of thought consist in, and to make use of the Scholastic terms used to describe them, and to this extent their work remains continuous with the tradition they officially reject. The mind understands, for example, when it receives impressions, and the way in which it does so is like, though not the same as, the way that wax receives the imprint of a seal. The will's consent to perceptions of the good is a movement, though not a physical one. Descartes and Malebranche persist in analysing thought in terms of imprints and motions, implicitly excepting this mode of analysis from their criticisms of the language of Aristotelian philosophy. Talk about substantial forms or formal causes may be gibberish, but motions of the mind are still acceptable currency. Their partial rejection of Scholastic accounts of the soul is, however, destabilized by the very upheaval to which they contribute, since criticism of the Schools proved hard to contain. Once its philosophical language was called in question, the terms in which thinking had habitually been discussed were liable to be re-examined, and in the eyes of at least some philosophers were found wanting.

It took a good deal of intellectual courage to challenge the distinction between perceptions and volitions, not only because this division had strong phenomenological backing, but also because it provided the basis for the conceptions of voluntary action on which Christian salvation was held to depend. Descartes's cautious orthodoxy and desire to avoid theological controversy, and Malebranche's intense religious faith, ensured that the will remained central to their conceptions of thought, and that volition survived as the epitome of the soul's activity. Philosophers who were, for one reason or another, less wedded to Christian dogma were in a better position to examine the character of will and understanding and the metaphors used to describe them. This chapter will

---

[1] *Ethics*, in *The Collected Works of Spinoza*, ed. E. Curley (Princeton, 1985), vol. i, I. P 15, s. 1.

be concerned with Hobbes and Spinoza, both loudly condemned as atheists, who produced searching and radical challenges to an Aristotelian understanding of these categories. Hobbes—presumably counting to some extent on the power of his patrons to protect him—combines acid hostility to organized religion with relentless criticism of the metaphors used to explain the mind, forging a thoroughgoing materialism in which the distinction between will and perception is all but obliterated. Spinoza, an excommunicated Jew living in and around Amsterdam, occupies an unusual position where the claims of dogma have little hold over him, and is able to formulate a distinction between the actions and passions of the mind detached from the division between volition and perception. By proposing solutions to the two problems we have identified—the relation between body and soul, and the character of the soul's thoughts—and combining these with an already-familiar conception of the body as extended and moving, Hobbes and Spinoza construct novel frameworks within which they locate and analyse the passions. Their approaches to the emotions therefore share the systematic character of those we have already discussed, but they take a step further away from Scholasticism and offer innovative interpretations of both the passions and passivity.

Hobbes's Analysis of Thinking as Motion

Hobbes's rejection of the Schools focuses with particular ferocity on the language they use. Error and ignorance may be cloaked, he reminds Bramhall, under grave Scholastic terms, 'and I do likewise entreat your lordship to take notice that the greatest fraud and cheating lurks commonly under the pretence of plain dealing. We see jugglers commonly strip up their sleeves and promise extraordinary fair-dealing before they begin to play their tricks.'[2] Among the tricks that incense Hobbes is the appeal to 'metaphysical motion' to explain the operations of the mind, and particularly the beginning of voluntary action. As we have observed, the mind is commonly held to move or incline toward the objects of its passions, although 'the Schools find in mere appetite to go, or move, no actual motion at all'. However, 'because some motion they must acknowledge, they call it metaphorical motion; which is but an absurd speech; for though words may be called metaphorical, bodies and motions cannot'.[3] Hobbes here grapples with a problem that his anti-Aristotelian contemporaries do not, on the whole, find unduly troubling. Descartes, for example, is prepared to countenance the idea of mental motions, both to characterize particular kinds of thinking and to explain how the soul can act on the body. He confesses in a letter to Henry More that 'the only idea I can find in my mind to represent

---

    [2] John Bramhall, *A Defence of True Liberty from Antecedent and Extrinsicall Neccessity* (London, 1655), 153.
    [3] *Leviathan*, ed. R. Tuck (Cambridge, 1991), 38.

the way in which God or an angel can move matter is the one which shows me the way in which I am conscious I can move my body by my own thought'.[4] The seeming naturalness of this way of construing our experience persuaded most philosophers that certain kinds of thinking could be interpreted as analogous to physical motions.

Because this stance is so pervasive, and underpins a conception of activity on which much else depends, the project of abandoning it is an extraordinarily radical one, and Hobbes is not always successful in carrying it through. When he sets out his position at the beginning of *The Elements of Law*, for instance, he distinguishes the motive power of the body from that of the mind,[5] and later offers separate definitions of the two: the motive power of the body is its strength or power to move other bodies, while that of the mind is its power to 'give animal motion to the body wherein it existeth'.[6] Such formulations are conventional, but are to some extent out of line with Hobbes's strenuous efforts to produce an account of thinking which does not rely on metaphysical motion. This in turn has an enormous impact on his treatment of the themes with which we are concerned: the bodily and psychological characters of passions, and the relations between them.

Hobbes holds that our sensory perceptions of colours, sounds, and so forth are caused by the actions of external motions on our sensory organs and nerves. His firm advocacy of this view is evident in a treatise on optics completed in 1645, where he proposes to sweep away the rubbish of other explanatory hypotheses, among them the old opinions that there are visible species, that there are 'millions of strings in the optic nerve, by which the object plays upon the brain, and makes the soul listen to it, and other innumerable such trash'.[7] Perceptions, along with the imaginings and memories that derive from them, are 'apparition[s] unto us of that motion, agitation, or alternation, which the object worketh in the brain or spirits, or some internal substance of the head'.[8] Moreover, the accidents and qualities we attribute to objects are 'seemings and apparitions', and the only things that are really in the world without us are 'those motions by which these seemings are caused'.[9] While Hobbes's analyses of the workings of the body are not as detailed as, say, those of Descartes, they are just as strongly committed to the view that the only power to be found

---

[4] Letter to More, 15 Apr. 1649, in *The Philosophical Writings of Descartes*, ed. J. Cottingham *et al.*, (Cambridge, 1984–91), iii. *Correspondence*, 375.

[5] Ed. F. Tönnies (2nd edn, London, 1969), 2. On the anti-Aristotelian character of Hobbes's psychology see T. A. Spragens Jnr., *The Politics of Motion: The World of Thomas Hobbes* (London, 1973), esp. 187–93.

[6] *Elements of Law*, 27–8.

[7] *A Minute or First Draft of the Optics*, in *The English Works of Thomas Hobbes*, ed. Sir William Molesworth (London, 1839–45), vii. 470. On the date of this work see J. Jacquot and H. W. Jones, Introduction to *Thomas Hobbes: Critique du 'De Mundo' de Thomas White* (Paris, 1973), 72–3.

[8] Hobbes, *Elements of Law*, 4.

[9] *Elements of Philosophy: The First Section, Concerning Body*, in *English Works*, ed. Molesworth, i. 7.

in bodies, human and otherwise, is motion. However, when he comes to talk about thoughts, Hobbes departs drastically from the theories that have been discussed so far. Whereas Descartes and Malebranche interpret thoughts as the soul's perceptions of, and responses to, states of the body, Hobbes appears to identify them with bodily motions. Sense, he explains in the English version of *De Corpore*, 'is some internal motion in the sentient, generated by some internal motion of the parts of the object, and propagated through all the media to the innermost part of the organ'.[10] However, as one would expect, this internal motion is not conceived as unidirectional. A human body does not passively receive the motions caused in it by external objects; it also resists or reacts 'by reason of its own internal natural motion', and it is from this reaction that 'a phantasm or idea hath its being'.[11] Sensory ideas, then, arise from the inter-action of external motion with internal bodily motion.

The most striking feature of this account is what it leaves out. There is no talk of the mind perceiving a motion and no discussion of transactions between body and soul. Instead, a sensory representation is analysed as a motion. As Hobbes concedes, there must be something distinctive about the motions of animal bodies to explain the experience of representations, since inanimate objects such as tables would otherwise be able to sense. After all, they too can be affected by, and react to, external motions. Sensing, he suggests, involves the capacity not just to experience phantasms, but to compare and distinguish them, which in turn presupposes that we can remember them. (Without this capacity we should be unable, for example, to discriminate between a sensory perception of a camel and of a horse.) Although inanimate objects react to external motions, the construction of their bodies does not enable them to retain motions, and they therefore do not have the phantasms that are the constituents of sense.[12] This argument does not altogether answer the objection, since it fails to close off the possibility that fleeting phantasms may occur in inanimate objects. A gap opens up between the occurrence of a phantasm, which coin-cides with the reaction of a body to an external motion, and the formation of concepts, which depends on the capacity of a body to retain the motion. Hobbes seems in fact to recognize some such distinction.[13] But he is mainly concerned to emphasize that human experience depends on an ability to retain phantasms, and so requires, and even consists in, a particular physical process.

The motions that constitute apparitions, phantasms, or conceptions in the brain do not stop in the head. They proceed to the heart, where they help or hinder the body's vital motion (the circulation of the blood),[14] causing alterations which

---

[10] Ibid. 391; cf. *Leviathan*, 14.   [11] *Elements of Philosophy: Concerning Body*, 391.
[12] Ibid. 393.
[13] Ibid. 394. Hobbes was a firm advocate of William Harvey's theories about the circulation of the blood. See ibid., Epistle Dedicatory, p. viii.
[14] Ibid. 407.

we experience as pleasure and pain, and as passion. It is significant that, whereas Cartesians hold that sensory perceptions and passions are both immediately preceded by motions in the brain, Hobbes views them as two stages of a single motion experienced as two kinds of thought as it interacts with different parts of the body. Upholding a popular view, he locates sense in the head and emotion in the heart, grounding this geography on the claim that the heart is the seat of the vital motion that keeps us alive, and with which the passions are closely connected. External objects therefore do not only cause sensory representations; in so far as the motions by which they are constituted affect vital motion, they also cause passions.[15] Furthermore, a comparable mechanism accounts for the emotions we experience in dreams. Reciprocal motions between the brain and the vital parts cause representations and affections whose content can be explained in physical terms, by the heat of the internal organs or the descent of different sorts of phlegm so that, for example, fearful dreams are attributable to a strong spleen.[16] As we saw in Chapter 5, Descartes distinguishes sensory perceptions from passions by appealing to the location of our ideas or representations: we experience sensory properties as qualities of external things, and experience passions as in the soul. Once again Hobbes offers a physical account of this difference. Phantasms appear to be outside us because they consist in reactions to a motion originating outside the body, whereas passions appear to be within because the motions that constitute them are in the body's internal organs.[17]

Our emotions are therefore conscious thoughts, which are our experience of bodily motions. But this experience is not, according to Hobbes, 'in' the soul as opposed to the body. Thoughts, Hobbes seems to be saying, just are motions, and this is as true of passions as of sensory perceptions. But if this is so, the character of our passions must somehow reflect the properties of bodily motions, as Hobbes in fact goes on to explain. The human body sustains certain patterns of internal motion, such as the circulation of the blood, which are essential to its proper functioning. When external motions impinge on it, they interact with its internal motions; as Hobbes puts it, the body has a capacity to resist change which he calls, translating the Latin *conatus*, endeavour. Sometimes endeavour is unconscious: for example, we are unaware of many of the expansions and contractions that go on in the body as it adjusts to changes in outside temperature. But in other cases it is 'helped by the motions of sense'. A motion in the brain that is experienced as warmth, for instance, may carry on to the heart where it is experienced as discomfort or pain, and an agent who feels this may move from a sunny corner into the shade.

The disposition to respond to conscious feelings of pleasure and pain begins, Hobbes believes, 'even in the embryo; which while it is in the womb moveth

---

[15] Ibid. 28, 31.   [16] Ibid. 9.

[17] On these processes see D. Sepper, 'Hobbes, Descartes and Imagination', *Monist*, 71 (1988), 526–42.

its limbs with voluntary motion, for the avoiding of whatsoever troubleth it or for the pursuing of what pleaseth it'.[18] Humans are equipped from their conception with a capacity to preserve the integrity of their bodies and keep them functioning, which works both through conscious and unconscious motions. Conscious endeavour is at first extremely rudimentary—foetuses and babies experience a comparatively limited range of phantasms or conceptions as pleasurable or painful. But as we gain experience we come to know more about what will prove pleasant and harmful, and our first endeavour is gradually refined.[19] Endeavour is, moreover, the basis of the passions, for 'when it tends towards such things as are known by experience to be pleasant, it is called *appetite*, that is, an approaching; and when it shuns what is troublesome, *aversion*, or flying from it'.[20] As we learn to discriminate between different kinds of appetite and aversion, we experience a broadening range of passions, 'all of which consist in appetite and aversion, except pure pleasure and pain'.[21] While some of our simplest appetites and aversions are experiences of present endeavour—sadness, for example, is our experience of the body failing to maintain itself in the face of an external motion—many of them are grounded on our ability to compare old motions (memories) with new ones (sensory perceptions and imaginings). Hope, for example, is an appetite for a future pleasure, and to experience it we must be able to form some expectation on the basis of our current state and our experience of the past. But all these ingredients—remembered pleasures, past events, present perceptions, expectations—must, according to Hobbes, be construed as bodily motions. Our interpretation of the world as containing things that are good or bad for us is in some way identical to a physical feedback mechanism which progressively refines our responses to the motions of our bodies.

With this interpretation of the passions, Hobbes transposes a number of familiar arguments about the soul or mind into a bodily key. But the continuity between his view and those of his dualist contemporaries is nevertheless striking. Like Descartes and Malebranche, he holds that the human body resists change, and that the passions assist it to do so. Their function is to encourage us to avoid things that are harmful to the body, and to pursue things that are good for it. Also like Descartes and Malebranche, he does not interpret this requirement narrowly. We are understood to be promoting the good of the body when we get angry with people who disagree with our philosophical opinions, for example, as much as when we long for a sustaining meal. However, Hobbes carries this line of argument further than the philosophers discussed

---

[18] *Elements of Philosophy: Concerning Body*, 407.
[19] See P. Hurley, 'The Appetites of Thomas Hobbes', *History of Philosophy Quarterly*, 7 (1990), 391–407. For the limitations of this account of our responses see T. Sorell, *Hobbes* (London, 1986), 82–7.
[20] *Elements of Philosophy: Concerning Body*, 407.   [21] Ibid. 409.

in Chapter 5, for whereas they have resources to distinguish between the emotions of the body and those of the soul, and to argue that the two can diverge, Hobbes does not. If passions are just our experience of bodily motions, and if there is no soul to reflect on or interfere with them, it follows that all our emotions must be explained in the same way. Even our most cerebral passions— a desire to learn geometry, for example—must be understood as the operations of a *conatus* or endeavour which is, ontologically speaking, corporeal, and consists of interacting sets of motions.

While this seems to be Hobbes's view and while he defends a mortalist position in part III of *Leviathan*, any interpretation along these lines must be partly pieced together from his silences. These were, however, clearly heard by those of his contemporaries who branded him an atheist, holding his views to be so out of line with the doctrines of the various Christian sects as not to fit any of them, so that it is not anachronistic to attribute to him a form of materialism which is at odds with a Christian outlook. All the same, it remains difficult to see what metaphysical claims are secreted in Hobbes's texts, largely because, although he sometimes asserts that sense, for example, is motion, he does nothing to explain how this should be understood. Are they identical? And if so, how? This central issue is further muddied by the fact that the explanatory force of much of Hobbes's work, including his analysis of the passions, relies on our familiarity with patterns of thought and their relation to action. It is by considering sensory perceptions, memories, and passions phenomenologically that we can grasp what Hobbes has to say about them, and much of his discussion relies on the assumption that we can attend to our thoughts and modify one in the light of the other. How this reflexivity translates into physical causes and effects remains hazy and inconclusive. And so, consequently, does the relation between thoughts and motions.

Passions as Appetites

Appetite and aversion are, then, our conscious awareness of the body's endeavour to maintain itself, and since the internal motions that constitute endeavour persist as long as the body continues to function in the manner that qualifies it as existing, we can never be without a susceptibility to passion. When the internal motions that are our appetites and aversions cease, we die, and become corpses rather than human beings. But as long as they continue, we are subject to passion, to short-term satisfaction allied to lifelong insatiability. As Hobbes puts it in chapter 11 of *Leviathan*, '[n]or can a man any more live whose desires are at an end, than he whose senses and imaginations are at a stand. Felicity is a continual progress of the desire from one object to another; the attaining of the former, being still but the way to the latter.'[22] Here, as elsewhere, appetite is identified with desire, and construed as a ceaseless striving to acquire and secure the means to a contented life.[23] Hobbes grounds his account of this aspect of our passions on a broader notion which he calls power, identifying the powers of the body as nutritive, generative, and motive, and that of the mind as knowledge.[24] Beyond these, however, are further powers that accrue to people who possess riches, places of authority, friendship or favour, and good fortune, all of which play a vital part in our quest for self-preservation. Once we have begun to learn from experience about the good and harm that other people can do to us, they become the objects of our appetites and we assess them as potential allies or enemies, depending on their power. Our estimations of power are thus an aspect of our own endeavour; to secure our own contentment, we evaluate the power other people have in relation to our own, and come to learn that—as well as knowledge or physical strength—wealth, authority, and friendship are forms of power. To recognize that another person possesses more power than one does oneself is, Hobbes tells us, to honour them. 'To honour a man (inwardly in the mind)', he claims in *The Elements of Law*, 'is to conceive or acknowledge that that man hath the odds or excess of power above him that contendeth or compareth himself.'[25] Moreover, the fact that a person is perceived to be worthy of honour often serves to sustain their power. To take a comparatively crude example, a poor man's recognition that a rich one can ruin him may prompt the first to take care not to offend the second, thereby sustaining the latter's security. But Hobbes also has in mind here, as chapter 10 of *Leviathan* attests, the more insinuating patterns of recognition that surround the notion of esteem and make us intensely responsive to the implications of many kinds of power.[26] Because the recognition that other people honour us upholds whatever power we have, we experience it as pleasurable. And 'in the pleasure men have, or displeasure from the signs of honour or dishonour done to them, consisteth the nature of the passions in particular'.[27] Our susceptibility to passion is, then, a susceptibility to honour which is itself a manifestation of a susceptibility to power. This is in turn the conscious aspect of endeavour, our overriding disposition to preserve ourselves.

This interpretation of the passions is especially clearly reflected in the first two particular emotions that Hobbes lists in chapter 9 of *The Elements of Law*[28]—glory and humility. Glory is defined as 'that passion which proceedeth from the imagination or conception of our own power, above the power of him that contendeth with us', and which 'by them whom it displeaseth is called pride [and] by them whom it pleaseth . . . is termed a just valuation of

---

[22] p. 70.   [23] Ibid.
[24] *Elements of Law*, 34. See R. Rudolph, 'Conflict, Egoism and Power in Hobbes', *History of Political Thought*, 7 (1986), 73–88.
[25] p. 34.   [26] See Ch. 7, below.   [27] *Elements of Law*, 36.   [28] Ibid. 36–7.

himself'.[29] It is opposed to humility or dejection, the passion 'proceeding from apprehension of our own infirmity'.[30] These definitions set the scene for the rather more conventional interpretations of courage, vengefulness, anger, hope, and so on, that Hobbes takes from Aristotle's *Rhetoric*.[31] However, while he defines hope, for example, as expectation of good to come, his summing-up reminds us that this is to be understood as the expectation of increased power. Man's life, Hobbes claims, is like a race which 'we must suppose to have no other goal, nor other garland, but being foremost'. The passions are all aspects of this headlong dash, so that

To endeavour is appetite.
To be remiss, is sensuality.
To consider them behind, is glory.
To consider them before, humility.
To lose ground with looking back, vainglory. . . .
To be in breath, hope.
To be weary, despair.
To endeavour to overtake the next, emulation.
To supplant or overthrow, envy. . . .
Continually to out-go the next before, is felicity.
And to forsake the course, is to die.[32]

By contrast, the discussion of the emotions in *Leviathan* does not accord priority to glory and humility or dejection, but instead identifies as principal or simple passions appetite, desire, love, aversion, hate, joy, and grief.[33] Glory appears as a form of joy—'the joy arising from imagination of a man's own power and ability'—and dejection as the kind of grief that arises from 'opinion of want of power'.[34] In this text Hobbes brings his list of principal passions more closely in line with those of his contemporaries; but he does not revise his account of what the passions are, and they remain manifestations of an underlying and insatiable striving for power.[35]

As this analysis implies, our passions are conceptions of things as good or bad, where the good and evil in question are relational. The fact that appetites are our experience of interactions between our own bodily motions and those of external bodies is mirrored in their character as interpretations of the good and harm that things can do us by virtue of the power they possess in relation to our own. Things we perceive as good for us—and consequently love, desire, or rejoice in—are therefore those which we perceive as able to sustain

[29] Ibid. 37.   [30] Ibid. 38.
[31] As originally noted by L. Strauss, *The Political Philosophy of Hobbes: Its Basis and its Genesis*, trans. E. M. Sinclair (Chicago, 1963), 36–41.
[32] *Elements of Law*, 47–8.
[33] p. 41. On this shift see A. Pacchi, 'Hobbes and the Passions', *Topoi*, 6 (1987), 111–19; G. B. Herbert, *Thomas Hobbes: The Unity of Science and Moral Wisdom* (Vancouver, 1989), 92 f.
[34] *Leviathan*, 42.   [35] Ibid., chs. 6 and 10.

or increase our power. Hobbes here imposes a distinctive interpretation on the familiar view that the passions dispose us to protect our bodies; but once again he diverges from the other philosophers we have discussed by refusing to distinguish the relational perception of the good contained in the passions from any conception of things as good or bad in themselves.

Every man for his own part calleth that which pleaseth and is delightful to himself, GOOD; and that EVIL which displeaseth him. In so much that while every man differeth from other in constitution, they differ also from one another concerning the common distinction of good and evil. Nor is there any such thing as . . . simply good. For even the goodness which we attribute to God Almighty, is his goodness to us. And as we call good and evil the things that please us and displease; so we call goodness and badness the qualities or powers whereby they do it.[36]

Whereas Orpheus, say, will be good for those who can benefit from his power and bad for those who can be damaged by it, and may also be good for a particular person at one time and bad for them at another, God, we may suppose, is always good for everyone. This is not to say, however, that he is simply good, or good in himself. It is rather to acknowledge that there is an unusual degree of convergence in the evaluations of God made by people who recognize his unlimited power and beneficence.

According to Hobbes's account, passions are manifestations of an underlying striving for power, and dispose us to act in such a way as to promote it and resist its loss. They are thoughts; but etymologically, at least, they carry connotations of motion. The words 'appetite' and 'aversion', Hobbes points out, 'we have from the Latins; and they both of them signify the motions, the one of approaching the other of retiring'. The motions in question cannot, however, be 'metaphorical'—there is no question of interpreting them as Malebranche does, for example, as inclinations of the mind. They must therefore be physical, and Hobbes consequently goes on to identify passions, our endeavours toward or away from objects, as 'the small beginnings of motion, within the body of man, before they appear in walking, speaking, striking and other visible actions'.[37] Passions are therefore thoughts which issue in action, but it remains to see what other characteristics they have, and particularly how they fit the conventional distinction between perceptions and volitions. Are they perceptions to which we must assent? Or are they volitions—acts of assent or inclination? Hobbes's answer is that they are neither. Volitions, he argues, are indeed the immediate antecedents of action; but this is not because they are a special kind of thought which comes into play in order to assess the reliability of our perceptions. When we deliberate about what to do, we consider a sequence of alternating appetites and aversions; for example, the thought of how pleasant it would be to go back to sleep is followed by the recollection

---

[36] *Elements of Law*, 29. See also *Leviathan*, 39.   [37] *Leviathan*, 38.

that I have to go out in half an hour; this is soon overwhelmed by a feeling of warmth, but gives way to an anxiety about being late. At some point, this mental toing and froing comes to an end, and the 'last appetite or aversion, immediately adhering to the action or the omission thereof' is, according to Hobbes, 'what we call the will'.[38] Just before I get up I decide or will to do so. This act of willing is only distinguished, however, by its position in the sequence of thoughts that precedes action; otherwise there is nothing special about it, and it is like any other appetite or aversion. Passions, then, incorporate some of the features that other philosophers attribute to perceptions and some that they reserve for volitions. Like perceptions, they are ideas that represent things as good or bad for us; but like volitions they are appetitive and can move us to action. Whereas Descartes argues that two components—a perception and a volition—precede action, Hobbes obliterates the distinction around which this view is organized. Our passions are not representations, waiting to have their truth or falsity affirmed; instead they are already conceptions of how things are, and are thus already affirmations.[39]

This view has several important consequences. To begin with, it implies that, contrary to the Cartesian view, willing and perceiving are one and the same. In place of a mind whose power to think works in two cooperating ways, we have a mind with a single power to form thoughts, which give rise to other thoughts and sometimes to actions. Secondly, Hobbes denies that any of our thoughts are 'free' in the sense of uncaused. There are no self-caused volitions —only appetites which are themselves our experience of the causally determined motions of our bodies. As we shall see in subsequent chapters, this revised conception of the passions has a significant effect on discussions of the part they play in the explanation of action. More relevant to our current concerns, however, are its implications for established interpretations of the difference between action and passion. As we have found, this distinction is often aligned with the division between perceptions, which are understood to be passive, and volitions, which are perceived as active. But once this distinction collapses, we are left with the question: Is there any remaining sense in which some thoughts can be said to be more active than others? From a causal point of view, Hobbes will argue, there is not, since all thoughts are caused, and all are capable of causing further thoughts. Moreover, sensory perceptions and passions are simply two stages of motions, one giving rise to the other. What about the claim, though, that some passions help our vital motion and others hinder it, so that some augment the power for which we strive whereas others diminish it? Significantly, Hobbes does not use the language of activity and passivity to characterize this difference. He does not say, for example, that we

[38] Ibid. 44.
[39] See R. Tuck, 'Hobbes' Moral Philosophy', in T. Sorell (ed.), *The Cambridge Companion to Hobbes* (Cambridge, 1996), 184–6.

are more active when we rejoice than when we grieve, and eschews the implication, embraced by other writers, that when we increase our power we increase
our perfection, and approach the divine. Instead, Hobbes takes the unusually
single-minded view that actions and passions are causes and effects. Considered
as a cause, a thought is active; considered as an effect, it is passive. But these
characterizations derive from its position in a process, not from the qualities
inherent in the thought itself.

   This bold, but also bald, materialist interpretation of the passions does indeed
sweep away a great deal of what Hobbes would no doubt describe as trash. But
in doing so it creates its own problems. On the one hand, it rests on an identification of body and mind which remains to be explicated. On the other hand,
Hobbes's steadfast refusal to apply the distinction between activity and passivity within the realm of thought proved hard for his readers to swallow. These
two problems exercise Spinoza who, reflecting on Hobbes's work, produces
a yet further conception of the place of the passions in the body and mind.

Spinoza on the Identity of Body and Mind

Spinoza's account of body and mind is embedded in a broader metaphysical
conception of substance and a related view of knowledge. To appreciate what
he has to say about humans, we need to begin by sketching aspects of his philosophy which may seem irrelevant to the problem in hand, but are in fact pre-
conditions of understanding how he deals with it. Many issues converge here,
and an attempt quickly to outline them cannot capture all their complexity or
do justice to the debates surrounding their interpretation. But they can, perhaps, provide a strategic sense of Spinoza's approach, indicating the features
of his position that bear most closely on his analysis of the passions or, as he
prefers to say, the affections.

   Starting, then, with the character of knowledge, one of the first axioms laid
out in the *Ethics* tells us that knowledge of an effect depends on, and involves,
the knowledge of its cause.[40] The search for knowledge continually pushes us
back along causal chains as we ask about the cause of a particular item, the
cause of that cause, and so on. If this enquiry is to answer to Spinoza's conviction that we can attain an adequate understanding of nature and come to rest,
the regress created by our quest for causes must end in something causally
and explanatorily self-sufficient, which completes our knowledge of the effects
that flow from it. Like many of his contemporaries, Spinoza holds that the
regress must end in substance, but he takes this requirement especially seriously. It is not enough, for example, to claim that the Cartesian notion of

---

[40] *Ethics*, I. A 4.

extended substance forms a self-explanatory ground on the basis of which we can arrive at an understanding of bodies; for extended substance in turn depends on God and is therefore not the end-point of the explanatory causal chain. Nor is it enough to push back to an anthropomorphic notion of God the Creator, because, although we can mouth words such as 'God creates and maintains the world by his will', our inability to understand how God could do such a thing means that the causal connection we posit is in the bad sense occult. We are looking for a notion of substance both conceptually and ontologically self-sufficient, which can serve as the intelligible explanatory basis of nature. As Spinoza puts it, 'By substance I understand what is in itself and is conceived through itself, i.e., that whose concept does not require the concept of another thing, from which it must be formed.'[41]

What could such a substance be like? One of the first tasks Spinoza undertakes in the *Ethics* is to show that it must be unique. If substance is to form a single explanatory point of closure, we have to get away from the Cartesian picture of a universe in which there are numerous distinct substances whose interconnections cry out for explanation. It is hard to see that any finite kind of stuff could answer to this requirement, for it would always be possible to ask about its cause. Spinoza therefore articulates a conception of substance as itself a causal order, as the most general—and from an explanatory point of view the most powerful—set of causal concepts which govern the totality of everything that exists.[42] How, though, does this function as the stopping-point of explanation, so that it is otiose to ask what caused it to be? Here it is important that substance, as Spinoza understands it, is not an entity separate from the various things there are in nature, as the Judaeo-Christian God is separate from his creation. On the contrary, it is the order to which natural things conform, and exists in so far as they instantiate it. We do not have to trace the causal relations between natural things, and then show that they are causally related to something else called substance. Rather, when we trace the relations between natural things, we are already presupposing its existence. Tracing these relations is not, moreover, just a matter of picking out their immediate causes. It involves coming to see how particular causal connections are instances of laws, which are in turn instances of more general laws. The process of arriving at ever more powerful and inclusive explanations would come to a stop if we could arrive at explanatory principles powerful enough to explain everything,

[41] Ibid. 1. D 3.

[42] See E. Craig, *The Mind of God and the Works of Man* (Oxford, 1987), 46–7; L. E. Loeb, *From Descartes to Hume: Continental Metaphysics and the Development of Modern Philosophy* (Ithaca, NY, 1981), 104–5; G. Lloyd, *Part of Nature: Self-Knowledge in Spinoza's 'Ethics'* (Ithaca, NY, 1994), 7–10. For more detailed discussion of Spinoza's argument see H. E. Allison, *Benedict de Spinoza: An Introduction* (New Haven, 1987), 44–63; A. Donagan, *Spinoza* (Hemel Hempstead, 1988), 77–95; E. Curley, *Behind the Geometrical Method* (Princeton, 1988), 3–39; R. S. Woolhouse, *Descartes, Spinoza, Leibniz: The Concept of Substance in Seventeenth-Century Thought* (London, 1993), 28–53; 88–93; 150–63.

to remove all sense of puzzlement about nature, and this, according to Spinoza, is what substance does. It consists in the explanatory principles that govern and explain everything there is. So when we work back along explanatory causal chains, we reach a point at which we have no need to go further, and the question 'But what explains that?' becomes pointless. If we were to arrive at this level of insight we should understand perfectly how nature operates, and this would be to understand in the only possible way why it operates as it does.

Substance is not just a static, abstract statement of the most powerful causal concepts by which nature is governed; it is the actual instantiation of those concepts in nature. For some seventeenth-century philosophers, Descartes included, the fact that nature conforms to laws is due to God's volitions, which provide the metaphorical push that starts nature up and keeps it going. Spinoza, however, urges us to see the problem in a different way. Substance does not have to be moved by something else, such as God's will, since it contains its own dynamic principle. And because the causal order of nature is a logical order, from which it is possible to derive complete explanations of all natural phenomena, it is capable of satisfying all our intellectual curiosity.

Spinoza adds to this account the claim that substance is identical with God, so that God is the unchanging causal order of nature. But for substance or God to satisfy the requirements we have just set out, it must be able to explain all the kinds of questions we pose about the world, all the kinds of experience we find puzzling. For instance, it must be able to account for our experience of the world as extended as well as our experience of our own thoughts, and it must do so in a way we find intelligible. Spinoza takes it that thought and extension are so different in kind that we simply cannot see how they could be causally interconnected.[43] Substance, therefore, must be able to accommodate and explain distinct and irreducible types of natural phenomena, and it can do this because it is not the sort of thing that can be entirely captured under one description. This view is expressed in the claim that substance has more than one attribute, where an attribute is 'what the intellect perceives of a substance as constituting its essence'.[44] So it is possible to perceive substance as constituted by various essences, including the two with which human intellects are acquainted—thought and extension. We humans can conceive substance as the order governing all extension, in which case it completes our explanations of corporeal bodies. The attribute of extension thus resembles Descartes's notion of extended substance in that there is nothing outside it. But, unlike Descartes, Spinoza treats the attribute of thought in the same

---

[43] *Ethics*, I. A 5.
[44] Ibid. I. D 4. On this difficult claim see W. Kessler, 'A Note on Spinoza's Concept of Attribute', in M. Mandelbaum and E. Freeman (eds.), *Spinoza: Essays in Interpretation* (La Salle, Ill., 1975), 191–4; J. Bennett, *A Study of Spinoza's 'Ethics'* (Cambridge, 1984), 60–6; Curley, *Behind the Geometrical Method*, 23–30; Donagan, *Spinoza*, 69–73; Woolhouse, *Descartes, Spinoza, Leibniz*, 34–51.

manner: substance conceived under this attribute is the order governing all thinking. When we shift from one attribute to the other, we offer two explanatory accounts of the same order, two descriptions of the same totality. Each captures the whole of nature, viewed from a certain perspective, in its causal web. But each is limited in the sense that there are aspects of reality which it fails to encompass. An account of the extended properties of the world, however comprehensive, tells us nothing about thinking, and vice versa. Moreover, since substance has to be able to close off all possible explanations, Spinoza stipulates that it can in principle be perceived not just under the two attributes with which we are familiar, but under infinite attributes, that is to say under all the attributes there are. It is designed to deal not just with the puzzles we actually have, but with all those that any intellect could possibly have.

Elaborating this explanatory aspiration, Spinoza tells us first that God is the immanent cause of everything. All the causal chains we trace back in our search for knowledge terminate in God or Substance; and because it is incompatible with explanatory adequacy to detach God from the effects he produces, he is an immanent cause.[45] Secondly, infinitely many things follow from God's nature.[46] That is to say, we can infer from substance a set of implications rich enough to ground all our explanations. These implications or modes are defined by Spinoza as 'affections of a substance, or that which is in another through which it is conceived'.[47] They are said to be of two kinds. Infinite modes follow from the 'absolute nature' of God's attributes, and are eternal. Finite modes also follow from the attributes, but are limited by other finite modes.[48] A movement of a particular leaf, for instance, is caused by the wind, and so on back. How, then, do causal chains of finite modes relate to infinite modes, and thus to substance? To explain a particular event, it is not enough to cite another particular event as its immediate cause. We obtain a better understanding of nature when we see particular events as instantiating lawlike generalizations; to put it differently, we see that finite modes instantiate infinite modes. To take one of Spinoza's examples, we explain the behaviour of particular bodies by appealing to the properties of other particular bodies; but these particulars all exemplify the general laws governing physical motion and rest.

We have, then, the claim that substance is the causal order governing the totality of nature. But it can only be described in more detail from a particular point of view, under an attribute. The explanatory connections we identify under each attribute are irreducible descriptions of a single causal order; they are not simply different descriptions of the totality of nature, but different descriptions of the order to which it conforms. So any mode of one attribute —say a mode of extension—will match up with modes of each of the other

---

[45] *Ethics*, I. P 18.   [46] Ibid. I. P 16.   [47] Ibid. I. D 5.

[48] See G. Deleuze, *Spinoza et le problème de l'expression* (Paris, 1968), 174–298; Allison, *Benedict de Spinoza*, 63–74; Donagan, *Spinoza*, 102–7; G. Lloyd, *Spinoza and the 'Ethics'* (London, 1996), 42–5.

attributes. And the causal relations between the modes of extension will be mirrored in all the other attributes. One consequence is that the modes of extension map on to the modes of thought. As Spinoza expresses it, 'the order and connection of ideas is the same as the order and connection of things'.[49] For every mode of substance viewed under the attribute of extension there is a corresponding idea—a mode of it viewed under the attribute of thought. This is true not just for simple modes of extension such as the shapes and motions of the very smallest bodies, but also for complex modes such as the bodies of human beings. A human body is a composite containing parts of many different kinds which constitute an individual by virtue of the fact that these parts conform to a relatively stable pattern of motion and rest, and the body as a whole correlates with an idea of the whole.[50] The same goes for all complex bodies, right up to the totality of nature itself, so that humans are in this respect in no way exceptional. Moreover, it is not only the modes of extension that are correlated with ideas. All modes of all attributes have matching descriptions in the attribute of thought, so that it contains an idea of the entire order of nature, viewed in every possible way. Spinoza calls the idea of this totality of knowledge God's intellect.

The fact that every mode of extension is correlated with a mode of thought implies that the whole of extended nature is also thinking. Spinoza is not claiming here that plants, tables, or the hearts of mammals think as human beings do. He is pointing out that ideas of all these things exist in God's intellect, so that a clump of moss growing on a roof-tile, for example, is also an idea. But what sort of idea? As we have already seen, the ideas with which bodies correlate mirror their complexity. Because a human being is a very complex body, the idea of it is also complex, and this latter complexity in some way accounts for properties of human thinking such as consciousness. By contrast, the body of a clump of moss and the idea corresponding to it are, comparatively speaking, quite simple. And while we cannot say much about what simple ideas are like, we can infer that they differ substantially from thinking as we experience it.[51]

This beautiful synchronism between the attributes of thought and extension sets the scene for Spinoza's discussion of the relation between the human body and the human mind. The idea corresponding to the human body, he tells us, is the human mind. 'The mind and the body are one and the same individual, which is conceived now under the attribute of thought, now under the attribute of extension.'[52] As we know, the human body is a composite, made up of many smaller bodies which 'communicate their motions to one another in a certain fixed manner'.[53] The corresponding idea, which constitutes

---

[49] *Ethics*, II. P 7.
[50] M. Gatens, 'Spinoza, Law and Responsibility', in *Imaginary Bodies* (London, 1996), 110–13.
[51] See Allison, *Benedict de Spinoza*, 96–100; Lloyd, *Spinoza and the 'Ethics'*, 38–41.
[52] *Ethics*, II. P 21 s.   [53] Ibid. II. P 24.

the mind, is similarly complex, composed of 'a great many ideas' of the composite individuals of which the body is made up.[54]

How, though, are we to make sense of this view that the mind is the idea of the body? On the one hand, since the order and connection of ideas is the order and connection of things, there is in God's intellect a complete idea corresponding to the human body and its interactions. God has an idea of all the bodies of which the human body is composed, all the bodies with which it interacts, and all the laws relating them.[55] We can say, then, that the mind is God's idea of the body.[56] And we can use this to interpret Spinoza's assertion that whatever happens in the body is perceived by the mind.[57] But this is to use the term 'mind' in a technical way which departs from our normal usage; and the question remains whether we can make anything of the claim that *our* minds, as we can experience them, are the ideas of *our* bodies, and that whatever happens in *our* bodies is perceived by *our* minds. Spinoza relies on the first of these claims to explain familiar features of our experience—for example the fact that each of us is conscious of her own body, so that I have an idea of the pain in my foot and not of the pain in yours.[58] But it remains to see how they are to be understood.

The claim that the human mind is the idea of the human body appears initially to fall prey to several obvious objections. It seems evident, first of all, that many of our ideas are not 'of' the body but of things external to it—we have ideas of physical objects, natural processes, and abstract entities. In addition, many events occur in our bodies of which we have no conscious ideas at all; for example, we are not conscious of all the processes that Spinoza's contemporaries described as movements of the animal spirits. There seems, then, to be a mismatch between our minds and bodies, at least as we ordinarily understand them, which makes nonsense of Spinoza's view. To deal with the first of these objections, Spinoza implicitly urges us to revise our everyday conceptions of both the mind and the body by paying attention to the idea of the body that we derive from our senses, memory, and imagination. It is true that we ordinarily assume that our senses and memory give us ideas of external physical objects, but this is a misconstrual. Following the lines we have already traced in Descartes's and Malebranche's accounts of secondary qualities, Spinoza claims that our senses yield ideas, not of external things in themselves, but of their relations with our bodies; in fact, 'the ideas that we have of external bodies indicate the condition of our own body more than the nature of the external bodies'.[59] This interpretation suggests that the ideas we derive from imagination and usually regard as ideas 'of' external things are better understood as ideas of the body's relation to external things. So in this sense they

[54] Ibid. II. P 15.   [55] Ibid. II. P 19.   [56] Ibid. III. P 1.   [57] Ibid. II. P 12.
[58] Ibid. II. P 13.   [59] Ibid. II. P 16. c2; see also P 18 s.

can be understood as among the ideas of the body that, according to Spinoza, constitute the mind.

What, though, of the second objection—the claim that many things happen in our bodies of which we have no idea at all? Up to a point, Spinoza concedes this. He agrees that the human body is made up of many smaller bodies of which, although there is an idea of them in God's intellect, we either have no idea, or only an exceedingly attenuated one. For example, I might have no idea of the homoeostatic mechanisms by which the body maintains its temperature, and yet have an idea of some of their components, such as shivering or sweating. But in considering what is involved in possessing the idea of the body which constitutes the mind, Spinoza focuses less on the body's parts than on the body as a whole and its interactions with the rest of the world. Rather than adopting the specialized approach of the anatomist, he emphasizes the commonplace knowledge of our bodies that we gain through sensory experience in order to reach the view that we only have an idea of the body in so far as it affects and is affected by other things. We do not first have an idea of the body, for example through bodily sensations, and then get ideas of other things in the world through sensory perceptions. Instead, we get ideas of our bodies and external things simultaneously, through their causal interactions. The resulting idea that constitutes the mind is not, therefore, of an isolated entity; rather it is an idea of the human body as part of a net of causal interactions.[60] Once again, this outline suggests a way to interpret the claim that our minds are our ideas of our bodies. At the same time it begins to suggest what Spinoza might mean when he claims that there is an idea in the mind of everything that happens in the body. The preceding argument claims that many of our ideas are derived from sensory experience and are of the causal interactions between our bodies and the rest of the world. If Spinoza also holds that all sensory experience is conscious, it will follow that we have ideas of all our sensory experience, so that there are ideas of all the body's interactions with the world. As far as the imagination is concerned, there is an idea in the mind of everything that happens in the body.

These arguments may enable us to grasp what Spinoza is driving at. But it is hard to see that they make his position persuasive. Even if we take account of the claim that our ideas of external things are better understood as ideas of our bodies, and of Spinoza's emphasis on the body as a whole and its relations to the world, there still appears to be too much of a gap between the idea of the body that (according to Spinoza) constitutes the human mind, and the body itself—an unequivocal and extremely complex physical object. Why, for

---

[60] See A. Rorty, 'Spinoza on the Pathos of Idolatrous Love and the Hilarity of True Love', in R. C. Solomon and K. M. Higgins (eds.), *The Philosophy of (Erotic) Love* (Lawrence, Kan., 1991), 360–5; Lloyd, *Part of Nature*, 10–25; M. Gatens, 'Power, Ethics and Sexual Imaginaries', in *Imaginary Bodies*, 125–45.

example, should we turn our backs on the fact that there are many aspects of our bodies of which we have no idea at all? Why should we accept Spinoza's implausible claim that we have ideas of all the causal interactions between our bodies and other things? These problems continue to loom large, so that we are liable to be drawn back to the view that the idea of the body is the complete idea in the divine intellect rather than the human mind.

To defuse these criticisms and gain a deeper appreciation of Spinoza's position, it is helpful to remember that, while we can posit the idea of the body that is in the divine intellect, we do not actually possess it. We can conceive of a complete account of the parts of the body, the whole that they constitute, and the relations of this whole with other things, but our own knowledge falls far short of this and is, by comparison, drastically incomplete. As Spinoza expresses the point, the ideas in the divine intellect are adequate, whereas the ideas that finite human intellects acquire through the imagination are inadequate. The inadequacy or incompleteness of the latter stems from the fact that they are relational. As we have seen, they are ideas of the causal connections between our bodies and external bodies which tell us something about the latter (namely how they affect us) and something about our own bodies (namely how they are affected). But ideas of this kind are distorted in the sense that they do not tell us how things are independently of their relations. In addition, they are patchy; they only chart some of the causal properties of the bodies in question, some of the ways in which they affect and are affected by each other. They therefore fail to delineate fully the causal properties which constitute the nature of a body, fail to map the effects that can be clearly and distinctly perceived through the idea of that body alone. In developing this argument, Spinoza takes the familiar view that our sensory experience of secondary qualities gives us only a partial and relational knowledge of external things, and reads this idea back on to the body. The knowledge of our own bodies acquired from our sensory encounters with physical objects is no fuller or clearer than our knowledge of the objects themselves.

In so far as we learn about the external world through the imagination, our ideas are inadequate. This also applies to our idea of the body, which does indeed fall far short of the adequate idea in the divine intellect.[61] If we were like God we would possess a complete idea of the body, but as it is we can only conceive of such an idea. If we were like God our minds would be infinitely more powerful, but as it is, our understanding of the world is partial and confused. Spinoza therefore agrees with the objection raised earlier. He acknowledges the gap between our idea of the body and the complete idea of it in the divine intellect. And he acknowledges the correspondence between this complete idea and the body itself. But he also holds that the human mind is the idea

---

[61] *Ethics*, II. P 29. See Lloyd, *Part of Nature*, 43–75.

of the human body. To put it the other way round, there is some physical
entity—the human body—identical with the human mind. Our main clue in
trying to work out what sort of an entity this might be is Spinoza's assurance
that it is identical with our idea of it, which we know to be inadequate. We
possess an incomplete idea of the human body, derived from imagination. So
the body corresponding to this is presumably equally incomplete, made up of
just those parts and interactions of which we have any knowledge. It is just the
body as we know it, the body of which we have an idea. Such an entity may
seem perilously unstable, changing as our ideas of it change. And in this respect
it is certainly removed from a conception of the body as a stable, enduring
object with properties that are independent of our perception of them. But this
seems to be an unavoidable implication of Spinoza's conception of our inadequate understanding as rooted in the causal relations between our bodies and
our environment, a conception which is in turn central to his analysis of the
mind as the idea of the body.

By conceiving the mind and body as matching attributes—one of thought,
the other of extension—Spinoza transforms the question of how they are related.
The problem is no longer to find a connection between two independent entities, but to work out how two disparate descriptions can be descriptions of the
same thing. How can a thought be an idea of the body? How can a bodily
motion be a thought? This change of approach brings with it many perplex-
ities; but if we assume, as Spinoza does, that they can be dealt with, it also has
far-ranging implications for an understanding of the passions. Any particular
thought, according to Spinoza, is a finite mode of the attribute of thought,
identical with a finite mode of the attribute of extension. More specifically,
a particular person's thought is an idea of an event in their body. Taking as
an example a thought which is a passion, it is possible to give a complete
psychological explanation of, say, a person's anger by citing its psychological
causes, and a complete physical explanation of the bodily event that their anger
is an idea of. What we cannot do is analyse the passion, Cartesian style, into
physical and psychological components, since the possibility of any intelligible connection between them is ruled out. By arguing that this is true of all
thoughts, Spinoza abandons any distinction between thoughts that do and do
not depend on the body. Although he defends the possibility of a kind of existence to which the body is comparatively unimportant at the end of the *Ethics*,
his argument implies that all thoughts—whether judgements of the understanding, sensory perceptions, or passions—will be ideas of the body. Presumably
the phenomenological differences between them reflect the fact that they are
ideas of different kinds of bodily events; but there are no thoughts which, like
the pure perceptions countenanced by Descartes and Malebranche, lack any
bodily counterpart. Spinoza's analysis of the relation between body and mind
therefore already tells us a good deal about the passions. But he goes on to

provide a more detailed account of their character when he turns to discuss the causal relations between thoughts, and to distinguish active from passive kinds of thinking.

Passions and Conatus

As we have seen, many of our ideas are inadequate: they are ideas not of things as they are in themselves but of things as they affect our bodies, and they provide only a patchy and distorted grasp of the world. Some of our thoughts, including some traditionally classed as perceptions, must, it seems, be inadequate. Our sensations, sensory perceptions, and memories, along with the fantasies we spin from them, are all ideas of things as they appear to us, shaped by the responses of our bodies to a range of stimuli. If we contemplate the task of explaining a bodily state of which we have an inadequate idea—say the bodily state I experience as a sensory perception of a beech tree—it is clear that we shall have to appeal to at least two causal factors: the beech tree and my body. Shifting into the attribute of thought, it is equally clear that in order to explain my idea of a beech tree we have to appeal to my mind (the idea of my body) and the idea of the beech tree. Ignoring, for the moment, the laborious duplication in which Spinoza's separate attributes involve him, we can see that in neither case am I the sole cause of the idea or bodily state in question. My body cannot produce the physical state corresponding to the idea of the beech tree unless it is, as Spinoza puts it, acted on by a beech tree. Nor can my mind perceive a beech tree unless it is acted on by another idea. Putting these claims together, Spinoza concludes that when we are the partial or inadequate causes of a state, whether of the body or mind, we are acted on.[62]

In this abstract and rather forbidding analysis, Spinoza captures some familiar connotations of passivity. One of these is causal. We are acted on or passive when something is done to us that we could not have brought about by ourselves. A second incorporates Hobbes's claim that 'the agent hath power if it be applied to a patient; and the patient hath power if it be applied to an agent'.[63] In order to be acted on we have to be capable of *re*acting, and because our reaction is a necessary condition of the effect it is part of the cause. So we are acted on when we are the partial cause of an effect. Furthermore, both these interpretations of passivity are contrasted with a conception of action: a thing acts when it is the sole or adequate cause of an effect.

As well as being acted on when we experience sensations, sensory perceptions, and so on, Spinoza holds that we are acted on when we feel passions or affections. Our affections are, therefore, as their name implies, ideas of the

---

[62] *Ethics*, III. D 1.   [63] Hobbes, *Elements of Philosophy: Concerning Body*, 129.

way that other things affect us, and presuppose a capacity on our part to react. The character of this reaction is, moreover, what distinguishes passions from perceptions of other kinds. According to Spinoza, the reactions that are our passions are a manifestation of a striving to persevere in our being, which is our essence. As such, they are an instantiation in humans of a feature of all natural things. Substance itself, the causal subsystems that it contains, and particular things, all strive to persevere in their being. The whole of nature exhibits this striving or *conatus*, which constitutes the essence of the whole and each of its parts, so that everything possesses some power[64] to maintain itself and resist destruction. In the case of bodies, human and otherwise, it seems reasonable to suppose that the *conatus* is manifested, for example, in the ability to resist change that is acknowledged, as we saw in Chapter 4, by proponents of the new corpuscular science. In the case of minds, Spinoza argues that our strivings to persevere in our being by reacting to other things are our passions. Our loves and hatreds, hopes and fears, are therefore all manifestations of the disposition to maintain and increase our power, which is our essence.[65] In ex- pounding this view, Spinoza is anxious to emphasize that our ideas of external things are not merely received, like pictures projected on a wall, but are nuanced interpretations of the capacities of things around us to sustain or damage our power to persevere in our being. It is misleading, he says, to describe them as perceptions since this term carries too many connotations of passivity and 'seems to indicate that the mind is acted on by its object'. Instead, they should be called conceptions, a term which 'seems to express an action of the mind'.[66]

How exactly does our *conatus* shape our responses? The striving of the mind and body together, Spinoza tells us, is called appetite, and includes all the capacities for self-maintenance that make us the individuals we are, under the attributes of both thought and extension. The striving of the mind alone is called will. And when appetite is conscious it is called desire (*cupiditas*).[67] Desire is therefore a principal manifestation of our *conatus*, and it consequently belongs to our nature to respond to the world desiringly in order to maintain our power. This key claim portrays humans as having an irrepressible and tenacious hold on life which can only be eclipsed when they are destroyed by something more powerful than themselves. What may appear to be forms of self-destruction, such as anorexia or suicide, can only be explained in terms of external causes against which we are bound to struggle to the last.

While desire, our *conatus* itself, is the most fundamental of our passions, it is complemented by two others which mark the successes and failures of our

---

[64] Usually *potentia* though sometimes *vis.*
[65] See A. Matheron, 'Spinoza et le pouvoir', *Nouvelle critique*, 109 (1977), 45–51; M. Della Rocca, 'Spinoza's Metaphysical Psychology', in D. Garrett (ed.), *The Cambridge Companion to Spinoza* (Cambridge, 1996), 192–237.
[66] *Ethics*, II. D 3.   [67] Ibid. III. P 9 s.

attempts to maintain ourselves: when our power increases we feel joy (*laetitia*) and when it decreases we feel sadness (*tristitia*). Taken together, these three principal passions, each of which has many varieties, are therefore our experience of our disposition to try to persevere in our being, and of our victories and defeats in this process.[68] Each emotion felt by an individual records the level of their power in relation to the power they possessed previously. Someone whose power diminishes to a particular level from a higher one will feel *tristitia*, whereas someone else whose power increases to the same level will experience *laetitia*. In this respect our passions reflect our individual histories. They depend on how powerful we were in the past.

Spinoza's definitions of particular passions are grounded on the claim that our striving for power is manifested in our responses to the world around us. Love, for example, is what we feel when an external cause increases our power, and is consequently a kind of joy—joy with the accompanying idea of an external cause. Hatred is sadness accompanied by the idea of objects that diminish our power. Envy is hatred of other people whose happiness makes us sad because it lessens our power. These definitions retain the familiar notion that the passions are functional, and are ideas of things as beneficial or harmful to us. But instead of simply asserting that we are disposed to preserve ourselves, Spinoza interprets the function of the passions as an expression in humans of a more general disposition—the disposition of all natural things to persevere in their being. Humans, then, are part of nature, and their passions are part of a much larger pattern of causal regularities. By integrating the passions into a broader metaphysical scheme, Spinoza also puts a particular interpretation on the good that our passions move us to pursue, which is both relational—we are on the look-out for things that are good for us—and shaped by our *conatus* in that the things that are good for us are those that enable us to maintain and increase our power to persevere in our being. The passions are therefore thoughts that dispose us to pursue this power. Unlike the advocates of the Aristotelian tradition, however, and, to a lesser extent, Descartes, Spinoza does not specify that they dispose us to protect the power of the body. His identification of body and soul allows him to abandon the always-shaky distinction between the good of the body and that of the soul, and to argue that each person strives for whatever they think will increase their power as a finite, embodied intelligence. The passions, in short, cater for the whole self.

Spinoza agrees with his contemporaries that the differences in people's passions are to be explained by their bodily constitution and temperament—which for him come close to being descriptions of the same thing under different attributes—by their experience, and by unreflective principles of association and comparison based on our perceptions of resemblances. If an object and a

---

[68] See Lloyd, *Spinoza and the 'Ethics'*, 73–83; Allison, *Benedict de Spinoza*, 124–40.

passion are juxtaposed, the association sticks: someone who was once terrified by a bird may continue to find birds terrifying.[69] If an object and a passion are juxtaposed, and we later encounter something that resembles that object, the associated passion will come to mind: a woman may feel affectionately towards a girl who looks like her daughter.[70] Finally, we imitate the affects of others. If we encounter an object like ourselves (i.e. another person) who is joyful or sad and for whom we have no particular feelings, their passion will infect us: a man who comes across a boy crying on the street will pity him, and the exuberant singing of a passer-by will cheer him up.[71] Like the writers already discussed, Spinoza takes it that our passions are shaped both by the more-or-less accidental associations which are a feature of individual experience, and by more general patterns of feeling which are found in most people. The bodily manifestations of passions ensure that we read them in others and respond in predictable ways. Both types of regularity are presumably to be explained as aspects of our *conatus*, and in the first case it is relatively easy to see how this might work. Our disposition to associate objects and passions is a way of learning from experience which usually works to our advantage, and its occasional idiosyncratic consequences, such as a man's irrational antipathy to birds or cats, are just the price we pay for a basically functional disposition. Our mimetic traits are, however, more puzzling. It is not immediately obvious how our disposition to feel sad at others' sadness helps us to persevere in our being, since sadness itself is a reduction in power. When we pity someone, Spinoza argues, the reduction in our own power caused by their sadness prompts us to try to increase our own power by destroying whatever it is that makes them sad. For example, pity for a frozen vagrant may prompt St Francis to give him half his cloak so that, by relieving the vagrant's cold, St Francis himself may feel better. Pity therefore leads to benevolence; but Spinoza does not argue, as Malebranche surely would, that this pursuit of the common good is itself a function of the passions, built into our *conatus*. On the contrary, he claims that the mimetic disposition that makes us benevolent also has notably antisocial consequences. When we see that someone enjoys something (when for example Lancelot sees the joy that Arthur takes in Guinevere) we want to enjoy what they enjoy, and so become envious and ambitious.[72] Our passions therefore do not dispose us to pursue the common good, and because we are enormously sensitive to the feelings expressed by others, they often dispose us to pursue our own good in ways that damage people around us. As a disposition to maintain and increase our power, there is a certain toughness in the *conatus*, which is reflected in the 'automatic' dispositions to which we are naturally prone.

These dispositions operate all the time, but by no means exhaust the workings of the *conatus*. While some of our passions are arbitrary sympathies and

---

[69] *Ethics*, III. P 14.   [70] Ibid. III. P 16.   [71] Ibid. III. P 27.   [72] Ibid. III. P 32.

antipathies, most are richer and more discriminating interpretations of the good and harm that the world may do us. As Spinoza emphasizes, our loves and hates, griefs and joys are for the most part not feelings we passively find ourselves experiencing, but conceptions to which we actively contribute. It follows that, to gain a clearer understanding of the passions as a particular type of thought or idea, and to appreciate the sense in which they are passive, we need to try to grasp what Spinoza means by a 'conception'.[73] This we can do by considering how conceptions fit into his broader account of the kinds of thought in the mind. More particularly, we can begin to see what conceptions are once we appreciate how Spinoza undercuts the distinction between perceptions and volitions, and in doing so breaks with both an Aristotelian and a Cartesian analysis of the soul.[74]

The salient properties of the will, according to Descartes, are its capacity to assent to judgements and the freedom with which it does so. Spinoza, however, wholeheartedly disagrees with the second of these characterizations, and claims that the will 'requires a cause by which it is determined to exist and produce an effect in a certain way'.[75] As finite modes of thought, volitions must be caused by other finite modes, contributing to a sequence that exemplifies the overarching causal order of the attribute of thought. The significance of this claim is twofold. On the one hand, Spinoza here incorporates volitions into the causal order of substance, ensuring that the whole of the human mind is a part of nature and subject to its laws. On the other hand, he rejects the theological doctrine of voluntarism, and with it the view that nature is to be explained by an appeal to God's infinite will. Not even God can be said to will freely, since the volitions contained in the totality of substance are, like its motions, causally determined, natural events. They are the manifestations of a causal order which is the divine intellect, and there is therefore no threat that they will turn out only to be explicable as the apparently arbitrary volitions of an incomprehensible deity.

Volitions, then, have causes and are thoughts. But what kind of thoughts? Here Spinoza follows Descartes's view that the mind wills when it 'affirms or denies something true or something false'. He takes care to point out the divergence between this conception of the will and the one favoured both by Scholastic Aristotelians such as Aquinas and by Malebranche, for whom it is an

---

[73] Latin *conceptus*. Ibid. II. D 3.

[74] See Lloyd, *Part of Nature*, 77–104; Gatens, 'Spinoza, Law and Responsibility', 109–13; J. Cottingham, 'The Intellect, the Will and the Passions: Spinoza's Critique of Descartes', *Journal of the History of Philosophy*, 26 (1988), 239–57.

[75] *Ethics*, I. P 32. See also II. P 48 where Spinoza also claims that there are no faculties of the mind. There are in the mind only particular volitions, desires, loves, etc. So faculties such as the will or understanding 'are either complete fictions or nothing but metaphysical beings or universals which we are used to forming from particulars. So intellect and will are to this or that idea, or this and that volition, as "stone-ness" is to this or that stone, or man to Peter and Paul.' (II. P 48 s.)

impulse or appetite closely akin to a desire. Spinoza is insistent that a volition is not 'the desire by which the mind wants a thing or avoids it'.[76] But he is also unhappy with the view that there is a kind of thinking—willing or affirming or assenting—that is distinct from perceiving. In the Cartesian picture of the soul, judgement requires both perception and volition.[77] For example, I may perceive a green beech tree, assent to or affirm this perception, and thus arrive at a confused judgement that the tree is green. One might wonder, however, whether judgements really require two separate kinds of thought. Spinoza's way of putting this problem is to ask whether ideas already involve affirmations in so far as they are ideas.[78] He concludes that they do. For they are not images or pictures, passively waiting for the mind to affirm their truth or falsity. They are already conceptions or thoughts about how things are or are not, and are therefore already affirmations.

This conclusion has several important consequences. It implies that, contrary to Descartes's view, willing and perceiving are one and the same.[79] In place of a mind whose power to think works in two cooperating ways, we have a mind with a single power to form ideas from which other ideas follow. Rather than analysing judgements as the outcome of perceptions and acts of assent, we need only appeal to conceptions. All thoughts, sensory perceptions, memories, passions, pure perceptions, and so forth are therefore of a single kind. They are all affirmations or judgements,[80] so that we affirm or judge whenever we perceive or imagine,[81] and our passions, too, possess this basic character. To love something is to judge that it will increase one's power, to hate something is to judge that it will do the opposite, and so on.

In arguing that there is no distinction within the mind between perceptions and volitions, Spinoza breaks with a strand of the Scholastic conception of the soul that had continued to cling to even some of the more determined opponents of Aristotelianism. Philosophers who make great strides in unifying the mind and transcending a conception of its separate though communicating powers continue to have pressing reasons for retaining the distinction between these two kinds of thought, and as long as this remains in place, the threat of separate powers looms. It is hard, for example, to reconcile Descartes's insistence that volitions and our perceptions of volitions are really one and the same thing[82] with his claim that perception and volition are quite distinct sorts of operation, one parasitic on the other.[83] Spinoza cuts through this aftermath of Aristotelianism by denying that thinking involves these two operations, which he merges into one. Perception, as he repeatedly reminds us, takes on some of

---

[76] Ibid. II. P 48 s.
[77] Descartes, *Principles of Philosophy*, in *Philosophical Writings*, ed. Cottingham *et al.*, i. 34.
[78] *Ethics*, II. P 49.   [79] Ibid. II. P 49 c.   [80] Ibid. II. D 3.   [81] Ibid. I. P 49 s.
[82] Descartes, *The Passions of the Soul*, in *Philosophical Writings*, ed. Cottingham *et al.*, i. 19.
[83] Id., *Principles of Philosophy*, I. 32.

the active quality previously attributed to willing, while willing is assimilated into the causal process of thinking, which becomes inherently affirmative. So although we still have thoughts of different kinds and can, for example, distinguish memories from pure perceptions, these are no longer seen as amalgamations of two components, perception and will.

Spinoza's Stoic reduction and unification of the powers of the mind radically affects the sense in which thinking can be understood as active or passive.[84] By abandoning the distinction between active volitions and passive perceptions, he gets rid of one influential way of discriminating passivity from activity in favour of the view that all thoughts are caused and can be causes. Is there, then, any remaining sense in which some thoughts are more passive than others? We saw earlier that some of our thoughts occur when we are acted on, and Spinoza contrasts this condition with a kind of thinking that he describes as acting. We arc actcd on when we are only the partial or inadequate cause of a thought or idea, so that the idea cannot be explained by appeal to the mind alone. But when we possess adequate ideas which *can* be explained by the mind alone, we act. What might this be like? First of all, an idea can only be explained by the other ideas that cause it; so if an idea is to be explained by the mind alone, it must be explained by an idea which is part of the complex idea that makes up the mind. And since the mind is the idea of the body, this is to say that one idea of the body must be explained by anothcr idea of the body. It is difficult, here, to do more than move the counters around, but Spinoza's view seems to be this. When I have an inadequate idea of a cat, I have an idea that causally depends on both an idea of the cat and an idea of my body. But when I have an adequate idea of, say, a triangle, I have an idea which is not causally dependent on ideas of the relations of my body with other things but is caused by my mind alone. As well as the causal relations between the body and other things, certain causal processes go on within the body, comparatively independently of its environment. The ideas of these processes form comparatively self-contained causal chains, which we experience as logical sequences of ideas, each one deriving entirely from ideas that do not depend on the ways we are affected by the external world. In so far as it possesses these adequate ideas the mind is able, so to speak, to generate ideas out of itself; and when it thinks in this fashion, it acts.[85]

This conception of the mind's activity is, to a certain extent, familiar. Whether a particular thought-process is active or passive depends on how the ideas that it contains are caused. When Spinoza claims that, in order for a

---

[84] See P. O. Kristeller, 'Stoic and Neo-Stoic Sources of Spinoza's *Ethics*', *History of European Ideas*, 5 (1984), 1–15; S. James, 'Spinoza the Stoic', in T. Sorell (ed.), *The Rise of Modern Philosophy* (Oxford, 1993), 289–316.

[85] See Donagan, *Spinoza*, 136–40; Allison, *Benedict de Spinoza*, 101–9.

thought-process to be active, the ideas in it must be caused by the mind itself, he picks up a trait often attributed to volitions, namely that they are self-initiating or self-causing. Equally, when he claims that passive processes occur when the mind is acted on by ideas of other things, he utilizes the standard association between passions and effects. The unusual feature of his position is that he does not predicate activity and passivity of thoughts differentiated by function, but makes the activity of a thought depend on its causal history. Because adequate ideas are entirely caused by other ideas in the mind, and because the mind is conscious of all its ideas, an adequate idea is complete in the sense that all its causal antecedents are known. Unlike an inadequate idea, it is not patchy, and is therefore not distorted. So the difference between ideas of these two kinds is in the end epistemological rather than psychological—it is a difference between ideas that we know, in the sense just outlined, and ideas that we do not.

It follows from this account that, along with various other kinds of thought, our passions are inadequate ideas that we acquire when we are acted on, which are distinguished from fantasies, sensory perceptions, and so forth by the fact that they are manifestations of our *conatus*. As long as we strive to persevere in our being, we experience passions; and because, as finite beings dependent for survival on the world around us, we never cease to strive in this way, we experience passions all the time. Our passionate responses are therefore not only excited by certain types of experience, but are always operating, although the histories of particular individuals will ensure that their passions are specific and articulated. If the grieving Orpheus proves completely indifferent to his friends' attempts to comfort him, this is not because his *conatus* has ceased to work, but because he does not at the moment conceive comfort as the sort of good that will increase his power.

So far, we have traced the ways in which Spinoza modifies traditional understandings of passivity within the mind. We are passive when we are partial causes and are acted on by external things. And our judgements are passions when they are manifestations of our *conatus* which conform to these two criteria. There is, however, a further crucial connotation of the opposition between activity and passivity which is all but obliterated in Spinoza's philosophy: the association of mind with activity and passivity with body. As we have seen, this remained influential among those mechanical philosophers who conceived bodies, including human ones, as passive because they have no power to move themselves, and who contrasted this feature of the material world with the capacity of human minds to will. For Spinoza, however, there can be no such asymmetry. The body and mind are one thing viewed under two attributes. Moreover, the *conatus* is a single power manifested in both attributes; whatever bodily events constitute the body's striving to persevere in its being are matched by ideas that constitute the same striving in the mind. Our transitions from joy to sadness and sadness to joy correspond to decreases and increases in our bodily power. As Spinoza puts it, 'the idea of anything that increases or diminishes, aids or restrains our body's power of acting, increases or diminishes, aids or restrains, our mind's power of thinking'.[86]

Just as it was hard to articulate a conception of the mind as the idea of the body, the claim that bodily power corresponds with psychic power resists common sense. Surely a cancer can diminish my bodily power long before I have any idea of it; and surely many of my emotions make no difference to my physical strength and health? To gain a better appreciation of Spinoza's position, we need to explore several lines of thought. One is to try to make some pre-theoretical sense of the idea that our passions reinforce or undermine our physical power. Love, for example, can be empowering when it fills the lover with vitality, determination, and purposefulness. Equally, some forms of sadness are marked by lassitude and a diminished perceptiveness that can be construed as a reduction of our power to persevere in our being. The insensibility of grief or the blindingness of rage overwhelm our ordinary abilities to perceive and reflect, leaving us physically as well as psychologically exposed and incapable. Generalizing, we might say that sad people are more prone than others to illness, self-neglect, and injury whereas happy ones are more healthy and resilient. Turning to the physical side, we can also sketch correspondences between bodily changes and the passions, which play a role in early-modern treatises on the subject. Like many of his contemporaries, Spinoza probably believed that certain physical states can be correlated with a feeling of well-being, that melancholy coincides with disease, and so on. If this is right, our problem is not that Spinoza is maintaining something altogether implausible. It is rather that he seems to be exaggerating when he claims that *all* passions are simultaneously changes in bodily power and vice versa. We are aware of the play of our passions, but in many cases we have no idea how to identify increases and decreases of bodily power that purportedly accompany them.

Spinoza would, I think, agree with this last point. Because our ideas of our bodies are inadequate, we have, in his view, very little conception of what the body can and cannot do. But the argument for the match between bodily and psychic power does not derive from our limited experience, and is not damaged by our incapacity to give a phenomenological account of its manifestations. Rather, it is an implication of the parallelism between the attributes of thought and extension. If the order and connection of ideas is the same as that of things, there must be a physical description of any causal connection between ideas, and vice versa. And if the mind is the idea of the body, any causal connection between ideas in the mind must be matched by a causal connection between physical states in the body. Finally, if the *conatus* of the mind is the *conatus*

---

[86] *Ethics*, III. P 11.

of the body, increases or decreases in the power of one must be matched by increases or decreases in the power of the other. This argument is much more strongly founded than the inadequate ideas we patch together in imagination; so our task is to try to bring our understanding of ourselves in line with it.

Spinoza here postulates a perfect match between causes and effects in the body and the mind, as well as between the activity and passivity ascribed to them. The claim that the mind acts when it possesses adequate ideas has its counterpart in the claim that the body acts when it is an adequate cause. The claim that the mind is acted on when its ideas are inadequate corresponds to the claim that the body is acted on when it is an inadequate cause. And because mind and body are the same thing described under different attributes, they can only act or be acted on together. Each is as powerful or powerless as the other, and nothing is left of the contrast between the passive body and the active mind. There is, however, something in Spinoza's discussion that this interpretation fails to capture, a remaining asymmetry which suggests that some sense of the mind as more active than the body survives in his philosophy.[87] While Spinoza is committed to the view that the strivings of the mind and body correspond, he nevertheless emphasizes the mind's capacity to reflect on its own ideas. Our responses to the world are the outcome of various informal but complex interpretations and calculations. But these are not just about ways of maintaining the power of the mind; they are also about ways of preserving the body. We think about ourselves as embodied creatures whose preservation depends on mind and body together, and these thoughts form an important element of our *conatus*.

The implication that the mind can reflect on and take account of the body emerges in Spinoza's claims that '[t]he mind, as far as it can, strives to imagine those things that increase or aid the body's power of acting'[88] and 'When the mind imagines those things that diminish or restrain the body's power of acting, it strives, as far as it can, to recollect those things that exclude their existence.'[89] These propositions, like many of those that succeed them in the *Ethics*, are liable to mislead twentieth-century readers by suggesting that the mind occupies itself with fantasies designed to sustain the body. We have to remember that the imagination, for Spinoza, encompasses sensory perception, sensation, and memory, as well as what we call imagination.[90] (So, for example, the claim that 'he who imagines that what he loves is destroyed will be saddened'[91] tells us that a person will be saddened if they find or see that something they love has been destroyed.) Read in this way, the claim that the mind strives to imagine things that will increase the body's power of acting is

---

[87] See Lloyd, *Part of Nature*, 121–41.   [88] *Ethics*, III. P 12.   [89] Ibid. III. P 13.
[90] On the history of this view see J. M. Cocking, *Imagination: A Study in the History of Ideas* (London, 1991).
[91] *Ethics*, III. P 19.

somewhat more approachable, and charts the part played by the mind in our everyday attempts to keep out of trouble. Suppose that conversation with a particular acquaintance generally lowers your spirits (as we still say). You catch sight of her coming down the street and, deciding to pretend you haven't seen her, put on a preoccupied expression, gaze past her, and begin to walk more quickly. Since Spinoza holds that there are no causal connections between things and ideas, he will analyse this sequence into two causal chains. On the one hand, your inadequate idea of the acquaintance prompts a decision which causes ideas of your own body looking preoccupied and so forth. On the other hand, a motion resulting from the interaction of your body with that of the acquaintance causes other bodily motions such as those in the legs when you speed up. Both these sequences are manifestations of your *conatus*. But the explanatory lead, so to speak, is taken by the mind, since it is your knowledge of the effect this acquaintance usually has on you, together with your desire to avoid it, which cause you to pretend you haven't seen her. You decide to try to protect yourself from the sadness or diminution of power that a conversation with her is likely to bring. In doing this, however, you simultaneously strive to protect yourself from the diminution of bodily power that is the counterpart of all sadness. So in trying to avoid the passion of sadness, you simultaneously strive to avoid encountering things that will decrease the body's power of acting.

It may be objected that, in cases like this one, increases and decreases of the body's power of acting are simply counterparts of the mind's efforts to persevere in its being by pursuing joy and eschewing sadness. This is true. But it is not difficult to imagine cases where the mind reflects directly on the welfare of the body. When a prisoner tries to find a way to untie the ropes binding her wrists and ankles, she strives to imagine things that will increase the body's power of acting. So does a woman who thinks to herself that, as soon as she gets home, she will try to get rid of her headache by lying down for half an hour. In these cases, too, we appeal to the mind's capacity to reflect strategically on its ideas of the body. So, although Spinoza holds that there must be some physical equivalent of this process, he gives the mind a certain primacy.

A second sign of the asymmetry in our grasp of the bodily and psychic workings of the *conatus* surfaces in Spinoza's accounts of these two strivings for power. The *conatus* of a body consists, as we have seen, in its disposition to persevere in its being by maintaining a certain proportion of motion and rest. Correspondingly, we might construe the mind's *conatus* as consisting in the disposition to maintain its power by avoiding sadness. In fact, however, Spinoza speaks of the mind's *conatus* as a striving not just to maintain but to increase its power. As well as trying to keep out of the way of sadness, we try to make ourselves as joyful as possible. Why does Spinoza introduce this asymmetry, which sits so uncomfortably with his claim that the striving of body and mind is a single power viewed under distinct attributes? Why does he not say either that both mind and body strive to persevere in their being by maintaining their power, or that they strive to persevere in their being by maintaining or increasing it? Spinoza's analysis of the passions seems to commit him to the second of these alternatives. If joy and sadness are respectively increases and decreases of power, and if it is a fact that we experience both, then these psychic fluctuations must have some correlate in the physical workings of our bodies. It must be possible to make sense of the claim that human bodies, at least, are disposed not merely to resist motions that disturb the proportion of motion and rest by which they are individuated, but also to increase their stability by strengthening their power of resistance. This suggestion is not particularly implausible; but Spinoza does not make it. And it seems possible that his asymmetric presentation of the *conatus* of human beings reflects some remaining commitment to the old division between the passive body and the active mind. As Spinoza's contemporaries would have agreed, the body has a certain power to maintain itself. But the mind's creative ability to reflect on its own thoughts gives it more than this. It enables it to increase its power of self-preservation.

PART III

7

Passion and Error

In the introduction to the *Port Royal Logic*, Arnauld and Nicole bemoan the rarity of a capacity for accurate judgement. Common sense, they warn, is not as common as people think, and its absence explains not only the mistakes we make in the sciences, but the many errors that afflict us in everyday life. Groundless quarrels, baseless lawsuits, rash judgements, and ill-planned ventures all arise from an inability to distinguish truth from falsehood, and from a vanity and presumption which drives us to make decisions at random rather than admit that we are too ignorant to arrive at an informed judgement.[1] While a familiarity with principles of correct inference can do something to counter these deficiencies, logicians have vastly exaggerated their efficacy, ignoring the painful but obvious fact that people educated in logic often reason as badly as anyone else. Formal rules are therefore not enough to promote reason. What is needed is an art of thinking, a method for improving our judgement which will bear on all aspects of our lives and grapple with two sources of our errors: our susceptibility to false appearances, and the disorder of our wills that is manifested in *amour propre*, interest, and passion.[2] Returning to this theme, the authors of the *Logic* take up a now-familiar argument that our passions trick us into believing that our relations with the world around us are states of the world itself. How often, they ask, do we see people who are incapable of recognizing any good in those for whom they have conceived an aversion, or who have in some way gone against their feelings, desires, or interests? The unfortunate object of their passion is represented as reckless, proud, ignorant, and lacking in faith, honour, or conscience. Consider, too, how love alters our attitudes. Because the beloved is exempt from all faults, everything they desire is justified and attainable, while everything they are averse to is both unreasonable and impossible.[3] These dispositions are perhaps already enough to unsettle our sanity; but they are augmented by an *amour propre* which makes us profoundly opinionated and resistant to learning. The conviction that our own emotional responses are correct persuades us that people whose feelings differ from ours are mistaken. Basking in our own intelligence, we convince ourselves that we only have to announce our opinions for everyone else to

---

[1] *La Logique ou l'art de penser*, ed. P. Clair and F. Girbal (Paris, 1981), 16–18; trans. and ed. J. V. Buroker as *Logic or the Art of Thinking* (Cambridge, 1996), 6.
[2] Ibid. 261; trans. Buroker, 204.   [3] Ibid. 262–3; trans. Buroker, 205.

agree; out of envy and jealousy we are loath to admit that other people are superior in knowledge or feeling;[4] and from fear of appearing ignorant, we reason like this: 'Si cela était, je ne serais pas un habile homme.'[5]

The association of the passions with error is, of course, both ancient and commonplace. The standard opposition between reason and the passions already implies their irrationality, and as we saw in Chapter 1, this conception is regularly strengthened and reinforced by descriptions which represent them as pathological, wayward, vicious, and overpowering. The passions distort our understanding, lead us astray, sweep us off the deck of the good ship *Reason*, and consign us to the restless waves. There is, however, something ritualistic about these ubiquitous images since, as we saw in Part II, early-modern philosophers do not in fact regard the passions as relentlessly unreasonable. On the contrary, whether or not they classify passions as judgements, they agree that they are complex, subtle responses in which many aspects of our characters and environments are registered. The problem is not so much that they are straightforwardly irrational as that they are designed to realize rather restricted goals. By working to protect us from bodily and psychological harm, they effectively shield us from painful insights, cocooning us in a world of half-truths from which we cannot escape without a struggle.

The various ways in which the passions incline us to error will be explored later in this chapter. The assumption that they lead us astray raises, however, a further set of epistemological questions which are the subject of the rest of Part III: Can we overcome the errors to which our passions expose us by overcoming the passions? And if not, how can we manipulate them so that they contribute to, or at least do not undermine, the search for truth? A number of recent interpreters have focused their accounts of seventeenth-century philosophy on the opposition between reason and passion, and have concluded that one of the questionable achievements of this period is a conception of neutral scientific reasoning drained of emotion, together with an image of science as a means to control a disenchanted world.[6] These readings, I shall suggest, vastly underrate the sophistication of seventeenth-century attempts to deal with the relations between passion and scientific or philosophical enquiry, and fail to take account of the role of the affections in the acquisition of knowledge. To overcome error, as Arnauld and Nicole point out, we need a love of truth, a particular emotional disposition that will guide our thoughts and actions. Far from divorcing reason and passion, philosophers of this era offer a rich set of interpretations of what such a love might be like, and of the habitats in which it might grow and flourish.[7]

[4] Ibid. 266; trans. Buroker, 206–7.   [5] Ibid. 264; trans. Buroker, 206.
[6] See Ch. 1 nn. 8 and 66.
[7] For some discussion of this theme see B. Shapiro, *Probability and Certainty in Seventeenth-Century England* (Princeton, 1983).

Recognition and appreciation of this strand of thought may have been hindered by the character of twentieth-century epistemology, which until recently tended to focus on the character of knowledge itself rather than on the conditions in which it can be acquired.[8] A further obstacle may have been the widespread interest in early-modern scepticism.[9] Important as this is, an emphasis on sceptical problems has tended to distract attention from the extent to which seventeenth-century philosophers assume that knowledge is within our reach, and aim to investigate how it can be acquired. While some—notably Descartes—confront the epistemological problem of fending off the sceptical demon, many others regard the main obstacles to knowledge as psychological. To acquire *scientia*, we must transform our own unruly dispositions, learning to identify and combat the errors to which our passions expose us; moreover, the crises of confidence we are liable to undergo in the course of this process are not lapses of faith in the possibility of knowledge, but doubts about our ability to triumph over the destructive aspects of our own natures.

Later in Part III I shall explore three different—though to some extent complementary—attempts to see how the destructive potential of the passions can be contained and harnessed in the quest for knowledge. Chapter 8 discusses the view that we can escape and combat the passions with a kind of reasoning that is emotional but not passionate. Chapter 9 considers the idea that, although our passions are always with us, we can harness the habits of thought in which they consist and employ them in the service of demonstrative knowledge. Chapter 10 explores a conception of knowledge which is not opposed to reason but is itself a kind of feeling, and argues that seventeenth-century conceptions of knowledge are pulled between two conflicting ideals—a vision of knowledge as separation and a conception of understanding as unification—which have yet to be reconciled.

That our passions are a source of error is taken for granted by seventeenth-century philosophers, many of whom chart and analyse the kinds of mistakes to which they expose us. Among these, the most widely recognized is perhaps the habit of interpreting the world in the light of our emotions. When the soul is stirred by passion, as Charron remarks, our senses 'do see and hear everything otherwise than as they are'.[10] The main use we make of our love of truth, Nicole gloomily insists, is to persuade ourselves that what we love is

---

[8] This approach is exemplified by the quest for necessary and sufficient conditions for knowledge. See e.g. A. J. Ayer, *The Problem of Knowledge* (Harmondsworth, 1956); E. Gettier, 'Is justified true belief knowledge?', in A. Phillips Griffiths (ed.), *Knowledge and Belief* (Oxford, 1967), 144–6; R. Nozick, *Philosophical Explanations* (Oxford, 1981), 172–96.

[9] For a classic account of the centrality of scep[ticism in thi]s period see R. Popkin, *The History of Scepticism from Erasmus to Spinoza* (Berkeley and Los Ange[les,] [...] id., *The Third Force in Seventeenth-Century Thought* (Leiden, 1992).

[10] *Of Wisdome*, trans. S. Lennard (London, 1608), 38; cf. Aristotle, *On Dreams*, in [...] *Works of Aristotle*, ed. J. Barnes (Princeton, 1984), vol. i, 460[b]1–16.

true.[11] When the soul is full of passion, according to Reynolds, 'the more clear and naked brightness of truth is suspended and changed'.[12] Passion, Hobbes explains, gives rise to dogmatical learning 'in which there is nothing not disputable because it compareth men, and meddleth with their right and profit in which, as oft as Reason is against a man, so oft will a man be against Reason'.[13] These uniformly pessimistic assertions are wryly anticipated in Bacon's claim that

The human understanding is no dry light, but receives an infusion from the will and affections; whence proceed sciences which may be called 'sciences as one would'. For what a man had rather were true he more readily believes. Therefore he rejects difficult things for impatience of research; sober things, because they narrow hope; the deeper things of nature from superstition, the light of experience from arrogance and pride, lest his mind should seem to be occupied with things mean and transitory; things not commonly believed, out of deference to the opinions of the vulgar. Numberless, in short, are the ways, and sometimes imperceptible, in which the affections colour and infect the understanding.[14]

We are subject to this kind of error, Wright suggests, because passions consume us and prevent us from considering the reasons for or against a view. They blind the wit, 'as he which shutteth up another man's eyes maketh him blindfold, not by taking away the power of feeling but only by hindering it from action'. And even when the understanding tries to get a grip on an affection, 'the imagination putteth green spectacles before the eyes of our wit, to make it see nothing but green, that is, serving for the consideration of the passion'.[15]

As these disparate sources suggest, the belief that the passions lead us astray is deeply entrenched and habitually articulated with the help of a range of equally well-established metaphors. Most persistently, as one would expect, passion is portrayed as blindness and contrasted with the brightness and clarity of vision that is associated with knowledge. Once again echoing an old thought, Bacon describes prejudices, lusts, passions, partial affections, and appetites of honour and interest as clouding the mind and obscuring the light of truth.[16] His image of passions darkening the mind like clouds over the sun, along with Wright's description of them as a blindfold, allude to the externality of the passions, the implication that they come between us and truth; but they also suggest that the passionate lose their bearings. Like travellers lost in a mist, we no longer know where we are or what direction to take. The same idea is also conveyed, along with a greater emphasis on the power of the affections,

[11] *Essais de morale* (Paris, 1672), iii. 35.
[12] *A Treatise of the Passions and Faculties of the Soul of Man* (London, 1640), 69.
[13] *The Elements of Law*, ed. F. Tönnies (2nd edn, London, 1969), Epistle Dedicatory, p. xv.
[14] *Translation of the Novum Organum*, in *Works*, ed. J. Spedding *et al.* (London, 1857–61), iv. 57.
[15] *The Passions of the Mind in General* (2nd edn 1604), ed. W. W. Newbold (New York, 1986), 128.
[16] *The Advancement of Learning*, ed. G. W. Kitchin (London, 1973), 56.

in the claim that the passions 'dazzle our minds with false lights, cover it and fill it with darkness'.[17] Knowledge, it seems, does not just depend on light, but on the degree of light that enables us to see clearly, so that error can arise from too much, as well as too little, illumination. Exploring still further this set of optical images, early-modern writers compare passion to colour. Bacon's description of passion as infecting or colouring understanding,[18] and Wright's comparison of the passions to green spectacles, draw on a conception of colour as giving things emotional character and thereby misrepresenting them. This image draws together many interwoven connotations, some of which will occupy us later on, from alchemy, from rhetoric, and from painting, where colour is held to be positively dangerous.

[F]or although there be sometimes in lineal pictures . . . a deceitful similitude of life and motion . . . coloured pictures for all that, as they show a more lively force in the several effects and properties of life and spirit, so do they most commonly ravish our sight with the bewitching pleasure of delightsome and stately ornaments. A discreet and wary moderation therefore . . . may not be forgotten here.[19]

In all these contexts, colour is associated with artifice and thus with deception, and opposed to the naked and transparent truth.

While these ubiquitous images portray the passions as intrinsically distorting, obscuring, and misleading, it remains to see how they inform and are reinforced by a more wide-ranging philosophical understanding of the passions as threats to knowledge. How do these metaphors retain their power and centrality? How do philosophers articulate them in their accounts of the errors to which emotion exposes us?[20] Since our encounters with the world are held to be shaped by our individual passions, and since it is accepted that our passions are likely to mislead us, the conclusion that we are commonly deceived follows without trouble. But what kinds of error are involved here? And how do they flow from the characterizations of the passions we have encountered? In this chapter I discuss four kinds of mistake to which our passionate natures make us prone.

Error and Projection

A first kind of error to which the passions expose us derives from the view discussed in Part II that the passions themselves are akin to secondary qualities

---

[17] Nicolas Malebranche, *De le recherche de la vérité*, ed. G. Rodis Lewis, in *Œuvres Complètes*, ed. A. Robinet (2nd edn, Paris, 1972), i. 67; trans. T. M. Lennon and P. J. Olscamp as *The Search after Truth* (Columbus, Oh., 1980), 17.

[18] See J. C. Briggs, *Francis Bacon and the Rhetoric of Nature* (Cambridge, Mass., 1989), 70–1.

[19] Franciscus Junius the Younger, *The Painting of the Ancients* (Farnborough, 1972), 285.

[20] For further discussion of this theme see J. Barnouw, 'Passion as "Confused" Perception or Thought in Descartes, Malebranche and Hutcheson', *Journal of the History of Ideas*, 53 (1992), 397–424.

and are relational—they record connections between external motions and motions in our bodies. Eurydice's fear of the snake, for instance, is her experience of a motion determined by both the snake and aspects of her own bodily constitution. As Malebranche explains,

The most general cause of the errors of our senses is . . . that we attribute to objects outside our bodies sensations that are really in our souls. We attach colours to the surfaces of bodies, scatter light, sounds and smells in the air and fix pain and tickling sensations in the parts of the bodies that are changed by motions in the bodies they encounter. More or less the same is true of the passions. We rashly attribute to objects which cause, or seem to cause them, all the dispositions of our hearts—our goodness, our gentleness, our malice, our bitterness, and all the other qualities of our minds. The object which arouses a passion in us seems to us somehow to contain within itself that which it awakes in us when we think about it.[21]

Versions of this view are upheld, as we have seen, by Descartes and Spinoza, as well as by Malebranche, so that, in addition to expressing a common outlook, they encounter common problems of interpretation. One of these concerns the persuasiveness of Malebranche's analogy. In normal conditions, he argues, we generally interpret colours and other secondary qualities as properties of the external world, and nothing in our everyday perceptual experience makes it plain that objects only look coloured because this is how humans are disposed to experience certain sets of cerebral motions. Similarly, Malebranche seems to be saying, individuals attribute emotional qualities to objects in the world. People who agree that a snake is green may not agree that it is frightening, but a person who finds it frightening will ordinarily not be aware that their fear is partly the fruit of their own dispositions. This last claim is only partly convincing, however, since we quite often acknowledge that our passions are special to us and born of our experience. Indeed, Descartes points to an important disanalogy with sensory properties when he emphasizes that we locate the passions in the soul; whereas our experience of secondary qualities encourages the belief that we are passively receiving perceptions of external objects, our experience of passions as in the soul itself should alert us to their relational character.

To deal with this problem, a Cartesian can allow that, because we make imperfect use of our ability to understand our own passions, we commit errors of the kind Malebranche describes. I may conclude that he is hateful, she is adorable, or it is terrifying, oblivious of the perspective built into these judgements. It remains to ask, however, what sort of error is embodied in this habit, and here we can distinguish two strands of criticism. First, and most obviously, our disposition to project our emotions sustains a philosophical misunderstanding

---

[21] *De la recherche*, ii. 113; trans. Lennon and Olscamp, 370. See also T. M. Schmaltz, 'Malebranche's Cartesian and Lockean Colours', *History of Philosophy Quarterly*, 12 (1995), 387–403.

of our own nature and our relation to the world. If Eurydice judges that the snake itself is frightening, she makes a philosophical mistake in failing to see that the property in question is really relational. Errors of this sort are significant in two connected ways: they contribute to a false view of the external world by attributing to it properties it does not possess, and they maintain a mistaken conception of human affections. But they may still strike us as rather arcane by comparison with the practical benefits we derive from our passions. Although Eurydice misconstrues the components of her fear, she is right, from a practical point of view, to be frightened of the snake. What do our philosophical mistakes matter, as long as our passions fulfil their function of enhancing our well-being as embodied creatures?

The writers under discussion all believe that these mistakes are significant, and defend their view by pointing to a connection between philosophical error and its practical counterpart. To be sure, there are cases like that of Eurydice where a lack of theoretical understanding does not prevent us from feeling emotions appropriate to our circumstances. As her story shows, her fear of the snake was well judged. But when, as often happens, our passions are either inappropriate or less appropriate than they might be, philosophical ignorance impedes our capacity to modify them. Our blindness to the fact that it takes both a subject and an object to make a passion stands in the way of our ability to identify those dispositions in ourselves which cause us to perceive others as frightening, lovable, and so on, and this in turn cuts us off from the kinds of critical reflection that alter our emotional responses.

A philosophical grasp of the components of our passions also enables us to avoid a further kind of mistake and another source of harm. As long as we think of passions as properties possessed by things in the world, independently of us, it comes easily, as Malebranche explains, to think of them as available to be perceived by everyone. 'For the same reason that we think all men receive the same sensations from objects as we do, we think that all men are agitated by the same passions for the same things . . . that they love what we love and desire what we desire.'[22] Putting the point slightly differently, we can say that our disposition to be led astray by our passions is a disposition to understand ourselves—wrongly—as plain mirrors that simply reflect the world, thereby attributing too hastily to ourselves the position of a passive subject of scientific knowledge.[23] To rid ourselves of this deep and pervasive kind of misunderstanding, we must first recapture the relational, situated character of our experience by learning to think of other people and things as frightening, hateful, or whatever in relation to ourselves. Moreover, we must learn that, since our passions depend on and vary with our constitutions and characters

---

[22] *De la recherche*, ii. 113; trans. Lennon and Olscamp, 370.
[23] Bacon, *Advancement of Learning*, 132: The mind is like 'an enchanted glass, full of superstition and imposture'.

and therefore differ from person to person, emotional consensus is not to be expected. In reconnecting ourselves with the world around us and shedding the illusion that our perspective is neutral, we acquire the means to think critically about the relations between external things and our bodies. Even if we do not know exactly how these connections occur, or exactly what connects with what, we are no longer condemned to accept passions, and the mistakes embodied in them, at face value.

Fundamentally, then, the error of projection consists in a functional natural trait which is at the same time a limitation, in a disposition to evaluate things in relation to ourselves without being aware that we are doing so. This is the problem Bacon identifies when he says that 'perceptions as well as of the sense as of the mind are according to the measure of the individual and not according to the measure of the universe', a passage quoted with approval by Malebranche.[24] Because we fail to realize that we are making judgements about the value that things as we perceive them possess in relation to ourselves, we both misunderstand what the passions are, and mistake the value things have for us for the value they have in themselves.

While these dangers are fairly widely recognized and discussed, some philosophers, including Hobbes, identify a further kind of error to which projection exposes us. In addition to interpreting as monadic properties that are in fact relational, we also tend, Hobbes argues, to fantasize whole objects answering to our passions. For example, we are prey to extreme anxiety about our future security, an anxiety so intense that it 'must needs have for object something'.[25] Rather than confronting this fear, we often invent a terrifying object of it, some 'power or agent invisible'[26] to be avoided or appeased, and in doing so fill the world with entities that simply do not exist. The fear of things invisible, Hobbes pointedly remarks, 'is the natural seed of that which everyone in himself calls religion; and in them that worship, or fear that power otherwise than they do, superstition'.[27] Our passions, then, do not only distort our understanding of the properties of objects; they also cause us to misinterpret the objects themselves.

Errors of Time and Scale

While many of our ideas of sensible things are suffused with emotion, it is widely assumed by early-modern philosophers that our strongest passions are provoked by objects actually present to our senses. Generally speaking, the

---

[24] Malebranche, *De le recherche*, i. 278; trans. Lennon and Olscamp, 136: 'Omnes perceptiones tam sensus quam mentis sunt ex analogia hominis, non ex analogia universe.' See Bacon, *Translation of the Novum Organum*, 54.

[25] *Leviathan*, ed. R. Tuck (Cambridge, 1991), 76.   [26] Ibid.

[27] Ibid. On superstition see D. Johnson, *The Rhetoric of Leviathan: Thomas Hobbes and the Politics of Cultural Transformation* (Princeton, 1986).

passions aroused by sensory perceptions are more forceful than those associated either with memory or fantasy. This orientation is beautifully captured in Hobbes's description of memory as 'decaying sense'. The phantasms of memory, he tells us, 'are as if worn out with time . . . For there is in memory something like that which happens in looking upon things at a great distance; in which as the small parts of the object are not discerned by reason of their remoteness; so in memory, many accidents and places and parts of things . . . are by length of time decayed and lost.'[28] Hobbes relies on a common and influential device when he portrays the past as spatially remote. As well as describing the perceptual qualities of memories, this image is also used to convey their emotional quality, so that remembered passion is conceived as fading as it recedes into the distance. Fantasy, that mixed bag of reveries, storytelling, and speculation about the future, is more equivocal, but at least in some cases one can make sense of the central idea that the emotions these thoughts arouse are less vivid than those evoked by sensory experience. Finding oneself trapped in a burning building, for example, is more terrifying than imagining it.

As Hobbes's account implies, the view that certain kinds of thought are emotionally more intense than others aligns with the view that the temporal focus of the passions is on the present. The weaker emotions associated with memory are, by definition, of the past; and imaginative speculation about the future also provokes comparatively faint affections. Pascal urges an Augustinian modification of this perspective, pointing out that our strongest passions are directed not so much to the present moment as to the near future and near past. Our desires are for future states, but we tend to be preoccupied by short-term goals; likewise, our love, sorrow, and anger focus more readily on the recent or very recent past than on things as they are absolutely now. In fact, the present is a sort of blank we find too painful to contemplate.[29] Many philosophers, however, are content to regard the present as the focus of intensity of our passions. Spinoza, for example, is quite clear that 'Other things equal, the image of a future or past thing . . . is weaker than the image of a present thing; and consequently, an affect towards a future or past thing is milder, other things equal, than an affect towards a present thing.'[30] Moreover, we are more intensely affected by the near past and future than by distant things; the forcefulness of our experience focuses on the present and then fades out in both temporal directions.[31]

Malebranche, ever the champion of divine wisdom and benevolence, defends this arrangement. It is important that we should be particularly moved by our

---

[28] *Elements of Philosophy: The First Section, Concerning Body*, in *The English Works of Thomas Hobbes* ed. Sir William Molesworth (London, 1839–45), i. 398. See also *Leviathan*, 15–16.

[29] Blaise Pascal, *Pensées*, trans. A. J. Krailsheimer (Harmondsworth, 1966), 47.

[30] *Ethics*, in *The Collected Works of Spinoza*, ed. E. Curley (Princeton, 1985), vol. i. IV. P 9.

[31] Ibid. IV. P 10.

sensory perceptions, because our well-being depends on our ability to respond to the things around us; we cannot afford to be more enthralled by a memory than alarmed by a bolting horse. But while this state of affairs is on balance advantageous, it also exposes us to error.[32] In interpreting the world, we take more account of things that are present to the senses and the passions they excite, of things that happened recently, and of the near future, than of distant thoughts and feelings. Our judgements are therefore continually skewed towards the here-and-now and are in this way unreliable. As Bacon also puts it, 'affection beholdeth principally the present . . . ; reason beholdeth the future and sum of time. . . . And therefore the present filling the imagination more, reason is commonly vanquished.'[33] It is vanquished and overcome because the liveliness and forcefulness of our ideas of the present lead us to generalize too rapidly and to neglect that 'going to and fro to remote and heterogeneous instances by which axioms are tried, as if by the fire'.[34] In short, our passionate involvement with the present makes us sloppy in our inductive habits. At the same time, it makes it difficult for us to generate strong feelings about the future, for example to fear punishment in the afterlife.[35] Error arises, then, not just from the inherent incompleteness of the experience from which our feelings arise, but also from the temporal focus of the passions themselves, which shapes whatever experiences we have.

If time introduces one kind of distortion and thus error into our passions, scale is the source of another. There is in many seventeenth-century writers on the passions a conviction that our emotions are determined by our perception of the greatness or smallness of things in relation to us, accompanied by a general view that these assessments are inaccurate. Descartes, for example, remarks almost in passing that the passions are intrinsically excessive in that they usually cause the goods and evils they represent to appear greater and more important than they actually are.[36] Hobbes argues that we assess the power of others in relation to ourselves, so that 'to value a man at a high rate is to honour him; at a low rate to dishonour him. But high and low, in this case, is to be understood by comparison to the rate that each man setteth on himself.'[37] This strand of thought is perhaps most thoroughly developed by writers who explore the notions of *grandeur* or greatness, and smallness or *petitesse*, terms which are used to describe both physical and metaphorical size—the vastness of the heavens, the insignificance of a peasant, a magistrate's authority, or the degree of someone's virtue. Underlying them is the idea that our

---

[32] *De la recherche*, i. 177; trans. Lennon and Olscamp, 79–80.

[33] *Advancement of Learning*, 147.   [34] Bacon, *Translation of the Novum Organum*, 56–7.

[35] See e.g. Pascal, *Pensées*, 427.

[36] *The Passions of the Soul*, in *The Philosophical Writings of Descartes* ed. Cottingham *et al.* (Cambridge, 1984–91), i. 138. See also id. Letter to Princess Elizabeth, 15 Sept., 1645, in *The Philosophical Writings*, iii. *Correspondence*, 267.

[37] *Leviathan*, 63.

affections are comparative, so that what we feel about other people and things depends on how they compare with us. This is a deep-seated trait, a fundamental aspect of the way we understand the world. But it also leads us to make significant and pervasive mistakes.

The orientation of our passions toward greatness is an aspect of our disposition to differentiate between the novel and the familiar. When we are struck by something new or surprising we experience *admiratio* (translated as 'admiration' or 'wonder' in English and as *l'admiration* in French), a passion which fixes our sense-organs so that we pay attention to the object in question.[38] While sheer novelty is the defining cause of wonder, it is also habitually a response to scale. Descartes, who designated *l'admiration* the first of the passions—the one we experience when we first perceive an object—adds without comment that we wonder at *grandeur* or *petitesse*, and consequently specifies esteem and contempt as the main modifications of this passion.[39] These are in turn subdivided according to their objects: esteem and contempt for ourselves are vanity and humility, while esteem and contempt for others are veneration and scorn.[40] In Descartes's account, this group of passions have a problematic status, since they do not involve any evaluation of their objects as good or evil, beneficial or harmful. This puts them at odds with the Cartesian definition of passions as affections which prompt us to do what is good for our nature, so that they sit uncomfortably on the borderline of Descartes's category. As feelings we experience within the soul they are encompassed by it, but as emotions not concerned for our good they are excluded.

Although Descartes does not resolve this tension, his distinction between the forms of wonder and all the other passions nevertheless makes some sense. It is perhaps not so hard to see how wonder itself can be devoid of moral evaluation. It arises when people encounter something so alien that they have no means to evaluate it, as when the Aztecs first set eyes on Spanish firearms, or when we are so taken by the novelty of a thing that the question of whether it is good or bad simply does not arise. Imagine an inhabitant of Rome in 1667 coming around a corner and confronting Bernini's newly installed Egyptian obelisk, mounted on the back of a stone elephant. The situation is slightly less straightforward when we come to objects which are novel by virtue of their combinations or contexts, for here the imagination has some experience to go on. Since in these cases we have the means to make rudimentary assessments

---

[38] On the significance of this first passion see B. Timmermans, 'Descartes et Spinoza: De l'admiration au désir', *Revue internationale de philosophie*, 48 (1994), 275–86; L. Irigaray, *An Ethics of Sexual Difference*, trans. C. Burke and G. C. Gill (London, 1993), 77–80. For its place in what he calls a rhetoric of attention see T. Carr, *Descartes and the Resilience of Rhetoric* (Carbondale, Ill., 1990), 52–4.

[39] Irigaray speculates interestingly as to whether contempt for the small may underlie our comprehension of sexual difference, measured by standards of more and less. See Irigaray, *Ethics of Sexual Difference*, 76.

[40] *Passions of the Soul*, 53–5.

of good and harm, wonder will be accompanied by other passions; but Descartes may still argue that wonder itself remains indifferent to perceived evaluative distinctions.

What, now, about esteem—wonder at the *grandeur* of others? Can we esteem someone without judging them in some way good? And can we feel contempt or scorn for someone without thinking them inferior in the sense of less good? Taking the first of these, esteem appears, on the face of things, to be intimately connected with moral judgement. Esteem for the *grandeur* of a great philosopher, say, is not akin to wonder. It does not consist in feeling overwhelmed by the sheer impressiveness of her astonishing appearance but in admiration for her insight and achievements, emotions which in turn presuppose that these qualities are of value. But are they of moral value, concerned with good and evil, benefit and harm? Yes. Her learning, devotion to the pursuit of truth, inventiveness, and so on are surely as morally valuable as many of the qualities Descartes regards as components of passions such as desire or ambition.

This strand of argument pulls against Descartes's claim that esteem does not involve moral assessment by suggesting that there are at least some cases where it does. But this is not the whole of the story. Esteem—*l'estime*—is related to *estimer* and stands, for Descartes and his contemporaries, somewhere between estimation and admiration. It carries connotations of giving an opinion on something, assessing it perhaps by estimating its size or weight, as well as connotations of value. When Descartes says that esteem does not involve considerations of perceived good or evil, he is surely drawing on this ambivalence. Esteem for *grandeur* can amount to no more than the recognition that someone possesses a lot of something by the going standards, whether power, jewels, learning, or sheer bulk. Equally, it can consist in appreciation of their non-moral qualities, as when someone is esteemed for their exquisite clothes. But because both these kinds of assessment shade swiftly into evaluation of the good or harm someone may do us, there is no firm boundary separating them from their moral counterpart. It is difficult to exclude moral evaluation from esteem and contempt. And it is therefore difficult to sustain Descartes's view that the latter are distinct passions, but are not concerned with our good and harm.

This tension is reflected in Malebranche's more elaborate discussion of the wonder we feel for *grandeur* and *petitesse*.[41] True to his Cartesianism, he begins by defining *l'admiration* in a now-familiar fashion as a feeling of pleasure in the mind that we experience when we see something for the first time, see a familiar thing in unfamiliar circumstances, come upon a new idea, or perceive a new connection between ideas.[42] Wonder itself, he goes on, considers things

---

[41] On this theme see G. Rodis Lewis, 'Malebranche "moraliste"', *XVIIe Siècle*, 159 (1988), 175–90.
[42] *De la recherche*, ii. 119; trans. Lennon and Olscamp, 375.

as they are in themselves, or as they appear to be in themselves, and takes no account of their relation to us or of whether they are good or bad.[43] But when the things we admire appear great, wonder is followed by esteem or veneration, and when they appear insignificant it gives way to contempt and scorn.[44] Wonder at ourselves produces a whole range of passions. Admiring our own perfection, we feel among other things pride or self-esteem and contempt for others. A just view of our own *grandeur* produces self-respect; admiration of our strength breeds a pleasure in our independence and boldness. But if we are struck by our imperfections, our passions are debilitating: we feel sadness, self-disgust, respect for others, humility, and so forth. The picture of our own *petitesse* produces abjectness, that of our weakness, fear.

Although Malebranche is more expansive than Descartes in listing the modifications of wonder, the general picture they offer is the same. Both writers take it that we wonder at *grandeur* and *petitesse* and that this produces several distinct emotions, depending principally on whether we are contemplating ourselves or something else. That we make comparative judgements of relative *grandeur* therefore seems to be taken for granted; but Malebranche goes beyond the Cartesian account in providing three separable explanations of why this is so.

First, our disposition to compare ourselves with other people and things, and the emotions to which this gives rise, form an aspect of our search for God. Disordered as it is, the human will has some idea of the good that will enable it to rest, and therefore directs itself towards a being that is infinite— perfect, boundlessly wise, eternal, omnipotent, and so on. At the same time, the will directs itself away from beings that are obviously finite, i.e. small. But its imperfections are such that when we are presented with ideas of things that appear great in comparison with ourselves, we perceive them as possessing some likeness to God and feel for them some of the passions that should properly be reserved for him. The will 'loves whatever is great, extraordinary or contains the infinite, because, not having found its true good in ordinary and familiar things, it imagines it will find it in things that are unknown to it'.[45] This disposition makes people excessively susceptible to the *grandeur* of objects other than God. For example, they are prone to revere astronomy because this science considers great and magnificent objects which are infinitely above everything around us.[46] As a counterpoise to their love of *grandeur*, people are disposed to disdain things which clearly lack any resemblance to God, including things that are small. They are, for instance, ordinarily scornful of insects. 'Because animals are small in relation to our bodies, we are led to view them as absolutely small, and consequently as despicable because of their smallness,

---

[43] Ibid. 119–20; trans. Lennon and Olscamp, 375–6.
[44] Ibid. 120; trans. Lennon and Olscamp, 376.
[45] Ibid. 5; trans. Lennon and Olscamp, 269–70.
[46] Ibid. i. 21, trans. Lennon, xxvi. Ibid. ii. 127; trans. Lennon and Olscamp, 382.

as if bodies could be small in themselves.'[47] Malebranche complements this analysis with an account of the bodily motions that accompany our ideas of *grandeur* and *petitesse*, appealing to the latter to help explain why it is that we are unduly preoccupied by sensible things that possess *grandeur*. Because the idea of *grandeur* is always matched by a great deal of motion in the animal spirits, things that are great appear to us as stronger, more real, and more perfect, and also excite stronger passions than small things, the ideas of which are only accompanied by small motions.[48]

These two arguments are joined by a third which deals not so much with the *grandeur* of other things as they appear to the soul as with the *grandeur* of the soul itself. One could say, Malebranche suggests, that the passions reason to themselves something like this:

I have to judge things on the basis of the ideas I possess, and of all my ideas the most sensible ones are the most real, because they strike me most forcefully. So I have to judge on the basis of those. When something I wonder at contains a sensible idea of greatness I ought to judge according to that idea; so I must esteem and love this *grandeur*, and pay attention to its object. In effect, the pleasure that I feel when I contemplate this idea is a natural proof that it is good for me to attend to it. After all, it seems to me that I become greater when I think about it and that my mind expands when it embraces an idea of something so great. The mind ceases to exist when it thinks of nothing; if the idea of which it thinks grows larger, it seems to me that my mind grows with it, and that it becomes smaller and more confined if it focuses on a smaller idea. Maintaining this great idea is, then, maintaining the *grandeur* and perfection of my being, which I then have reason to wonder at. . . . I am something great by virtue of my connection with great things. In a way, I possess them through the wonder I feel for them.[49]

In this soliloquy, the figure of Passion traces the intricate, self-aggrandizing reflexivity of the soul. The esteem that the soul feels for objects it perceives as great spreads, so to speak, and attaches to the soul itself, encompassing both subject and object. Esteem consists in a unification of the soul with its object, which is a kind of possession. The soul here employs Malebranche's view that affections can pass from person to person, as when you communicate your sadness to me. Emotions are portrayed as free-floating, as states of mind that must initially correlate with the motions of a particular body but that, once created, can leave it, thereby becoming separated from their original objects. Your sadness at the death of a friend may lose its specificity when it passes to me, and I may attach it to something completely different, say the dark days of February. The figure of Passion now turns this interpretation back upon the self. Esteem is initially stimulated in one soul by an idea of the greatness

---

[47] Ibid. i. 91; trans. Lennon and Olscamp, 31.   [48] Ibid. ii. 120; trans. Lennon and Olscamp, 381.
[49] Ibid. 133; trans. Lennon and Olscamp, 387.

of an external object; but once the emotion has arisen, the soul can attach it to itself, blurring the boundary between self and other.

By letting go of the authorial voice and putting this speech into the mouth of Passion, Malebranche distances himself from what is surely one of the most interesting consequences of his analysis of the passions. When these are classified as perceptions, we are prone to conceive of them as representations, comparable to sensory perceptions, memories, and so on. A sound I hear is a sound of something, even if I cannot give an accurate account of its source. Similarly, my sadness has an object, even if my analysis of it is partial and distorted. But if the passions involve modifications of the will—if they are feelings we somehow bring to bear on perceptions—a passion can exist over time, attached now to this object, now to that, now to no object in particular. Passions can follow their own dynamic sequences within the soul, interacting with, but not simply reflecting, the sequences of ideas in the understanding. Moreover, their bodily manifestations allow them to move from person to person, spinning an affective net which both ensnares and supports us.

Why, then, is Malebranche so tentative, so defensive in his exploration of this view? The answer returns us to our epistemological theme by way of Malebranche's deep suspicion of this tendency to sustain and protect the pleasure we take in contemplating our self-image by associating it with *grandeur*. While he is impressed by the extent to which we do this, Malebranche shares with his contemporaries a conviction that it leads us astray. For all their seductiveness, the arguments enunciated by Passion are deceptive and lacking in solidity.[50] Our susceptibility to *grandeur* dazzles and overthrows our reason and is, in fact, a susceptibility to several types of error.[51]

Because we are so easily moved by thoughts belonging to the imagination, we readily conflate *grandeur* with goodness. In beings other than God there is no reliable correlation between comparative scale and comparative value. The belief, for example, that the stars are a proper object of veneration—or are even of great significance because they are in human terms large—is simply a mistake. Secondly, our disposition to measure things in relation to ourselves, to adopt a human perspective, is at odds with the God's-eye view that constitutes truth and thus knowledge. The passions we feel for things that appear to us to possess *grandeur* conceal from us their—and our own—insignificance in the divine scheme of things. Equally, our contempt for things that we take to be insignificant is an exaggerated and erroneous response which hides their worth as elements of God's creation. Insects, Malebranche reminds us, are breathtakingly beautiful and diverse.[52] Incorporated in this sense that *grandeur* distorts our assessment of the significance of things is a horror at its self-centred

---

[50] Ibid. 134; trans. Lennon and Olscamp, 387–8.
[51] Ibid. 32; trans. Lennon and Olscamp, 296.
[52] Ibid. i. 90–1; trans. Lennon and Olscamp, 31.

perspective. By measuring other things in relation to ourselves, *grandeur* focuses on the *moi* in a manner that offends against the Christian aspiration to self-annihilation and identification with the divine. Arnauld and Nicole spell out their distaste for Montaigne, whose harping on about himself appears to them a kind of impiety,[53] and their view is shared by Malebranche who announces sternly—if rather priggishly—that 'if it is a defect to speak of oneself often, it is an affront, or rather a kind of folly, to praise oneself all the time as Montaigne does, for this is not only a sin against Christian humility but also an insult to reason'.[54] *Grandeur*, as Nicole insists, is opposed to almost all the Christian virtues.[55] Finally, our passions are direct or indirect responses to the sensible properties of things—we are moved by physical size, displays of wealth, the gorgeous robes of an official. But this attentiveness to the sensible makes us correspondingly insensitive to the intelligible realm, and thus blind to truths that only the intellect can comprehend. By the standards of the senses, vastness or honours appear greater and more real than virtue and justice.[56]

The particular kinds of things that strike us as possessing *grandeur* so shape our passions that these overarching errors take characteristic forms. They are manifested first of all in our attempts to acquire scientific knowledge, many of which are deeply misguided. Initially, we are drawn to the large, and also to the historically remote and the exotic.[57] Malebranche not only condemns astronomers who spend their lives 'hanging on the ends of telescopes', but, with a dig at the likes of Montaigne, ridicules the fashionable interest in cabinets of curiosities, in strange customs, and in the study of antiquity: 'Respect, mixed with stupid curiosity, makes us search for old medals though they are encrusted with rust, and carefully preserve the lantern and worm-eaten slipper of some ancient.'[58] Studying such objects, scholars transfer to themselves the *grandeur* they see in them, thus buoying up their self-esteem or vanity. Moreover, their knowledge of such apparently impressive things wins them the admiration of other people, whose deference further increases their own scholarly self-satisfaction. Finally, even the deferent admirers grow in self-esteem by associating themselves with purportedly learned scholars; for they, too, attach to themselves the respect they feel for the scholars and their pursuits.

These *faux savants*, as Malebranche calls them,[59] do not of course produce unadulterated falsehoods; they assemble all sorts of facts about Chinese artefacts, Athenian history, or Indian religions. In Malebranche's disparaging account,

---

[53] *Logique*, 269.　　[54] *De la recherche*, i. 364; trans. Lennon and Olscamp, 187.

[55] *Essais de morale*, ii. 234.

[56] Malebranche, *De la recherche*, ii. 127; trans. Lennon and Olscamp, 381.

[57] Descartes seems to allude to this view when he remarks that we regard difficult problems as more attractive than simple ones. *Rules for the Direction of the Mind*, in *Philosophical Writings*, ed. Cottingham et al., i. 33.

[58] *De la recherche*, i. 282; trans. Lennon and Olscamp, 138–9.

[59] Ibid. 287; trans. Lennon and Olscamp, 141.

their activities are united by an interest in large measurements, whether of size, age, or distance, which bestow *grandeur* on a wide variety of objects. For instance, while one might expect a coin or an amulet to excite disdain on account of its *petitesse*, Malebranche appeals to its antiquity to capture it in the capacious net of *grandeur*. This free and easy use of a single category strains an already-questionable psychological thesis by extending the claim that people are disposed to feel esteem for things larger than themselves to the claim that they esteem objects with temporally or spatially distant origins. It is not obvious, however, that early-modern theorists of the passions can argue straightforwardly for this point of view. Apart from the problem already mentioned (that one would expect comparatively small objects to arouse scorn) there is the difficulty that our passions for the far away and long ago are normally weaker than those for present objects and states of affairs. If an assessment of an amulet focuses on its spatially and temporally distant origins, our feelings for it, whatever they are, should surely be relatively faint and insignificant.

The impression that Malebranche's interpretations of *grandeur* and the fame of the *faux savants* are over-neatly tailored to one another is reinforced when he shifts his ground and provides a further string of reasons for disparaging antiquarian studies. Their first failing is that they deal with subjects about which we can only gain opinion. Because the study of sensible things does not, by itself, produce the certainty that is the mark of true philosophy, conclusions about them lack solidity, and are consequently less valuable than findings based on incontrovertible first principles. The motives of *faux savants* are also suspect. Their work is not only initially inspired by a passion—their admiration for certain objects—but is sustained by a passion—the self-esteem they gain from it, which itself breeds error. This emotional investment in their opinions guides their research and conceals from them the value of the quest for higher truths. Moreover, since the *grandeur* of the objects they study is itself an illusion, based on an unreflective acceptance of the world as it appears to us, their self-esteem is a kind of charade—a charade which infects their admirers, whose reverence for arcane knowledge in turn stifles their interest in true philosophy.

As well as aiming to expose the pretensions of many of his contemporaries, Malebranche's attack serves the polemical purpose of vindicating the acumen and emotional purity of students of mechanism. Philosophers who study the principles governing tiny particles of matter resist both the blandishments of *grandeur* and the emotional pull exerted on us by the sensible world in order to concentrate on the purely intelligible. In so far as their conclusions are grounded on incontrovertible principles, they possess the certainty that the findings of the *faux savants* lack; and as to motivation, mechanists are not spurred on by the attention of crowds of admirers, since the objects they study do not in general excite or impress. As Malebranche explains, 'Knowledge of opinions is more useful for causing admiration than knowledge of true philosophy.'[60] The dynamic which enhances the reputation and self-esteem of false scholars simply fails to operate. By analysing the relations between *grandeur* and scientific enquiry, Malebranche implicitly takes a stand in an intellectual, and broadly political, debate about the proper direction of scientific research, aligning himself firmly with a mechanist approach. His advocacy of the New Science rests not only on the epistemological status of its results, but also on the related psychological dispositions of its practitioners. Mechanists who interest themselves in the very small have to be able to turn their backs on *grandeur* as this is generally interpreted, a feat which requires emotional strength and application. To acquire scientific knowledge we have to avoid the error of giving in to one of our most pervasive passions—a natural disposition to be impressed by relative size.

This, however, is not the end of the story, since a related and more central manifestation of our perception of *grandeur* is to be found in our attitudes to social rank. Here the same sequence of emotions that sustains the reputation of counterfeit scholars operates to the advantage of princes, officials, and the nobility. The trappings of rank—decorated harnesses, dazzling clothes, the splendour of palaces, or the solemnity of judicial courts—breed reverence in courtiers, lesser officials, and hangers-on, who increase and sustain their own self-esteem by their association with people of high status. The sentiments of a prince, for instance, 'will always be in fashion, his pleasures, passions, games, speech, habits and generally all his actions'.[61] So much so, that courtiers are slaves to a prince's opinions: 'they pass from an inclination to philosophy to an inclination to debauchery, and from a horror of debauchery to a horror of philosophy.'[62]

Malebranche's contempt for courtiers is palpable. Their devotion to the *grandeur* of the prince overwhelms their critical faculties and sets them on a course of mindless servility. But they are only some of the most extreme victims of a phenomenon by which we are all affected.

The reputation of being rich, learned, or virtuous produces in the imagination of those around us, or who are closest to us, dispositions that are very advantageous to us. It prostrates them at our feet; it excites them in our favour; it inspires in them all the impulses that tend to the preservation of our being, and to the increase of our *grandeur*. Therefore men preserve their reputation as a good that they need in order to live comfortably in the world.[63]

---

[60] *De la recherche*, 282; trans. Lennon and Olscamp, 138. Cf. Descartes, *Discourse on the Method of Rightly Conducting one's Reason and Seeking the Truth in the Sciences*, in *Philosophical Writings*, ed. Cottingham *et al.*, i. 147.

[61] Malebranche, *De la recherche*, i. 335; trans. Lennon and Olscamp, 169.

[62] Ibid. 336; trans. Lennon and Olscamp, 169–70.

[63] Ibid. ii. 26; trans. Lennon and Olscamp, 290.

Here, as more famously in the work of Pascal, and less famously in the work of Hobbes, we find the idea that *grandeur* is a kind of power, and that the passions it evokes can readily be manipulated. Men who have *grandeur*, Malebranche tells us, do their best to preserve it. Magistrates, as Pascal adds, know how to use the powerful effects of visible greatness.

Their red robes, the ermine in which they swaddle themselves like furry cats, the law courts where they sit in judgement, the fleur de lys, all this august panoply was very necessary. If physicians did not have long gowns and mules, if learned doctors did not wear square caps and robes four times too large, they would never have deceived the world which finds such an authentic display irresistible. If they possessed true justice, and if physicians possessed the true art of healing, they would not need square caps; the majesty of such sciences would command respect in itself. But, as they only possess imaginary sciences, they have to resort to these vain devices in order to strike the imagination, which is their real concern, and this, in fact, is how they win respect.[64]

By exciting our affections, *grandeur* creates the effects of authority, power, and knowledge; and yet this is all, like the Emperor's new clothes, a kind of error or illusion to which we are exposed, and expose ourselves, by the vividness of our imagination and eagerness of our passions.

The disposition to evaluate things by comparison with ourselves leads us, then, to assessments that are mistaken or at best ill-founded. Some of these errors arise when we take ourselves as a fixed point: measured against the self-image of a cobbler, the magistrate in his scarlet and ermine takes on the qualities of greatness. But seventeenth-century analyses of *grandeur* further unsettle the scale of comparison around which the term is defined when, employing Malebranche's third argument, they turn it back on to the self. We do not simply feel passions for other people and things that reflect their *grandeur* in relation to us. Simultaneously, we assess our own *grandeur* in the same passionate light as we bring to bear on the rest of the world. Both terms of the comparisons we make are thereby rendered unstable. This further complexity draws our attention once again to the fact that the self experiencing passion is not simply a detached rational maximizer aiming, however ineptly, at its own well-being. It is formed by its own passionate history, and may therefore be timorous, ambitious, loving, or mean. As well as directing its passionate nature outwards, it brings it to bear on itself, so that timorous people are liable to underestimate their own powers, proud people want to think well of themselves, and so on.

Among the passions to which our nature disposes us is vanity or vainglory, a disposition to think excessively well of ourselves by being thought well of.[65]

[64] *Pensées*, 44. See C. Lazzeri, *Force et justice dans la politique de Pascal* (Paris, 1993), 39–55.
[65] Malebranche, *De la recherche*, i. 289 f; trans. Lennon and Olscamp, 143. Cf. Hobbes, *Leviathan*, 46; Spinoza, *Ethics*, IV. P 58.

We initially evaluate ourselves from the standpoint of others who evaluate us; if they admire us, we take on this assessment. What is emphasized here is the relational character of *grandeur* and the passions that contribute to it. I admire the magistrate, and as long as I admire him I am deferent to his opinions, anxious for his approbation, desirous of pleasing him—in short I sustain his *grandeur* not only by the way I behave, but also by the way I feel. The magistrate's *grandeur* therefore depends to some extent on me—indeed, it is hard not to think anachronistically of Hegel's master and slave when reading Malebranche's analysis of this dependence. 'The general of an army depends on all his soldiers because they all hold him in regard. Often, this slavery produces his valour [*générosité*], and the desire for the esteem of those who have him in view often obliges him to sacrifice other, more reasonable and more pressing desires.'[66]

Why, though, do Malebranche and his contemporaries regard the self-esteem which arises from the *grandeur* of public officials, scholars, and so on as generally excessive, erroneous, vain? After all, one might argue along Hobbesian lines that the power of such people is real enough, so that their self-esteem, or as Hobbes calls it, their glory, is perfectly appropriate. The first part of the answer lies in the mismatch we have already considered between the objects of *grandeur* and the passions they evoke. Admiration and reverence should be proportional to the greatness of an object. To revere God, or to revere someone for their authentic wisdom, is appropriate. But to revere a pompous fool on account of his scarlet robes, or a would-be savant for his spouting of ancient texts, is not. The next stage of the answer makes use of the idea that the ineptness of our passions, our disposition to love badly, extends to ourselves. Just as we are prone to be dazzled by the trappings and performances of others, so our own deceive us. The magistrate is impressed by his robes, the counterfeit scholar by his ingenuity and learning; they lose sight of themselves as ordinary men tricked out in a little brief authority. While these self-assessments are no less ludicrous and off the mark than comparable assessments of others, this fact is especially difficult for us to recover and apply. As Pascal remarks, 'That something so obvious as the vanity of the world should be so little recognised that people find it odd and surprising to be told that it is foolish to seek *grandeur*; that is most remarkable.'[67]

The difficulty we experience in realizing that the *grandeur* we attribute to ourselves and others consists not in an accurate understanding of properties that they actually possess, but in properties we attribute to them on the basis of our own passions, is an instance of the objectification which, we found earlier, is seen as a central feature of our psychology. We are prone to admire others for their *grandeur* and to admire the same trait in ourselves. What we

---

[66] *De la recherche*, ii. 84; trans. Lennon and Olscamp, 343.   [67] *Pensées*, 16.

fail to see is that *grandeur* itself is not a property of them or us, but consists in a set of relations underpinned by certain dispositions—in an initial disposition to evaluate comparatively and a susceptibility to scale; in the reverence and submission that these dispositions create; and in the pride and self-esteem that they engender. If people came to see the magistrate as a man much like themselves, his *grandeur* would collapse. To understand the way that *grandeur* works, and to overcome the errors embodied in our passions, we have to come to think of ourselves relationally, as creatures who feed emotionally off each other, often against our better judgement. At the same time, we have to learn to question our natural disposition to evaluate objects on the basis of their size, and to circumvent our feelings of esteem and deference for social rank.

It remains to ask, however, how far we should try to offset these tendencies, and indeed, to what extent this is possible. As we saw in Chapter 5, Malebranche argues that our inclination to feel submissive in the face of people more powerful than ourselves is both natural and generally well adapted; so we presumably should not root it out completely. If the passions are to function as they should and promote our well-being as embodied creatures, we need to remain susceptible to *grandeur* in the sensible world while avoiding esteem or disdain that is excessive or inappropriate. But when is esteem excessive? When is it inappropriate? A courtier might well protest that his well-being depends on exactly the kinds of deference and admiration that Malebranche and his fellow philosophers regard as erroneous. And Malebranche would no doubt reply that the courtier is more deeply implicated in the dynamics of *grandeur* than he cares to acknowledge. Both might be right. Underlying their diverging viewpoints, however, there is an ambivalence within Malebranche's account, a pull between the claim that the passions sustaining deference are God-given and functional, and the claim that they promote a corrupt society. To survive, we need to be susceptible to the *grandeur* of powerful people and things. At the same time, this very susceptibility creates in us damaging social and intellectual loyalties.

Overcoming the errors associated with *grandeur* is therefore a delicate business. In social life, we must become capable of interrupting the sequence of emotions sparked off by our initial esteem for size; although we may tug our forelocks in the face of power, we must learn not to transfer our admiration for the mighty to ourselves, and must avoid self-sustaining patterns of attachment. At the same time, we must cultivate the right kinds of susceptibility to relative scale. This requirement is important in all walks of life, but is particularly pressing in philosophy. Christian philosophers such as Descartes and Malebranche, and non-Christians such as Spinoza, agree that *grandeur* attaches to the infinite, and that God, however understood, is worthy of esteem. Moreover, this correct interpretation of scale overrides all the others, and is manifested in relative indifference to social rank or physical size. Natural philosophers

who devote themselves to studying comparatively small objects such as insects
or atoms do not become impervious to *grandeur*; instead they interpret it in a
different way, transferring the *grandeur* of God to his entire creation, rather
than simply to those parts of it which are, by human standards, large. This
move enables Malebranche to claim that the disposition to respond to things
in terms of scale is a deeply rooted psychological trait and explains a wide
range of attitudes, some well judged, others mistaken. True philosophers who
bring their philosophical understanding to bear on *grandeur* itself are able to
transform our flawed disposition to take account of the relative size of sensible things into a fruitful understanding of scale, which rises above our sensible horizons and sloughs off the errors they engender. A sceptic might wonder
whether, given the terms of this account, there could be a godless mechanist
whose interest in the very small was not sustained by an appreciation of the
vastness of creation and the puniness of humankind; or whether the vastness
of nature itself could excite a secular esteem, manifested in a fascination with
some of its tiny parts. But these are not among the problems addressed by
Malebranche.

Error as Inconstancy

We need finally to consider a further feature of the passions which undercuts
our ability to acquire knowledge: their intrinsic restlessness, captured in the
analogy between passions and waves driven by the wind[68] and more solemnly
enunciated in Bacon's claim that the affections abhor lengthy investigation.
Why are the affections so changeable? One explanation, which itself divides
into several strands, relies on the claim that they register bodily motions and
change as these change. Since the animal spirits are continually on the move,
so are our passions.[69] First, our emotions are easily disrupted because our most
powerful passions tend to be evoked by our sensory perceptions, which are
themselves subject to changes over which we have only limited control. Sounds,
scents, or bodily sensations can easily spark off associations and alter the
weather of our souls, so that we find ourselves feeling unaccountably irritable,
low, or serene, regardless of the task in hand. The same is true, secondly, of
our other ideas of sensible things, so that fantasies and uninvited memories can
also have this effect. Thirdly, the passions have their own dynamic patterns,
as, for example, when pleasures pall and give way to new desires.

   The fact that the passions are rarely still, combined with their forcefulness,
enables them to undercut our efforts to achieve understanding by damaging

---

[68] e.g. Spinoza, *Ethics*, III. P 59 s.
[69] Descartes, Letter to Princess Elizabeth, 1 Sept. 1645, in *Correspondence*, 264.

our concentration. Even if we can settle our affections sufficiently to embark on the demanding intellectual labour of searching for truth, their instability ensures that they are unlikely to stay quiet for long. Malebranche is eloquent on this score. The least impression from the senses or passions, he tells us, breaks the mind's closest attention, and the flow of spirits and blood sweeps the mind along with it, pushing it continually toward sensible objects. Only rarely does the mind think of resisting, because it is too pleasant to follow this flood of feeling, and too exhausting to oppose it.[70]

A further explanation for this feature of our passions derives from the view that they are caused by modifications of the will. Because, as we have seen, the will is never satisfied, our loves and joys quickly grow stale, and unless God's grace enables the will to find the good for which it is searching, it is condemned to wander. Its very restlessness 'is one of the principal causes of our ignorance and of the errors into which we fall about an infinity of subjects'.[71] This inefficiency, if you like, is made worse by the quality of the will's own passion, for it does not search idly, diligently, or carefully, but is parched by a burning thirst, driven by anxiety and desire. In its desperation, it fixes now on this, now on that, barely pausing to see what it has found, perpetually goaded by its own disappointment.[72]

When it is extreme, this restlessness of the passions is akin to madness. As Hobbes explains, to have passions indifferently for everything is giddiness and distraction;[73] and people who, 'entering into discourse, are snatched from their purpose by everything that comes into their thoughts, into so many, and so long digressions and parentheses that they utterly lose themselves', are subject to a folly which is sometimes caused by excessive wonder or want of experience, sometimes by an eccentric perception of *grandeur* 'by which that seems great to him which other men think a trifle'.[74] Madness and knowledge are here held to be opposed. By making us restless, our passions undermine the steadiness and concentration that the pursuit of knowledge requires.

The aspects of the passions explored in this chapter suggest that they are far from friendly to knowledge-seekers. They distort our image of the world by the self-centred perspective they impose: feeling varies with time, space, and scale, all of which are measured from the body. Their restless dynamic kidnaps concentration, condemning us to fragmented and transitory *aperçus*. Moreover, these unreliable emotions contribute to an objectified conception of the world which we must overcome if we are to understand the part we ourselves play in constructing what we take to be reality. The passions, it seems, are an epistemological disaster. And yet, since we sometimes manage to lessen our ignorance, they presumably do not form a total barrier to knowledge. One

[70] *De la recherche*, i. 469; trans. Lennon and Olscamp, 249.
[71] Ibid. ii. 5; trans. Lennon and Olscamp, 270.
[72] Ibid. i. 405–6; trans. Lennon and Olscamp, 212. [73] *Leviathan*, 54. [74] Ibid. 51.

way to escape them, examined with particular care by a number of seventeenth-century philosophers, is to cultivate a kind of reasoning that is proof against their malign influence. This possibility will be explored in Chapter 8. Another tactic, not incompatible with the first, is to use the passions to initiate and sustain our search for knowledge. The various passions capable of kindling our interest and reviving our flagging enthusiasm will be discussed in Chapter 9. Finally, some seventeenth-century philosophers regard knowing as an emotional state. A particular emotional temperament is not, for them, merely a condition of knowledge but an aspect of knowledge itself. Their position is the subject of Chapter 10.

8

Dispassionate Scientia

When Bacon remarks in *The Advancement of Learning* that 'they be the clouds of error which descend in the storms of passions and perturbations',[1] he poses an obvious problem: if passion damages and hinders our attempts to acquire knowledge, how can its destructive potential be deflected or contained? Anyone who aspires to understanding must, it seems, confront this problem, and seventeenth-century philosophers inherit and elaborate a range of solutions to it, all tailored to an overarching conception of the kinds of insight that we are capable of achieving. In everyday life, we work with ideas derived from sensory experience which may be more or less well supported but fall short of certainty. Ordinarily, we reason about these ideas, that is to say, we subject at least some of them to critical reflection, as when I ask myself whether that bird really is a sparrowhawk, or wonder whether those are tears of grief or joy. A capacity for informal reasoning is thus a 'natural' skill which we exercise with more or less care and determination in the normal course of events. We are also able, however, to think critically about the standards we use to assess our ideas, a second-order reflectiveness that enables us to articulate and refine them into codified rules for arriving at conclusions that are not just highly probable but certain. By applying such standards conscientiously, we can, in the view of many early-modern philosophers, recognize clear and distinct ideas for what they are, and formulate truth-preserving rules of inference. Thus equipped, we can move from one true idea to another, either starting with principles and following out chains of inference proceeding from them, or starting with a conclusion that stands in need of establishing, and trying to fill in the chain that leads back from it to the relevant principles. Either way, the truth of any one idea is guaranteed by its place in a sequence and is ultimately anchored in a principle which, being self-evident, needs no demonstration.

To rest secure in this orthodox conception of *scientia*, its advocates needed to be able to reassure themselves that we can purge our reasoning of the distortions and errors generated by the passions. But since these are acknowledged to play a powerful and pervasive role in our thought, there are no grounds for expecting that this will be easy or straightforward. The problem of how to

[1] Ed. G. W. Kitchin (London, 1973), 56.

tame or transcend the passions in order to attain an unbiased understanding of ourselves and the world therefore loomed large, and several solutions, or part-solutions, were proposed. The most ambitious of these, organized around the distinction between *scientia*—certain knowledge—and *opinio*—knowledge which is probable—will occupy us in the first part of this chapter.

Sensible and Intelligible Ideas

Many early-modern philosophers take it for granted that we can only be certain that a claim is correct if we are sure that our understanding of it is not distorted by the errors to which our emotions expose us. *Scientia* must therefore be free from the epistemological effects of passion. To see why knowledge of this sort is regarded as attainable, it is helpful to begin by considering the distinction between intelligible and sensible ideas which is used to mark a division between ideas of things that can be sensed, and ideas of things—whether virtues, numbers, thoughts, or God—that are in principle imperceptible. Sensible ideas are of several kinds: while our most basic way of acquiring them is through sensory perception, we can also have ideas of sensible things we are not actually perceiving, by remembering or imagining them. I imagine rose-red Petra as a city I could see with my own eyes; and even when I remember a conversation, for instance, without entertaining any visual or auditory image, I remember it as something I sensed while it was occurring. Ideas of sensible things, or ideas immediately derived from them such as memories, are contrasted with pure perceptions—ideas that either do not depend on sensible ideas at all or are related to them more remotely. Using the stronger version of this contrast, Descartes explains that our sensible ideas of roughly triangular things do not help us to gain an idea of a perfect triangle.[2] Echoing his view, Malebranche asserts that the mind does not need to form corporeal images in the brain to represent spiritual things, universals, common notions, the idea of a perfect being, or the idea of extension.[3] All these ideas are gained by the understanding or intellect on its own, and their objects, along with the ideas themselves, are described as intelligible. As Descartes's example suggests, the standard of scientific knowledge is set by mathematics, which deals with intelligible objects: with perfect figures, numbers, and various operations, none of them sensible. If other kinds of enquiry are to lay claim to scientific status, they too must

---

[2] *Objections and Replies to the Meditations*, in *The Philosophical Writings of Descartes*, ed. Cottingham, *et al.* (Cambridge, 1984–91), i. 262, 'Fifth set of Replies'.

[3] *De la recherche de la vérité*, ed. G. Rodis Lewis, in *Œuvres complètes*, ed. A. Robinet (2nd edn, Paris, 1972), i. 66; trans. T. M. Lennon and P. L. Olscamp as *The Search after Truth* (Columbus, Oh., 1980), 16.

meet this standard.[4] Hence the conception of moral science as dealing with various abstract virtues and a non-sensible notion of the good. And hence the Cartesian conception of natural philosophy as the study of mathematically defined bodies. We have ideas of particular sensible things, such as this gold ring or that gold salt-cellar, and from these we form a sensible idea of gold as a metal that is yellow, shiny, soft, and so on. But this latter idea plays a comparatively marginal role in natural science, which works with an intelligible idea of the metal, defining it in terms of the sizes and motions of its particles. We cannot perceive this idea with our senses, and must rely on the eye of the mind instead.

How, though, are these two kinds of ideas, sensible and intelligible, related to our passions? As we have already seen, our strongest affections are held to be excited by things that are present to sense, whereas weaker passions are integral to memory and imagination. Much of the store of sensible ideas that underpins our everyday knowledge of the world and guides our actions will therefore be passionate, and the beliefs or opinions we derive from it will be susceptible to the distortions these passions impose. Turning to *scientia*, we need to ask whether the fact that this focuses on ideas of intelligible things has any bearing on the resistance of scientific enquiry to passion, and this question is best approached by considering what it is about our ideas of sensible things that excites our emotions. Sensory perceptions are held to evoke strong passions because their objects are present and, being present, are in a position to benefit or harm us now. Moving on to other kinds of sensible ideas such as memories and fantasies, their power to arouse affection derives from the fact that, although their objects are obviously not present, these ideas are nevertheless grounded on sensory perception in that they are memories of things perceived and fantasies about things with perceptible elements. When we remember sensible objects and states of affairs, we sometimes visualize them in a certain spatial relation to us—for example, I may remember looking at Bernini's obelisk from a particular angle or hearing a flute concerto from the back of the room. Equally, some of our fantasies incorporate spatial relations between ourselves and other things: I may imagine Mount Everest rising above me, or a friend opening the door to let me in. Needless to say, not all our memories or fantasies involve this sort of imagery, but even in cases where it does not occur there may be something that marks a memory, say, as a recollection of something sensible. When we remember sensible things, we conceive of them as objects that were present to us, that is, as things that once stood in a certain spatial relation to us. We may not recall what this spatial relationship was, but

---

[4] Descartes, *Rules*, in *Philosophical Writings*, ed. Cottingham *et al.*, i, rule 12. The relation of mathematics to the sciences in the early-modern period is much debated. See S. Gaukroger, *Descartes: An Intellectual Biography* (Oxford, 1996), 104–86; W. R. Shea, *The Magic of Numbers and Motion* (Canton, Mass., 1991).

we nevertheless understand the objects in question as the sorts of things to which we can be, or once were, spatially related. A comparable point holds for many of our fantasies and speculations about the future. Consider, for example, imagining oneself walking along an Amsterdam canal in 1654, or wondering with whom one will have supper.

It is in virtue of this feature that sensory perceptions, memories, and fantasies of sensible things all excite our affections. Our strongest passions are integral to sensory perceptions because these represent things that can help or hurt us at the moment, to which we would do well to attend if we are to preserve our well-being. When nothing in the immediate environment arouses any significant emotion (the room is quiet and still, its contents anodyne) we nevertheless remain attuned to the present, disposed to respond to an alarming noise or an opening door. Weaker passions come with memories and imaginings, which are conceptual simulacra of sensory perceptions and mimic the properties of the present. Remembering an occasion when he was slighted, a man may feel again the anger that consumed him at the time and rehearse the more-or-less well-judged passions which contributed to his attempt to foster his well-being; but the anger and its bodily manifestations are fainter now. Similarly, so one may hope, the wonder I experience when I imagine Mount Everest is nothing to what I would feel if I were to see the real thing. This analysis is deeply contentious. It is arguable that it overemphasizes the visual and thus the spatial character of remembering and imagining, and that it offers an unduly simple account of the relations between our responses to present and absent objects. Nevertheless, it provides a way to explain and defend the hypothesis that sensible ideas arouse our passions and intelligible ones do not. Sensible ideas arouse our passions because they are ideas of things which either do or can occupy the same spatial field as we do, and are therefore capable of affecting us for good or ill. Given that our passions are designed to ensure that we attend to our well-being as embodied creatures, their objects are the sorts of things about which it makes sense to feel emotions such as fear or envy. Intelligible ideas, by contrast, lack spatial location in relation to us; although a particular imperfect triangle can be in front of me or to the left, an idea of a perfect triangle cannot. And something to which I have no spatial relation cannot affect my body, and thus cannot directly arouse my passions. Even the idea of extension—itself spatial—is not spatially related to *us*. To contemplate it, we have to form an intelligible idea which does not represent extension as itself possessing spatial relations to other things.

If sensible and intelligible ideas have incommensurable spatial properties, their temporal qualities are similarly divided. In the preceding chapter we saw that our passions for objects that are present are generally held to be more intense than those for things in the past and future. We can now see that we feel passions about past or future states when our memories or fantasies are of sensible objects which were or could be present, and which therefore did, or could, help or harm us. Once again, however, there is a strong contrast with intelligible ideas, which—being eternal or unchanging—have no temporal relation to us at all. As such, they are not the sorts of ideas that arouse passion.

These arguments suggest that intelligible ideas possess features which make them resistant to passion. The passions run off them like water off a duck's back and, in so far as *scientia* consists in the perception of intelligible ideas and their relations, it too will give the passions nothing to grip on to. The view that the intelligible ideas linked together in scientific demonstrations do not excite passion might seem to solve our problem: if *scientia* does not move the emotions it will not be susceptible to the errors that flow from passion-laden ideas. But this conclusion is double-edged. If the intelligible ideas that contribute to this kind of knowledge do not arouse desires or pleasure, a further question arises: what prompts us to bother with *scientia*? What sort of hold does it have over us? What moves us to struggle our way through demonstrations to an understanding that guarantees itself as correct? A first reply falls back on the view that, even if *scientia* itself is passion-free, our affections play a vital part in promoting and sustaining our search for understanding. We come equipped with passions which make us responsive to the world around us and set us on the path to learning. As we saw in Chapter 5, *admiratio* or wonder is thought to be peculiarly well adapted to this task,[5] since it is what we feel for things that strike us as novel or surprising, and by prompting us to learn and retain new information it sows the seeds of a more systematic kind of knowledge. As Hobbes explains, 'it excites the appetite of knowing the cause',[6] and as Descartes points out, people who lack it are usually exceptionally ignorant.[7] Wonder is therefore agreed to be useful, but its status remains debated, and the uncertainty surrounding it betrays a deep anxiety about the wisdom of depending on passion to gain *scientia*. On the one hand, there seems to be no alternative; but on the other hand, there remains a significant danger that the errors attaching to passion will damage the purity of our perceptions.

Several attempts to neutralize this threat can be found in early-modern discussions of wonder and the passions connected with it. To take a notable example, Descartes tries to break the association between the character of the bodily motions caused by passions and the changeability of the passions themselves by attributing to wonder certain physiological peculiarities. Whereas all the other passions are accompanied by changes in the heart or blood, wonder alone consists in a rush of spirits to the brain which serves to deprive the body of the means to consider anything else. It does not prompt us to move, nor

---

[5] The idea that philosophy begins in wonder goes back to Plato (*Theaetetus* 155d) and is reiterated by Aristotle (*Metaphysics* 982^{b}12).

[6] *Leviathan*, ed. R. Tuck (Cambridge, 1991), 42.

[7] *The Passions of the Soul*, in *Philosophical Writings*, ed. Cottingham *et al.*, i. 75.

do we blush, tremble, or display any other corporeal sign of emotion. Instead, when wonder strikes us, the concentration of spirits in the brain keeps our sense-organs trained on whatever it is that has arrested our attention.[8] Rather puzzlingly, Descartes goes on to qualify this account by allowing that wonder is, after all, compatible with movement, and contrasting it with astonishment, an excessive version of the same passion which immobilizes us completely. Wonder at Bernini's obelisk may prompt me to walk round it and look at it from all angles; but if I am astonished I will simply gawp at one elevation, too overwhelmed to investigate further. The view that there are two ways of respond-ing passionately to the unfamiliar, one excessively constant, the other constructive and appropriate, is fairly common. Bacon, for instance, had made use of the same distinction, explaining that 'astonishment is caused by the fixing of the mind on one object of cogitation, whereby it doth not spatiate and transcur, as it useth; for in wonder the spirits fly not, as in fear; but only settle and are made less apt to move'.[9] Malebranche appeals to a different, but strictly com-parable and indeed overlapping, pair of passions. When we wonder, we become attentive, and the object of our emotion is represented distinctly (*nettement*) to the mind. But only when wonder makes us curious (*curieux*) do we examine an object from all sides and put ourselves in a position to make a reliable judge-ment about it. So it is only when wonder provokes curiosity that we embark on the kind of exploration from which we can learn.[10]

The physiological configuration of wonder outlined by Descartes, and adapted by Malebranche, is designed to emphasize the features that fit this passion to be the well-spring of knowledge. Since *admiratio* is itself a kind of attentiveness or concentration, it can defeat the restlessness that is otherwise a hallmark of the affections and contributes to their power to hinder enquiry. Moreover, wonder is in the head. It is untainted by the bodily motions that trouble and distract us. These cerebral connotations come to the surface in Malebranche's characteristically nervous hope that, as long as we are careful, we may be able to enlist wonder in the search for truth since, of all the passions, it least affects the heart, and therefore does not excite motions which corrupt reason.[11] But while its stillness distinguishes it from the other passions and carries connota-tions of tranquillity which ally it with knowledge, the strong connection between passion and movement puts this interpretation under considerable strain.

An indication that the struggle to detoxify wonder or admiration could not easily be resolved is evident in a dispute as to whether it is a passion at all. Descartes argues, as we have seen, that the movement of the animal spirits to

    [8] Ibid. 71.
    [9] *Sylvana Sylvanum or a Natural History in Ten Centuries*, in *Works*, ed. J. Spedding *et al.* (London, 1857–61), ii. 570.
    [10] *De la recherche*, ii. 132; trans. Lennon and Olscamp, 386.
    [11] Ibid. 130; trans. Lennon and Olscamp, 385.

the brain in which wonder consists is enough to qualify it as a passion. But two of his most careful readers were less sure. Malebranche sits on the fence, allowing that wonder is a passion, though an imperfect one.[12] Spinoza resolves the problem differently, concluding that wonder is not an affect after all. Our train of thought is held together by the associations between our ideas, but when we encounter something new, we acquire an idea which we do not associate with anything, so that the train of our thought is broken and sticks at the alien idea until it can move forward again.[13] This state of affairs provokes wonder which is not, however, a passion, because it cannot be construed as a feeling that marks an increase or decrease in our power, or as a manifestation of our striving for power. On the contrary, it is an interruption of these.[14] Spinoza's analysis, which takes seriously the claim that wonder is provoked by complete novelty, once again underlines the connection of passion with movement, both from one idea to the next and within the body.

A further sign of the difficulties involved in enlisting the passions to promote *scientia* can be found in disagreement over exactly which passions can best play this role. Malebranche, doubting whether so static an affection as wonder can fulfil the task allotted to it, opts for a slightly more mobile passion— curiosity.[15] In doing so, however, he steps out on to dangerous ground. For the very mobility that makes curiosity attractive simultaneously introduces the destabilizing restlessness which is one of the passions' principal flaws and can give rise, as Hobbes explains, to 'a defect of the mind which men call levity, which betrayeth also mobility of the spirits, but in excess'.[16] For Hobbes, as for Malebranche, levity is distinct from the passion of curiosity, a hunting-out of causes and effects which, as Hobbes puts it, 'is nothing but seeking, or the faculty of invention, which the Latins call Sagacitas and Solertia'.[17] These writers turn the mobility of curiosity into a strength by identifying it with the inferential movement from cause to effect, and with the way the mind ranges over hypotheses as it searches for these deductive connections, 'as a spaniel ranges the field, till he finds a scent; or as a man should run over the alphabet, to start a rhyme'.[18] Perhaps the most determined exponent of this interpretation is Hobbes, who gives curiosity a special status. Unlike passions such as joy or sadness, it is only possessed by humans, who are unique in their desire to know natural causes.[19] It is because they are endowed with curiosity

---

[12] Ibid. 119; trans. Lennon and Olscamp, 375.

[13] *Ethics*, in *The Collected Works of Spinoza*, ed. E. Curley (Princeton, 1985), vol. i, III. P 52.

[14] Ibid. III. Definition of the Affects, IV, p. 532.

[15] For a comparable account of the role of curiosity see Bernard Lamy, *Entretien sur le science* (1684), ed. F. Girbal and P. Clair (Paris, 1966), 54–8.

[16] *The Elements of Law*, ed. F. Tönnies (2nd edn, London, 1969), 50. At the limit, excessive mobility of the spirits and passions is seen as a kind of madness, a conception of insanity explored in Michel Foucault's account of asylums as a way to confine the mad, to enforce stillness on them. See his *Madness and Civilisation: A History of Insanity in the Age of Reason*, trans. R. Howard (London, 1967).

[17] *Leviathan*, 21. [18] Ibid. 22. [19] Ibid. 42.

PLATE 3. Jean Cousin the Elder, *Eva Prima Pandora* (*c*.1549)

that people impose names, and are thus capable of arriving at the definitions that are the beginning of philosophy.[20] This benign reading is set against a range of more ominous interpretations of curiosity which emphasize the very changeability that *scientia* is supposed to overcome.[21] Reynolds, for example, describes it at one point as *ambulatio animae*, the walking up and down of the soul or ranging of a mind that lacks purpose and concentration, and elsewhere glosses it as prying into other people's business.[22] Still more pessimistically, Burton identifies curiosity as the source of all sin, the passion that prompted Pandora to open the box and release disease into the world.[23] These connotations of curiosity are portrayed in a mysterious painting by Jean Cousin the Elder, inscribed *Eva Prima Pandora*,[24] of a beautiful and impassive woman reclining on the ground, her head framed by a rocky arch beyond which is a stretch of water and, far in the distance, a city. (See Pl. 3.) On her right side

---

[20] *Elements of Law*, 45. Here Hobbes identifies curiosity and admiration.

[21] Augustine, *Confessions*, v. 3; x. 35. See also H. Blumenberg, *The Legitimacy of the Modern Age*, trans. R. M. Wallace (Cambridge, Mass., 1983), 309–23. On the history of these aspects of curiosity see R. Newhauser, 'Towards a History of Human Curiosity: A Prolegomenon to its Medieval Phase', *Deutsche Vierteljahrsschrift für Literaturwissenschaft und Geistesgeschichte*, 56 (1982), 559–75; L. Marin, 'Mimesis et description: Ou la curiosité à la méthode de l'âge de Montaigne à celui de Descartes', in E. Cropper *et al.* (eds.), *Documentary Culture: Florence and Rome from Grand Duke Ferdinand I to Pope Alexander VII* (Baltimore, 1992), 23–47; N. Kenny, ' "Curiosité" and Philosophical Poetry in the French Renaissance', *Renaissance Studies*, 5 (1991), 263–76.

[22] *A Treatise of the Passions and Faculties of the Soul of Man* (London, 1640), 175.

[23] *The Anatomy of Melancholy*, ed. T. Faulkner *et al.* (Oxford, 1989–94), i. 122 f.

[24] The painting (*c*.1549) is in the Musée du Louvre.

are the accoutrements of Eve—she holds an apple branch, and leans her elbow on a skull, reminding us that through her we are mortal. On her left, in accordance with Renaissance retellings of the story of Pandora, are two vases: a highly decorated red one which stands on a step more or less at the centre of the composition and is open, and a partially concealed white one over which she places a hand, around which a snake is entwined. The complex iconography of this picture has been much studied, and various hypotheses have offered to explain it.[25] The association of Pandora with Eve, and of both with evil, is not, however, in doubt. Pandora is exquisitely beautiful, but deadly; her disobedient curiosity releases unhappiness into the world, which itself becomes still, sombre, and lifeless—a living tomb.

When wonder gives rise to curiosity, it is succeeded by a profoundly ambivalent passion, replete with the risk of error. Moreover, even philosophers who believe that wonder alone can stimulate an interest in knowing the causes of things are forced to admit that the search on which it launches us is at the same time a sequence of further passions. If we are to acquire more than the promise of knowledge, it is generally agreed, wonder must give way to a desire to grapple with problems, to persist in our attempts to solve them or pursue the implications of our current understanding; and desire, as we have seen, is also dangerous. It is, after all, only a fragile and defeasible passion which has built into it a potential for error that threatens to undercut its very aim. The attempt to ground the pursuit of knowledge on our passions consequently strikes many philosophers as inherently unstable and unsatisfactory, a compromise which cannot guarantee that our attempts to acquire *scientia* will not be wrecked by undetected error. If intelligible ideas do not themselves excite joyfulness or desire, so that these qualities must be generated from outside by passions, the prospects for scientific understanding are poor. We consequently find in seventeenth-century philosophy an argument to the effect that our dependence on passion can be minimized and counterbalanced by reason itself, which has a power both to constrain and excite our emotions. Even if the pursuit of understanding begins in wonder, and is correspondingly vulnerable, it rapidly evolves into a form of investigation which is free from passion and the errors it induces.

Intellectual Emotions

One influential interpretation of the features of reasoning that make it resistant to passion draws to some degree on an older conception of ecstasy or rapture, a condition in which we leave sense behind us, outrun our bodies,[26] and

---

[25] See E. and D. Panofsky, *Pandora's Box* (New York, 1965), 55–67. On the vases see ibid. 14–26; J. Guillaume, 'Cleopatra Nova Pandora', *Gazette des Beaux-Arts*, 80 (1972), 185–94.
[26] Reynolds, *Treatise on the Passions*, 8–9.

are carried outside ourselves.[27] This phenomenon is described in more sober terms, and from the viewpoint of an external observer, by Descartes, who explains that 'When the soul is distracted by an ecstasy or deep contemplation, we see that the whole body remains without sensation, even though it has various objects touching it.'[28] While the bodily insensibility that betrays religious or intellectual rapture is acknowledged to be an extreme and comparatively rare state of withdrawal, something comparable to it is nevertheless regarded as an aspect of the kind of reasoning that constitutes *scientia*. To be sure, reasoning of this sort does not involve the complete shutting-down of the body; but it nevertheless requires a retreat from the thoughts that the body provokes in us, together with a meditative attentiveness to the clear and distinct ideas revealed by the light of the mind. This common view is widely expressed. It is implicit in the opening of the *Meditations*, where Descartes spells out for his readers the conditions most conducive to philosophical thought. 'So today I have expressly rid my mind of all worries and arranged for myself a clear stretch of free time. I am here quite alone, and at last I will devote myself sincerely and without reservation to the demolition of my opinions.'[29] It is also articulated by Malebranche, who urges us that 'those who wish to approach the truth in order to be illumined by its light must begin by depriving themselves of pleasure. They must carefully avoid everything that touches or agreeably distracts the mind. For the senses and passions must be silent if one wishes to hear the word of truth, since retreat from the world and contempt for all sensible things are as necessary for perfection of the mind as for the conversion of the heart.'[30] In fact, Malebranche is confident that, if only we could retreat entirely from sensation and passion and escape 'into ourselves', we would easily discover the most abstract and difficult truths known and would never fall into error.[31] But he also realizes, of course, that this is impossible; however much we withdraw, our senses and emotions remain with us, and we can sometimes be put off by the least flash of light, the buzzing of a fly, or a sudden recollection.[32] So while solitariness and peace of mind may encourage intellectual concentration, they cannot guarantee it.[33]

[27] See e.g. Aquinas, *Summa Theologiae*, ed. and trans. the Dominican Fathers (London, 1964–80), 1a. 2ae. 28.

[28] *Optics*, in *Philosophical Writings*, ed. Cottingham *et al.*, i. 164.

[29] *Meditations on First Philosophy*, in *Philosophical Writings*, ed. Cottingham *et al.*, ii. 12. See also *Discourse*, ibid. i. 116.

[30] *De la recherche*, ii. 50 f; trans. Lennon and Olscamp, 314.

[31] Ibid. 51; trans. Lennon and Olscamp, 314. Ibid. i. 16; trans. Lennon and Olscamp, p. xxiii.

[32] Ibid. i. 25; trans. Lennon and Olscamp, p. xxix. Descartes makes the same point. 'It seems to me very true that, as long as the mind is united to the body, it cannot withdraw itself from the senses whenever it is stimulated with great force by internal or external objects.' Letter to Arnauld, 29 July 1648, in *Philosophical Writings*, ed. Cottingham *et al.*, iii. *Correspondence*, 356.

[33] On Descartes's use of an Augustinian notion of meditation and revelation see G. Hatfield, 'The Senses and the Fleshless Eye: The *Meditations* as Cognitive Exercises', in A. O. Rorty (ed.), *Essays on Descartes' Meditations* (Berkeley and Los Angeles, 1986), 45–79.

Fortunately, perhaps, our capacity to pursue *scientia* does not depend entirely on minimizing the distractions stemming from the body. Reasoning itself, like ecstasy, is held to have compelling qualities which, once we have embarked on it, encourage us and help us to withstand the disruptive onslaughts of passion. The attractiveness of reasoning and the power it exerts over us are initially conveyed through several metaphors which we have come across already. Most familiar is the association of reason with sight (and, less prominently, with hearing),[34] the counterpoint between the clear-sightedness of intellection and the fogginess of other kinds of thought. Blind desire, blind curiosity, blind passion, and blind Cupid are commonplace images. Sensory perception, too, is blind, as Descartes implies when he remarks that living without philosophizing is like having one's eyes closed and never trying to open them.[35] More strangely still, the limitations of sight are brought out in Descartes's self-consuming analogy between rays of light and a blind man's stick.[36] The ostensible point of the comparison is to show, among other things, how light passes instantaneously from the sun to the eye, just as movements at the point of the stick are transferred simultaneously to the blind man's hand. But it conveys much more than this. Our eyes are no better at providing satisfactory representations of the world than the scrapings of the stick so that as long as we depend on them we shall be stumbling around in the dark. Only when we learn to reason clearly shall we be cured, like the blind men to whom Christ restored their sight, and step into the light; and just as no one who can see would choose blindness, reason removes difficulties and holds out opportunities previously beyond the bounds of imagination. The new level of capability and vision into which it releases us makes the idea of nostalgia for our previous selves hard to take seriously.

This optimistic view of the power of reason is advocated in more detailed portrayals of its constraining force. The conviction that, as Reynolds expresses it, 'things presented to the mind in the nakedness and simplicity of their own truth, do gain a more firm assent . . . and fixed intuition . . . [than] those things which come mixed and troubled, dividing the intention of the mind between truth and passion'[37] rests on a visual dialogue between the mind and the things presented to it in the nakedness of truth, and draws once again on familiar images of the passions. The ability of naked ideas to claim our attention and assent is presented as stemming from the fact that, being free from passion, they are not 'troubled' or 'divided'.[38] Lacking the restlessness that is integral

---

[34] Cf. the passage quoted above in which Malebranche speaks of the need to cultivate the capacity to hear the truth.

[35] *Principles*, p. 180, pref. to the Fr. edn. On Descartes's conception of vision see M. Merleau-Ponty, 'The Eye and the Mind', trans. C. Dallery, in J. M. Edie (ed.), *The Primacy of Perception* (Evanston, Ill., 1964), 159–90; D. Judowitz, 'Vision, Representation, and Technology in Descartes', in D. M. Levin (ed.), *Modernity and the Hegemony of Vision* (Berkeley and Los Angeles, 1993), 63–86.

[36] *Optics*, 153.   [37] *Treatise of the Passions*, 70.

[38] Cf. Malebranche, *De la recherche*, ii. 162; trans. Lennon and Olscamp, 414.

to ideas mixed with passion, they possess a kind of steadiness and purity which works on the mind in several ways. Their stability allows it to contemplate them. Their purity ensures that they are accessible to it, regardless of its own dispositions. Moreover, these characteristics in turn evoke steadiness and concentration in the contemplating mind, which consequently gains a firm intuition of the ideas in question. Elements of this transference are reiterated in Descartes's account of intuition,[39] the conception of a clear and attentive mind which proceeds solely from the light of reason, as opposed to the fluctuating testimony of the senses or the deceptive judgement of the imagination. Once more, we find the light of reason purified, so to speak, of sense and passion. Furthermore, intuition is so easy and distinct that there can be no room for doubt about what we are conceiving. Although Descartes here attributes the traits of reason to the mind rather than its ideas, the traits themselves are all in place. The light of reason does not fluctuate—it is steady. Nor is it deceptive —it reveals truth in all its nakedness. The mind that conceives in accordance with the light of reason is correspondingly clear and attentive, and this state makes indubitable understanding not only possible but effortless.[40]

These interactions are also implicitly at work in Malebranche's claim that clear and distinct ideas have a hold over us because, once we understand something clearly, the will can no longer desire any further elucidation of it and gives its assent. The sheer transparency of the truth constrains volition so that, although it remains free, it no longer has any grounds for prolonging its search. Here the steadiness of the ideas presented to the will is matched by the steadiness of the will when it finally comes to rest, a stillness which guarantees that our knowledge of truths is stable and free from fluctuation. Malebranche presents the ideas on which the will settles as in some sense complete: the will cannot require any further elucidation of them because it already knows all there is to know. Like the view that the understanding submits to truth, this argument presupposes that the will can identify a point at which it is rightfully satisfied, and the restless yearnings which give rise to our passions are stilled. For 'it is necessary, as it were, that the will stops uselessly agitating and exhausting itself, and acquiesces with full assurance that she is not mistaken, since there is nothing else to which she can direct the understanding'.[41]

The compelling quality of the pure perceptions revealed by reason derives, too, from the deductive relations between them. While the notion of deduction is understood in various ways,[42] it is agreed that demonstrations consist of

---

[39] *Rules*, rule 14.

[40] On the irresistibility of reasoning in Descartes see L. E. Loeb, 'The Priority of Reason in Descartes', *Philosophical Review*, 99 (1990), 3–43; F. Van de Pitte, 'Intuition and Judgment in Descartes' Theory of Truth', *Journal of the History of Philosophy*, 26 (1988), 453–70.

[41] *De la recherche*, i. 53; trans. Lennon and Olscamp, 9.

[42] See S. Gaukroger, *Cartesian Logic: An Essay on Descartes' Conception of Inference* (Oxford, 1989).

chains of truth-preserving inferences from self-evident premisses. Moreover, these chains interconnect, so that demonstrative knowledge is often seen as forming a whole or totality (or, according to a tradition followed by Descartes, a tree).[43] The contrast between this all-encompassing knowledge and our confused, passionate ideas is sometimes conceived in musical terms, harmonious, orderly knowledge being set over against discordant, cacophonous passion. Bacon resorts to this image when he casts Orpheus, the master of all harmony, as Universal Philosophy.[44] But another characteristic of harmony is that it moves us, and this fact is used to suggest that the very structure of demonstrative reasoning determines its impact and explains our susceptibility to it.[45] Working alongside this metaphorical application of the effect that music has on us is a more wholehearted and metaphysical conception of harmony which is particularly central to Spinoza's *Ethics*. According to Spinoza, the clear, adequate ideas with which we reason demonstratively belong to a totality identical with God's thoughts or God's mind. So when we infer one adequate idea from another, we think some of God's thoughts, and in this way begin to merge with God or nature by partaking of his (or its) perfection and power. The knowledge that this is what reasoning is gives rise to a joy, stemming this time from the capacity to blur the boundaries of the self, and become a part of the greatest totality of all. Our joy comes not from hearing the harmony of a whole distinct from us, but from our incorporation in the harmonious whole itself.

These images go some way to suggesting how the process of reasoning and the ideas it yields can exert a strong hold over us. But there is a further dimension to the view that reasoning constrains, one that returns us to the analogy between reason and rapture. Early-modern philosophers who make use of this idea draw on a long tradition which incorporates both the Stoic view that understanding is a condition in which passion is transcended and replaced by intense and tranquil happiness, and Aristotle's claim that, although our grasp of eternal things is slight, they give us 'from their excellence, more pleasure than all our knowledge of the world in which we live; just as a half glimpse of persons we love is more delightful than an accurate view of other things, whatever their number and dimensions'.[46] While Aristotle here attributes the joy that accompanies reason to the qualities of its objects (we reason about

---

[43] R. Ariew, 'Descartes and the Tree of Knowledge', *Synthese*, 92 (1992), 101–16.

[44] *The Philosophy of the Ancients*, in *Works*, ed. J. Spedding *et al.* (London, 1857–61), vi. 720–2. On Orpheus see D. P. Walker, *The Ancient Theology: Studies in Christian Platonism from the Fifteenth to the Eighteenth Centuries* (London, 1972), 22–41; N. Rhodes, *The Power of Eloquence in English Renaissance Literature* (Hemel Hempstead, 1992), 3–8.

[45] The capacity of music to move us is widely discussed in this period. See e.g. Marin Mersenne, *Les Préludes de l'harmonie universelle* (Paris, 1634). For further discussion see D. A. Duncan, 'Mersenne and Modern Learning: The Debate over Music', in T. Sorell (ed.), *The Rise of Modern Philosophy* (Oxford, 1993), 89–106.

[46] *On the Parts of Animals*, in *The Complete Works of Aristotle*, ed. J. Barnes (Princeton, 1984), vol. i, 644^{b}32–645^{a}1.

eternal things that possess excellence and worth), seventeenth-century philosophers tend to add the idea that we feel joy in the intellectual operations of
our minds. It is the activity of reasoning, as much as the resulting knowledge,
that moves us; and the fact that we take delight in the process of understanding
means that our emotions prompt us to continue reasoning, to pursue inferences, and to expand our knowledge.

The two most careful and sustained expositions of this view are given by
Descartes and Spinoza, each of whom distinguishes passions from internal or
intellectual emotions. Their accounts of the intellectual emotions differ, however, in ways which bear particularly on the emotional aspect of the contrast
between *scientia* and *opinio*. For Spinoza, our inadequate ideas produce passions
and our adequate ones intellectual emotions. Only in so far as we reason with
adequate or complete ideas do we escape the passions and the errors that go
with them, and the balance between passions and intellectual emotions therefore varies with the extent of our understanding. For Descartes, by contrast,
the internal emotions are part of the business of thinking. We experience them
when we judge clear and distinct ideas; but we also experience them when
we assess confused ideas derived from everyday experience. The scope of the
internal emotions consequently extends beyond *scientia*, although these feelings are particularly intense when we assent to clear and distinct ideas. Each
of these views offers an answer to the question, 'What moves us to pursue
scientific knowledge?', and I shall consider each in turn.

Descartes: Joyful Volition

It is important to Descartes's account of the mind as an integrated whole that
all our thinking is done by a single cognitive power, the operations of which
are distinguished by the various kinds of ideas on which it works. When the
mind contemplates the ideas assembled in the common sense it sees, hears,
etc.; when it attends to ideas in the imagination it remembers or imagines;
when it focuses on ideas that are not in the body it understands.[47] Contemplating or focusing on ideas is, for this cognitive power, a matter of awareness
(the mind is aware of these distinct kinds of ideas as distinct), of inference (the
mind connects one idea to another), and of criticism (the mind makes more
or less rigorous judgements as to the content and reliability of its ideas). These
components combine in a single process which is itself emotional—it is imbued
with what Descartes calls *émotions intérieures* that are excited 'in the soul only
by the soul itself' and, unlike passions, do not depend on motions of the
animal spirits.[48]

[47] *Rules*, 42.   [48] *Passions of the Soul*, 147.

When Descartes introduces these emotions in *Les Passions de l'âme*, he describes them as the soul's perceptions of its own operations—of its volitions and of all the imaginings and other thoughts which depend on them.[49] Moreover, these perceptions are intimately linked to volitions (Descartes remarks that the two are really one and the same thing) which are in turn of two kinds—the actions of the soul which terminate in the soul itself, and the actions of the soul which terminate in the body. Because these perceptions and volitions have the soul as their cause, and occur independently of any motions of the animal spirits in the body, they are not accompanied by passions. So there is a class of thoughts which is free from the passions' more destructive consequences.

The perceptions and volitions caused by the soul alone include a kind of second-order consciousness of all our thoughts: we cannot think without being aware that we are thinking, and because the soul always perceives and judges its own thoughts it is always active in the sense of entertaining thoughts caused by the soul alone. In addition, Descartes mentions two further kinds of thought that are independent of the body. There are the perceptions and volitions which arise when we will to apply our minds to objects which are not sensible but intelligible, such as geometrical figures, extended bodies, or virtues. And there are the perceptions and volitions that occur when we set ourselves to imagine something that does not exist, such as an enchanted castle or a chimera.[50] The first of these cases serves to emphasize the claim we have been exploring—that our intelligible ideas are independent of the body, and thus of passion. So, too (as the second case indicates), are the operations that involve taking ideas derived from sensory experience and reordering them. This last capacity is not a specialized kind of thinking in which we engage occasionally, nor, as Descartes's example suggests, is it special to fictional imagination. Rather, it is active much of the time, for instance when we reflect on possible courses of action, or generate hypotheses on the basis of experimental evidence. So the mind always contains thoughts caused by the soul itself; and they are all imbued with *émotions intérieures*, with a kind of joy that the mind takes in its own operations. This delight is, moreover, independent of the content of its thoughts; whether it rejoices in what it judges to be good or grieves in what it judges to be bad, the soul takes pleasure in its awareness of its own activity.

The independent operations of the soul are thus a source of joy. When we reason with intelligible ideas, reflect on ideas derived from sense, or bring the will to bear on our perceptions, we experience a delight which motivates us to persist in these kinds of intellectual activity. How, though, are the *émotions intérieures* related to our passions? As Descartes takes pains to emphasize, the two are intimately interconnected. For example, when we hear good news, the mind makes a judgement about it and, finding it good, rejoices with a joy that

<hr />

[49] Ibid. 19.   [50] Ibid. 20.

is purely intellectual and so completely independent of the body that 'the Stoics could not have denied it to their Sage, although they wished him to be free of all passion'. But the same event also causes changes in the body that we experience as passionate joy.[51] In this case, the judgement of the mind endorses the passion, and both are feelings of joy; but this need not always be so. Descartes illustrates the dislocation that can occur between passions and *émotions intérieures* by means of two examples. First, reading a story or going to the theatre often arouses passions in us, but our very awareness of them causes an internal joy. The terror, for instance, that we feel in the theatre is sealed off from, and does not destroy, the pleasure we take in feeling it. Second (a more perplexing case), a man who is happy that his wife has died may be moved to genuine sadness at her funeral. At the same time, however, 'he feels a secret joy in his innermost soul, and the emotion of this joy has such power that the concomitant sadness and tears can do nothing to diminish its force'.[52] He grieves; but his grief does not touch his joy (relief? glee?) that his wife is dead. The line drawn in these examples between passions and internal emotions is not altogether easy to trace. Why, after all, should we not say that they are cases of conflicting passions? Descartes would presumably reply that internal emotions are produced in the soul by the soul itself. If the widower's joy accompanies an involuntary memory of his wife's complaining, together with his realization that he will never have to humour her again, it may be classifiable as a passion caused by the motions of his pineal gland. But if it accompanies a judgement based on a reflective assessment of his marriage, it may stand at one remove from these bodily events and be said to lie in the soul alone. The widower's joy is then intellectual or internal.

Intellectual emotions occur alongside passions, then, as when the widower feels both grief and joy. The soul experiences *émotions intérieures* upon perceiving its own passions, and the *émotions intérieures* in turn produce passions so that, in practice, we often cannot distinguish the emotional responses caused by the soul alone from those caused by the soul–body composite. However, it remains to ask whether the two kinds of affect simply interact, or whether the intellectual emotions possess some distinctive power which offsets the force of the passions and protects us from the errors to which they make us prone. In discussing the pleasure we gain from reasoning, Descartes claims that the internal emotions touch us more closely ('nous touchent de plus près'), and consequently have more power over us than the passions that occur with them.[53] But because the pleasures they cause are so closely attached to the will, it is

---

[51] *The Principles of Philosophy*, in *Philosophical Writings*, ed. Cottingham *et al.*, vol. i, IV. 190. This English trans. is less emphatic than the French. When the soul finds that the news is good, 'elle s'en rejoit *en elle-même*, d'un joie qui *est purement intellectuelle*, et tellement indépendente des émotions du corps, que les Stoïques n'ont pû la dénier a leur Sage, bien qu'ils ayant voulu qu'il fût exempte de toute passion'. *Œuvres de Descartes*, ed. C. Adam et P. Tannery (Paris, 1964–74), ix. 311.

[52] *Passions of the Soul*, 147.   [53] Ibid.

not immediately clear that the intellectual emotions encourage us to reason correctly, in accordance with the standards of *scientia*, as opposed to prompting us to reason in a relaxed and approximate fashion. The wide scope of the *émotions intérieures* is evident in Descartes's analysis of virtue, which consists, he tells us, in two connected skills—in judging what is best and in acting in line with our judgements.[54] As he explicitly points out, virtuous judgement does not require *scientia*, since we are only required to judge as well as we can, to use whatever critical powers we possess to the best of our ability. The emphasis is rather on strength of will, since virtue requires us to act on our considered judgement. When we become virtuous, however, we gain immense emotional rewards, since we experience a satisfaction which has such a power to make us happy that the most violent efforts of the passions are powerless to trouble the tranquillity of the soul.[55]

To achieve such happiness we must, obviously, be capable of resisting the blandishments of the passions, and here the extra strength of the *émotions intérieures*, the fact that they touch us more closely, will presumably help us. Moreover, as soon as we are in a position to overcome some of our passions, our awareness of their impotence and of our power to overrule them will itself strengthen our intellectual joy.[56] But we still need to consider how this kind of happiness is related to knowledge, since, as we have seen, the style of reasoning required for virtue may fall far short of *scientia*. If virtuous reasoning, which may include judgements that are mistaken, yields such intense emotional satisfaction, what prompts us to search for the clear and distinct ideas that are the mainstay of certain knowledge? Is the draw of *scientia* purely intellectual, or does it possess some distinctive emotional features which make it attractive to us? Descartes's musings on his own philosophical life suggest that he must have an answer to this question. Extolling his own method, he records that since beginning to follow it he has felt a contentment so extreme that he does not believe it possible to experience a sweeter or more innocent one on earth.[57] And in a disquisition on philosophy as the supreme good, he claims that the pleasure of seeing the world instead of walking around with our eyes closed is as nothing compared to the satisfaction we gain from the knowledge that philosophy gives us.[58] But what is it about philosophical reasoning that makes it so outstandingly pleasurable? Part of the answer lies in a set of connections between understanding, perfection, and volition. When we perceive clearly and distinctly, our ideas engage the will, over which they exert a strong hold. We not only judge that something is the case, which is itself pleasurable, but also judge that our judgement is correct, which intensifies our pleasure still further. In addition, when our judgements are unqualified, as they are when we assent to clear and distinct ideas, it is easier for us to act on them,

---

[54] Ibid. 148.   [55] Ibid.   [56] Ibid.   [57] *Discourse*, 124.
[58] *Principles*, p. 180, pref. to the Fr. edn.

since we do not suffer any residual doubt which can weaken our assent. The possession of clear and distinct ideas thus increases our ability to act on our best judgements, which is an integral part of virtue, and at the same time increases the happiness that virtue brings.[59]

Descartes is committed, then, to the view that the kinds of ideas that do not depend on the body arouse *émotions intérieures*. Since these ideas are present in our minds all the time, both because we are always aware of our own thoughts and because we often reflect on our experience, the pleasure they bring is familiar to everyone. It motivates us to engage in a range of critical thinking, formal and informal, and provides us with a means to counter and alter the passion caused in us by bodily motions. To put it another way, the *émotions intérieures* arouse our interest in all kinds of thinking that depend on the soul alone, and do not just excite our enthusiasm for the comparatively rarefied demonstrations that are the highpoint of *scientia*. This analysis presupposes a fairly inclusive view of the kinds of thoughts that can increase our understanding, and are thus an integral part of philosophizing. To arrive at *scientia*, we need to make inferences from sensible ideas, as when we reflect on our experience of bodies in order to arrive at laws of motion. We also need to work out the relations between purely intelligible ideas, as when we construct mathematical proofs. Our interest in both these kinds of thinking is excited and sustained by *émotions intérieures* which, by being pleasurable in themselves, excite a desire for further pleasure of the same kind—a desire to keep on reasoning.

The intellectual emotions direct our desires and counteract our concern with bodily pleasures; they motivate us to pursue virtue and to take an interest in our own intellectual capacities. In so far as they encourage us to reflect on the place of our passions in our broader experience and modify our emotional habits, they foster circumstances in which we are better placed to overcome passionate error. And they become more intense as our ability to act on our best-considered judgement increases, a capacity which is in turn strengthened by the clear and distinct ideas of *scientia*. Intellectual joy is focused, then, on volition—on the operation that Descartes identifies as the activity of the soul. And it is because *scientia* contributes to the soul's activity that we experience our knowledge of it as pleasurable. The self-affirmation implicit in the unqualified assent that the will gives to clear and distinct perceptions is reflected in the intellectual joy that accompanies it, and is correspondingly intense.

Spinoza: Joyful Understanding

A comparable view is enunciated by Spinoza, although, as one would expect, this does not depend on a distinction between understanding and will, but

---

[59] *Passions of the Soul*, 49.

relies instead on two types of interpretation.[60] We have already found that, because most of our ideas are in Spinoza's view incomplete or, as he prefers to say, inadequate, they contribute to an understanding of ourselves and the world which is patchy and in this sense distorted. To escape from this limited view we must begin to decipher the causal relations concealed in our inadequate ideas, gradually learning to distinguish our own bodies from the objects we encounter, and to separate aspects of ourselves from aspects of the world. Moreover, if we pursue this quest far enough, we may acquire ideas that are complete or adequate.[61] The task of replacing our inadequate ideas with adequate ones is, however, at the same time a process of affective change, in which our passions give way to stronger, non-passionate emotions of joy and desire. Adequate ideas are not only pleasurable, but excite a distinct kind of affection which Spinoza characterizes in terms of the central opposition between activity and passivity. Whereas we experience passions when we are acted on, the joy and desire that accompany adequate understanding are what we feel when we act.[62]

This view is deeply embedded in Spinoza's philosophy, and follows from the doctrines already discussed in Chapter 6. These views help us to see, first of all, why the transition from inadequate to adequate knowledge is an emotional one, and also why it is joyful. The passions, we need to remember, are manifestations of the *conatus* that is our essence, affections that we experience as we strive to increase our power on the basis of inadequate ideas. Desire is our consciousness of our perpetual effort to preserve our power, while joy and sadness mark our successes and failures. As we enlarge our stock of adequate ideas, our partial, passionate interpretations of the world give way to complete or adequate ones which enable us to make reliable judgements about the capacity of objects to help or harm us. In place of the limited power deriving from our inadequate ideas and expressed in our passions, we gain a greater and more secure power, grounded on a full and adequate understanding. Moreover, this increase in our power is expressed in an alteration in our emotions, principally in the growth of an intense joy.[63]

The distinguishing feature of this joy or delight, which marks it out as an active emotion and separates it off from its passionate counterpart, is the fact that it derives from ideas that are adequate, and its intensity is directly correlated with the qualities that adequate ideas possess. Because adequate ideas reveal

---

[60] On Spinoza's and Descartes's approaches to this issue see J. Cottingham, 'The Intellect, the Will and the Passions: Spinoza's Critique of Descartes', *Journal of the History of Philosophy*, 26 (1988), 239–57.

[61] *Ethics*, II. P 38 c.   [62] Ibid. III. D 2; P 1.

[63] Ibid. III. P 58; P 59; v. P 20 s (v). See G. Lloyd, *Part of Nature: Self-Knowledge in Spinoza's Ethics* (Ithaca, NY, 1994), 105–18; A. Donagan, *Spinoza* (Hemel Hempstead, 1988), 136–40; A. Matheron, 'Spinoza and Euclidean Arithmetic: The Example of the Fourth Proportional', trans. D. Lachterman, in M. Grene and D. Nails (eds.), *Spinoza and the Sciences* (Dordrecht, 1986), 125–50.

themselves to be true, yield chains of further conclusions, and are eternal, they give rise to a kind of knowledge or understanding which is itself a formidable kind of power and, more than anything else, enhances our capacity to persevere in our being. And precisely because this sort of knowledge increases our power, we experience it as joy. Passionate and non-passionate joy are therefore both manifestations of our *conatus;* but whereas our passions are our responses to a fluctuating and precarious power grounded on the inadequate understanding we gain from our sensory experience of ourselves and the world, the power we gain from our adequate ideas is by comparison secure and, in Spinoza's view, much more effective. The joy that accompanies it is consequently the strongest we are capable of experiencing, and grows with our adequate knowledge. Phenomenologically, it may not be very different from some forms of passionate delight but it remains distinct by virtue of its causal history.

In human beings, the process of replacing inadequate with adequate understanding is always incomplete so that, however wise and knowledgeable people may become, they will continue to be passionate, and will remain vulnerable to loss of power.[64] In so far as they have adequate ideas, however, the sadness that loss of power engenders can be modified by the pleasure they take in understanding the things that are happening to them. For example, an angry and vengeful official may damage and undermine the professional reputation of her colleagues, reducing their power and causing them to suffer sadness— they may, for instance, come to hate or fear her. But if they possess adequate ideas of her anger and its causes, and of the aspects of their own characters that excite it, their fear, say, will be modified by a kind of joy or satisfaction in the control that their understanding gives them. They are not simply victims of this anger. Because they understand it, they possess some power to deflect it, avoid it, or constructively challenge it, and in this respect their understanding yields an instrumental power. Whether a particular person will succeed in escaping from the errors that are part and parcel of the passions will depend on the content and extent of their adequate ideas. A woman who has an adequate knowledge of a range of mathematical problems, but does not understand much about her own anger, may well fall prey to this passion; and in general our rather fragmentary adequate ideas will often be insufficient to modify our passions and protect us from losses of power that are in principle avoidable. Since many of our ideas remain inadequate, this vulnerability never goes away, and even the most devoted philosopher may misinterpret the world in a way that diminishes his or her power. Nevertheless, it is part of Spinoza's view that, as our stock of adequate ideas increases, so does our power and the intellectual joy we derive from it. As understanding gets under way, the

---

[64] Spinoza. *Ethics,* IV. P 4.

non-passionate emotions also take hold and become a more powerful force in directing our thought and action.[65]

Spinoza's account of the emotional transformation that reasoning brings has a good deal in common with that of Descartes: for both philosophers, the affections integral to intellectual activity are outstandingly pleasurable, and create in us a desire for a type of knowledge which protects us from various kinds of error, among them those into which we are led by our ordinary passions; and for both philosophers, the process of modifying our passions is itself an emotional one. Beyond this, their positions diverge significantly.[66] First, their dramatically different views of the relation between body and mind, discussed in Chapters 5 and 6, have an immediate impact on their analyses of passionate and non-passionate emotion. In Descartes's case, the *émotions intérieures* are distinguished, as we have seen, by the fact that they attach to ideas that are caused by the soul alone. The essential difference between these affections and the passions lies in their point of origin, in the fact that passions originate in the body and are states of the soul–body composite, whereas *émotions intérieures* are states of the soul. This conception is transformed by Spinoza, for whom intellectual emotions, as much as passions, are ideas of our bodies. Reasoning with adequate ideas is, in his view, neither more nor less embodied than any other kind of thinking. To put it another way, it is no more true of reasoning than of any other kind of thinking that it occurs 'in the mind'. This difference also bears on the way these two philosophers understand the process by which we learn to resist our passionate impulses. According to Descartes, the passions and *émotions intérieures* are separate forces, and although the *émotions intérieures* are intrinsically the stronger of the two, they are often overcome. Only by developing our capacity to will are we able to strengthen our interior joy to a point where it can keep the passions at bay. This account is dominated by an image of a battle in which the mind may eventually triumph over the body, and is completely rejected by Spinoza, for whom the passions are not vanquished but modified. As we acquire adequate ideas and increase our power, our emotions change. The old passions do not lurk in our bodies, waiting for an opportunity to overwhelm us. While we may remember what it was like to feel them, the emotions which engage us answer to our increased understanding of our relations with the world around us.[67]

A second contrast concerns the kind of power that reasoning yields—what it is we are joyful about when we learn to modify our passions. As we found

---

[65] See A. O. Rorty, 'Spinoza on the Pathos of Idolatrous Love and the Hilarity of True Love', in R. C. Solomon and K. M. Higgins (eds.), *The Philosophy of (Erotic) Love* (Lawrence, Kan., 1991), 357–65; G. Lloyd, *Spinoza and the 'Ethics'* (London, 1996), 83–98; S. James, 'Power and Difference: Spinoza's Conception of Freedom', *Journal of Political Philosophy*, 4 (1996), 210–21.

[66] See Lloyd, *Part of Nature*, 77–147.

[67] On this contrast see J.-M. Beyssade, 'L'Émotions intérieures/l'affect actif', in E. Curley and P.-F. Moreau (eds.), *Spinoza: Issues and Directions* (Leiden, 1990), 176–90.

earlier on, the focus of interior joy in Descartes's work is volition; it is principally the assent given by the will, the rather narcissistic pleasure that the
mind takes in its own autonomous operation, that is accompanied by interior
joy. Consequently, the more we strengthen our wills by learning to act on our
best-considered judgements, the more joyful we become. Because understanding
is a means to this end we have an indirect reason for enlarging it, namely that
this helps us to gain the will-power which secures our happiness. In Spinoza's
case, however, our reason for increasing our understanding is direct, since
it is understanding itself which strengthens our power and makes us joyful.
Although Spinoza and Descartes disagree about the location of the power that
enables us to overcome passion, and thus about the character of the emotion
that is part of it, they share a general conviction that the power in question
provides us with a kind of independence. This link emerges in Descartes's
adherence to the view that the will is self-caused; uniquely among our thoughts
it can activate itself, so that we may will, for example, to start thinking about
grammar, or walk into the garden. As the growth of interior joy strengthens
our ability to will, we become more autonomous, increasingly able to control
the way we respond to all our perceptions including the passions, and in this
sense more independent, both of the world around us and of our bodies. In
Spinoza's work, some of the features Descartes attributes to volition are transferred to adequate ideas. While our inadequate ideas are confused conceptions
of the relations between our bodies and external objects, of which we are only
the partial cause,[68] our adequate ideas can be understood through our nature
alone.[69] When we make inferences from one adequate idea to another, the
causes of the second idea are all in our minds, and our thinking is therefore
independent of the external objects that impinge on us. Once again, we find
an image of autonomy or self-containedness; although in this case understanding
is not conceived as a retreat from the body, it nevertheless exhibits a kind of
independence of the world beyond the body, and this is one aspect of the
increased power that increased knowledge brings.[70] These differences are central
to the conceptions of activity around which Spinoza and Descartes organize
their philosophies. For Descartes, activity consists in volition, so that we become more active as we become able to act on our best-considered judgements.
For Spinoza, activity consists in understanding, and we become more active
as we increase our adequate ideas. But for both, increases in activity are accompanied by an intensification of joy.

The view that our capacity to concentrate on reasoning is enhanced by the
emotions that accompany it obviously presupposes that these emotions are
pleasurable, and it is striking that the writers discussed in this chapter are

---

[68] Spinoza, *Ethics*, III. D 2.   [69] Ibid.
[70] On Spinoza's view that the mind can exist without the body see R. J. Delahunty, *Spinoza* (London,
1985), 279–305; Donagan, *Spinoza*, 197–207; Lloyd, *Spinoza*, 109–31.

convinced that, regardless of what we come to know, the activity of knowing is a kind of rejoicing. This is, in a way, surprising. If, like Spinoza, one abandons the special relationship between God and humankind in favour of the view that people are just small fragments of a universe in no way adjusted to their purposes, it is not obvious why knowledge of one's own condition should make one joyful. Why should coming to see oneself as tiny, fragile, and unprotected be exhilarating, rather than frightening or depressing? Spinoza's answer is that the joy we experience when we realise that we have correctly understood our own position derives from the part this knowledge plays in increasing our power. We empower ourselves by way of understanding, however gloomy the news we come to understand. In this account, our dim impression of the totality to which knowledge belongs and the prospect of immersing ourselves in it function as an inspiration—or perhaps as a passionate, desirous hope. They hold no terrors, and the pains of intellectual labour appear as intervening passions rather than emotions belonging to knowledge itself. Spinoza's optimism, like that of Descartes, is also linked to the view that when we reason we act, which is in turn embedded in an outlook that associates activity with perfection. For Descartes, as for his Scholastic predecessors, to become more active is to become more like God, and the more that humans are able to govern their wills, the more active and perfect they are. How could this increase in perfection be experienced as unhappiness or sadness? Spinoza, too, argues in parallel fashion that we act in so far as we have adequate ideas, and that as we increase our adequate ideas we become more perfect by increasing our capacity to think the thoughts in the divine intellect. Once again, action partakes of the divine, and thus of happiness.

A number of recent discussions of early-modern conceptions of knowledge have been keen to emphasize that demonstrative reasoning is habitually seen as a capacity of the mind which is independent both of the body and of emotion.[71] We are now in a position to see that this is an unwarranted oversimplification. According to both Descartes and Spinoza, reasoning excites emotions which are not passions, and it is therefore true to say that it is dispassionate. It is not, however, correct to equate lack of passion with lack of emotion, thereby concluding that reasoning is unemotional. On the contrary, the emotions excited by reasoning can be exceptionally intense, and even when this is not the case, reasoning is shot through with joy and desire. Turning to the claim that reasoning is divorced from everything bodily, we have seen that this is as far as possible from Spinoza's view. It is true that a good deal of support for it can be found in the work of Descartes, Malebranche, and other Cartesians, who argue unoriginally that the mind must withdraw from sense and passion in order to perceive clearly and distinctly, and sustain this thesis more originally with an absolute metaphysical distinction between body and mind. Even here,

---

[71] See Ch. 1, n. 68, above.

however, it is easy to exaggerate the strictness of their division, and to forget that although mind and body are conceptually distinct, their union ensures that they interact. As we have already seen, Descartes holds that all our thinking gives rise to intellectual emotion which in turn causes passions.[72] The same view is more forcefully expressed by Malebranche, who insists that

all the soul's inclinations, even those it has for goods that are unrelated to the body, are accompanied by disturbances in the animal spirits that make these inclinations sensible; since man is not a pure spirit, it is impossible for him to have an entirely pure inclination, unmixed with some passion, great or small. Thus, the love of truth, justice, virtue or of God himself is always accompanied by movements of the spirits that make this love sensible, although we are not aware of this because we almost always have livelier sensations . . . Since ideas of things that can only be perceived by the pure mind can be linked to traces in the brain, and the sight of objects we love, hate or fear through natural inclination can be accompanied by motion in the spirits, clearly the thought of eternity, the fear of hell, and the hope for eternal bliss (although these objects do not strike the senses) . . . can excite violent passions in us.[73]

This kind of interaction between the intellectual emotions and passions was also a feature of Aristotelianism, which continued to win adherents late into the seventeenth century. Charleton, for example, writing in the 1670s, explains that, when the rational soul understands supernatural things, it experiences metaphysical emotions. These are communicated to the sensible soul, where they produce the so-called Christian passions of piety, devotion, love of God, hatred of sin, repentance, hope of salvation, and fear of divine justice.[74]

Reasoning and the intellectual emotion that accompanies it are therefore not, according to this Cartesian view, sealed off from passion. Rather, the connection between them is close and reciprocal. In order to reason we have to do our best to ignore those thoughts which originate in the body and interfere with the difficult business of philosophizing. But at the same time we have to cultivate passions such as wonder and a desire for knowledge, which encourage us in this project. When we succeed and are able to reason critically about our ideas, our awareness of our own thought-processes gives rise to intellectual emotions which sustain intellectual enquiry; and these emotions in turn cause and strengthen our passions, reinforcing the joy we take in understanding and the desire to understand more. So although intellectual emotions have no bodily expressions, the fact that they are accompanied by passions ensures that reasoning can have physical effects, and philosophers, in the broad seventeenth-century sense of the term, can flush with excitement or feel a tightness in the chest as they grapple with particularly intractable problems. This connection between mind and body also provides a further insight into the question of how we are able to still the passions sufficiently to enquire after knowledge;

[72] *Principles*, IV. 190.   [73] *De la recherche*, ii, 86; trans. Lennon and Olscamp, 345.
[74] *A Natural History of the Passions* (London, 1674), 77–8.

for it suggests that, once we have begun, the intellectual emotions come to our aid by producing sympathetic and supporting passions. To be sure, there is nothing foolproof about this process; intellectual delight in doing philosophy can still be conquered by a passionate desire to lie in the sun. But our bodily passions are here conceived as capable of being influenced by, and cooperating with, the emotions of the mind.

The integrity of our embodied selves is therefore recognized by Descartes and his Cartesian followers, who appeal to it in explaining both what motivates us to acquire *scientia* and how it is that we are capable of pursuing it. If the truths of *scientia* are, in a sense, disembodied, the quest for them is not, and depends on the interconnection between body and soul. Moreover, this interconnection is emotional. It is partly because reasoning excites feeling that it constrains us or has a hold over us, and its hold is strengthened by the mutual relations between intellectual emotion and passions. Since the intellect is not an unfeeling judge, emotion accompanies all thought. While this point needs stressing, because it goes against some recent and influential interpretations of Descartes, it remains true that the Cartesian analysis of the emotions involved in reasoning is extremely cumbersome.[75] The transactions between passions rooted in bodily motions and intellectual emotions rooted in thought-processes belie the unity of the mind. In addition, the division between them —perhaps uncomfortably close to that between the sensitive and intellectual souls—is hard to identify. One aspect of this awkwardness—the association of passion with body, and intellectual emotion with mind—is recognized and transformed by Spinoza, who takes over many of Descartes's insights and incorporates them in a distinctive and emphatically non-Aristotelian theory of the soul. For Spinoza, however, as much as for Descartes, intellectual activity possesses a special emotional quality, which explains why we engage in philosophical enquiry, and glorifies the life of the mind.

The view that reasoning, and above all reasoning with intelligible ideas, excites in us a joy that moves us to pursue systematic scientific knowledge exerts a strong influence over the yearning imaginations of a number of early-modern philosophers. If abstract reasoning generates the most intense delight of which humans are capable, philosophers will find their task ever more absorbing and satisfying and will want nothing more than to carry it through towards a state of understanding and happiness. It is hardly surprising, however, that this image also excited a certain amount of scepticism. Many people educated in the arid art of Scholastic disputation had little love for philosophy, and were unpersuaded by the view that it opened the door to perfection and contentment. They took a rather different view of the emotional character of intelligible ideas, and consequently favoured a competing analysis of the relation between passion and knowledge.

[75] See G. Lloyd, *Part of Nature* (Ithaca, NY, 1994), esp. 90–7.

9

The Value of Persuasion

The task of ensuring that our knowledge is free from the distorting effect of passion is made difficult by the fact that the acquisition of *scientia* consists largely in the critical scrutiny of the sensible ideas to which our passions adhere. Even if some of our intelligible ideas are innate—as Descartes, for example, believes—and even if we acquire more intelligible ideas in the process of enquiry, we never transcend our dependence on the senses. This conviction is universally shared by early-modern philosophers, some of whom formulate it in terms of an explicitly Aristotelian division between the intellectual and sensitive souls. Charleton, for instance, explains that, while the sensitive soul can compound and divide notions of sensible things, only the intellect can review propositions conceived from the fantasy, judge them, and reorder them.[1] Others appeal to the messages passed between the senses, the imagination, and the understanding, as when Bacon describes the senses as an agent or nuncius sending over to imagination before reason has judged, or when Reynolds represents them as porters conveying ideas to the understanding.[2] A strictly comparable view is maintained by anti-Aristotelians who construe the erstwhile powers of the soul as distinct kinds of thought. In the preceding chapter, for example, we examined Descartes's claim that 'the intellect can either be stimulated by the imagination or act upon it. Likewise, the imagination can act upon the senses through the motive force, by directing them to objects, while the senses in their turn can act upon the imagination, by depicting the images of bodies upon it.' So, 'if the intellect proposes to examine something which can be referred to the body, the idea of that thing must be formed as distinctly as possible in the imagination. In order to do this properly, the thing itself which this idea is to represent should be displayed to the external senses.'[3] Regardless of how they put the point, all these writers present the intellect as a critical faculty with an ability to integrate ideas, including representations of the extended world. Fulfilling the first of these functions, it judges the ideas presented to it and

---

[1] *A Natural History of the Passions* (London, 1674), 49.
[2] Francis Bacon, *The Advancement of Learning*, ed. G. W. Kitchin (London, 1973), 120; Edward Reynolds, *A Treatise of the Passions and Faculties of the Soul of Man* (London, 1640), 3–4.
[3] *Rules for the Direction of the Mind*, in *The Philosophical Writings of Descartes*, ed. J. Cottingham *et al.*, 3 vols. (Cambridge, 1984–91), i, rule 12.

pronounces them dependable, fraudulent, a reasonable basis for inference, good grounds for action, and so forth. Fulfilling the second, it uses ideas it has assessed to expand, refine, or revise the knowledge it already possesses. Both operations obviously presuppose a grasp of standards of judgement which may vary from person to person (I may be satisfied by an idea that you regard as deeply suspect) and situation to situation (as Descartes points out, we sometimes have to make a decision quickly, and at other times aim at judgements that are conclusive).[4] But whenever we reason, we appeal more or less self-consciously to norms which the authors of logic manuals attempt to articulate and refine.

The sensible ideas that contribute so much to our understanding are, however, in many cases interwoven with passions, and are therefore subject to the distorting dynamics discussed in Chapter 7. An unacknowledged fear may, for example, draw a philosopher to the view that women are less capable of reasoning than men; the *grandeur* of the planets may encourage us to overrate their causal influence and correspondingly underrate that of the less impressive, distant stars. To avoid these biases and the errors they contain, we can subject scientific hypotheses to tough epistemological tests. But because our passionate ideas are not waiting quietly for reason to pronounce, but are already straining at the leash and tugging us after them, reason can only have an effect on agents who are able and prepared to give it space. Our passions are powerful exponents of certain inferences and conclusions—that this experiment is decisive, that argument unappealing, that particular person sure to be right. To get any critical distance on these affections we have to be able to refrain from taking them at face value and allow reason an opportunity to work. Once again, we face the central question: what gives us the capacity to rein in our passions and subject them to scrutiny? What makes us attentive and obedient to reason?

The preceding chapter considered two answers to these questions. One was that, when we retreat from the sensible to the intelligible realm, we start to work with ideas that are passion-proof. The other proposed that not all our emotions are passions, and that the activity of reasoning itself arouses in us internal or intellectual emotions. It must be admitted, however, that for all their meticulously mapped coherence there is something unconvincing about these solutions. If the passions really shape many of our ideas, and if they are potent and confident emotional forces, is it not implausible to claim that, like Daniel in the lions' den, the joyful pleasures of reasoning will tame them? In fact, is it not unduly artful to posit two kinds of emotion, passionate and intellectual, and call on the latter to control the former? Much wishful thinking is doubtless enfolded in this image of the overwhelming power of the intellect, but it is nevertheless greeted with scepticism by philosophers who agree that the passions make us prone to error, but do not believe that reasoning comes

---

[4] Id., *The Passions of the Soul*, in *Philosophical Writings*, ed. Cottingham *et al.*, i, 211.

complete with its own emotions. They offer a yet further solution to the problem from which we began, arguing that our ability to control our emotions and circumvent the errors to which they expose us is integral to the passions themselves. Since there is no escape into a realm of intellectual emotions and the passions are ever with us, we must employ and restrain them as best we can.

Knowledge and Power

An exceptionally wholehearted example of this approach is provided by Hobbes, who begins by analysing the modes of reasoning of which we are capable and the kinds of knowledge they yield. Sense and memory, he claims, can provide an absolute knowledge of fact 'as when we see a fact doing or remember it done', which concerns only the past and is history. In addition, they can provide the materials for a kind of reasoning or conjecture based on experience, called prudence—the presumption of the future contracted from the experience of time past and the presumption of the past from the present, on the basis of experience of the past.[5] Knowledge of fact and prudence are possessions of animals as well as humans, but there is also a kind of philosophical reasoning that requires language and is practised by humans alone.[6] This is called reckoning or the right ordering of names, and consists in inferring consequences from initial definitions.[7] While sense and memory are born with us and prudence is gained by experience, reason is only attained by industriously imposing definitions and working out rules of inference. The resulting knowledge of consequences, 'and dependence of one fact on another' is science, to which philosophers aspire.[8]

Hobbes's account of the epistemological character of science is notoriously puzzling.[9] It is, he argues, inferential or conditional knowledge, because it consists in knowledge of the causal relations between names, rather than in knowledge of whether particular events occurred. Science will not tell us 'that this, or that, is, has been, or will be; which is to know absolutely; but only that if this be, that is; if this has been, that has been; if this shall be, that shall be: which is to know conditionally'.[10] Judging from some of Hobbes's claims, the inferences it captures are certain. For instance, a man who is not only skilful in the use of weapons but possesses 'an acquired science of where he can offend, or be offended by his adversary', is infallible.[11] At other points, however, Hobbes draws back, conceding that correct definitions (unlike Cartesian clear and distinct ideas) do not reveal themselves as such, so that although individuals can

---

[5] *Leviathan*, ed. R. Tuck (Cambridge, 1991), 23.   [6] Ibid.   [7] Ibid. 32.   [8] Ibid. 35.
[9] See D. W. Hanson, 'The Meaning of "Demonstration" in Hobbes' Science', *History of Political Thought*, 11 (1990), 587–626 and 'Science, Prudence and Folly in Hobbes' Political Philosophy', *Political Theory*, 21 (1993), 634–64.
[10] *Leviathan*, 47.   [11] Ibid. 37.

do their best to reason correctly, even 'the ablest, most attentive and most practised men may deceive themselves, and infer false conclusions'.[12] Because nothing about the process of reasoning guarantees that reasoners will converge upon the truth, the want of a right reason constituted by nature means that the parties to a dispute must appoint an arbitrator or judge whose decision they are prepared to abide by. Certainty, here, consists in the word of an authority.

This appeal to socially constructed truth, alongside Hobbes's claim that geometry is 'the only science that it hath pleased God hitherto to bestow upon mankind',[13] suggests that our attempts to reason are subject to serious impediments, among which are our passions. As we have already seen, knowledge of causes and effects increases our ability to control what happens to us, and releases us from dependence on the possibly misleading authority of other people.[14] Our interest in acquiring this kind of knowledge is grounded on a restless desire for power after power, an unquenchable appetite for preserving and increasing such control as we possess which is modulated by curiosity or love of the knowledge of causes,[15] and by a disposition to believe that, if something began at a particular point, there must have been a cause which determined it to begin then. These dispositions make us inquisitive; but they also make us anxious. 'For being assured that there be causes of all things that have arrived hitherto or shall arrive hereafter, it is impossible for a man, who continually endeavoureth to secure himself against the evil he fears, and procure the good he desireth, not to be in a perpetual solicitude of the time to come.' Like Prometheus, whose liver regenerated at night so that it could be devoured by the eagle during the day, 'that man which looks too far before him . . . hath his heart all the day long gnawed on by fear of death, poverty, or other calamity; and has no repose, or pause of his anxiety, but in sleep'.[16]

The only reliable antidote to fear of the future is, in Hobbes's view, knowledge of causes and effects; but this insight may be concealed from us by our very anxiety which, 'as it were in the dark, must needs have for object something'.[17] Rather than tracing our fear to our own incapacity to tolerate ignorance, the habit of projecting it on to imagined entities (discussed in Chapter 7) often undermines both prudence and science. Concern for our own protection breeds a desire to be able to control what will happen to us in future, which may move us to acquire scientific knowledge of causes and effects. But because our concern for our future is strong, and our awareness of our ignorance and impotence correspondingly lively, it can manifest itself as anxiety, the very intensity of which stands in the way of its own alleviation. Gnawing at us, it destroys the concentration and peace of mind that enable us to investigate ourselves, formulate definitions, and work out their consequences. Passion here

[12] Ibid. 32.   [13] Ibid. 28.   [14] Ibid. 73.   [15] Ibid. 74.   [16] Ibid. 76.
[17] Ibid. 76.

promotes two connected errors: it short-circuits the patient and methodical investigation that science requires; and it posits 'things invisible' on inadequate grounds. As the objects of strong emotions, these entities then enter into further, unscientific explanations.

Our desire for knowledge of causes and effects is, therefore, both sustaining and menacing. Without it, we should be condemned to a state of dangerous ignorance; with it, we are vulnerable to an anxiety that works against our aspiration to protect ourselves with science. Somehow, we need to allay our fears so that we can concentrate on formulating definitions and drawing inferences, and among the qualities we should cultivate in order to do this is judgement.[18] Hobbes follows the classical rhetoricians in contrasting judgement, the capacity to discern differences between things, with fancy, the observation of likeness that gives rise to metaphors and similes.[19] Fancy, he explains, is paramount in poetry, orations of praise, invectives, and pleadings designed to disguise the facts, and has a marginal role in history. But in 'demonstration, in counsel and all rigorous search of truth, judgement does all; except sometimes the understanding have need to be opened by some apt similitude; and then there is so much use for fancy. But for metaphors, they are in this case utterly excluded.'[20] His aim here is not to deny that an appreciation of difference is simultaneously an appreciation of similarity. The limited use of fancy in the rigorous search for truth is rather a rejection of metaphor which, as Charleton later explains in a similar context, is 'equivocal and introductory to fallacy'.[21] Science, as Hobbes understands it, rests on definitions, and defining a term is a process of distinguishing it from other terms and breaking it down into its components, hedging it about (to speak metaphorically) and identifying its limits. The motto of the philosopher-scientist, we might say, should be 'Only disconnect'. Within such a project, the use of 'metaphors, tropes and other rhetorical figures, instead of words proper' is destructive, because they blur the very boundaries that definitions are intended to create.[22]

By cultivating judgement, we can train ourselves to make distinctions which serve to undo some of our more destructive passions. For example, the errors into which we are drawn by our anxiety about the future can be avoided by people who distinguish this anxiety from its causes and objects. Having separated out these components, they are in a better position to consider the causal

---

[18] Ibid. 51.

[19] See Q. Skinner, *Reason and Rhetoric in the Philosophy of Hobbes* (Cambridge, 1996), 182–98.

[20] *Leviathan*, 52.

[21] *A Brief Discourse Concerning the Different Wits of Men* (London, 1669), 26–7; cf. Malebranche, *De la recherche de la vérité*, ed. G. Rodis Lewis, in *Œuvres complètes*, ed. A. Robinet (2nd edn, Paris, 1972), i. 313; trans. T. M. Lennon and P. J. Olscamp as *The Search after Truth* (Columbus, Oh., 1980), 157.

[22] *Leviathan*, 35. On changes in Hobbes's attitude to the use of figurative language in science see Skinner, *Reason and Rhetoric*.

relations between them, and less likely to jump to the conclusion that there exists an invisible power of which they are rightly afraid. But whereas Descartes and Spinoza regard this kind of untangling as part of an escape from passion, a transition to adequate or clear ideas the contemplation of which brings intellectual joy, Hobbes takes another view. He believes that the differences in people's natural wit—in their capacities for judgement, and, incidentally, for fancy—lie in their passions and principally in the strength of their desires for various forms of power, including wealth, knowledge, and honour. Someone who does not desire any of these things cannot have much judgement. For without a strong desire people lack both a motive to make distinctions and the steadiness and direction to pursue them and work out their consequences.

This argument contains several important and connected claims. One is that the only cure for the restlessness of our thoughts is a strong passion capable of focusing our attention and keeping it fixed on some end. There is nothing special about the definitions with which we reason that enables them to hold our attention. A second claim is that the process of reasoning does not itself induce distinctive emotions. We remain interested in reasoning, and find it pleasurable, when we regard it as a means to satisfy our curiosity or desire for knowledge of causes and effects. Thirdly, Hobbes attributes to the passion of curiosity some of the traits that Descartes and Spinoza reserve for the intellectual emotions. Just as the latter take the view that everyone experiences some intellectual emotions, Hobbes claims that all people possess some curiosity; although their interest in natural causes is usually limited, they are inquisitive about the causes of their own good or evil fortune.[23] Moreover, where Spinoza notes that the intellectual emotions do not pall, Hobbes describes curiosity as a lust of the mind 'that by perseverance of delight in the continual and indefatigable generation of knowledge, exceedeth the short vehemence of any carnal pleasure'.[24] Fourthly, these characteristics do not detract from the fact that curiosity is a passion, a desire for one kind of power which competes with others. We desire to know causes and effects when, and in so far as, we interpret this knowledge as a way to increase our power. Hobbes hastens to add, however, that 'the sciences are small power', since only those people who have to some degree mastered them appreciate the fact that they are empowering.[25] Whereas the power that derives from wealth, for example, is a species of *grandeur* that increases as it 'procureth friends and servants', the power of philosophy is for the most part invisible and therefore limited. Nevertheless, knowledge confers some power and is therefore not entirely negligible, partly because it can play an instrumental role in achieving more substantial forms of social and political control. A prince, for example, may acquire mathematical skills which enhance his glory and reputation.

---

[23] *Leviathan*, 57, 76.   [24] Ibid. 42.   [25] Ibid. 63.

Reasoning therefore provides us with a distinctive method for checking the everyday understanding of causal connections that we derive from experience. Formulating definitions forces us to re-examine our ideas and classify them more minutely than we otherwise would; tracing the relations between definitions refines our understanding of causes and effects; and applying definitions encourages us to perceive distinctions we might otherwise overlook. Science, the outcome of reasoning, is much better grounded than prudence, the grasp of causal relations we base on experience, but it is not guaranteed to be free from error. As Hobbes points out, we know that even the best-informed people can make mistakes, and even the fact that everyone agrees about a definition does not make it correct. Moreover, when an intractable disagreement between two parties is resolved by an arbitrator, there is surely a chance that the conclusion by which everyone agrees to abide will be wrong. All the same, reasoning is the best method available to us, if only we can school ourselves to subject our judgements to its standards. Like the philosophers we considered in the last chapter, Hobbes claims that our initial desire to reason stems from a passion—curiosity—and that the capacity to reason varies—some people have better judgement than others, some have a strong fancy, some are dull, others steady. These differences lie in our passions, which are in turn explained primarily by differences in our bodies and educations. Where Hobbes differs from the philosophers discussed in Chapter 8 is in his conviction that passions not only initiate, but also sustain, an interest in reasoning. Rather than being initially motivated by passion and then graduating to a level where reasoning is also driven by intellectual emotion, we depend entirely on our desires. All that moves us to subject our beliefs to the standard of scientific reasoning is our desire for power, either a desire for the small power of science itself, or a desire for another sort of power to which science is a means. While Hobbes does not claim that scientific enquiry is really a quest for something else—power—he does regard scientific investigation as aimed at knowledge under a certain description, namely knowledge-as-power.

For writers who agree with Hobbes's conclusion, the only way to encourage scientific knowledge is to arouse and sustain the passions that move us to reason by nourishing a desire for understanding in the face of the lure of more glamorous and spectacular kinds of power, 'as when a man, from the thought of honour, to which he hath an appetite, cometh to the thought of wisdom, which is the next means there; and from there to the thought of study, which is the next means to wisdom, etc'.[26] This view differs radically from the one discussed in the preceding chapter, though in practice the two approaches overlap, since advocates of intellectual emotion also recognize the motivating force of passion. While they hold that it is epistemologically soundest to be moved by

---

[26] Id., *The Elements of Law*, ed. F. Tönnies (2nd edn, London, 1969), 13 f.

intellectual emotion, they allow that we need to manipulate the passions to get ourselves and others to stick at the arduous task of reasoning, and concede that we may sometimes have to appeal to base motives. Malebranche, for instance, directs us to rely as much as possible on the passions that are the counterparts of intellectual emotions, such as the desire to make good use of our minds and to free it from prejudices and errors,[27] but he admits that, since these are often fluctuating and faint, we sometimes have to take the more dangerous course of appealing to 'less reasonable' passions. 'Vanity, for example, excites us much more than love of truth, and one regularly sees people who apply themselves diligently to study as long as they have someone to whom they can relate what they have learned, but abandon study completely when there is no one to listen to them.'[28] As Malebranche's concession indicates, it is generally agreed that the passions have a part to play in exciting a love of learning. However, the Hobbesian view that they alone can perform this role is also embedded in a further debate about the pains and pleasures of scientific enquiry. While advocates of intellectual emotion regard this as intrinsically pleasurable, and while advocates of the Hobbesian position allow that it is pleasurable when it satisfies our overriding desire for power, a third school of philosophers take the view that it is positively unpleasant and unrewarding.

The Thorny Rule of Reason

A popular early-modern conception of reason as severe, rigorous, strict, massive, exact, and above all unpersuasive[29] is memorably captured in Philip Sidney's portrait of the Philosopher who, 'setting down with thorny arguments the base rule, is so hard of utterance and so misty to be conceived, that one that hath no other guide but him shall wade in him until he be old, before he shall find sufficient cause to be honest'.[30] Reasoning, as this picture suggests, is exceptionally arduous; but worse than that, submission to its rules grates on the imagination and fails to excite any kind of love or delight, so that it is simply a mistake to believe, as many learned men have done, 'that where reason hath so much over-mastered passion, as that the mind hath a free desire to do well', there the light of nature will shine.[31] On the contrary, *scientia* leaves us for the most part unmoved.

No doubt this complaint is in part a protest at the peculiarly unwelcoming style of much Scholastic philosophy, as Charron implies when he reassures his readers in the preface to *La Sagesse* that 'philosophy such as this book teacheth

---

[27] *De la recherche*, ii. 164; trans. Lennon and Olscamp, 415.
[28] Ibid. 163; trans. Lennon and Olscamp, 414.   [29] Reynolds, *Treatise of the Passions*, 21.
[30] *The Defense of Poesie*, in *The Prose Works*, ed. A. Feuillerat (Cambridge, 1962), iii. 13–14.
[31] Ibid. 19.

is altogether pleasant, free, buxom, and, if I may say so, wanton, too; and yet notwithstanding puissant, noble, generous and rare'.[32] But it also runs deeper than such an interpretation suggests. The point is not merely that philosophy fails to arouse our interest when it is wrapped up in opaque and obfuscatory language. It is rather that there is something inherently arid about even the most pellucid reasoning. In consequence, we can only be won over to philosophical enquiry by eloquence or the art of persuasion without which, Bacon tells us, we would be lost. Because the affections raise such mutinies and seditions, 'reason would become captive and servile if eloquence of persuasions did not practise and win the imagination from the affections' part and contract a confederacy between the reason and imagination against the affections'.[33]

The view that reasoning either leaves us indifferent or repels us challenges the claim that it arouses pleasurable intellectual emotions. In addition, the view that we have to be won over to scientific enquiry by eloquence runs counter to the claim that the rigorous pursuit of truth requires judgement rather than fancy. The point is frequently put in exactly these terms, for example by Reynolds, who explains that 'It often cometh to pass that some plausible fancy doth more prevail with tender wills than a severe or sullen argument, and hath more powerful insinuations to persuade, than the peremptoriness of reason hath to command.'[34] Philosophy, in short, cannot rely on judgement alone, and must borrow the tools of the Poet, who 'doth not only show the way, but giveth so sweet a prospect into the way as will entice any man to enter it'.[35] She must use eloquence to move people to reason, and to embrace the conclusions to which their reasoning leads.

Despite their stark differences, this solution to the problem of arousing and sustaining our interest in scientific enquiry is grounded on the same premisses as the approach preferred by Descartes and Spinoza. Demonstrative reasoning, we saw earlier, is held to consist in the perception of connections between intelligible ideas which are in turn contrasted with sensible ones. The division ensures that, while our sensible ideas excite passion, intelligible ideas are passion-proof. Some philosophers regard this feature of intelligible ideas as an advantage and an opportunity. The fact that they are resistant to passion creates a conceptual seed-bed in which intellectual emotions can take root and grow. Others, however, regard it as a liability. The resistance of intelligible ideas and chains of inferences to passion has the undesirable consequence that we are simply not moved by them. They do not excite interest, love, or desire. By comparison with the sensible ideas that do arouse our emotions, they strike us as rebarbative, so that, as Malebranche expresses it, 'an abstract, metaphysical, purely intelligible principle appears without solidity to carnal eyes, or to minds

---

[32] *Of Wisdome*, trans. S. Lennard (London, 1608), sig A 7[r–v].
[33] *Advancement of Learning*, 147.   [34] *Treatise of the Passions*, 19.
[35] Sidney, *Defense of Poesie*, 19.

that see only through their eyes. Nothing in this dry and abstract principle will quiet the restlessness of the will.'[36] One explanation of our failure to be moved by scientific enquiry therefore appeals to the fact that the ideas it involves are intelligible rather than sensible. But this analysis dovetails with a second, which draws on the view that we feel more vehemently about the here and now than about the spatially or temporally distant. Abstract truths do not excite us because they appear remote;[37] they lack the vividness and immediacy that engage our passions and 'are only seen, as it were, at an infinite distance and so appear to the soul proportionately lessened'.[38] The apposite contrast here is sometimes between present and absent ideas, sometimes between those that are near and those that are far away; but both oppositions rely on related conceptions of location and distance. Moreover, each interpretation of the problem carries with it a possible solution. Reflecting on the first, we arrive at the idea that, if our intelligible ideas could somehow be made sensible, they would become present and excite our passions; drawing on the second, we reach the conclusion that, if our ideas of intelligible things could be brought nearer, they would arouse stronger passions and gain our attention. In both cases, the tools of the poet can help.

Poetry, orations, invectives, and pleadings require, as we found Hobbes reiterating, a strong fancy or ability to discern similarities. By devising similes and metaphors, and employing a variety of other linguistic devices, a rhetorician or poet can represent abstract, intelligible ideas in terms of sensible ones, and can associate distant things or events with those that are recent or familiar.[39] Both strategies make objects present by enabling an audience to picture or imagine them, and, for the reasons we have just explored, making things present or near at hand simultaneously makes them the likely objects of passion. This set of techniques makes use of habits of association that, as we saw in Part II, are firmly embedded in human nature. At the simplest level a poet can trade on an established connection between an object and a passion, say between fear and monsters, and by associating one object with another, succeed in transferring the emotion from the first to the second. If jealousy, for example, is a monster, it too becomes fearful. Advocates of this and similar techniques are well aware that they do not only work through the medium of words, and many of them agree that the foremost, because literal, example of such a strategy is Christ's incarnation in which the Word becomes flesh. As Malebranche explains, 'The light illuminating all men shone upon their darkness without dispelling it—they could not even see it. Intelligible light had to

---

[36] *De la recherche*, ii. 7; trans. Lennon and Olscamp, 271.
[37] Ibid. i. 407; trans. Lennon and Olscamp, 213.
[38] Pierre Nicole, *Essais de morale* (Paris, 1672), ii. 56.
[39] See the outstanding discussion in D. K. Shuger, *Sacred Rhetoric: The Christian Grand Style in the English Renaissance* (Princeton, 1988), 193–227.

veil itself and make itself visible; the Word had to be made flesh, and hidden and inaccessible wisdom had to be taught to carnal man in a carnal manner.'[40] Humans, of course, lack the power to render the intelligible sensible, but they can create rituals to bring things alive, as the sacraments, for example, bring Christ nearer in visible and sensible things.[41] (Watching the raising of the host makes the Last Supper present and enlivens a congregation's emotional appreciation of the torment and generosity of Christ's sacrifice.) Most important of all, they can arouse emotions by the art of persuasion, which makes 'absent and remote things present to your understanding'.[42] The so-called 'figures' of rhetoric serve to ornament unadorned and naked intelligible ideas and present them to the imagination dressed in terms to which it can respond, associating sensible ideas with bare intelligible ones and thereby arousing passion. In this way, people can be moved to accept arguments and conclusions about the non-sensible realm.[43]

This ancient view is a commonplace of early-modern writing, spelled out and alluded to in a wide variety of contexts.[44] Among self-consciously philosophical authors, there are some, as we have already seen, who make it explicit. Adding examples, Bacon tells us that the business of rhetoric is to make virtue visible. For 'seeing that she cannot be showed to the sense by corporal shape, the next degree is to show her to the imagination in lively representation'.[45] In the same vein, Charleton asserts that the power of the ornaments of speech 'over the affections of the greater part of mankind . . . is so great that the whole art of oratory is founded thereon, and he that is the most excellent in that art, who by the help of those images of things absent formed in his imagination, doth represent them in so lively colours, that they appear present'.[46] As these claims suggest, the success of persuasion is explained by the fact that it exercises the imagination. But its efficacy is also sometimes attributed to the character of the will. Because liberty is natural to the will, it responds best to an approach 'which doth offer least force unto its liberty; which is done rather by an argument of delight than of constraint, and best of all when a rational and convincing argument is so sweetened and tempered, to the delight of the

---

[40] *De la recherche*, ii. 8; trans. Lennon and Olscamp, 272. This point is widely made. See e.g. John Smith (who attributes it to Augustine) in *The Excellency and Nobleness of True Religion*, in C. Patrides (ed.), *The Cambridge Platonists* (Cambridge, 1969), 146.

[41] John Donne, *The Sermons of John Donne*, ed. E. M. Simpson and G. R. Potter (Berkeley and Los Angeles, 1953–62), v. 144.

[42] Ibid. iv. 87.

[43] On Quintilian's formative discussion of this technique see Skinner, *Reason and Rhetoric*, 182–8.

[44] On the history of rhetoric and different styles of persuasion see Shuger, *Sacred Rhetoric*, 14–54; B. Vickers, 'The Power of Persuasion: Images of the Orator, Elyot to Shakespeare', in J. M. Murphy (ed.), *Renaissance Eloquence: Studies in the Theory of Renaissance Rhetoric* (Berkeley and Los Angeles, 1983), 411–35. On Aristotle and persuasion see L. A. Green, 'Aristotle's *Rhetoric* and Renaissance Views of the Emotions', in P. Mack (ed.), *Renaissance Rhetoric* (Basingstoke, 1994), 1–26. On rhetoric in France see M. Fumaroli, *L'Âge d'éloquence* (Geneva, 1980).

[45] *Advancement of Learning*, 147.   [46] *Brief Discourse*, 20–1.

hearer, that he shall be content to entertain truth, for the very beauty and attire of it, so you shall not know whether it were the weight of the reason that overruled, or the elegancy that enticed him'.[47]

For some writers, then, passions are an essential ingredient of reasoning, without which it could neither set sail or make any headway.[48] Moreover, even philosophers who do not share this view often agree that appeals to sensible ideas provide a vital explanatory prop which aids students who have not yet acquired the intellectual and emotional self-control to reason at will. As we have already seen, Hobbes allows that in some cases 'the Understanding hath need to be opened by some apt similitude; and then there is so much use for Fancy'.[49] The same problem is acknowledged by Descartes, who explains that 'our mind is unable to keep its attention on things without some degree of difficulty and fatigue; and it is hardest of all for it to attend to what is not present to the senses or even the imagination'.[50] This being so, we must help it out, by using, for instance, arithmetical and geometrical examples, the 'outer garment' of algebra, which 'clothe and adorn it so as to make it easier to present to the human mind'.[51] A concern to assist reason surely also underlies Descartes's advice that we should begin our study of the order that character-izes all sciences with the 'simplest and least-exalted arts, and especially those in which order prevails—such as weaving and carpet-making, or the more feminine arts of embroidery, in which threads are interwoven in an infinitely varied pattern'.[52] In these arts, order is sensible—we can see it with our eyes in the arrangement of the threads. By studying it in these contexts, we can accustom ourselves to perceiving it, and later apply this skill in more abstract domains.

Although he comments on it only occasionally, Descartes makes extensive use of what is perhaps the main technique for rendering intelligible ideas sensible—the use of simile.[53] If we want to engage the imagination, he remarks, we must take care that the similes we employ are not too simple, since 'most minds lose interest when things are made too easy for them'. Nor must they be too uniform; to present a picture which pleases, an author must 'use shadows as well as bright colours'.[54] In a letter written in 1638, Descartes makes it clear that he regards the use of analogy as an important explanatory device; he would go so far as to say, he tells Morin, that when someone makes an assertion

---

[47] Reynolds, *Treatise of the Passions*, 19. On rhetoric and philosophy see B. Vickers, 'Rhetoric and Poetics', in C. B. Schmitt and Q. Skinner (eds.), *The Cambridge History of Renaissance Philosophy* (Cambridge, 1988), 715–45.

[48] For discussion of this theme in Locke see M. Losonsky, 'John Locke on Passion, Will and Belief', *British Journal for the History of Philosophy*, 4 (1996), 267–83.

[49] *Leviathan*, 52.

[50] *The Principles of Philosophy*, in *Philosophical Writings*, ed. Cottingham *et al.*, vol. i, 1. 173.

[51] Id., *Rules*, rule 17.   [52] Ibid. 35.

[53] See the excellent discussion in P. France, *Rhetoric and Truth in France: Descartes to Diderot* (Oxford, 1972), 40–67.

[54] *The World*, in *Philosophical Writings*, ed. J. Cottingham *et al.*, i. 97.

concerning nature that cannot be explained by an analogy, the point is false.
The analogies in question must, however, meet certain standards; they must
not replicate the bad habits of the Schools by appealing to one kind of thing
to explain another, such as explaining intellectual matters by means of physical ones or substances by means of accidents, but must 'compare movements
only with other movements, or shapes with other shapes'.[55] Sticking to this
rule, Descartes fills his works with vivid images, representing the human body
as like the automata in the royal gardens,[56] the fire in the heart that causes
bodily motion as like an ordinary wood fire,[57] the heart and arteries as like the
bellows and pipes of a church organ,[58] and the circular motions of bodies as
like fish swimming in the pool of a fountain.[59] These analogies, and others like
them, form a crucial part of what rhetoricians call *ornatus* and *ornamenta*. But
to say that they are ornamental is not to say that they are decorative, and from
a philosophical point of view dispensable.[60] On the contrary, they are a vital
part of persuasive argument or exposition, for unless the imagination can picture the subject under discussion, the mind will have difficulty in attending
to it. Visual images therefore make it easier for us to conceive the properties
and relations of intelligible things. But because sensible ideas arouse our
passions, they simultaneously excite in us emotions such as pleasure or desire.

For authors such as Descartes this technique is only intended to be trans-
itional. The passion aroused by sensible images is meant to pass to the intelligible ideas they represent, so that the images themselves can eventually be
discarded or at least only imagined intermittently. When he excites our interest
in the behaviour of bodies in air by getting us to imagine fish in a fountain,
Descartes aims to enable us to think about the behaviour of the bodies
themselves. From time to time we may need to return to the fish or some
other image. But as we go on, our capacity for abstract thinking increases. The
technique of representing an intelligible idea by a sensible one revolves around
the assumption that two ideas can be in certain respects alike—for instance,
the motions of fish in a pool of water, like those of bodies, are circular. The
sensible idea is held to be more accessible because it is imaginable; and although
many of the philosophers whose work has been discussed in this section are
emphatic that ideas are not visual images, they seem in this context to rely on
the fact that, although sensible ideas are not identical with visual or auditory
images, they can be accompanied by them. Moreover, we can be reminded of
a sensible idea in a manner which prompts us to visualize it in a certain way.
When a philosopher describes particles of wood floating upward in a fire, the

[55] Letter to Morin, 12 Sept. 1638, *Correspondence*, 122.
[56] *The Treatise on Man*, in *Philosophical Writings*, ed. Cottingham *et al.*, i. 99, 100–1.
[57] *Passions of the Soul*, 8–10, cf. *World*, 83.   [58] *Treatise on Man*, 104.   [59] *World*, 86.
[60] *Ornatus* is used in classical Latin to describe the weapons and accoutrements of war. On this
metaphor and its use by the classical rhetoricians see Skinner, *Reason and Rhetoric*, 48–9.

image we form is likely to contain the details that have been mentioned. For example, I will probably form an image of a fire which is sufficiently near for me to 'see' particles rising above it. How, though, do such images represent ideas of intelligible things? Presumably, part of the process of coming to see intelligible things as similar to sensible ones consists in forming related images, as when my image of the fire prompts me to form an image of the fire in the heart. Perhaps I visualize tiny, leaping flames, drained of colour and unsustained by any detectable fuel, burning in the heart and creating warm currents in the blood. This image is not identical with my idea of the fire in the heart.[61] But it is held to be able to alter and strengthen it. Having visualized the fire in the heart, I gradually become able to think about its operations without visualizing it. I simply think in an abstract way about its motions and their effects.

What, though, about the emotional aspect of this process? Here the crucial mechanism seems to be one we have already discussed—our natural disposition to transfer passions from one object to another that resembles it. As well as bringing this to bear on external things, as when we find ourselves listening with pleasure to a stranger whose voice reminds us of a friend, we bring it to bear on ideas, so that a person whose fear is excited by one idea will transfer the emotion to other ideas she finds similar. To manipulate this disposition, all we have to do is to represent one idea as like another, and although, as we have just seen, it is not perfectly clear how we do this, the fact *that* we do it is taken for granted. If I experience the idea of a fire as beautiful and fascinating, and if you can persuade me that this idea is similar to that of the fire in the heart, my emotions will attach to the latter idea, and I will contemplate it with pleasure and interest.

As we have seen, early-modern writers describe the technique we are exploring in two ways. Symbols and figurative language make the intelligible more accessible by making it imaginable or present; they also make it accessible by bringing ideas of distant things closer. In so far as these descriptions can be held apart, many of the techniques recommended and used by Descartes seem to fit the first; they represent things that are not accessible to sense in sensible terms. However, the notion of moving things around in the sensory field— bringing them closer or sending them further away—has further connotations which play still more intricately on the natural dispositions of the passions. Since bringing an idea closer also has the effect of making it look larger, the idea that we feel strong passions for things that are near is intimately related to the idea that the passions of esteem and veneration are aroused by things that look large. The techniques for bringing things nearer are therefore liable also to excite the passions surrounding *grandeur* and *petitesse*, so that several

---

[61] For philosophers such as Descartes, who reject the view that ideas are images the relation between the two becomes problematic and it becomes correspondingly harder to explain how persuasion works.

of the distorting dispositions explored in Chapter 7 start to operate. Our sensitivity to sensible ideas brings worldly things close to us and gives us lively desires for them. These are further strengthened by the perception that other people desire them too, which activates the dynamics surrounding *grandeur*. As Nicole analyses it, 'it is enough that anything be esteemed and sought after by others to make us believe that it deserves to be so, since by having it we look on ourselves as surrounded by the crowd of people who judge advantageously of us, and account us happy in being owners of it'. In this way, we rate things 'not by their true, intrinsic value, but by that they carry in the opinion of others'.[62] *Grandeur*, as we have seen, is a treacherous quality, and our vulnerability to it gives rise to interests and relationships with other people which divert us from true understanding. This seems to imply that the technique we are now considering is similarly dangerous. Precisely because we easily admire things that appear literally or metaphorically large, we need to be very careful how we apply the techniques that bring our ideas of things closer, for once they are close, they will excite strong admiration.

This peril is well understood. But the art of altering our passions by moving things around in our imagined sensory field is held to be a useful tool none the less. The persuasive techniques I have discussed are widely regarded as an essential part of philosophy, the only reliable means to attract and sustain interest in true learning and knowledge. At the same time, though, they are subject to suspicion, and tend to be condemned even by those who manipulate them most skilfully. Hobbes gives a decidedly cautious welcome to fancy, conceding in the Review and Conclusion of *Leviathan* that 'Reason and eloquence, (though not perhaps in the natural sciences, yet in the moral) may stand very well together.'[63] Descartes, despite his brilliant use of imagery, flatly defends the superlative persuasive power of reason. 'Those with the strongest reasoning and most skill at ordering their thoughts so as to make them clear and intelligible are always the most persuasive, even if they speak only low Breton and have never learned rhetoric.'[64] And Malebranche, for all his appeals to imagination, condemns orators or those known as *grands parleurs* for their superficiality. Good minds, he insists, easily remark the differences between things. But superficial ones, which occupy themselves with imagining resemblances, only see things fleetingly, indistinctly, and from a great distance.[65] Part of this shared hesitation stems from the conviction that the use of visual images can prove self-defeating. The mathematical analysis of the ancients, Descartes points out, 'is so closely tied to the examination of figures that it cannot exercise the intellect without greatly tiring the imagination'.[66] Malebranche expresses

---

[62] *Essais de morale*, ii. 58.   [63] pp. 483–4.
[64] *Discourse on the Method of Rightly Conducting one's Reason and Seeking the Truth in the Sciences*, in *Philosophical Writings*, ed. Cottingham *et al.*, i. 114.
[65] *De la recherche*, i. 313; trans. Lennon and Olscamp, 156.   [66] *Discourse*, 118.

the same view in a highly rhetorical style. We must be careful not to overload Truth with ornament in case she should appear like one of those people so covered with gold and precious stones that they themselves are less noticeable than their costume. Rather, 'we must dress Truth like the doges of Venice, who are required to wear an utterly simple gown and cap which only serves to distinguish them from ordinary people, in order that one can concentrate on their faces with attention and respect, rather than dwelling on their clothes'.[67]

There are, then, two versions of the widespread view that, to pursue knowledge with any consistency and determination, we have to rely on the motivating force of our passions. For Hobbes, scientific enquiry, like everything else we do, must spring from a desire which moves us to formulate definitions and work out causes and effects. To excite this desire, we must appeal to other passions such as anxiety or fear. The search for knowledge is in this respect like any other activity, and there is no reason to think that the pleasure we gain from it will necessarily be greater than the satisfactions of wealth, rank, or reputation. Hobbes's attempt to cut philosophy down to size is, however, if anything less deflating than the view that reasoning is so strict that it easily induces tiredness and despair.[68] To make it manageable, let alone pleasant, the intelligible ideas it requires us to grasp must be made sensible and represented by images that arouse appropriate passions such as love and desire for knowledge. We must make use of the fact that passion attaches to the ideas we derive from sense, imagination, and memory; and at the same time we must be careful that sensible images strengthen, but do not overwhelm, the intelligible ideas they are intended to represent.

This latter view can be espoused either as a first step towards arousing the intellectual passions that accompany reasoning proper, or as the only available means to create the emotions that move us to pursue knowledge. The second of these conceptions obviously carries the implication that acquiring, possessing, and using knowledge are passionate activities which depend on the existence of a certain range of desires and on certain kinds of frustration, pleasure, and enjoyment. Knowledgeable people, and people who want to become knowledgeable, will possess a distinctive range of passions and susceptibilities to passion, and these will be central to their characters. They will know certain things and have certain feelings about their knowledge. They will also possess certain desires to maintain, use, or increase their understanding. These capacities depend, however, on their continuing passivity—on their exposure and sensitivity to the sensible ideas we derive from our embodied existence and which are perhaps the most important way in which we are acted on. The capacity to pursue

---

[67] *De la recherche*, II. 167; trans. Lennon and Olscamp, 417. On the rhetorical style employed by Malebranche see T. Carr, *Descartes and the Resilience of Rhetoric* (Carbondale, Ill., 1990), 89–124.

[68] Reynolds, *Treatise of the Passions*, 21.

scientific understanding is therefore not, according to this view, a matter of escaping the sensible and entering an active, quasi-divine realm, but is continuous with passive thought and feeling. The active connotations of philosophical enquiry are lost, or compromised, and knowledge is both sustained by, and a manifestation of, desire.

So far, I have spoken of knowledge and passion as distinct, although occurring together. Because it is accompanied by passion, knowledge is never a matter of acquaintance with an otherwise inert set of interconnecting propositions. But it is not itself an array of emotions. The philosophers whose work has been central to this chapter are strongly drawn to this conception of understanding, and distinguish the demonstrations that are the content of knowledge from the feelings associated with knowing them. This view of the matter is, however, under some strain. For it exists alongside a very different conception of knowledge as passion which will be the subject of the next chapter.

IO

Knowledge as Emotion

Alongside the view that passions can motivate us to acquire knowledge, and that intellectual activity is itself accompanied by pleasurable affections, we find in seventeenth-century philosophy a further, internally complex conception of knowledge which is still more closely linked to emotion. To know something, according to this account, it is not enough to understand it or be able to prove it—one must also be capable of acting on it. The ability to act, however, depends on the possession of appropriate volitions, which are in turn conceived as identical with emotions, or as so closely connected that the two always occur together. Either way, action and emotion are both intrinsic to knowledge, and can be used as criteria for distinguishing it from epistemically inferior states. The fact that people may be incapable of acting on claims they profess to know is an indication that they have not attained knowledge after all. Equally, the presence of certain emotions (typically love) can be evidence for the correctness of a particular view.

This heady analysis draws on two palimpsestic traditions—Platonism and Augustinianism. From Plato, early-modern philosophers inherit a hierarchical conception of knowledge as love, which many of them put to work in their interpretations of the relation between natural and moral knowledge.[1] Superimposed on this is the influence of Augustine (famous for his remark that Plato is the most nearly Christian of the pagan philosophers)[2] whose doctrine of the will lends authority to the association between emotion and volition.[3] Error, as Augustine sees it, lies not so much in misperception as in the disorder of the human will, in our inability to keep our volitions, and hence our actions, in line with our understanding. But since we experience volitions as emotions, this failing is simultaneously an emotional one, an inability to feel appropriate loves and hatreds. To bring order to our wills, we must do our best to redirect our emotions so that we love and hate the right things, and although Augustine thinks that our ability to achieve this end is limited, he nevertheless believes that we have a responsibility to make whatever progress we can.

---

[1] On the history of Platonism see D. P. Walker, *The Ancient Theology: Studies in Christian Platonism from the Fifteenth to the Eighteenth Centuries* (London, 1972), esp. 164–93; P. Merlan, *From Platonism to Neo-Platonism* (The Hague, 1968); A. Baldwin and S. Hutton (eds.), *Platonism and the English Imagination* (Cambridge, 1994).

[2] *City of God*, 8. 2.   [3] See Ch. 5 nn. 101 and 105.

Only by learning to reshape our feelings, then, can we produce the orderly volitions that are intrinsic to knowledge. This approach has a significant influence on both Catholic and Protestant writers in the seventeenth century, where it is most prominent in discussions about knowledge of the good. Many of the philosophers who adopt it make a more-or-less explicit division between theoretical and practical knowledge, taking the view that, while it may be possible to possess purely theoretical knowledge of the natural world, knowing God and understanding virtue are practical skills which manifest themselves in action. A division along these lines is obviously convenient, but it also raises the question of how theoretical and practical knowledge are related, and this problem is a subject of debate.[4] In some cases, as we shall see, the two kinds of knowledge are integrated into a Platonist hierarchy, a progression of types of knowledge and love.

Knowledge as Will

The conviction that virtue depends on a knowledge of God which can never be gained simply 'by our acquaintance with systems and models of divinity' or 'by our skill in books and papers',[5] is shared by the group of English Protestant philosophers known as the Cambridge Platonists,[6] and is relatively systematically explored by Henry More, for whom virtue consists both in following right reason and in the tranquil happiness this inspires. While understanding the good is a rational enterprise,[7] knowledge of virtue consists in more than bare definitions, since it is an ability to prosecute the good which gives rise to joys that cannot be uttered.[8] Moreover, the experience of these joys is not an aspect of understanding; instead, it occurs in what More calls the boniform faculty of the soul—a faculty which 'much resembles the will' and enables us to enjoy the good.[9] Thus far, More seems to espouse the view that knowledge of virtue consists in understanding accompanied by emotion. When we understand what is and is not good, we are moved to follow the good by the volitions of the boniform faculty, which we experience as emotions. But this reading is unsettled

---

[4] See R. Hoopes, *Right Reason in the English Renaissance* (Cambridge, Mass., 1962); L. Mulligan, '"Reason", "Right Reason" and "Revelation" in Mid-Seventeenth Century England', in B. Vickers (ed.), *Occult and Scientific Mentalities in the Renaissance* (Cambridge, 1984), 357–401; J. Morgan, *Godly Learning: Puritan Attitudes towards Reason, Learning and Education, 1560–1640* (Cambridge, 1986), 41–61.

[5] Ralph Cudworth, *A Sermon Preached before the House of Commons*, in *The Cambridge Platonists*, ed. C. A. Patrides (Cambridge, 1969), 108. See S. Darwall, *The British Moralists and the Internal 'Ought', 1640–1740* (Cambridge, 1995), 109–47.

[6] On Cambridge Platonism see E. Cassirer, *The Platonic Renaissance in England* (London, 1953); S. Hutton, 'Lord Herbert of Cherbury and the Cambridge Platonists', in S. Brown (ed.), *The Routledge History of Philosophy*, v. *British Philosophy and the Age of Enlightenment* (London, 1996), 20–42.

[7] More, *An Account of Virtue or Dr. More's Abridgment of Morals put into English*, trans. E. Southwell (London, 1690), 12, 15.

[8] Ibid. 9.   [9] Ibid. 6.

by More's further claim that the standard of right reason is the intellectual love that moves the boniform faculty. If we ask how we know that we are reasoning correctly, the answer lies in 'the relish and intrinsic feeling' of the boniform faculty.[10] So while the boniform faculty follows the judgements of right reason, the judgements of right reason submit to the feeling of the boniform faculty. Intellectual emotion becomes the test of goodness.

Other Cambridge Platonists combine this view of the epistemological significance of emotion with a greater emphasis on the connection between knowledge and action. According to Benjamin Whichcote, for example, unless knowledge goes forth into act, it does not sanctify, and truth is held in unrighteousness.[11] People who have a theoretical understanding may have 'a religion to talk of and profess, a religion to give them a denomination'.[12] But they lack 'the sense of God', the strong and vigorous inclination towards him which enables us to participate in his nature and brings with it the truest pleasure and satisfaction.[13] The claim that, where religion is concerned, speculative knowledge is not enough is more vehemently reiterated by Ralph Cudworth, who allies its limitations to the inadequacy of words to capture spiritual truths. 'Cold theorems and maxims, dry and jejune disputes, lean syllogistical reasonings, could never yet of themselves beget the least glimpse of true heavenly light, the least sap of saving knowledge in any heart.' But this is because 'words and syllables, which are but dead things, cannot possibly convey the living notions of heavenly truths to us'.[14] Cudworth's argument, later echoed by his colleague Henry More,[15] seems to draw here on the view of demonstration that we find, for example, in Hobbes—the view that this sort of thinking consists in studying the relations between definitions or words rather than the relations between ideas. The force of his condemnation also rests, however, on a distinction between the dead and the living, which is aligned with that between representations and our experience of sensory properties.

A painter that would draw a rose, though he may flourish some likeness of it in figure and colour, yet he can never paint the scent and fragrancy; or if he would draw a flame, he can never put a constant heat into his colours; he cannot make his pencil drop a sound, as the echo in the epigram mocks him—'If you wish to paint a likeness, paint a sound' . . . Neither are we able to enclose in words and letters, the life, soul and essence of any spiritual truths, and as it were incorporate it into them.[16]

The essence of spiritual truths is here compared to the scent of a rose or the heat of a flame, to the vivid, sensory properties that move us to action. Religious

[10] Ibid. 156.
[11] *The Use of Reason in Matters of Religion*, in *The Cambridge Platonists* ed. Patrides, 42. On Whichcote see R. A. Grene, 'Whichcote, the Candle of the Lord and Synderesis', *Journal of the History of Ideas*, 52 (1991), 617–44.
[12] Whichcote, *Use of Reason*, 72.   [13] Ibid.   [14] Cudworth, *Sermon*, 92.
[15] More, *Account of Virtue*, 9.   [16] *Sermon*, 92.

knowledge resembles these in being a kind of sensible awareness of God which Cudworth and the other Cambridge Platonists persistently describe in terms of taste, touch, and smell, as well as through visual and auditory images. As Cudworth puts it, 'the spirit of divine truth cannot sufficiently express itself in words and sounds, but it will best declare and speak itself in actions: as the old manner of writing among the Egyptians was, not by words but things'.[17]

The view that we should be perfecting our practical rather than merely speculative knowledge is also eloquently defended by John Smith, according to whom 'That is not the best and truest knowledge of God which is wrought out by the sweat and labour of the brain, but that which is kindled within us by an heavenly warmth in our hearts.'[18] Like Whichcote and Cudworth, Smith distinguishes understanding the truth from living the good, but also like them, he sees the two as intimately connected. Truth and love, Cudworth tells us, are two of the most powerful things in the world, and when they both go together, cannot easily be withstood.[19] More than this, Smith claims, truth and goodness can in themselves never be disunited; 'they grow both from the same root and live in one another'.[20] These writers adhere to the Augustinian view that the transition from truth to goodness lies in the transformation of the will. The source of our unhappiness, in Cudworth's view, is self-will. 'When we have cashiered this self-will of ours, which did but shackle and confine our souls, our wills shall then become truly free, being widened and enlarged to the extent of God's own will.'[21] For Smith, also, our deficiencies lie principally in our volitions. 'We want not so much means of knowing what we ought to do, as wills to do that which we may know.' Furthermore, both writers equate possessing a good will with joyfulness. Smith describes this state as 'the true perfection, sweetness, energy and loveliness . . . that can no more be known by naked demonstration, than colours can be perceived by a blind man'.[22] Cudworth characterizes it as the Law of Love, 'a kind of musical soul, informing the dead organs of our hearts, that makes them of their own accord delight to act harmoniously according to the rule of God's word'.[23]

These explications draw on a view discussed in the preceding chapter, that reasoning alone is powerless to move us. Rather than identifying the aridity of reason as an obstacle to the pursuit of knowledge, however, the Cambridge Platonists emphasize that it is an obstacle to knowledge itself, which consists in more than a grasp of logical connections, and requires emotion. Their identification of knowledge and feeling resembles the view that understanding

---

[17] Ibid. 108.
[18] *The True Way or Method of Attaining to Divine Knowledge*, in *Cambridge Platonists*, ed. Patrides, 129.
[19] *Sermon*, 118.   [20] *True Way*, 130.   [21] *Sermon*, 99.   [22] *True Way*, 139.
[23] *Sermon*, 124.

arouses intellectual emotions; but there are nevertheless significant differences between the two. The advocates of intellectual emotions defend two central claims: first, that all speculative knowledge, whether of the natural or moral sciences, excites intellectual joy; secondly, that the mind rejoices in the operation of its own understanding. Both these positions are questioned by the Cambridge Platonists. Knowledge of the natural world does not, as they see it, depend on intellectual emotion, and may arise from lean syllogistical reasonings, whereas moral knowledge consists in a certain emotional temperament. In the case of moral knowledge, moreover, we experience intellectual joy when we will correctly rather than when we merely understand. The perceptions that constitute our acquaintance with systems and models of divinity, for example, may leave us completely unmoved, and it is only when we experience volitions or emotions that we can really be said to know.

These distinctions remain relatively clear and tidy as long as we compare the Cambridge Platonists with Spinoza, one of the two philosophers discussed in Chapter 8, but they become muddier when we turn to Descartes. For Descartes, as we have seen, the intellectual emotions are primarily associated with volition, and it is by learning to control our wills so that we can act in accordance with our best-considered judgements that we become truly happy. Cartesianism thus coincides with Cambridge Platonism in so far as both hold that virtue consists in the ability to control the will. They diverge, however, in the aspects of volition that they emphasize, and in the relations they posit between willing and knowledge. For Descartes, the will rejoices in its own proper activity which is to assent to judgements, and, albeit only indirectly, the acquisition of knowledge strengthens its joy. For the Platonists, by contrast, there is a gap between reason on the one hand, and love or knowledge, on the other. Because reasoning itself does not engage the will and cannot create the ability to act on our understanding, the question of how to achieve the one is consequently no longer the same as the question of how to achieve the other. We face a new problem: how is the love that constitutes knowledge of virtue to be created and disseminated?

Since this kind of knowledge consists at least in part in the acquisition of appropriate emotions towards things, it seems that, in order to overcome error, we must redirect our passions. One way to bring about this change, liberally employed by the philosophers we have just considered, is to resort to the persuasive devices catalogued by rhetoricians. A judicious selection of symbols and figures of speech can change an audience's picture of the world and the way they feel about it. The desire to create practical knowledge also licenses the use of other techniques, however, which play in yet further ways upon our passions. First, among the traits that can be tapped to redirect our emotions is our disposition to love things that we perceive as like ourselves. This durable view is found in Plato, and had been used by Plutarch to explain solidarity within animal species—elephants, for example, love elephants, and eagles eagles. In humans, a comparable tendency works in a more fine-grained fashion, and arises not only from propinquity of natures but also from sameness of manners,[24] so that learned people tend to get on with one another, students make friends with students, and soldiers with soldiers. Once we have become aware of it, we can manipulate this disposition, changing a person's passions by presenting others as more like or unlike them than they had believed. The paramount example of this strategy draws on Christ's Incarnation since, in becoming man, God made himself like us, and by coming to see him as capable of our enjoyments and suffering we can intensify our love for him. But it also has secular applications, as Thomas Wright reminds us when he remarks that 'if thou wilt please thy master or friend, thou must apparel thyself in his affections . . . ; and as this means fostereth flattery if it be abused, so it nourisheth charity if it be well used'.[25] Like all the persuasive techniques we have considered, this one is double-edged. Cudworth, for example, rails against those who present God as nothing but an image of themselves which 'Narcissus-like, they fall in love with'. However, in the same passage he praises the Gospel as a source of divine knowledge on the grounds that it is 'nothing else, but God descending into the world in our form, and conversing with us in our likeness, that he might allure us, and draw us up to God, and make us partakers of his divine form'.[26]

A second way to redirect the emotions is to appeal to their mimetic quality. Although I may have no particularly strong passions for an object, once I perceive that you love it I will take on your emotion and begin to love it too. This use of this trait is a standard rhetorical device, and, as we saw in Chapter 5, it is built in to seventeenth-century theories of the bodily manifestations of the passions. Malebranche, for example, explains how it operates when one person is directly present to others. '[A] man who is convinced by what he says usually convinces others, as an impassioned man always arouses their emotions; and even if his rhetoric is irregular he will be no less persuasive. This is because his presence and manner make themselves felt, and excite men's imaginations more strongly than a solider but coolly-delivered discourse which does not flatter the senses or strike the imagination.'[27] Henry More assumes an understanding of this device in his didactic poem 'Cupid's Conflict', in which Cupid spells out to the virtuous poet Mela the delights and advantages of lustful passion. If I made you burn with love, Cupid tells him,

[24] e.g. Edward Reynolds, *A Treatise of the Passions and Faculties of the Soul of Man* (London, 1640), 88.

[25] *The Passions of the Mind in General* (2nd edn 1604), ed. W. W. Newbold (New York, 1986), 160.

[26] *Sermon*, 101.

[27] *De la recherche de la vérité*, ed. G. Rodis Lewis, in *Œuvres complètes*, ed. A. Robinet (2nd edn, Paris, 1972), i. 329; trans. T. M. Lennon and P. J. Olscamp as *The Search after Truth* (Columbus, Oh., 1980), 165–6.

All sexes, ages, orders, occupations
Would listen to thee with attentive ear,
And eas'ly moved with thy sweet persuasions,
Thy pipe would follow with full merry cheer.[28]

The same disposition is held to work through the mediation of painting, as is evident, for example, in Poussin's explanation of his refusal to embark on a picture of the road to Calvary. '[Painting] the Crucifixion', he writes, 'made me ill, I took such pains over it, but the carrying of the cross would finish me off. I would not be able to withstand the deep and distressing thoughts with which it is necessary to fill one's mind and heart in order to paint such sad and gloomy subjects with any conviction.'[29]

This technique is therefore used in various contexts, including preaching, where it forms the basis of a tradition of Christian oratory which flourished particularly in English Puritan circles. At the centre of this practice is the idea that a preacher who is actually in the grip of a passion and expresses it in his words and gestures will excite the same emotion in his audience so that, as Perkins puts it, the fire in his heart kindles the love of God or hatred of sin in his congregation.[30] To imprint a passion in another, 'it is requisite it first be stamped in our hearts; for through our voices, eyes and gestures, the world will pierce and thoroughly perceive how we are affected'.[31] For this method to succeed, the preacher must appear ardent but artless, since once a congregation becomes aware of the devices he is using to arouse them they will be distracted from his passion, and the transfer of emotion will not take place. There is consequently an emphasis on sincerity and expressiveness, and on the use of a felt, if irregular, rhetoric, as opposed to a polished and carefully contrived style. Ideally, in fact, a preacher should not have to work to achieve emotional effects; instead the Holy Spirit should bestow on him the fiery heart and burning tongue[32] that enable him unselfconsciously to pour out his feeling. When skilfully used, this method is acknowledged to be extremely powerful, capable of working violently on an audience and stirring up vehement passions. Thomas Wright regales his readers with his recollections of

a preacher in Italy who had such powers over his auditors' affections, that when it pleased him he could cause them to shed abundance of tears, yea, and with tears dropping down their cheeks, presently turn their sorrow into laughter; and the reason was because he himself was extremely passionate, knowing moreover the art of moving the

---

[28] In *Cupid's Conflict* annexed to *Democritus Platonnisans*, ed. P. G. Stanwood (Berkeley and Los Angeles, 1968), 12.

[29] Poussin to Stella in *Actes*, ed. A. Chastel (Paris, 1960), ii. 219.

[30] *The Art of Prophesying*, in *The Workes of that Famous and Worthie Minister of Christ, in the University of Cambridge, Mr. William Perkins* (Cambridge, 1609), ii. 70.

[31] Wright, *Passions of the Mind*, 212.

[32] Perkins. Quoted in Shuger, *Sacred Rhetoric: The Christian Grand Style in the English Renaissance* (Princeton, 1988), 231.

affections of those auditors; and besides that, the most part were women that heard him (whose passions are most vehement and mutable) therefore he might have persuaded them what he liked.[33]

As Wright's anecdote illustrates, exhortations of this kind are designed to arouse not just positive emotions such as love of God or hope of salvation, but also negative ones such as fear and self-loathing. 'The way to obtain a good assurance indeed of our title to heaven', Cudworth reminds the members of the House of Commons, 'is not to clamber up to it, by a ladder of our own ungrounded persuasions; but to dig as low as hell by humility and self-denial in our own hearts.'[34] The transition from error to knowledge is here seen as an emotional journey in which self-satisfaction must give way to hopelessness and hope be crushed by fear before these feelings can begin to be replaced by appropriate loves and hatreds. Rather than inducing tranquil and pleasurable affections, increasing knowledge stirs up a range of emotions, aroused by a rhetoric that 'urges things contrary to human sense, and bitter and distasteful to the depraved and misguided nature of men: as the contempt of wealth, scorn of honours, flight from pleasure, hatred of parents, love of enemies'.[35]

The prevalence of this technique among the English Puritan sects attracted forceful opponents who condemned such enthusiasm, as it was called, on both religious and epistemological grounds and criticized the view that emotion is integral to knowledge. The stirring-up of passionate religious conviction threatened, on the one hand, the authority of priests and the doctrines of the Church. On the other hand, it also claimed to vindicate a conception of knowledge as feeling which seemed to bypass reason. The claim to be able to feel the truth amounted to an extreme subjectivism which struck many philosophers as a dangerous travesty of religious knowledge, and was fiercely contested on two grounds. Henry More articulates the first of these when he defines enthusiasm as 'a full but false persuasion in a man that he is inspired' and attributes this error to the excesses of the imagination, and particularly to melancholy, which makes men prone 'strongly and peremptorily either to believe or disbelieve a thing' and also makes them eloquent and persuasive.[36] The problem here is not that inspiration does not occur, or that love which is also knowledge does not reveal itself as such, but that it is difficult to identify. A different kind of objection is voiced by Locke, in the chapter that he wrote for the fourth edition of *An Essay Concerning Human Understanding*, published in 1700.[37] There

---

[33] *Passions of the Mind*, 90.   [34] *Sermon*, 94.

[35] Ludovicus Carbo, *Divinus Orator, vel de rhetorica divina libri septem* (Venice, 1595), 32. Quoted in Shuger, *Sacred Rhetoric*, 131.

[36] *Enthusiasmus Triumphatus*, ed. M. V. De Porte (Berkeley and Los Angeles, 1966), 10–11. See R. Crocker, 'Mysticism and Enthusiasm in Henry More', in S. Hutton (ed.), *Henry More (1614–1687): Tercentenary Studies* (Dordrecht, 1990), 137–55.

[37] See W. Von Leyden, *John Locke: Essays on the Law of Nature* (Oxford, 1954), 60–80.

are, Locke tells us, only two proper grounds for assenting to a proposition. One is that we have reasons for it—proofs or arguments which support it and command a certain degree of assent. The other is that it is part of revelation, one of the truths communicated directly to us by God, 'which reason vouches the truth of, by the testimony and proof it gives that they come from God'.[38] Enthusiasm, or the belief that one's own impulses are divinely inspired, is not, however, a proper ground of assent. People who believe themselves inspired 'feel the hand of God moving within them, and the impulses of the spirit, and cannot be mistaken in what they feel . . . [W]hat they have a sensible experience of admits no doubt, needs no probation. Would he not be ridiculous who should require to have it proved to him that the light shines, and that he sees it?'[39] It is this very certainty, the fact that enthusiasts see no need to consider whether they perceive an inclination in themselves, or the spirit of God moving that inclination, that makes them so intransigent and dangerous.[40]

Locke here condemns the unreflective attitude that enthusiasts take towards their own emotions. But he also implies that there is in the emotions themselves nothing to reflect on. They contain no evidence about their own origins, so that in order to assess whether a truth has been revealed by God we have to look beyond the truth itself to the testimony of reason. When the words of enthusiasts are stripped of the metaphors of seeing and feeling, all they amount to is the claim that 'they are sure because they are sure; and their persuasions are right only because they are strong in them'.[41] But these similes 'so impose on them, that they serve them for certainty in themselves and demonstration to others'. This scepticism about the epistemological significance of the metaphors employed by enthusiasts no doubt underpins Locke's more general view that rhetoric is a powerful instrument of error and deceit.[42] And yet, in explaining this judgement, he acknowledges the characteristics which give it such force and convince other philosophers that it can be put to benign use. It has to be faced, Locke concedes, that rhetoric pleases. 'Eloquence, like the fair sex, has too many prevailing beauties in it, to suffer itself ever to be spoken against. And 'tis vain to find fault with those arts of deceiving, wherein men

---

[38] *An Essay Concering Human Understanding*, ed. P. H. Nidditch (Oxford, 1975), IV. xix. 4.

[39] Ibid. 8.

[40] Attacks on enthusiasm are widespread. See Walter Charleton, *The Darkness of Atheism Dispelled by the Light of Nature: A Physico-Theological Treatise* (London, 1652), pref.; Robert Boyle, *Some Considerations on the Reconcileableness of Reason and Religion*, in *Works*, ed. T. Birch (London, 1772), iii, esp. 518–19; John Wilkins, *Sermons Preached upon Several Occasions* (London, 1682), 400, 407–8; Hobbes, *Leviathan*, ed. R. Tuck (Cambridge, 1991), 57, 258–9. See Mulligan, '"Reason", "Right Reason" and "Revelation"', 357–40. On earlier debates in England see D. K. Shuger, *Habits of Thought in the English Renaissance: Religion, Politics and the Dominant Culture* (Berkeley and Los Angeles, 1990), 17–68.

[41] *Essay*, IV. xix. 9.

[42] Ibid. II. x. 34. For the place of this discussion in Locke's philosophy see the outstanding essay by J. Tully, 'Governing Conduct: Locke on the Reform of Thought and Behaviour', in *An Approach to Political Philosophy: Locke in Contexts* (Cambridge, 1993), 179–241.

find pleasure to be deceived.'[43] Passion, in short, is out of line with truth, and the pleasures of knowledge can easily be overruled by those attaching to error.

While religious enthusiasm served to discredit the identification of knowledge and feeling, and to consolidate the view that knowing depends on the possession of other kinds of evidence, it would be a mistake to allow the historical importance of this trend within seventeenth-century philosophy to overshadow the extent to which knowledge and emotion were regarded as inextricably intertwined, to the point of being almost identical. As we have seen, a range of philosophers continued to believe that religious and moral knowledge require an inner transformation of emotion and will. They therefore remained interested in the character of this transformation, and the question of how it could be brought about. Because their investigations of these issues both shaped and were shaped by their views about the links between knowledge of the natural world and knowledge of the good, they provide insights into the connections between feeling and knowledge as a whole.

Love as the Highest Kind of Knowledge

For some philosophers, the distinction between knowledge of nature and knowledge of God belongs within a hierarchical order of stages through which the soul can ascend in its search for perfection. A number of versions of this doctrine were espoused during the seventeenth century. One cluster of interpretations is basically Platonist in allegiance, and draws from chronologically scattered sources the common conviction that because reason yields only one, relatively poor kind of knowledge, the mind must move out beyond it to a knowledge more akin to feeling. Only love or knowledge of the heart can yield true insight into the nature and commands of God, and thus into the good. Among the defenders of this view, John Smith, a fellow of Queens' College, Cambridge whose *Select Discourses* were published posthumously, reworked a series of doctrines attributed to Plato and Plotinus in the name of (Protestant) Christianity. Smith's argument for the limitations of reason displays what is by now a familiar concern with the role of piety in a Christian life: it emphasizes that to possess moral knowledge is to be able to act rightly; and to act rightly is to lead the kind of godly life described in the New Testament. Smith starts from the fact that 'there are some radical principles of knowledge that are so deeply sunk into the souls of men, as that the impression cannot easily be obliterated', of which 'the common notions of God and virtue . . . are more perspicuous than any else'.[44] These impressions, however, grow faint and

---

[43] *Essay*, II. x. 34.   [44] *True Way*, 138.

inefficacious if we do not make use of them; and they are especially prone to be weakened by our bodily passions. To retain our natural grasp of virtue, we must withdraw from sensuous encounters, for only then can we begin to acquire knowledge of the divine world which will bring with it virtuous emotions.[45] People who are able to take this advice have already embarked upon an ascent through four types of knowledge, and have passed beyond the lowest level, where reason is subject to passion, to the second phase. Here, reason has won enough ground to enable them to have clear and steady impressions of virtue and goodness, and from this point they may rise to a third level at which 'their inward sense of virtue and moral goodness [are] far transcendent to all mere speculative opinions of it', but not yet so secure as to be proof against pride, conceit, and other varieties of self-love. Finally, a person 'running and shooting up above his own logical or self-rational life' may achieve union with God, and become 'amorous of Divine Beauty, beautiful and lovely'.[46]

For Christian Platonists, the transformation embodied in these four stages has a mystical quality which is an aspect of faith. Those who have not yet gained divine knowledge must have faith in the possibility of doing so while lacking anything more than a schematic sense of what they are striving to achieve. Among the claims they must take on trust is the view that it is possible to acquire a non-propositional kind of knowledge which is experienced as love. As Richard Hooker had already put it, they must 'hope against all evidence of believing'.[47] In his efforts to explain this idea, Smith plays in a manner by now familiar upon a variety of conventional contrasts. He is emphatic that moral knowledge is not mere knowledge *that*, but knowledge of *how* to live a virtuous life. At the same time he undermines the sceptical contrast between sensing and knowing by using metaphors of sight and taste to convey the quality of divine truth.[48] In addition, he reverses the traditional associations of knowledge and emotion with the head and the heart: the best knowledge—knowledge of God and morality—originates in the seat of the emotions, the heart.

The view that knowledge lies beyond the reach of reason is not only explored by writers who identified themselves as Platonists, and indeed any distinction between Platonists and non-Platonists in this matter is a somewhat artificial one. Plato's doctrines had been widely adapted by Christian thinkers, and Augustine, in particular, had made some aspects of Platonism his own. In the seventeenth century, the overlap between philosophers in the Augustinian and Platonist traditions emerges particularly clearly in the works of French writers sympathetic to Jansenism. Unsurprisingly, the latter group tend to reflect the Augustinian emphasis on man's fallen nature. And, partly because they

---

[45] Ibid. 139.   [46] Ibid. 142.
[47] 'Of the Certainty', in *The Works of Mr. Richard Hooker*, ed. J. Keeble (7th edn, Oxford, 1888; repr. New York, 1970), iii. 70–1.
[48] *True Way*, 128.

regard human corruption as central to our own self-understanding, they share
with the Platonists the view that there are moral truths that reason is incapable of discerning. By far the most sustained and original treatment of this
theme is that of Pascal, who brings to it a rhetorical clarity foreign to the sermons and discourses of English Platonism in this period.[49] While Pascal places
reason in a hierarchy of types of knowledge and value, he goes on to delineate
its limits in its own terms. Confronting the advocates of the belief that we can
grasp the requirements of a moral life by reasoning, he appeals to reason itself
to explain just how their view is deficient.

In his *Pensées* Pascal distinguishes three orders—the order of the flesh, the
order of the mind, and the order of charity—each of which constitutes a system of values and ends and possesses its own *grandeur*.[50] The carnal order allots
value to worldly things and recognizes the *grandeur* of those who wield temporal power. The order of the mind esteems intellectual achievements such as
argument and discovery, and is exemplified, in Pascal's view, by Archimedes.
Finally, the order of charity or the will values only divine things. Its *grandeur*—
wisdom—resembles the wisdom of God and its exemplars are Christ and
the saints. Each order incorporates a method of investigation and justification.
Unsurprisingly, perhaps, the values of the carnal order are recognized by the
eyes, and more generally by the senses. Reason, the 'eyes of the mind', enables
us to appreciate and justify intellectual achievement. And lastly faith, 'the eyes
of the heart', reveals to us the religious values of the order of charity. These
three moral schemes are incommensurable, in the sense that the values embedded in one order cannot be appreciated from the perspective of a lower one,
and yet they can nevertheless be compared. When the comparison is made,
wisdom far outstrips either carnal or intellectual greatness, and Pascal assumes
that this supreme value is the only end of a truly moral life, the only source
of real happiness. We should therefore make it our goal. But this conclusion
obviously poses a problem. If we are burdened with the unenlightened values
of the body or the intellect, we shall be unable to appreciate the significance
or rewards of wisdom, and will therefore have no reason to pursue it.

The resolution of this dilemma is a prominent theme of the *Pensées*. Implicitly taking the view that one can only ascend the hierarchy of orders one stage
at a time, Pascal concentrates on the plight of those who inhabit the order of
the intellect and confidently put their trust in reason. The only way to convince
them of the poverty of their ends is to borrow their own tools and persuade
them by reasoned argument that they have rational grounds for distrusting
reason.[51] Pascal accordingly offers several kinds of grounds for doubting its

---

[49] On Pascal's debt to Augustine see P. Sellier, *Pascal et St. Augustin* (Paris, 1970).
[50] Trans. A. J. Krailsheimer (Harmondsworth, 1966), 308, 933. See P. Topliss, *The Rhetoric of Pascal*
(Leicester, 1966), 129–36.
[51] *Pensées*, 174. Pascal attributes this view to Augustine.

sufficiency. The least ambitious—a familiar repertoire of Pyrrhonist tropes—persuade us that reason is extremely unreliable.[52] They are complemented by a more telling discussion of the psychological difficulty we encounter in trying to excise all non-rational elements from our judgements. The capacity of humans to conform to reason is jeopardized by the fecundity of the imagination, which all but swamps it with vivid yet extraneous items of evidence. The philosopher standing on a wide plank over a ravine, for example, is, despite himself, prey to an irrational fear of falling. While his reason assures him that the danger of losing his balance is negligible, his imagination portrays this terrifying possibility in lurid colours.[53]

Humans are thus burdened by emotional and cognitive dispositions which make it extremely difficult for them to reason, so much so that it would be fruitless to try to explain their behaviour as the outcome of rational judgement. Equally, it would be a sign of vanity to suppose them capable of becoming rational, since dispassionate inspection reveals that they are powerless to reform their natures. This pessimistic view, so common among Christian moralists, is elaborated in the *Pensées* when Pascal embarks upon a further argument to the effect that, even if we were capable of using our reason properly, it would not meet the standard of certainty usually claimed for it. Here the criticism of reason shifts from a psychological to an epistemological plane, and once again Pascal follows in the footsteps of Pyrrhonism.

The chief obstacle standing in the way of certainty is, Pascal claims, the first principles from which reasoning proceeds. For the conclusion of a syllogism to be secure, its premises must be certain; but the first principles on which all our reasoning is ultimately founded are not themselves known by reason. If the art of demonstration is not to be undercut, their truth must be guaranteed by some other means. What could this be? One way to avoid the problem would be to claim, as Descartes did, that first principles are known by intuition. But Pascal argues that this is tantamount to dogmatism, since the intuition that the principles are true does not amount to proof, and reason tells us that we should not be prepared to accept unproven propositions. Another way out would be to draw the sceptical conclusion that there is no justification for first principles. But Pascal argues that this, too, is unsatisfactory, because we are by nature incapable of suspending belief about such fundamental matters.[54]

The proper response is to allow that, while we do indeed know the first principles on which we base demonstrations, we do not know them by means

[52] Ibid. 21.

[53] Ibid. 44. See G. Ferreyrolles, 'L'Imagination en procès', *XVIIᵉ Siècle*, 177 (1992), 468–79; A. McKenna, 'Pascal et le corps humain', *XVIIᵉ Siècle*, 177 (1992), 481–94; P. Sellier, 'Sur les fleuves de Babylone', in D. Wetsel (ed.), *Meaning, Structure and History in the Pensées of Pascal* (Paris, 1990), 33–44.

[54] *Pensées*, 110, 131. See T. M. Harrington, 'Pascal et le philosophie', in J. Mesnard *et al.* (eds.), *Actes du colloque tenu à Clermont-Ferrand 1976* (Paris, 1979), 36–43; J.-L. Marion, 'L'Obscure évidence de la volonté: Pascal au delà de la "Regula Generalis" de Descartes', *XVIIᵉ Siècle*, 46 (1994), 639–56.

of reason. 'We know the truth not only through our reason, but also through our heart. It is through the latter that we know first principles, and reason, which knows nothing about them, tries in vain to refute them . . . Principles are felt, propositions proved, and both with certainty though by different means.'[55] While it is not at all clear that Pascal has here escaped the dependence on intuition which he earlier condemned as dogmatism, he evidently wishes to defend the cognitive status of a certain kind of feeling. He seeks to persuade us that, since we already depend on diverse cognitive principles, we should not shrink from admitting that reason is only one source of knowledge.

At the same time, sober and unflinching reflection on our state should, in Pascal's view, convince us that we are incapable of gaining more than a very modest knowledge of nature.[56] But once we realize that anything more is beyond our grasp, we shall be prone to suffer a kind of frustration in the face of our own impotence. Our limited powers of reasoning are sufficiently strong to enable us to understand the difference between knowledge and opinion. And this understanding in turn enables us to conceive the possibility of a complete and securely founded knowledge, guaranteed by reason through and through. Such cast-iron certainty is the object of intense desire. But the very powers of reasoning which enable us to conceive it also show us that it can never be attained.[57] Reason thus has the special characteristic of revealing its own limits, and although Pascal occasionally discusses this in a matter-of-fact tone of voice as something we must just settle down and accept, he more often speaks of the juxtaposition of power and powerlessness as a source of anguish. 'We desire truth, but find in ourselves nothing but uncertainty. We seek happiness, but find only wretchedness and death. We are incapable of not desiring truth and happiness and incapable of either certainty or happiness. We have been left with this desire as much as a punishment as to make us feel how far we have fallen.'[58]

Yet out of anguish comes a new kind of understanding. For once we ask ourselves why we have both an ability to reason and an inability to carry our reason to its natural conclusion, we shall see, according to Pascal, that this paradoxical state of affairs must be explained by the Fall.

Is it not as clear as day that man's condition is dual? The point is that if man had never been corrupted, he would, in his innocence, confidently enjoy both truth and felicity, and, if man had never been anything but corrupt, he would have no idea either of truth or bliss. But unhappy as we are . . . we have an idea of happiness but we cannot attain it. We perceive an image of the truth and possess nothing but falsehood, being equally

---

[55] *Pensées*, 110; cf. 513. See J. Yhap, *The Rehabilitation of the Body as a Means of Knowing in Pascal's Philosophy of Experience* (Lewiston, NY, 1991); J. La Porte, *Le Cœur et la raison selon Pascal* (Paris, 1957); P. Sellier, 'Le cœur chez Pascal', *Cahiers de l'association internationale des études françaises*, 40 (1988), 285–95; M. Warner, *Philosophical Finesse: Studies in the Art of Rational Persuasion* (Oxford, 1989), 152–208.

[56] *Pensées*, 199.   [57] Ibid. 131.   [58] Ibid. 401.

incapable of absolute ignorance and certain knowledge; so obvious is it that we once enjoyed a degree of perfection from which we have unhappily fallen.[59]

In order to understand ourselves, we must acknowledge the duality within our nature. But Pascal goes on to insist that this correct self-description is not susceptible to rational justification. It will only be acceptable to those who believe the story of the creation told in the Bible, and since the truth of this story cannot be demonstrated, such a belief must rest on faith. Moreover, when we accept the story of the Fall, we accept the doctrine of the transmission of sin. And, as Pascal comments, 'nothing is more shocking to our reason than to say that the sin of the first man has implicated in its guilt men so far from the original sin that they seem incapable of sharing it. This flow of guilt does not seem merely impossible to us but indeed most unjust.'[60] Nothing in reason can convince us of the veracity or the justice of God's decree that Adam's sin should be transmitted. But unless we accept its veracity we are left with no way of explaining our dual nature. And to accept its veracity without accepting its justice would be to settle for an unjust God—a possibility not contemplated by Pascal. In his view, therefore, we are committed to accepting both that Adam and Eve fell from grace and that their sin descends to us. But in doing so we abandon reason, which is powerless in this arena, for faith.[61]

It is therefore by turning inward upon ourselves that we are able to understand the contradictions that are part of our nature and see how to resolve them. Pascal's stress on self-knowledge here owes something to Montaigne, and although he fiercely repudiates the secular tone and argument of the *Essais*,[62] he shares the view that self-knowledge gives rise to both practical and philosophical benefits and may even lead one to the truth. To achieve self-understanding in this latter sense, however, one must recognize the limits of reason and submit to faith. God will help those who sincerely attempt to conquer the polar vices of pride and despair,[63] and set themselves to believe the central truths of Christian religion. For he will give them grace—the overwhelming desire to love God and lead a pious life—which will enable them to conform to the laws of Christian morality.

This conclusion muddies the opposition between reason and passion. To be sure, the passions remain destructive of both rationality and piety. But reason, the surviving fragment of our prelapsarian condition, appears in a more equivocal light. While it is still acknowledged to be active, its controlling quality

[59] Ibid. 131.   [60] Ibid.

[61] See C. M. Natoli, 'Proof in Pascal's *Pensées*: Reason as Rhetoric', in Wetsel (ed.), *Meaning, Structure and History*, 19–34.

[62] Pascal, *Entretien de M. Saci*, in *Œuvres complètes*, ed. L. Lafuma (Paris, 1963), 291–7, 293. On Pascal and Sacy see D. Wetsel, *L'Écriture et le reste: The Pensées of Pascal in the Exegetical Tradition of Port Royal* (Columbus, Oh., 1981).

[63] *Pensées*, 354.

is no longer seen as the benevolent means to virtue. Instead, our ability to use reason to quash the passions is now presented as one aspect of an undue confidence, arrogance, and pride, itself a consequence of our fallen nature. Our busy attempts to impose rational order on the world are therefore self-defeating in that they conceal from us the centrality of faith, and thus ensure that our attempts to gain knowledge of the moral law laid down by God are perpetually frustrated. Virtue will not, then, be achieved by means of the active processes of reasoning. Rather, it issues from a constructive form of passivity which Pascal describes as submission.[64] To be passive, therefore, need not be a bad thing. On the contrary, it is only through submission that we can transcend the order of the mind and recognize the supreme values embodied in the order of charity. We must put our faith in feeling.[65]

The view that emotions are intimately connected to volitions enabled the philosophers I have discussed in this chapter to make space for a conception of knowledge as feeling. As we have seen, most of them draw a distinction between two kinds of knowledge—the demonstrative knowledge we can attain through the human power of reasoning, and the emotional knowledge lying at the very edge of our natural capabilities. While we can work towards the emotions that arise when we learn to love the good, only divine grace enables us to complete and sustain this transformation of feeling, which is at the same time a shift to a different order of knowledge. Embodied in this account is a cross-cutting interpretation of the view that perfection lies in activity, and that as we become more nearly perfect we gradually leave behind the passive aspects of our nature.

This interpretation begins with the claim that the emotions that constitute knowledge are not passions deriving from our sensible perceptions of the relations between our bodies and external things. Instead, they are the fruit of our capacity to withdraw from sense, to rise above the order of the flesh, and to love not just what appears beneficial to our embodied natures, but the true good. Perfection increases, it seems, as we become dominated by what Malebranche calls natural impulses, the volitions to the true good with which God has equipped us. This view identifies virtue with the possession of a will which is rightly directed, where its right direction is to face away from the sensible and towards the intelligible. But we have to be careful not to overemphasize the extent to which the conceptions of loving knowledge that we have explored focus on the intellect. The knowledge in question is, after all, characterized as knowledge of the heart, and it consists in feeling and action. To appreciate it, we need to take account of the fact that its advocates muddle the association of passivity and ignorance with the body, and of activity and knowledge with the mind, to create a transgressive category of supremely active emotion with strong bodily connotations, which is also knowledge. Rather than being left

<hr />

[64] Ibid. 167, 170, 188.   [65] Ibid. 821.

behind, the body is, so to speak, taken over by the properties traditionally ascribed to the soul.

A second aspect of loving knowledge lies in its link with the will. As we have already seen, willing is widely regarded as acting, not just because volitions move us to action, but also because they are conceived as the thoughts through which the mind exercises control over itself. The more we are able to act voluntarily, the more perfect and independent the mind becomes. However, the notion of independence I have introduced here also has to be handled with care. The process of becoming more perfect is, according to this model, a move away from the impulses of the body. We become to some degree independent of our bodies as we become less trusting of, and less responsive to, our senses and passions, and learn to appreciate the domains into which they yield no insight. Of course, we still depend on our bodies for survival. But we develop a greater capacity to think critically about the information they provide and the demands they impose, and to act on the judgements at which we arrive. At the same time, perfection is conceived as unification. As we come to love the good, there are several senses in which we merge with God. First, we will as he wills and love what he loves. Next, our emotions and actions contribute to a harmonious pattern intended by God and realized by the virtuous. Thirdly, in so far as love of the good is created and strengthened by grace, it consists in God's bringing it about that our wills and his should coincide. In this last idea, the association of perfection and activity is, as Pascal makes clear, undercut. To become active, we must be passive in the sense of submitting ourselves to God and allowing his grace to work in us. And in fact, the conception of virtue as unification carries with it the passive connotations of being taken over by, and incorporated in, something much larger than ourselves.

The ingrained distinction between reason and faith around which this sharp division between demonstrative and emotional knowledge is organized is to a great extent marginalized by early-modern philosophers who are interested in extending and vindicating scientific knowledge. We see this in a range of otherwise diverse Christian philosophers. Descartes, for example, classifies *la morale* —'the highest and most perfect moral system, which presupposes a complete knowledge of the other sciences and is the ultimate level of wisdom'[66]—as a science. Locke, likewise, defends the possibility of a science of ethics accessible to reason. For these authors, knowledge of the good is demonstrative, and whatever emotional impact it has on us is a consequence of this fact. Nevertheless, the boundary between a theologically inspired conception of knowledge of God and a scientific knowledge of nature is not always clear-cut, and some authors who subordinate feeling to reason retain the connection of knowledge with unification. This is clearest, as one would expect, in works which self-consciously attempt to graft science on to religion. Malebranche, for instance,

---

[66] *Principles*, p. 186, pref. to the Fr. edn.

argues that, in applying ourselves to universal sciences such as mathematics and metaphysics, we apply our minds to God in the purest and most perfect way of which we are capable, and perceive the intelligible world that God himself knows.[67] Scientific knowledge unites us with God by enabling us to know as he knows, and this sort of knowledge in turn excites a love of the intelligible which mirrors God's own love. A less explicitly theological version of this view is also expressed in Descartes's account of the dialogue between passion and intellectual emotion. Intellectual love of things that we judge to be good gives rise, as we have seen, to a corresponding passionate love. But the passion of love is, as Descartes defines it, an emotion of the soul which impels it to join itself willingly to objects that appear agreeable to it.[68] Elaborating, Descartes explains that, when we join ourselves willingly to an object, we consider ourselves as henceforth joined with it 'in such a manner that we imagine a whole, of which we take ourselves to be only one part, and the thing loved to be the other'.[69] So to love something is to regard oneself as united with it. And since this passion accompanies the intellectual love that the perception of the good arouses in us, our knowledge of the good brings with it a conception of ourselves as part of a larger whole.

At one level, this strand of Descartes's thought can be seen as a reworking of the Christian conception of the blessed united with God. But it would be a mistake to try to separate the influence of this tradition too sharply from the legacies of Platonism and Stoicism, each of which holds out an image of knowledge as joyful unification. Spinoza's work certainly suggests that the conception of knowledge as unity sketched by Descartes was ripe for incorporation into a more wholeheartedly Stoic picture. Understanding, as Spinoza sees it, gives us a grasp of the causal laws that constitute both the natural order and the mind of God. As we understand, we become progressively united with God or nature; and as we merge, our intellectual joy becomes more pervasive and intense. Here we see the Christian doctrine in the context of which we began our discussion of the relation between knowledge and emotion transformed into a non-Christian view which in turn exerted a considerable influence on deism, and was in this way reincorporated into Christianity.

Knowledge, Love, and Power

The sensitivity with which seventeenth-century philosophers explore the connections between emotion and knowledge, and the theoretical complexity

---

[67] *De la recherche*, ii. 110; trans. Lennon and Olscamp, 367.

[68] *The Passions of the Soul*, in *The Philosophical Writings of Descartes*, ed. J. Cottingham *et al.* (Cambridge, 1984–91), i. 79. See A. Gombay, 'Amour et jugement chez Descartes', *Revue philosophique de la France et de l'Étranger*, 178 (1988), 447–55.

[69] *Passions of the Soul*, 80.

they bring to bear on it, has been largely overlooked in the recent exegetical literature. A misreading of Descartes's analysis of *scientia* as the transparent, emotionless reasoning of a disembodied mind has gained currency and been attributed to the period as a whole. At the same time, it has been claimed that the New Science engendered a conception of knowledge aimed at the control of nature, thereby ushering in the instrumentalism and individualism of the modern era. Needless to say, these interpretations are not unfounded. But neither are they just. In this and the preceding two chapters I have argued that the first of these interpretations distorts Descartes's account of the emotions that accompany reasoning, and have aimed to dispel any impression that such a view dominates early-modern philosophy. The connections I have explored between reason and passion also serve to place in a broader and somewhat destabilizing context the claim that knowledge comes to be regarded in this period as a body of information independent of the knowing subject, which can then be used to control nature. This view, I shall next suggest, is regarded with deep ambivalence. It is subject to several interpretations, some of which threaten the power of the knower, and the separation of knowledge from its object.

The acquisition of knowledge is, as we have seen, widely held to release powerful emotions. Knowledge changes us and, with or without the help of divine grace, makes us happier than we were before. By looking at the various ways in which this happiness is portrayed, and what it is about, we can gain some insight into the conceptions of knowledge to which it is allied. At the same time, we are able to see how these conceptions are contested and the happiness that accompanies them fissured. For Cartesians, knowledge of ourselves, of the rest of nature, and of our relations to the external world is a source of intellectual joy. The exercise of our mental capacities is itself pleasurable. And through this exercise we also acquire an understanding of our powers and their limits. Descartes's account of the control over our bodies and external things that he expects his philosophy to produce is celebrated:

Through this philosophy we could know the power and action of fire, water, air, the stars, the heavens and all the other bodies in our environment, as distinctly as we know the various crafts of our artisans; and we could use this knowledge—as the artisans use theirs—for all the purposes for which it is appropriate, and thus make ourselves, as it were, the lords and masters of nature. This is desirable not only for the invention of innumerable devices which would facilitate our enjoyment of the fruits of the earth and all the goods we find there, but also, and most importantly, for the maintenance of health which is undoubtedly the chief good and the foundation of all the other goods in this life.[70]

---

[70] *Discourse on the Method of Rightly Conducting one's Reason and Seeking the Truth in the Sciences*, in *Philosophical Writings* ed. Cottingham *et al.*, i. 142–3.

However, as well as residing in an instrumental power to manipulate our environment and bodies, the happiness that knowledge brings derives from our appreciation of the limits of our power. Since there are many things we cannot in fact control, we need to learn to protect ourselves against disappointment. We have to learn that anything worth pursuing has to be such that its acquisition depends solely on ourselves, and train ourselves not to feel regret or self-reproach over things that depend on others.[71] This withdrawal and cultivation of autonomy, Stoic in inspiration, is a moral aspiration which Descartes calls *générosité*. But it is also a more broadly philosophical ideal which shapes scientific method and practice.

In his *Discourse on the Method*, Descartes presents his own scientific quest as solitary. Disputation of the sort practised in the Schools does not advance understanding, because each side tries only to win the debate.[72] Discussion and controversy are unprofitable distractions in which the search for truth is distorted by passion, whether in the form of friendship or malice.[73] Publication exposes one to the agony of misrepresentation when others seize on one's views and, like blind men who lure an enemy into a dark cellar in order to fight him on equal terms, force one to produce dangerous clarifications of one's position. There is even no point in relying on other people to perform experiments; not only are their observations usually mistaken or misleading, but they also 'wish to be rewarded by having certain difficulties explained to them, or at any rate by compliments and useless conversations, which could not but waste a lot of time'.[74] Piling up the disadvantages of communal work, Descartes convinces himself that it is in everyone's interest that he should publish only the most fundamental of his principles and keep his further discoveries to himself.[75] The true philosopher is beset on every side by people in the grip of *grandeur*, who wish to parrot fragments of his views in order to appear learned. Like ivy clinging to a great tree,[76] they have the power to smother him and bring him down, and he therefore needs to devise a way of working which, since its success depends only on the philosopher himself, deprives them of the opportunity to harm him.

The method of turning inward to contemplate clear and distinct ideas, allied to the cultivation of the power to engage in this sort of reasoning at will, answers to Descartes's demand. (Admittedly, experiments have to be performed. But Descartes resigns himself to slow progress, rather than risking collaboration.)[77] To this extent he conceives the acquisition of knowledge as an achievement of intellectually isolated individuals. People who have reasonably well-ordered wills possess the capacity to increase their scientific understanding, and, for the sake of scientific progress and their own happiness, will do best to exercise

---

[71] *Passions of the Soul*, 156.   [72] *Discourse*, 146.   [73] Ibid.   [74] Ibid. 148.
[75] Ibid. 147. See P. France, *Rhetoric and Truth in France: Descartes to Diderot* (Oxford, 1972), 43–5.
[76] *Discourse*, 147.   [77] Ibid. 148.

this capacity alone. Someday, the New Philosophy will be sufficiently advanced to be made public; it will be so clear and comprehensive that everyone will be able to understand it.[78] But in the meantime knowledge is only safe in the possession of those few individuals who together form the embattled community of the wise. The figure of the philosopher here takes on some of the secret power of the magus. His knowledge of causes and effects makes him, as Bacon boasts, supremely powerful, since he alone can make reliable predictions and see how to intervene effectively in the course of events.[79] The image of knowledge and happiness as control, and hence as power, is therefore eloquently defended.

Even the advocates of this position, however, are troubled by a sense of fragility which undermines their confidence and introduces equivocation. One manifestation of this uneasiness surfaces in discussions of the happiness experienced by people who understand the limits of their own power and know what they can and cannot achieve. Either by itself, or allied to a strong will, their knowledge enables them to resist destructive passions such as fear, sadness, and despair, and to take a serene and tranquil pleasure in their own abilities. Unlike ordinary people, who are subject to a succession of fluctuating passions, their emotional temper is steady, like a still pond. But this very stillness is treacherous, since it also characterizes the pathological condition of melancholy, which particularly afflicts those 'whose vocation consisteth in study of hard points of learning'.[80] Melancholics 'are of a temper still and slow'[81] and their disease affects them with lethargy or heaviness.[82] Their grave and disturbing symptoms, which include delusion and hallucination, terror, distrust, despair, and rage, can arise when

the *curious* melancholy carries the mind into the sense of mysteries as exceed human capacity and is desirous to know more than is revealed in the word of truth; or being ignorant of that which is revealed through importunate enquiry, of a sudden falleth into that gulf of God's secret counsels which swalloweth up all conceit of man or angel; and measuring the truth of such depth of mysteries by the shallow model of his own wit, is caught and devoured by that which his presumptuous curiosity moved him to attempt to apprehend.[83]

At its worst, this disease brings the sufferer to a halt, so that in Dürer's famous engraving the figure of Melencolia sits slumped, her head on her hand, staring

---

[78] Ibid. 146.

[79] Bacon, 'For the chain of causes cannot by any force be loosed or broken, nor can nature be commanded except by being obeyed. And so those twin objects, human knowledge and human power, do really meet in one; and it is for ignorance of causes that operation fails.' *The Great Instauration: Plan of the Work*, in *Works*, ed. J. Spedding *et al.* (London, 1857–61) iv. 32.

[80] Timothy Bright, *A Treatise of Melancholy* (New York, 1940), 195.

[81] Ibid. 194.   [82] Ibid. 101.

[83] Ibid. 194. See B. Lyons, *Voices of Melancholy: Studies in Literary Treatments of Melancholy in Renaissance England* (London, 1971). On the relation between melancholy and enthusiasm see M. Heyd, 'Enthusiasm in the Seventeenth Century', *Journal of Modern History*, 53 (1981), 269–71.

PLATE 4. Albrecht Dürer, *Melencolia I* (1514)

fixedly ahead of her.[84] (See Pl. 4.) She is surrounded by regularly shaped blocks of stone and the tools for cutting them which, so Panofsky suggests, symbolize her skill at dealing with sensible things and her inability to deal with

---

[84] On the iconography of Melancholy and for a discussion of Dürer's engraving see E. Panofsky, *The Life and Art of Albrecht Dürer* (Princeton, 1955), 156–71.

intelligible ones—an incapacity to move from an understanding rooted in spatially located figures to a metaphysical grasp of non-extended ideas that is the source of her depression. Less acutely, perhaps, the overwhelming desire for arcane knowledge appears as a yearning for solitary ecstasy. Milton's Penseroso walks alone at night and begs the goddess Melancholy to enlighten him.

> Or let my lamp at midnight hour
> Be seen in some high lonely tower,
> Where I may oft outwatch the Bear
> With thrice great Hermes, or unsphere
> The spirit of Plato to unfold
> What worlds, or what vast regions hold
> The immortal mind that hath forsook
> Her mansion in this fleshly nook.[85]

The withdrawal from the world that the quest for knowledge requires can thus encourage in us ideas which make us ill. In addition, the withdrawal itself can prove unbearable. The repudiation of ordinary ways of understanding and feeling, including the distrust of the senses that Descartes discusses so calmly, are elsewhere seen as lonely and painful. As we have already found, in Chapter 10, Christian conceptions of salvation as the repudiation of the world and its pleasures are understood to be bitter and distasteful; and the natural counterpart of divine knowledge also involves losses, so that, while it may ultimately reconcile us to our limited power, it can induce a pathological state of impotence and despair.

Because knowledge of our power includes knowledge of its limits, it contains both the promise of *ataraxia* and the curse of melancholy and despair. The philosopher's strength is simultaneously a weakness, and his ability to control nature is threatened by passions which remove his ability to control himself. An understanding of our own fragility has many manifestations which undercut the confident assertions of independence that can be traced in the work of Bacon and Descartes. Most winningly, perhaps, Descartes's haughty rejection of the idea that anyone can help him is the prelude to an admission that he has changed his mind. If he does not publish his work, people may think his reasons for withholding it are discreditable. 'I am not excessively fond of glory', he protests.[86] Nevertheless, silence is not a sufficient defence against the meddling savants, who are liable to put a damaging construction on it. In addition, Descartes confesses, 'I am becoming more and more aware of the delay which my project of self-instruction is suffering because of the need for innumerable observations which I cannot make without the help of

---

[85] *Il Penseroso*, in *John Milton: A Critical Edition of the Major Works*, ed. S. Orgel and J. Goldberg (Oxford, 1991), 27–8.
[86] *Discourse*, 149.

others.'[87] The acquisition of knowledge must, after all, be to some extent a collective enterprise.

Descartes presents this grudging acknowledgement as a request for practical help and a justification for publication; once the readers of the *Discourse* see how far he has got, they may be interested in contributing to his projects, and, provided that they do not expect lengthy replies, he is prepared to respond to their objections.[88] But it perhaps also reflects the anxiety and sense of enormous responsibility that vitiate the pleasure of knowledge, when this is understood as power vested in the individual knower.[89] Knowledge is a burden which the philosopher may both wish to keep to himself and long to share, and the desire for a kind of understanding unmarred by desolate self-sufficiency is expressed in the powerful images of knowledge as unification discussed earlier in the chapter. Far from accentuating the boundary around the individual, knowledge, as these portrayals would have it, is a kind of fusion of the knowing subject with something much larger than itself. For the most part, this process is conceived as fusion with a benevolent and protecting God, worthy of unqualified veneration. And among non-Christian philosophers, fusion with nature is incorporation in a whole, the perfection of which gives us reason to love it. So happiness, according to these views, consists not in a complacent appreciation of our own paltry capacities, but in loving and identifying with what is truly powerful. Knowledge therefore remains a kind of power. But it is not the power of the individual over nature. Instead, it is an active submission to, and cooperation with, the power that is nature and is also divine.

And yet, we may well wonder whether this ideal of knowing is not as alarming as the isolation to which it is an antidote. The way in which it is conceived by seventeenth-century philosophers, and the care with which they oppose it to physical union, suggest that they find it at once alluring and disquieting. Unification offers a resolution to the pain of separateness, but at the same time threatens the boundaries that create the self. Separation re-establishes the boundaries, but at the cost of a protecting love. Both conceptions of knowledge are present and influential in early-modern philosophy, each answering to profound desires and high aspirations. But the tension between them remains unresolved—and indeed, Christian philosophers offer an explanation of why this should be so.

The separation between the spiritual fusion that constitutes knowledge and mere physical union is reflected with particular vividness in discussions about the relation between mother and child during pregnancy. Here, after all, is a paramount case of two beings who are for the moment one,[90] an image, one

---

[87] Ibid.   [88] Ibid. 149–50.   [89] Cf. Pascal, *Pensées*, 198.

[90] Malebranche endorses this view of mother and foetus in *De la recherche*, ii. 232–5; trans. Lennon and Olscamp, 112–15. See J. Kristeva, 'Motherhood according to Giovanni Bellini', in *Desire and Language* (New York, 1980).

might think, of the joy and completeness that awaits the seeker after knowledge. In fact, however, their relationship is widely represented as a source of distorting passion and bodily disfigurement which threatens the well-being of the child. These dangers arise from the purported fact that 'there is certainly a connection between all the movements of a mother and those of a child in her womb, so that anything adverse to one is harmful to the other'.[91] Although Descartes here presents the connection as reciprocal, attention focuses on the disastrous impact that mothers can have on their unborn children, an impact often illustrated by anecdotes. Malebranche's recollections are typical.

About seven or eight years ago I saw at the *Incurables* a young man who was born mad, and whose body was broken in the same places in which those of criminals are broken. He had lived for nearly twenty years in this condition: a lot of people saw him and the late queen mother, while she was visiting the hospital, was curious to see him and even to touch his arms and legs where they were broken. . . . [T]he cause of this disastrous accident was that his mother, knowing that a criminal was to be broken, went to see the execution. Every blow to this unfortunate man forcibly struck the imagination of the mother and, by a sort of counterblow, the tender, delicate brain of her child. The woman's brain fibres were unusually shaken, and perhaps broken in places, by the violent flow of spirits that the sight of such a terrible action produced, but their consistency enabled them to escape being entirely destroyed. The brain fibres of the child, by contrast, unable to resist the torrent of spirits, were completely dissipated, and the attack was sufficient to make him permanently lose his mind. That is why he came into the world deprived of sense. . . . At the sight of the execution, so liable to terrify a woman, the mother's animal spirits went violently from her brain to the parts of her body corresponding to those of the criminal, and the same thing happened to the child. But, because the bones of the mother were able to resist the force of the spirits, they were not damaged. Perhaps she did not feel the least pain or trembling in her arms and legs when they broke those of the criminal. But the rapid flow of the spirits was enough to sweep away the soft, tender parts of the child's bones. . . . It is worth pointing out that if this mother had determined the movements of the spirits towards some other part of her body by stirring them forcefully [*se chatouillant avec force*], her child would not have had broken bones.[92]

Malebranche is not alone in believing that the passions of pregnant women shape the bodies and brains of their children,[93] so that 'as there are hardly any women who do not have some weaknesses, and who have not been moved by some passion during pregnancy, there must be very few children whose minds have not been in some way distorted [*mal tourné*], and who do not have some dominant passion'.[94] More unusual is his view that this is how original sin is

---

[91] Descartes. *Passions of the Soul*, 136; cf. *Treatise on Man*, in *Philosophical Writings*, ed. Cottingham et al., i. 106.

[92] *De la recherche*, i. 239–40; trans. Lennon and Olscamp, 115–16.

[93] See also Reynolds, *Treatise on the Passions*, 25; Wright, *Passions of the Mind*, 140.

[94] *De la recherche*, i. 246; trans. Lennon and Olscamp, 119.

transmitted; the impressions made on the brains of Adam and Eve by sensible things were passed down to their children, and ever since, our mother's passions have ensured that we are born concupiscent. 'Thus, a mother whose brain is full of traces that are by their nature connected to sensible things, which she cannot efface because of the concupiscence within her, and whose body is not at all submissive to her, necessarily communicates these traces to her child, engendering a sinner even if she is righteous.'[95] But even without this theological twist, pregnancy is represented as a stage during which children are mentally and physically sullied rather than strengthened by their mothers' passions. No doubt these beliefs feed on and sustain men's distrust of the women who must bear their children. As Malebranche explains, 'The unity that we had with our mothers in their womb, which is the closest there can be between men [*sic*], has caused us the two greatest evils, sin and concupiscence, that are the source of all our misery. Nevertheless, in order for our bodies to be formed, this union had to be as complete as it was.'[96]

Physical union is here represented as a state of extreme vulnerability in which the child has no control over the shaping of its body, and is at the mercy of the animal spirits that course through it. Its lack of bodily boundaries makes it powerless to resist damage. Viewed like this, unity is terrifying, and discussions of the early stages of our lives are one context in which this fear is explored. Once born, we are subjected, according to Malebranche, to a second, though less damaging, union with our parents and nurses, who impose on us their beliefs and habits. And even when we escape this, our union with other men is close enough to harm us. For it leads us to esteem worldly things and ignore true ideas.[97] The search for knowledge is thus a flight from physical closeness, a matter of distancing ourselves from other bodies and overcoming the distorting passions that unity bequeaths to us. We have to erect boundaries not just around the body but around the mind to separate ourselves from the inescapable afflictions of sense.

Fear of bodily fusion therefore counterbalances the supreme happiness of losing oneself in God or nature, and images of knowledge as unification carry with them the anxiety that attaches to physical merging. This counterpoint is manifested in divergent readings of the episode in the Book of Genesis that was taken by many seventeenth-century writers to mark the very beginning of knowledge—the moment when Adam named the animals. One strand of interpretation, favoured by Calvin and perhaps most memorably expressed by Milton, links Adam's act of naming with his sexual desire and yearning for unification:

> I nam'd them as they passed, and understood
> Their nature; with such knowledge God endued

---

[95] *De la recherche*, i. 254; trans. Lennon and Olscamp, 123.
[96] Ibid. 377; trans. Lennon and Olscamp, 195.   [97] Ibid. trans. Lennon and Olscamp, 195.

My sudden apprehension: but in these
I found not what methought I wanted still.[98]

Because the animals are his inferiors, Adam can find in them no society, harmony, or true delight, and to satisfy him God creates Eve, 'bone of my bone, flesh of my flesh, myself',[99] who inspires in Adam the novel affections of love and amorous delight. In this dramatization, Adam's knowledge of the animals crystallizes for him what he lacks. The animals have mates, while he is alone, and while, as Adam explains, this is all right for God, who possesses no deficiency, it is not all right for man, who desires to be completed in sexual union. Knowledge therefore articulates an existing desire, and brings Adam to greater self-understanding of his insufficiency. Sexual union and the unification that comes from knowledge are here run together, a connection reiterated even in the works of philosophical authors who do their best to hold them apart, to separate the knowledge that Adam acquires when he names the animals from the desire that results in the creation of Eve.

Malebranche is quick to insist, as he lays out the damage to which union exposes us, that he is not talking about the unity of minds, from which we can learn, but only about the sensible variety,[100] and a similar barrier is implicit in Descartes's discussion of sexual union in *The Passions of the Soul*. As we have seen, Descartes allows that knowledge brings with it what he calls benevolent love (*l'amour de bienveillance*), and that loving benevolently is a matter of identifying one's own good with that of the object one loves. For example, 'the love of a good father for his children is so pure that he desires to have nothing from them, and he wants neither to possess them otherwise than he does, nor to be joined to them more closely than he already is. He regards them, rather, as other parts of himself, and seeks their good as he does his own, or even more assiduously.'[101] Sexual desire is not dissimilar, since it is a desire for completion. Nature has brought it about that 'at a certain age and time we regard ourselves as deficient—as forming only half of a whole, whose other half must be a person of the opposite sex'.[102] But there is an important difference. Sexual desire arises from attraction (*agrément*)—the passion we experience when our external senses, as opposed to our internal senses or reason, represent something as beneficial. It is the beauty or physical attractiveness of other people that excites our sexual interest and creates desire for bodily union. This surface phenomenon is, however, contrasted with the benevolent love that we feel when reason confirms that an object is good. Like the good father, we then

---

[98] *Paradise Lost*, in *John Milton: A Critical Edition*, ed. Orgel and Goldberg, VIII. 352–5. See J. R. Solomon, 'From Species to Speculation: Naming the Animals with Calvin and Bacon', in E. D. Harvey and K. Okruhlik (eds.), *Women and Reason* (Ann Arbor, 1992), 77–162.

[99] *Paradise Lost*, VIII. 495.   [100] Ibid. Milton also compares Eve to Pandora at IV. 714.

[101] *Passions of the Soul*, 81.   [102] Ibid. 90.

willingly regard ourselves as one with it, and embark on an intellectual union, free from any incestuous taint.

Fear of unity, then, is often expressed as a fear of the loss of bodily identity. The intensely desirable unity that knowledge brings has to be made safe by being separated off from bodily fusion and all its attendant dangers. Yet, because this division is never quite secure, even the loving union of minds is not free from anxiety, and the urge to re-establish boundaries and resort to the power that individual knowledge secures remains strong. In seventeenth-century philosophy we find a to-and-fro movement between these conceptions of knowledge and the pleasure it brings. Some authors emphasize one image over the other, so that it is fair to say, for example, that Pascal favours union and Descartes separation. But most, as we have seen, feel the attraction of both and strive to reconcile them. They aim to articulate a conception of knowledge which guarantees both control and love, separation and connection. Hence Spinoza's view that understanding maximizes our power to control our own emotions, maximizes our power to control what happens to us, enables us to become part of nature, and creates in us the greatest joy of which we are capable. This conjuring trick, and others like it, have their metaphysical problems. They spring, however, from a desire to resolve the dilemma created by the recognition that, in order to acquire knowledge, we must run the risks to which the passions expose us, while knowing at the outset that we are unlikely to be able to resist their strength and cunning. Milton's reading of Genesis tells the history of this flaw; Adam's insufficiency and desire for love can only be satisfied by Eve, who brings about his Fall, and with it the uncontrollable human passions that stand in the way of knowledge.

PART IV

Conflicting Forces:
The Cartesian Theory of Action

That people act on their passions is generally taken for granted. Were it otherwise, our affections would neither be dangerous nor efficacious in securing our
well-being, and their inherent and tantalizing ambiguity would be neutralized.
It is because they guide our behaviour, prompting us to speak rashly, to avoid
people we dislike, to get out of the way of poisonous snakes, or to protect
those we love, that our passions shape our lives, and a comprehensive understanding of them must consequently include some insight into their role as
antecedents of action. At one level, the assumption that passions are expressed
in actions gives rise to the question, How do passions cause physical motions
of the body? A number of seventeenth-century philosophers address this theme,
drawing on the analyses of mind–body interaction discussed in Chapters 5 and
6. For the most part, however, interest in the passions as antecedents of action
stems from the juxtaposition of two assumptions: that people can, and often
do, act on their passions; and that sometimes they do not. To understand the
character of action would be to understand how passions relate to other kinds
of thought, and how we are able at least some of the time to control and modify the expressive urge of our emotions. What do we control our passions with?
And what makes the difference between, say, stifling one's anger and giving
it full rein?

Seventeenth-century discussions of these connected themes are, as we have
seen, conducted against the background of a Scholastic Aristotelian philosophy
which both explicates and moulds everyday experience of psychological conflict and its relations with action. Its treatment of the relation between passion
and bodily motion is comparatively brisk. Aquinas, for example, argues that
passions occur in sequences, and that love and hatred give rise to desire and
aversion, motions of the sensible appetite accompanied by bodily motions which
in turn initiate the grosser motions we describe as actions, such as weaving a
tapestry or running away from a wolf. Much more attention is paid, however,
to the complex antecedents of action, and a variety of forms of conflict and
dislocation are worked out in terms of the tripartite soul, and the divisions
within its sensible and rational parts. On the one hand, reason can oppose

passion when the sensible appetite, manifested in the passions, conflicts with the will or rational appetite, so that, for example, someone may judge that they should do one thing but long to do another. On the other hand, we experience opposing passions when the irascible appetite within the sensitive soul opposes the concupiscible one, as when someone is torn between love and fear. This analysis of two distinct kinds of conflict remained popular among early-modern philosophers who were content to follow Scholastic tradition. Thomas Wright, for example, puts the point vividly when he remarks that the passions can rebel against reason, or brawl with one another 'like so many young crows, half starved, gaping and asking for food, every one more earnest than another to be satisfied'.[1] Both kinds of contest are, however, explicated in quasi-spatial terms, for it is when appetites or passions arise in separate parts or powers of the soul, each of which can function to some extent independently of the other, that they are able to remain unintegrated and in tension.

This way of accounting for complex patterns of motivation and action continued to be regarded as powerful and compelling. Writing in 1674, Charleton refers to the 'intestine war which every man too frequently feels within himself', and insists that it can only be explained by a divided soul. 'What then can remain to cause this dire war daily observed in us, betwixt the allurements of our sense, on one side, and the grave dictates of our mind, on the other, but two distinct agents, the rational soul and the sensitive, coexistent within us, and hotly contending about the conduct of our will?'[2] As we have already seen, however, this very separation was regarded by many seventeenth-century philosophers as a fatal flaw in Aristotelianism, to be avoided at all costs. To provide an adequate explanation of psychological conflict and its relation to action, it was necessary to abandon the Aristotelian approach and show how the thoughts within a unified soul could yet remain unintegrated and conflictual. The development of the so-called New Philosophy therefore had important repercussions for the philosophy of action by requiring a novel analysis of the relations between the antecedents of action, including the passions. Anti-Aristotelian philosophers faced the substantial task of developing an account which would do justice to our experience of psychological conflict without appealing to separate parts of the soul, or to illicitly independent powers such as the irascible and concupiscible appetites.

One way of tracing their attempts to rise to this challenge is through recurring discussions of a stock example—the lines that Ovid gives to Medea , 'Video meliora, proboque | Deteriora sequor' ('I see the better course, but follow the worse'). When Jason arrives at Colchis in search of the golden fleece, King Aeetes tells him that he and his Argonauts can have it if they perform a series

---

[1] *The Passions of the Mind in General* (2nd edn 1604), ed. W. W. Newbold (New York, 1986), 144.
[2] *A Natural History of the Passions* (London, 1674), Epistle Prefatory.

of prodigious tasks. Medea, Aeetes' daughter, knows that these will be too much for them, and also knows that duty requires her to support her father. But her sudden and overwhelming love for Jason moves her to try to help him carry off the fleece. The opening of book VII of the *Metamorphoses* describes her struggles with her oscillating feelings of love and duty. How foolish to fall in love with a stranger. Yet surely it would be wrong to let him suffer the cruel death planned by Aeetes. To interfere would be to betray her father's kingdom. But perhaps if she saves Jason he will betray her? No, she could find a way round that. But to leave her family for a foreign land? Well, her father is cruel and her home barbarous, her sister's prayers would be with her. Stop, all this is sinful. Expelling her love, Medea has before her eyes, Ovid tells us, a vision of what is right, of what filial modesty and affection require.

She was strong in her resolution now, and love had been routed and driven from her heart, when she caught sight of the son of Aeson. Her cheeks blushed scarlet, and then the colour drained from her face entirely. The passion that had been quenched was rekindled, and just as a tiny spark that lurks beneath a covering of ash is nourished by the wind's breath and, increasing as it is fanned, regains its original strength, so Medea's cooling love, which had seemed to be dying, blazed up anew at the sight of the young man, there before her in person.[3]

Medea's struggle, encapsulated in her lament, 'I see the better course, but follow the worse', exemplifies for early-modern philosophers the kind of psychological conflict between passion and reason, and passion and passion, that they need to explain if their interpretations of the unified soul are to possess the power of the Aristotelian theory they reject.

The urge to unify the mind also brings with it a policy of simplification. Most obviously, there is no longer any need to make each part of the soul independent by giving it a distinct set of powers. More generally, the aspiration to employ a smaller range of categories to explain the workings of the soul engenders a tendency to reduce and tidy up the overladen legacy of Aristotelianism. This wish has a marked effect on the philosophy of action, where it gives rise to a series of revised interpretations of desire and its relation to action and progressively increases its importance. These changes are of a piece with the unifying of the mind that is such a central feature of early-modern philosophy. But they are also independent of it, in so far as a philosopher could consistently advocate a unified theory of mind without adopting them. In fact, however, the two shifts occur roughly concurrently, and in order to appreciate the changing connections between passion and action it is necessary to pursue the implications of both. In this chapter and the next I shall trace them through the work of Descartes, Hobbes, Spinoza, and Locke, and will suggest that, taken together, they create the conditions for the emergence

---

[3] *Metamorphoses*, trans. M. M. Innes (Harmondsworth, 1955), 157.

of the twentieth-century orthodoxy that actions are to be explained simply by invoking beliefs and desires.

Volition, Passion, and Action

The aspiration to articulate a theory of action which makes no appeal to a divided soul is, unsurprisingly, uppermost in the work of Descartes, who not only dispenses with the view that the soul has separate parts, but also emphatically rejects the Thomist distinction between the concupiscible and irascible appetites. Dismissing his predecessors with characteristic hauteur, he emphasizes, and in fact exaggerates, the novelty of his position.

I am well aware that here I part company with all who have previously written on the passions. But I do so for good reason. For they derive their enumeration from a distinction that they draw, within the sensitive part of the soul, between the two appetites they call 'concupiscible' and 'irascible'. As I have already said, I recognise no distinction of parts within the soul; so I think their distinction amounts merely to saying that the soul has two powers, one of desire, the other of anger. But since the soul has in the same way the powers of wonder, love, hope and anxiety, and hence the power to receive in itself every other passion, or to perform the actions to which the passions impel it, I do not see why they have chosen to refer them all to desire or to anger. And besides, their enumeration does not include all the principal passions, as I believe mine does.[4]

Descartes's account of the differences between Thomism and his own position is of course correct. However, in developing his analysis he also tacitly takes over various aspects of Aquinas's view, among them the claim that the immediate antecedents of action are desires. For Descartes, as for Aquinas, desires are affections directed towards the future, and are embedded in sequences of passions. They therefore do not occur alone. Nevertheless, it is only when another passion, such as love, gives rise to a desire for an object that a person can act, and no action can occur without an antecedent desire. When nothing intervenes, desires therefore issue in actions; but, as we have seen, this process can be interrupted in a number of ways. According to Aquinas, a second conflicting passion may give rise to a conflicting desire which stands in the way of the action in question; or a rational judgement may give rise to a conflicting volition which has the same effect. But for Descartes, this last configuration (presupposing, as it does, sensitive and rational parts of the soul which can struggle with one another) is completely unacceptable. He therefore needs to find a way of explaining how conflicts between passions, and conflicts between passions and volitions, can occur within a soul containing mutually transparent thoughts.

---

[4] *The Passions of the Soul*, in *The Philosophical Writings of Descartes*, ed. J. Cottingham *et al.* (Cambridge, 1984–91), i. 68.

To solve this problem, Descartes allocates passions to the body. 'All the conflicts', he claims, 'usually supposed to occur between the lower part of the soul, which we call "sensitive", and the higher or "rational" part of the soul—or between the natural appetites and the will—consist simply in the opposition between the movements which the body (by means of its spirits) and the soul (by means of its will) tend to produce at the same time in the gland.'[5] For example, if Eurydice judges that she should stand still in order to avoid being bitten by a snake, but is too frightened to do so and backs away, her judgement originates in her mind, whereas her fear originates in her body and is her experience of the movements of her animal spirits. Descartes describes this state of affairs as a conflict between body and soul, thereby avoiding any conflict within the soul itself. But it would be more accurate to say that the conflict is between a state of the soul (in this case a volition) and a state which cannot be attributed to the soul or the body alone (in this case a passion). The conflict itself takes place in the pineal gland, which is pushed one way by the body and one way by the soul. But once we look more closely at the forces operating on it, this clear division mists over. A volition is a mode of thinking, and therefore belongs to the soul; but a passion is both a mode of thinking and a state of the body. While it is a bodily motion that manipulates the gland, this motion is accompanied by an emotion in the soul. So when Eurydice's pineal gland is pushed in two directions at once, she feels afraid and wants to back away, and simultaneously wills herself to stand still. Although Descartes describes this state of affairs as a conflict between soul and body, it seems that one could also legitimately describe it as a conflict which, though it does not originate in the soul, nevertheless occurs in the soul. But if we allow Descartes the benefit of the doubt, he is able to claim his prize—a theory of psychological conflict which nevertheless presupposes a fully integrated and unified soul.

In making this immensely significant move, Descartes overcomes what he regards as one of the most serious limitations of Scholastic philosophy. But while he purportedly gets rid of any division within the soul, he retains the view, also central to Scholasticism, that actions are to be explained as the outcome of a conflict between separate and competing forces. The site of the struggle has shifted from the soul to the pineal gland, and the opposing powers are now the forces exerted on it by the soul and body instead of the two antagonistic appetites of the soul. But passions and volitions continue to conflict, and the explanation of action rests on an analysis of the forces they bring to bear. Moreover, when Descartes explicates the relations between these, he follows the outlines delineated within the Scholastic tradition.

To trace these similarities, and articulate the Cartesian position, it will be helpful to take an example. If one of the Naiades who attend Eurydice desires

---

[5] Ibid. 47.

to listen to Orpheus playing his lute, then, other things being equal, she will do so. But the sequence of thoughts and motions which this involves can be interrupted in several different ways. It may be dissipated by more forceful motions that constitute a separate passion; if she hears a sudden scream, her desire to stay and listen to the music will probably give way to a desire to investigate the noise. Or it may be destroyed by her reflection that she should go to Eurydice. Here the sequence is more complicated: she judges that her desire to listen to Orpheus' playing is out of line with a pleasurable obligation, and this judgement gives rise to a volition. The volition gives rise to a movement of the pineal gland, thereby redirecting the animal spirits and causing her to set off for the grove in which Eurydice is to be found.

What, though, determines the force of these various desires and volitions? What, for example, ensures that the Naiad's desire to investigate the scream is strong enough to turn back the tide of animal spirits already flowing through her body as she moves towards Orpheus? The strength of our desires reflects, according to Descartes, the strength of the preceding passions from which they arise. The Naiad's desire to listen to the lute is caused by a preceding passion classified as some sort of love. Perhaps she hears its strains, is attracted by their beauty, and attraction gives way to a desire to hear more. Then she hears the scream. Sudden anxiety makes her run in the direction of the sound. Descartes assumes that the force with which the animal spirits flow through her reflects her emotional past: if screams have so far been associated with situations worthy of anxiety, this scream will excite the same passion and cause her to move accordingly. But her action will also be reinforced by her assessment of priorities—her judgement and accompanying volition that it is more import-ant to investigate the scream than to listen to the lute. Moreover, Descartes also holds that because sudden passions consist in sudden motions of animal spirits, they have extra force, as do the volitions associated with exceptionally clear, strong judgements. The sound of the scream therefore causes a sudden rush of spirits which makes the Naiad jump up.

In this case, there is no conflict between passion and judgement. The Naiad's desire to investigate the scream is stronger than the attraction exerted by Orpheus' music, and, as she runs in the direction of the sound, nothing makes her think that she is wrong to act on it. So while desire is a necessary condition of her action, we can only fully explain it by appealing to the passion that causes her desire, and the judgement and volition that cooperate with it. Explanatory weight is divided between the passion that initiates the action (the Naiad's anxiety) and the volition that endorses it, since both contribute to the force of the resulting desire.

In the example just discussed, the action to be explained was a response to an external stimulus- a scream. But as Descartes points out, actions can also be caused by our thoughts. Sitting on the grass listening to Orpheus playing his lute, the Naiad remembers Eurydice and gets up in order to go to her. This capacity to initiate actions is due to our active power of willing, to the activity of the soul 'which consists entirely in the fact that simply by willing something it brings it about that the little gland to which it is closely joined moves in the manner required to produce the effect corresponding to this volition'.[6] Thus, 'when we want to walk or move our body in some other way, this volition makes the gland drive the spirits to the muscles which serve to bring about this effect'.[7] If we set aside the mysterious capacity of the will to move the pineal gland, and instead focus on the structure of this explanation, we find that it contains the same ingredients as the case of the scream, although their causal order is reversed. The explanation of the action hinges on a volition, which is itself an act of assent to a judgement, that it would be right to join Eurydice. The volition causes a motion of the pineal gland, which is in turn transmitted to other parts of the body, and finally to the limbs. But these motions will simultaneously be experienced as passions; so the volition will cause a desire which, according to Descartes, reinforces the motion initiated by the will. In this way he arrives at the view that two distinct causal processes can result in action. Actions can originate in intellectual judgements and volitions that are backed up by passions, or they can originate in passions that are backed up by volitions.

As Descartes recognizes, a vital question remains to be considered: what happens when passion and intellectual judgement fail to coincide, as when a soldier wills himself to feel bold without managing to excite the corresponding passion? Taking up this issue, Descartes points out that the causal connections between passions and judgements are not always direct. In some cases, volition and passion match, as when a volition to stand up causes the corresponding desire, but in others the links are more circuitous. We cannot, for example, simply will ourselves to feel bold. Instead, '[w]e must apply ourselves to consider the reasons, object or precedents which persuade us that the danger is not great; that there is always more security in defence than in flight; that we shall gain glory and joy if we conquer, whereas we can expect nothing but regret and shame if we flee; and so on'.[8] Implicit in this analysis is the assumption that, unless we can modify our passions and bring them in line with our volitions, we shall not be able to act as our volitions dictate. For instead of being reinforced by the motions that are passions, the motions caused by our volitions will be opposed by contrary flows of animal spirits which will weaken them or dissipate them entirely. A judgement accompanied by a volition to run into the thick of battle may be undermined by the bodily trembling that results from fear, or completely destroyed by a terror that causes the soldier

---

[6] Ibid. 41.   [7] Ibid. 43.

[8] Ibid. 45. See also Letter to Princess Elizabeth, 8 July 1644, in *Philosophical Writings*, ed. Cottingham *et al.*, iii. *Correspondence*, 237.

to turn and flee, unless he can discover and learn to make use of the indirect links between volition and courage. Learning what to think about in order to make oneself feel bold is a way of learning to strengthen the power of the will, to weight the scales on the side of volition in a contest with passion in which the soul has the advantage of ingenuity. A seasoned soldier, for example, may well have at his command a set of techniques for suppressing anxiety before combat with which he can turn back the tide of his fear. In some situations, however, the passions possess the overriding advantage of strength. The soldier may believe that he ought to stand firm, and desperately desire to do what he conceives as his duty, and yet find himself overcome by a terror beyond his control.

When a passion is in full flood, Descartes concedes, it is often impossible to suppress it; sometimes no amount of ingenious willing can prevent us from feeling angry, loving, or afraid. '[T]he most the will can do while an emotion is at its most vigorous is not to yield to its effects and to inhibit many of the movements to which it disposes the body. For example, if anger causes the hand to rise to strike a blow, the will can usually restrain it; if fear moves the legs in flight, the will can stop them.'⁹ This partial remedy makes use of the idea that the transition from passion to action is a causal sequence of bodily motions. Someone who has given up the attempt to transform a passion such as anger can still will themselves not to strike. Their volition translates into movements of the body that do not confront the motions of the passion where they are most forceful, but attack them at a weaker point, in time to prevent them issuing in action. Pursuing his military example, Descartes implicitly portrays the understanding as a general, tactically controlling the forces that range back and forth through the body, estimating their strength, choosing the most likely point of attack, doing his best to avoid total rout.

This stress on the manipulation of bodily motion is particularly marked in one of Descartes's warmest and most personal letters of condolence, which nevertheless makes one hope that its recipient was feeling strong when he read it. Writing to his fellow-soldier Pollot to console him for the death of his brother, Descartes allows that some expression of grief is justifiable. 'I am not one of those who think that tears and sadness are appropriate only for women, and that to appear a stout-hearted man one must force oneself to put on a calm expression at all times.' There should, however, 'be some moderation in your feelings, and while it would be barbaric not to be distressed at all when one has due cause, it would also be dishonourable to abandon oneself completely to grief'. To comfort Pollot, Descartes reminds him that soldiers become inured to the deaths of their closest friends, and that he has already suffered, and survived, a serious setback.

---

⁹ *Passions of the Soul*, 46.

The loss of a brother, it seems to me, is not unlike the loss of a hand. You have already suffered the latter without, as far as I could see, being overwhelmed; so why should the former affect you so much more? If it is for your own sake, the loss of a brother is certainly the easier loss to make good, since acquiring a faithful friend can be as worthwhile as the friendship of a good brother. And if it is for your brother's sake . . . you know that neither reason nor religion gives us cause to fear . . . any harm.[10]

Having explained why Pollot should pull himself together, Descartes tells him how to set about it. 'Sir, all our afflictions, whatever they may be, depend only to a very small extent on the reasons to which we attribute them; their sole cause is the emotion and internal disturbance which nature arouses in us. For when this emotion is quelled, even though all the reasons we had earlier remain the same, we no longer feel upset.' The key to recovery is therefore to alter one's bodily state by using the understanding and volition to counter the movements that constitute our passions wherever they are most exposed. To understand how philosophers such as Descartes think about action, we perhaps need to try to imagine what it would be like to understand one's body as an unstable river system, prone to violent floods and tides, and one's deliberations as a more-or-less uneasy succession of ebbs and flows. When Poussin, for example, writes to a friend, 'the joy that has seized me is so great that it overflows on all sides, like a mountain stream which, after a long drought, fills with more rainwater than it can hold and suddenly bursts its banks' he is not speaking entirely metaphorically. The torrential rush he describes is an account of the movement of his own animal spirits.[11]

Alongside the defensive strategy of fending off the passions until they moderate or retreat, Descartes suggests that we can modify them by mentally separating the object of a passion from the passion itself and attaching the latter to a new object. 'Although the movements (both of the gland and of the spirits and the brain) which represent certain objects to the soul are naturally joined to the movements which produce certain passions in it, yet through habit the former can be separated from the latter and joined to others which are very different.'[12] We are used to the idea that animals can be trained: '[W]hen a dog sees a partridge it is naturally disposed to run towards it; and when it hears a gun fired, it is naturally impelled to run away. Nevertheless, setters are commonly trained so that the sight of the partridge makes them stop, and the noise they hear afterwards, when someone fires at the bird, makes them run towards it.'[13] Using comparable techniques we can self-consciously condition ourselves to admire what we used to envy, feel compassion for what we

---

[10] Letter to Pollot, Jan. 1641, in *Correspondence*, 167–8.
[11] Letter to Chantelou, Rome, 3 Nov. 1643, in *Nicolas Poussin: Lettres et propos sur l'art*, ed. A. Blunt (Paris, 1964), 81. On the antiquity of this theme see R. Padel, *In and Out of the Mind: Greek Images of the Tragic Self* (Princeton, 1992), 78–98.
[12] *Passions of the Soul*, 50.   [13] Ibid.

once scorned, or view with equanimity things that once induced panic and terror. Occasionally (an aversion therapist's dream) the reconnection happens all at once: 'When we unexpectedly come upon something very foul in a dish we are eating with relish, our surprise may so change the disposition of our brain that we cannot afterwards look upon any such food without revulsion, whereas previously we ate it with pleasure.'[14] Usually, however, we have to work to bring about transformations in our responses by redescribing the objects of our passions and surrounding them with new sets of associations until we come to feel differently about them.

Descartes's analysis of the struggle and deliberation that sometimes precedes action rests, then, on an account of the conflict between the will and powerful bodily motions over which we have only limited control. The body is, so to speak, already disposed to act, and although the soul can intervene to modify its motions and the actions they cause, it possesses its own emotional patterns and moods to which the soul can respond in various ways. It can sit back and endorse them uncritically, or it can actively refashion them, and itself, through the understanding and will. As we saw in Chapter 8, Descartes relies on the claim that voluntary control over one's passions and actions is intensely pleasurable in order to explain why people bother to try to cultivate this kind of power. Anyone who has discovered the internal joy that arises from the exercise of the will has, he suggests, an emotional reason to fashion their character by exploring the springs and levers that enable them to outwit their unwanted emotions. Most people, however, attain only imperfect control over their passions, and this is how Descartes explains Medea's betrayal of her father. Because our wills are not able to confront our passions directly, there is no point in her willing herself not to love Jason. Instead, she must assemble, as she does, a series of thoughts that may serve to counteract and alter her passion. This process is, however, far from foolproof.

[T]he will, lacking the power to produce the passions directly, . . . is compelled to make an effort to consider a series of different things, and if one of them happens to have the power to change for a minute the course of the animal spirits, the next one may happen to lack this power, whereupon the spirits will immediately revert to the same course . . . This makes the soul feel itself impelled, almost at one and the same time, to desire and not to desire one and the same thing; and that is why it has been thought that there are within the soul two conflicting powers.[15]

In a letter to Mersenne, Descartes implicitly applies this analysis to Medea's case. '[T]he intellect often represents different things to the will at the same time; and that is why they say "I see and praise the better, but I follow the worse." '[16]

---

[14] Ibid.   [15] Ibid. 47.   [16] Letter to Mersenne, May 1637, in *Correspondence*, 56.

Changing Antecedents of Action

As well as introducing a revolutionary interpretation of the conflict between the passions and the will, Descartes presses ahead with the project of unifying the mind by offering a more integrated account of the passions directly preceding action. Whereas Aquinas picks out both desire and aversion as immediate antecedents of action, Descartes collapses these into a single passion, *désir*.[17] He justifies the shift with the claim that, since good is a privation of evil and vice versa, 'it is always the same movement which gives rise to the pursuit of a good and at the same time the avoidance of the opposite evil'. For example, in pursuing riches we necessarily avoid poverty, and in avoiding illness we necessarily pursue health. So whereas there are, for Aquinas, two types of sequences of passions which lead to action, the first pivoting around desire, the second around aversion, Descartes reduces them to one.

Descartes's claim that good and evil are mirror images of each other is not entirely persuasive. To take one of his own examples, when the rich try to become yet more rich, it is hard to construe them as fleeing poverty. However, it is plausible to suggest that when people who are already rich pursue still greater wealth, they are avoiding something they regard as an evil, such as the embarrassment of being less well off than their friends, or the boredom that afflicts them when they stop trying to increase their wealth. Because the good they pursue and the evil they avoid are not opposites, it is an oversimplification to suggest that one can be decoded from the other; but it will often be true that both goals shape our desires, and thus help to explain our actions. As so often, Descartes here pursues a policy of integration: desire, as he understands it, encompasses both desire and aversion as understood by the Schools. When we avoid things we regard as evil, and when we pursue those we regard as good, we are moved to do so by a single passion; so, for example, desire can prompt me to get out of the way of a snake or to go to hear the music of Orpheus.

While this revision brings with it certain philosophical advantages, it has the effect of removing some of the content of the passion of desire. According to the Scholastic view, the affection which prompts us to avoid harmful things is distinct from the one that prompts us to pursue perceived goods; it feels different, and it has a different function, namely avoidance as opposed to pursuit. While desire carries spatial connotations of drawing nearer to an object, aversion consists in withdrawing from it, increasing the distance between object and agent. This differentiation makes room within the Scholastic model for the idea that it is possible to avoid evil without pursuing good, and vice versa. Because actions of these two types are caused by distinct affections, desire

---

[17] Hobbes retains the distinction between appetite and aversion. See *The Elements of Law*, ed. F. Tönnies (2nd edn, London, 1969), 28; *Leviathan*, ed. R. Tuck (Cambridge, 1991), 38.

and aversion, we understand them as movements to or from. For example, when fear prompts Eurydice to leap out of the way of the snake, she is moved to act by the passion of aversion. This emotion *is* a wish to avoid the snake, so that the idea of getting away from something is part of its content. While it may be true that we can also describe her action as the pursuit of a good, such as health, or life, this description is, emotionally speaking, negligible and does not explain her action. Equally, when she falls in love with Orpheus she is, as Aquinas would say, moved by a desire to try to possess her beloved. There is no emotional or motivational substance to the claim that she is, for example, simultaneously acting to avoid the evil of loneliness.

Descartes's view that a single passion—desire—prompts Eurydice both to move out of the way of the snake and to pursue her beloved loses this explanatory differentiation. The claim that an action resulted from a desire tells us nothing about what kind of action it was. And it becomes correspondingly difficult to give this passion any emotional content. We know, for example, that love and joy are broadly positive feelings, and hatred and sadness broadly negative ones. But in the case of desire, we do not even know this much. In defence of Descartes, we might argue that examples like those of avoiding the snake and pursuing the lover, where an action is explained by a virtually unqualified aversion or desire, are extremely unusual. Most of the time our emotions are balanced between considerations of advantage and harm, so that they more closely reflect Descartes's view that pursuit and avoidance are not separate activities but part of a single pattern of action. The very feature of the Scholastic account that appears a strength in the case of the snake—namely that this action is best understood as an attempt to *avoid* something—may elsewhere strike us as a weakness. For example, when Eurydice follows Orpheus out of the land of the shades, she desires both to be reunited with him and to escape from death. Pursuit of benefit and avoidance of harm are in this case integrated, so that it would be artificial to claim that one of them is uppermost. In directing our attention to this latter kind of case, Descartes implicitly urges his readers to abandon a view of the world as divided between perceived good and evil, between things to be avoided and things to be sought. Instead, he encourages them to understand their own actions as the outcome of a single emotional process which can always be described in two ways, as the pursuit of good or the avoidance of harm. Moreover, the fact that one evaluative pole can always substitute for the other is signalled by the fact that, under both descriptions, the action in question is caused by the same passion—namely desire.

While Descartes is thus concerned to provide a more unified schema of the passions giving rise to action, he nevertheless remains alive to the need to incorporate into his analysis the emotional diversity marked by the Scholastic notions of desire and aversion. This he does by redistributing the emotional weight contained in the sequences of passions that accompany action, and in particular by shifting the feelings contained in desire and aversion to the love and hatred that precede them. To see what is going on here, we need to remember that for Descartes, as for Aquinas, desires are always embedded in longer sequences of passions. Although Cartesian desire is a passion so general that its name gives little clue as to what it feels like or what sort of action it will provoke, it occurs in contexts which enable us to interpret it. For instance, when a desire is accompanied by hatred it will usually be more salient to describe it in terms of the evil to be avoided than in terms of the good to be simultaneously secured, and the opposite when it is accompanied by love. Equally, when it is followed by despair, it is pretty safe to assume that the object of the desire was not realized, and the opposite when it gives way to joy. At this exceedingly schematic level, Descartes shifts some of the content of Scholastic desire and aversion on to the passions surrounding Cartesian desire. Desire alone has less emotional content than its predecessors. But the whole sequence in which it occurs can take up the slack, by indicating what the emotional content of a desire must be.[18]

This redistribution is particularly evident in Descartes's discussion of attraction (*l'agrément*), the love we feel for beautiful things, and repulsion (*l'horreur* or *l'aversion*), our hatred for what is ugly. Both these emotions are responses to sensible appearances, to shapes, colours, smells, and so on, and according to Descartes the desires that arise from them are sharply differentiated.

For attraction and repulsion, which are indeed opposites, are not the good and the evil which serve as objects for these desires. Rather, they are two very different emotions of the soul which dispose it to pursue two very different things. On the one hand repulsion is ordained by nature to represent to the soul a sudden and unexpected death. Thus, although it is sometimes merely the touch of an earthworm, the sound of a rustling leaf, or our shadow, that gives rise to repulsion, we feel at once as much emotion as if we had experienced a threat of certain death. This produces a sudden agitation which leads the soul to do its utmost to avoid so manifest an evil. It is this kind of desire that we commonly call 'avoidance' [*la fuitte*] or 'aversion' [*l'aversion*].[19]

Aversion and its counterpart, the attraction 'ordained by nature to represent the enjoyment of what attracts us as the greatest of all the goods belonging to mankind', are therefore intense kinds of love and hate, which we experience as ardent yearning and revulsion. To return to the case of the snake, while Aquinas would have explained that Eurydice's fear gave rise to aversion, which caused her to try to leap out of its way, Descartes contends that what she feels for the snake is revulsion, and that this gives rise to a desire which causes her to

---

[18] See A. Matheron, 'Amour, digestion et puissance selon Descartes', *Revue philosophique de la France et de l'Étranger*, 178 (1988), 407–13.

[19] *Passions of the Soul*, 89.

move. The feeling of needing to get away has been shifted from the aversion that is the immediate antecedent of action to the hatred that precedes desire.

By including attraction and aversion in his list of passions, Descartes acknowledges an important range of emotions. But he also gives aversion a greater specificity than it possesses in the Scholastic model. While Aquinas regards it as an affection which may be intense, as with the snake, or barely conscious, Descartes recasts it in such a way that it is always perceptible. When we experience aversion or revulsion, we know it. But this passion occurs comparatively rarely because it is only caused by sensible things that strike us as ugly. In so far as our deliberations about good and evil are distanced from our immediate sensory perceptions, we will not experience aversion, and will form desires without the intervention of this kind of hatred. I cannot, it seems, feel revulsion for philosophy, although I can feel it for this particular philosophical book. Like possessive love, the objects of aversion will be sensible.[20]

This departure from the Scholastic conception of desire and aversion is, I shall suggest, one stage in a lengthy reconceptualization of desire which takes place throughout the seventeenth century and gives rise to a substantially altered philosophy of action in which desire plays an increasingly central role. It is complemented by another important change—this time in the part played by desire in the explanation of action. For Descartes, as for his Scholastic predecessors, desires are embedded in sequences of passions which, taken together, are contributory causes of action. Desires do not occur on their own and are distinct from the other passions with which they occur. For example, I can love something that I believe to be good: that's to say, I can consider myself joined to it. Equally, I can desire something: that's to say, I can want to have it in the future because I believe this will be to my advantage.[21] These passions are separate. But they habitually go together, because love for something gives rise to the desire to get into a state that will enable me to maintain the love.[22]

Descartes's theory of action therefore breaks in two important ways with Scholastic Aristotelianism. It identifies the conflicts between passion and volition that are held to precede some actions as contests between the soul and the body. And it merges the distinct passions of desire and aversion into the single passion of desire. While the Cartesian solution to the problem of how to avoid any appeal to a divided soul is not widely taken up, and while the Cartesian analysis of desire is not universally accepted, many philosophers embrace the spirit, if not the letter, of Descartes's proposals. Like him, they aim to produce a unified theory of the mind, powerful enough to explain a wide range of actions; and like him, they are struck by the advantages of a broader conception of desire. Taking up Descartes's problems, they propose a series of still more radical solutions that will be discussed in the next chapter.

---

[20] Ibid. 90.   [21] Ibid. 80.
[22] A. F. Beavers, 'Desire and Love in Descartes' Late Philosophy', *History of Philosophy Quarterly*, 6 (1989), 279–94.

12

Deliberating with the Passions

Descartes is not the only seventeenth-century philosopher to grapple with the limitations of the Scholastic explanation of action. Alongside the Cartesian attempt to deal with them, discussed in the preceding chapter, we find other proposals which focus more narrowly on the notion of desire, a passion which moves steadily to the centre of the stage until it is not just the immediate antecedent of action, but *the* antecedent of action, the driving force which shapes our responses and colours all our other emotions. Allied to this shift is a further change—the demise of attempts to explain action in terms of a conflict between passions and volitions, which itself rests on a move towards a still more integrated theory of the mind. Theories of action that incorporate these two changes give the passions a central explanatory role. But in order to play it, they have to be reconceptualized in a manner that breaks with the oppositions between activity and passivity which formed the starting-point of my account. The themes to be discussed in this chapter therefore mark the passing of the philosophical era with which this book is concerned, as one framework within which the passions are understood begins to give way to a contrasting one. Needless to say, this change does not happen all at once, nor does it give way to a single, universally accepted view, so that the theories that will occupy us here are in some ways tentative, and are fiercely opposed by philosophers who wish to maintain the ancient categories of action and passion that began to come under threat.

Hobbes, Descartes's near contemporary, abandons the Scholastic view that desires occur sandwiched between other passions in sequences that, taken as a whole, explain our behaviour. Instead, he gives a new priority to desire and aversion as the antecedents of action. The voluntary motions of our bodies 'such as to go, to speak, to move any of our limbs in such a manner as is first fancied by our minds' are, in his view, caused by thoughts which represent objects and states of affairs as advantageous or harmful. These thoughts are 'commonly called endeavour' which, 'when it is toward something is called appetite or desire'[1] and 'when the endeavour is fromward something, it is

---

[1] Although Hobbes distinguishes appetite and desire, explaining that desire is the more general term and appetite is usually reserved for hunger and thirst (*Leviathan*, ed. R. Tuck (Cambridge, 1991), 38), he nevertheless often uses appetite as a synonym of desire. See e.g. his definitions of passions, ibid. 42–4.

generally called aversion'.[2] The fact that Hobbes retains the distinction between desire and aversion should not distract us from the main feature of his position, which is to make these passions the antecedents of action. But so far this is completely conventional. It is only when Hobbes discusses the relation between desire and the other passions that the distinctiveness of his view begins to emerge, for he here analyses a set of eight 'simple passions'[3] as stages in the process of desiring and attaining an object. We start out with desire and aversion, which are themselves motions. We add the 'appearance or sense' of these motions, which we call delight or pleasure, and trouble of mind or pain. We therefore never experience desire without pleasure or aversion without pain. In addition, that which we desire we love, and that which we are averse to we hate. 'Desire and love' Hobbes says, 'are the same thing; save that by desire we always signify the absence of the object; by love, most commonly the presence of the same.'[4] And similarly for aversion and hate. Finally, the expectation of achieving or failing to achieve our desires gives rise to joy or grief.

The simple passions are thus organized around desire and aversion which are no longer the middle members of a sequence of emotions that is efficacious in bringing about action, but are *the* natural dispositions, *the* motivating forces, in terms of which the rest of our passions are to be characterized. Desire and aversion are what get us going, and the other simple passions are modifications of them. Moreover, other less basic passions are to be understood in terms of the simple passions, and thus in terms of this central pair. Hope, for example, is appetite with the opinion of obtaining an object; fear is aversion with opinion of hurt from it; desire of office or precedence is ambition, and so on. There is a significant contrast here with the classification of passions compiled by Descartes; for whereas Descartes distinguishes six primitive passions each of which has many modifications, Hobbes's passions are for the most part modifications of aversion or desire.[5]

Nor is this revision merely a matter of classification. By identifying desire and aversion with endeavour (his translation of *conatus*), Hobbes draws on a central Stoic doctrine—the idea that the force enabling each thing to maintain its identity can be understood as a kind of striving. We saw in Chapter 4 that Hobbes construes the endeavour of inanimate objects as the internal motions which enable them to resist change. Turning now to humans, he takes it that each person experiences some of the motions that constitute their *conatus* or endeavour as desires and aversions, as inclinations towards the things they think will sustain them and away from those they regard as potentially damaging. Endeavour, experienced as desire and aversion, is thus our most fundamental striving to maintain ourselves, and an ineradicable response to the world around

---

[2] Ibid. 38.   [3] Ibid. 41.   [4] Ibid. 38.
[5] See G. B. Herbert, *Thomas Hobbes: The Unity of Science and Moral Wisdom* (Vancouver, 1989), 97–8.

us. But because it is in humans a highly complex and articulated drive, it surfaces not only in desire and aversion themselves but in a whole set of finely tuned passions which vary with circumstance. The centrality Hobbes accords to this striving is dramatically brought home by his claim that to have no desire is to be dead;[6] but it is also vividly reflected in his account of our thought-processes, many of which are regulated, in his view, by some desire or design and consist in instrumental reasoning from means to ends. 'From desire arises the thought of some means we have seen produce the like of that which we aim at; and from the thought of that, the thought of the means to that mean; and so continually till we come to some beginning within our own power.'[7] As long as we live, we must continue to maintain ourselves in a changing environment, fending off threats and securing our position, so that we can never overcome the insatiable desires which drive us on from one goal to the next.

This Stoic-inspired analysis of desire as the primary passion which moves us to action is still more clearly expounded by Spinoza. Like Hobbes, Spinoza identifies the passion of desire with our *conatus* or striving to persevere in our being and grafts it on to the Cartesian view that desire and aversion are a single passion. Appetite, he claims, 'is the very essence of man, in so far as it is determined to do what promotes his preservation', and 'desire is appetite together with the consciousness of it'.[8] Furthermore, there is really no difference between appetite and desire, 'for whether a man is conscious of his appetite or not, the appetite still remains one and the same'.[9] Desire is therefore our experience of the striving for power that is our essence, and is one of three fundamental passions, the other two being the joy and sadness we feel as our power is increased or diminished. Hobbes's position is here simplified and consolidated in a further step away from the Scholastic interpretation of the passions and their relation to action, together with a further affirmation of the view that our actions are initiated and sustained by our desires.

This new understanding of the relation between desire and action is incorporated, in the work of both Hobbes and Spinoza, into an analysis of irresolution and psychological conflict which does not appeal to distinct and antagonistic forces, either in the mind, or in the mind and body. Where Descartes traces Medea's failure to act on her judgement to the effects of a contest between her passions and her will, Hobbes and Spinoza dispense with volitions and offer a different account of her difficulty. Hobbes's interpretation is rooted in his view that our ideas are motions in the brain[10] which, when they continue to the heart, give rise to passions,[11] and that these in turn are 'the first unperceived

---

[6] *Leviathan*, 54.   [7] Ibid. 21.
[8] *Ethics*, in *The Collected Works of Spinoza*, ed. E. Curley (Princeton, 1985), vol. i, III, Definition of the Affects, 531.
[9] Ibid.   [10] *The Elements of Law*, ed. F. Tönnies (2nd edn, London, 1969), 28.
[11] Ibid. 31.

beginnings of our actions'.[12] Action, Hobbes goes on, 'immediately follows with
the first appetite, as when we do anything upon a sudden'. When Eurydice sees
the snake, she immediately feels aversion (the first appetite) and leaps out of
its way. It may happen, however, that 'to our first appetite there succeedeth
some conception of evil to happen unto us by such actions, which is fear, and
withholdeth us from proceeding'.[13] In this case, appetite is succeeded by fear
'and to that fear may succeed a new appetite, and to that appetite another fear
alternately, till the action be either done, or some accident come between, to
make it impossible'.[14] This alternating succession of appetites and fears is deliberation, and we can deliberate about any action in the future which we believe
to be possible. So unless we act on our first appetite, we embark on a process
of deliberation, and only when this is somehow brought to a conclusion will
we act.

In discussing the end of deliberation, Hobbes introduces what was, perhaps,
the most startling of his philosophical innovations, the view that the appetite
or fear immediately preceding action is called will.[15] 'In deliberation', he claims,
'the last appetite or aversion, immediately adhering to the action, or to the
omission thereof, is that we call the will; the act (not the faculty) of willing.'[16]
Rather than opposing or proceeding from the will, appetite and aversion *are*
the will.[17] So in explaining action we no longer have to consider the interplay
of two forces, passions and volitions; instead, we have to attend to an alternation of passions. Suppose, for example, that a painting of Venice causes an
idea of the city, which in turn arouses a desire to see it. But the thought of
visiting Venice is followed by an idea of being alone there, and this cerebral
motion gives rise to a fear which replaces the desire. Thus begins a sequence
in which each passion displaces the one preceding it, as motions are transferred through the body from the brain. Whereas Descartes had presented deliberation as a conflict between motions with distinct origins, which is resolved
by their relative strength, Hobbes conceives the process as involving forces
of a single kind. The bodily motions that result in action are all passions. In
addition, the motions that are appetites and fears do not directly confront one
another. Each gives way, at least temporarily, to its successor. In this latter
account, deliberation is shaped by a series of conceptions which all give rise to
passions. But the passions do not, so to speak, fight back. Just as deliberation
consists in a sequence of ideas about the advantages and disadvantages of a
course of action, so it consists in a sequence of alternating appetites and fears.[18]

Like Hobbes's account of endeavour, this analysis is profoundly indebted
to Stoic conceptions of deliberation as a kind of oscillation. Indecision and torn

---

[12] Ibid. 61.   [13] Ibid.   [14] Ibid.   [15] Ibid. 62.   [16] *Leviathan*, 44.
[17] *Elements of Law*, 62–3.
[18] See T. Sorell, *Hobbes* (London, 1986), 92–5; T. Airaksinen, 'Hobbes on the Passions and
Powerlessness', *Hobbes Studies*, 6 (1993), 82–9.

feeling, Chrysippus tells us, are 'not the conflict and civil war of two parts, but the turning of a single reason in two different directions, which escapes our notice on account of the swiftness and sharpness of the change'.[19] When we deliberate, we are not tugged in two ways, but contemplate a sequence of scenarios, each of which portrays certain values and states of affairs. In the language used by Hobbes, we draw near to a picture of the future, retire from it to contemplate a different image, return to a picture rather like the first, and so on.[20] But in the end we settle on one portrayal. Hobbes makes his position clear in his comment on Medea's lines, 'I see the better course, but follow the worse', although he draws on Seneca's *Medea* rather than Ovid's, and refers to Medea's conflicting passions as she brings herself to kill her two sons. 'Pretty as it is', Hobbes objects, the indecision that Seneca attributes to her 'is not true; for though Medea saw many reasons to forbear killing her children, yet the last dictate of her judgement was that the present revenge on her husband outweighed them all.'[21]

The rhythm of embracing and denial which constitutes deliberation can itself be directed by the character of the ideas involved. A woman who finds herself contemplating a course of action involving a terrible risk, say the death of someone she loves, may be horrified and block off all further exploration of that avenue. The pattern of her deliberation is here shaped by the strength of her feeling, which is allied to her judgement that certain things are too valuable to be endangered. By contrast, another woman may force herself to work through a set of alternatives exhaustively out of a desire to be sure that the decision she arrives at is well grounded, a desire itself interwoven with her belief that this decision is vitally important to her life. The actual sequence of passions that constitutes a process of deliberation will therefore be shaped by an agent's experience, by her passions, and above all by her imaginative construction of where her present situation may lead. As Hobbes explains, 'the propounding of benefits and of harms, that is to say, of reward and punishment, is the cause of our appetite and of our fears, and therefore also of our wills, so far forth as we believe that such rewards and benefits as are propounded, shall arrive unto us. And consequently, our wills follow our opinions, as our actions follow our wills.'[22]

What, though, brings deliberation to a close and moves us to act? For Descartes, the answer lies in the force of the passions and will; once an internal

[19] Plutarch, 'De Virtute Morali', in *Moralia*, trans. W. C. Helmbold (Cambridge, Mass., 1962), vi. 441C, 441F. See M. Nussbaum, *The Therapy of Desire: Theory and Practice in Hellenistic Ethics* (Princeton, 1994), 384.

[20] These are Hobbes's verbs. See *Elements of Law*, 31.

[21] *Of Liberty and Necessity*, in *The English Works of Thomas Hobbes*, ed. Sir William Molesworth (London, 1839–45), iv. 265. See Seneca, *Medea*, in *Tragedies*, trans. F. J. Miller (Cambridge, Mass., 1917), i. 225–315.

[22] *Elements of Law*, 63.

motion is strong enough to cause the movements that constitute an action, it will be performed. But for Hobbes it seems that someone might deliberate back and forth indefinitely without ever reaching a decision. There are several possibilities here. Hobbes will agree that some deliberations are never resolved; I may keep wondering whether to go to Venice without ever reaching a decision one way or the other. A second possibility stems from the fact that many deliberations come to an end when they generate strong passions. Deliberation, as Hobbes sees it, presupposes an absence of what he calls 'suddenness' in our passions, a lack of the intensity and conviction that give rise to action. But it can itself generate suddenness: for example, thinking over a situation and wondering whether to see it this way or that, I may become increasingly persuaded by a particular interpretation and at the same time increasingly angry, to the point where I lose interest in deliberating about it any further and act. Here the growth of my conviction about how to see the situation and the growth of my passion proceed together. It would be misleading to say that I am progressively taken over by a passion which finally prompts me to act. Equally, it would be misleading to say that I consider the pros and cons and decide what to do. To capture Hobbes's view, we need to see deliberation as involving both an interpretative and an emotional change, and as issuing in action when both interpretation and feeling gain sufficient conviction to make further deliberation superfluous. This view of action connects to a third point—that people's disposition and ability to deliberate more or less thoroughly, and the style in which they do so, will be shaped by the experience and passions they already have. Some are cautious, others bold; some are gamblers, others risk-aversive; some are confident, others anxious. In addition to these character traits, individuals have to work with their existing attitudes to particular topics; deliberating about a given subject may be congenial to some and uncomfortable for others. In these and related ways, our histories feed into our patterns of behaviour and determine the points at which we act.

Among philosophers who share the view that action can be explained without recourse to the will, perhaps the most important is Spinoza. However, Spinoza's account of the antecedents of action diverges from the Hobbesian one by taking a further step towards the Stoic view that the passions are judgements. For Hobbes, ideas remain distinct from passions, although the two are causally connected. They represent different stages of motions radiating out from the brain into the rest of the body, ideas being motions in the head and passions motions in the heart. Spinoza reduces these two categories to one. Passions, in his view, are ideas. To love someone, for example, is to have a certain idea of what they are like which is interwoven with an assessment of their capacity to increase one's own power. Being sensitive and tender, they will not intentionally hurt one; being funny and easygoing, they enliven even the most dreary chores; being perceptive and observant, they awaken ideas and feelings that are pleasurable and exciting. Loving them consists in appreciating these qualities, and this feeling will change only as they change, or as we come to re-evaluate their character. If disappointment makes them bitter and cynical, we may find them less lovable than before. Or if remarks that might once have struck us as perceptive come to seem excessively critical and unkind, love may wane.

What, now, about deliberation? Although Spinoza does not explicitly describe deliberation as an alternation of passions, he shares Hobbes's view that it consists in a dynamic sequence of ideas. In so far as our ideas are inadequate, and hence passionate, our deliberations are based on a partial and to some extent distorted picture of the world. In so far as our ideas are adequate, they are more likely to result in actions that are well judged, both in that they realize the ends at which they were aimed, and in that they are aimed at ends which will effectively increase our power. As we saw in Chapter 8, both these types of ideas are affective and can therefore function as antecedents of action. On the face of things, Spinoza's division between two sorts of ideas, and two corresponding sorts of affects, threatens to open up a new division in the mind, and with it new forms of conflict as adequate ideas battle against inadequate, passionate ones. However, Spinoza does not see the problem in these terms. Rather, he regards ideas of both types as judgements, which occur in integrated processes of deliberation and collaborate to produce the conceptions of the world upon which we act. On the whole, adequate ideas possess a clarity and coherence which makes them more compelling than their inadequate counterparts, so that those who possess them will for the most part act wisely. For example, if Medea had had a more adequate idea of Jason and knew what a feckless adventurer he was, she might have found him less lovable. Our capacity to resolve conflicts of judgement therefore depends on our resources—on the information available to us, on our philosophical insight, and on our skill in disentangling the elements of a passion that lie in ourselves from those that lie in its object.

There is, however, a further problem which Spinoza addresses, using the standard example: namely, how to explain the fact that Medea knows she is going to help Jason even though she recognizes that she ought to obey her father. Her plight, as Spinoza presents it, stems from a phenomenon which we explored in Part III and which is vividly described by Ovid—the exceptional power that our passions have over us when we are in the presence of their objects. Left to herself, Medea is able to get her love for Jason in perspective and arrives at an adequate understanding of what she ought to do, but as soon as she sees him her resolution drains away and she recognizes that she is going to help him. It is because our temporal and spatial relations to other things direct our feelings for them and because the power of external causes may be greater than the power we derive from our knowledge of good and evil, that men are moved more by opinion than by true reason, and this is also why the true knowledge of good and evil arouses disturbances of the mind, and often yields to lusts of every kind. 'Hence that verse of the Poet, ". . . video meliora, proboque | deteriora sequor . . .".'[23] If humans were not located in time and space their judgement would be much more effective in guiding action, but as it is they are often knocked off course by the imperatives of the present. Ideally, we should deliberate from the atemporal perspective of our adequate ideas, but in practice we have difficulty in keeping this before our minds and lend extra weight to the here and now. Medea's anguish has to be understood in terms of the adequate and inadequate ideas which constitute her resources for reflecting on her situation, but do not enable her to think it through to a point where she is no longer susceptible to Jason's charms. This inability may be due to her lack of certain philosophical insights, such as an understanding of the tension between our ideas about the present and those about the comparatively distant future, or to her lack of skill in the kind of deliberation that effectively modifies passion. Agreeing with Hobbes, Spinoza takes it that both these related capacities are determined by her past, and by the resulting assemblage of ideas that is her mind.

An Integrated Mind and Voluntary Action

Philosophers who abandoned the view that volitions are a particular kind of thought and a distinct antecedent of action ran into fierce opposition, grounded on the claim that they were advocating a determinism which destroys the difference between the voluntary and involuntary, and with it a series of theological and more broadly philosophical distinctions. If people act on ideas which are themselves caused by preceding ideas, and if there is nothing outside the process of deliberation and action with which to oppose or redirect this causal progression, they appear to be wholly in the grip of their ideas and, on Hobbes's interpretation, wholly in the grip of their passions. How, then, are they to secure their salvation through free, virtuous action? And how is it possible to retain the self-evident boundaries between the inanimate and animate, between animals and people, or between immature and mature human beings? A hierarchical interpretation of nature which serves to legitimate the authority of rational men over the rest of creation is suddenly challenged.

The anxiety provoked by these issues is palpable, for example, in Bramhall's wide-ranging attack on Hobbes, whom he condemns as both unchristian and dangerously mistaken. By construing deliberation as the alternation of passions, and by treating it as a causal process, Hobbes has first of all dishonoured the

---

[23] Spinoza, *Ethics*, IV. P 17.

nature of man and made men 'but the tennis balls of destiny', the victims of causal processes beyond their control.[24] In addition, his neglect of the difference between spontaneous and free action has rendered the liberty of men 'brutish' and 'childish'.[25] We act spontaneously, in Bramhall's view, when we act in accordance with an intellectual or sensible appetite but do not deliberate. For example, when fear—'a perturbation arising from some expectation of imminent evil'[26]—makes a sheep run, its act is spontaneous. But we act freely when we deliberate, which in turn requires understanding.[27] The non-causal process of deliberating about what to do begins when the will, 'the Lady and Mistress of human actions', assents to a judgement proposed or represented to her by the understanding, and commands the understanding, 'her true counsellor, to deliberate about the ways of attaining a particular end'.[28] Thus instructed, the understanding may suggest two or three ways of attaining a goal, but in deciding between them the will has the power to do or forbear and to choose good or evil, and is not constrained by any advice that the understanding offers.[29] She elects or chooses, and only actions that derive from the exercise of this apparently capricious, feminine, but nevertheless morally vital power are free.

While children, animals, and fools act spontaneously on their passions, rational men are capable of deliberation and can thus act freely.[30] Hobbes's refusal to discriminate between actions of these two types strikes Bramhall as pernicious and indeed incredible. Willing, as Hobbes portrays it, consists in appetite. But if rational men act only on appetite, there is nothing to distinguish their actions from those of horses, bees, or spiders,[31] and the considered actions of a bishop or philosopher become as appetitive and spontaneous as those of a baby sucking at the breast.[32] As Bramhall's outrage testifies, people who believe that the moral supremacy of man lies in the liberty invested in the will are liable to find the Hobbesian doctrine deeply threatening. By collapsing volition into appetite, it seems to flatten out the distinctions that give men the freedom and autonomy that is the basis of their authority over the natural world. At the same time, it removes from within the human race the moral superiority of the rational over the foolish, and the adult over the young. For a bishop committed to believing that God speaks with the voice of little children, this last piece of levelling perhaps touched a particularly raw nerve, and, taken together, these revisions raised the disturbing spectre of a world in which the actions of animals, fools, children, and adults alike are deliberate, and in this respect free. All these actions would on the one hand demand the moral respect reserved in Bramhall's view for the free actions of adults. On the other hand, they would presumably be eligible for praise and blame. But

[24] Bramhall, *A Defence of True Liberty from Antecedent and Extrinsicall Necessity* (London, 1655), 60.
[25] Ibid. 10.   [26] Ibid. 43.   [27] Ibid.   [28] Ibid. 30.   [29] Ibid. 31–2.
[30] Ibid. 34.   [31] Ibid. 45.   [32] Ibid. 38.

the prospect of a world turned so thoroughly upside down cannot be taken seriously, and is presented as a *reductio ad absurdum* of Hobbes's position.

Bramhall's criticisms serve to point out the levelling consequences of measuring some of Hobbes's views against a conception of liberty he does not hold. If free action requires the operation of a free will, and if volition is simply the last appetite, then all thought-processes are equally unfree. But Hobbes is not, of course, a leveller. As far as he is concerned, animals are distinguished from humans, and children from adults, by the extent of their prudence, and by their power to arrive at definitions and deduce consequences in an orderly and scientific fashion. The fact that they are all capable of deliberation and willing does not undermine the intellectual and moral differences between them. This aspect of his dispute with Bramhall therefore centres on the characterization of moral differences between living things. According to Bramhall, the morally vital quality is freedom, which depends on the possession of powers to understand and will that lie outside the nexus of natural causation. According to Hobbes, the morally vital quality is the power to reason, which is itself part of causally ordered nature. Pushing back, we see that this disagreement in turn rests on a dispute about the character of determinism. Hobbes holds that his determinist theory of reason and action can accommodate the morally significant differences between kinds of living things that worry Bramhall, and can also account for the various sorts of indecision and mental conflict with which we are familiar. Bramhall argues, by contrast, that without the will we cannot make sense either of the moral differences between rational men and others, or of psychological struggle. To interpret these phenomena we need, in his view, a distinction between passion and will. In short, we need to retain a model of the mind in which more than one power contributes to the determination of action.

Bramhall here upholds a conservative criticism of what he perceives as an unduly Stoic interpretation of action.[33] Hobbes's mistake consists in straying from the entrenched view that the mind contains separate powers of passion and volition, and the simplest way to put this right is to revert to orthodoxy. However, rather than rejecting Hobbes's position outright, a more innovative critic might consider whether his arguments contain anything of which a less outrageous theory of action ought to take account. This is in fact the approach taken by Locke, whose discussion of this issue owes a good deal to Hobbes, and yet stops short of some of Hobbes's more shocking conclusions. In his *Essay Concerning Human Understanding*, Locke expounds the view that the will is the power of directing our operating faculties to some action,[34] the power to do or forbear, to continue or end the actions of our minds or motions of

---

[33] See ibid. 66, 89, 137–43. For Hobbes's reply see ibid. 85.
[34] Ed. P. H. Nidditch (Oxford, 1975), II. xxi. 40.

our bodies simply by thinking about it.[35] Volitions are therefore the bare thoughts that control action, something like choices or preferences. This position is, however, to be distinguished from another, with which Locke disagrees. 'I find the Will often confounded with several affections, especially desire; and one put for the other, and that by men who would not willingly be thought not to have had very distinct notions of things, and not to have writ very clearly about them.'[36] Expanding this implicit criticism of Hobbes, Locke points out that we know perfectly well that we can voluntarily perform actions which conflict with our desires. This shows, he argues, that willing and desiring are two separate acts of the mind, and that we have a power to act which is distinct from our desires, and indeed from any of our affections. Part of the problem with Hobbes's identification of volition and desire is therefore, in Locke's view, that it deprives him of the means to account for a familiar kind of conflict—cases where we want one thing but do another.

At the same time, Locke agrees with Hobbes's criticism of the traditional claim that the will is self-determined, and therefore agrees that we have to ask 'What is it that determines the will in regard to our actions?'[37] What makes us do or forbear, begin or end an action? Locke's reply is best taken in two stages. Our volitions, he first of all tells us, are determined by something called uneasiness, which he defines as 'all pain of the body, of what sort soever, and disquiet of the mind'.[38] The notion of uneasiness first appears in the *Essay* as a synonym for pain, and as one of the hinges on which our passions turn; sensation provides us with the simple ideas of pleasure-or-delight and pain-or-uneasiness, in terms of which Locke then defines our passions. For example, desire is the uneasiness a person feels upon the absence of a thing whose present enjoyment carries the idea of delight,[39] hatred is what we feel for things that are apt to produce uneasiness, sorrow is uneasiness of the mind upon the thought of a good lost, and so forth.

Returning to the claim that uneasiness determines the will, this would seem to suggest that volitions are determined by the various passions into which it enters. In fact, however, this is not quite what Locke goes on to say. When he turns to the explanation of volition, and thus of action, he emphasizes that

---

[35] Ibid. 5.

[36] Ibid. 30. On Locke on the passions see J. W. Yolton, *Locke: An Introduction* (Oxford, 1985), 19–24; P. A. Schouls, *Reasoned Freedom: John Locke and the Enlightenment* (Ithaca, NY, 1992), esp. 92–114.

[37] *Essay*, II. xxi. 31.

[38] Ibid. This discussion first appears in the 1690 edn. of the *Essay*, but is anticipated in Locke's journal for 1676. See W. von Leyden (ed.), *John Locke: Essays on the Law of Nature* (Oxford, 1954), 60–80. For further discussion about the development of the *Essay* see J. Passmore, 'Locke and the Ethics of Belief', in A. Kenny (ed.), *Rationalism, Empiricism and Idealism* (Oxford, 1986); M. Ayers, *Locke* (London, 1991), i. 110–12.

[39] *Essay*, II. xx. 6. See E. Vailati, 'Leibniz on Locke on Weakness of Will', *Journal of the History of Philosophy*, 28 (1990), 213–28.

only desires move people to act. 'But that which immediately determines the will to every voluntary action is the uneasiness of desire, fixed on some absent good.'[40] We therefore have the following argument. The will is determined by uneasiness. Uneasiness usually takes the form of a passion. So the will is determined by some passion. But not all passions are equally efficacious in this respect. And the passion that plays the pivotal role in the determination of the will is none other than desire, that is, 'an uneasiness in the absence of a thing whose present enjoyment carries the idea of delight'. As Locke explains, 'the will seldom orders any action, nor is there any voluntary action performed, without some desire accompanying it'.[41] Moreover, when we speak as though our wills were determined by other passions such as aversion, fear, or shame, this is because they are mixed with desire, and therefore contain the element of uneasiness that moves the will. 'These passions are scarce any of them, in life or practice, simple and alone and wholly unmixed with others . . . Nay there is, I think, scarce any passion to be found without desire joined to it.'[42] This apparently innocuous view suggests that it is unduly limited to think of the will as opposing the passions, since nothing less than a passion determines the will. Desire and volition are not opposed forces, but work together to cause our actions. We therefore have a new answer to the question: How are desires and volitions connected?, which relies once again on a more integrated picture of the thoughts that precede action. The will remains; but it is now submissive to desire and occupies the same position as Hobbes's last appetite.

The changing relations between volitions and desires traced throughout this section are reflected in a series of interpretations of the scope of voluntary action. As we have seen, explanatory theories of action are caught, in the seventeenth century, between a wish to overcome the problems associated with a segmented soul and the need to account for various familiar kinds of mental conflict. It must be possible to explain how people can resist their passions. And it must be possible to explain how people can change, for example by learning to counter certain passions or to overcome unwanted desires. But at the same time it must be possible to explain how they can act against their

---

[40] *Essay*, II. xxxi. 33.

[41] Ibid. xxi. 39. On Locke's analysis of action see J. W. Yolton, *Locke and the Compass of Human Understanding* (Cambridge, 1970), 138–59; V. Chappell, 'Locke on the Intellectual Basis of Sin', *Journal of the History of Philosophy*, 32 (1994), 197–208 and 'Locke on the Freedom of the Will' in G. A. J. Rogers (ed.), *Locke's Philosophy* (Oxford, 1994), 101–21; M. Losonsky, 'John Locke on Passion, Will and Belief', *British Journal for the History of Philosophy*, 4 (1996), 267–83. For broader discussions of the context of Locke's view see J. Colman, *Locke's Moral Philosophy* (Edinburgh, 1983), 206–34; J. Tully, 'Governing Conduct: Locke on the Reform of Thought and Behaviour', in *An Approach to Political Philosophy: Locke in Contexts* (Cambridge, 1993), 179–241; J. Dunn, ' "Bright enough for all our purposes": John Locke's Conception of a Civilised Society', *Notes and Records of the Royal Society of London*, 43 (1989), 133–53; W. M. Spelman, *John Locke and the Problem of Depravity* (Oxford, 1988); P. A. Schouls, 'John Locke: Optimist or Pessimist?', *British Journal for the History of Philosophy*, 2 (1994), 51–73.

[42] *Essay*, II. xxi. 39.

better judgement and, as we still say, give way to passions in spite of themselves, without reintroducing a range of separate powers in the soul. To some extent, these two aspirations pull against one another, because the positing of separate powers provides a way of characterizing mental conflict.

As we have seen, Descartes describes the division between the voluntary and the involuntary in a way that leaves space for an account of internal struggle and secures two important goals—the unification of the soul and an account of conflict and change. There are always some actions we can perform voluntarily, but the soul's capacity to observe, reflect on, and experiment with its bodily passions enables it to increase the range of actions it can bring about at will. Learning to do this can be a long and taxing process, and even as we progress there remains an uneasy territory in which will and passion fight it out and the voluntary and involuntary conflict. When a soldier manages not to run away from the fray, but is unable to enter the battle as boldly as he would like to because of the weakness in his knees, are his actions voluntary or involuntary? When an angry mother moves to smack her child but stops at the last moment, does she raise her arm voluntarily or involuntarily? Descartes does not insist on a straight answer to these questions, but offers us a way to explain actions as flowing from forces of both kinds. Voluntary action, according to this picture, is partly born with us; we have, from the start, a limited ability to act at will. But it is partly learned. We extend the scope of voluntary action by acquiring new skills—for example by learning to talk—and by learning to control our passions.

Philosophers such as Hobbes, who espouse a more integrated theory of the antecedents of action, are forced to provide a different account of this interplay between the voluntary and the involuntary. Since there is only one kind of immediate antecedent of action—in Hobbes's case the endeavour that encompasses both appetite and aversion—the contrast between voluntary and involuntary acts can no longer be drawn in terms of a distinction between passion and will. Nor does Hobbes draw it along another Cartesian line by appealing to the suddenness or deliberateness of an action, since in his view all actions are at some stage deliberated on.[43] Instead, he defines involuntary actions as those brought about by external force, and contrasts these with all other actions, which he classifies as voluntary. They are voluntary because they are all willed, in the Hobbesian sense that some appetite or aversion is their immediate cause.[44] This draconian revision seems on the face of things to sweep away the discriminations between different types of action that are so central to philosophers like Descartes in favour of the psychologically blank view that anything we are not physically forced to do, we do voluntarily. However, Hobbes is in fact far from insensitive to the kinds of conflict and struggle that

---

[43] Hobbes, *Of Liberty and Necessity*, 243–5.   [44] *Leviathan*, 145–6.

Descartes and his Scholastic predecessors discuss. He is perfectly well aware that some actions are sudden, others not; that some are the outcome of long and difficult deliberations, while others result from quick and easy decisions; and that while some are performed without regret, others are deeply unsatisfying. In addition, he recognizes that we are sometimes in a position critically to assess our beliefs and desires before acting on them, and are sometimes condemned to act on irrational projections beyond our immediate self-understanding.

Although Hobbes acknowledges these differences, he does not want to characterize them by saying that some actions are more voluntary, or willed, or free than others. In rejecting these descriptions, he also gives up the idea that action can result from an internal struggle that the agent may win or lose. To be sure, we speak in these terms. But to describe oneself as conquered or overwhelmed by passion is, strictly speaking, a piece of inaccurate and exculpatory self-dramatization. How, then, should we interpret human actions? To act voluntarily, according to Hobbes, is to act on the last appetite that arises from a longer or shorter process of deliberation, during which we assess the likely outcomes of competing passions. The soldier who runs away acts at a point when he desires to avoid getting hurt more than he desires to fight. The soldier who rushes into battle acts when his desire to fight is more compelling than his desire to flee. And the soldier who stays but is too scared to fight boldly presumably finds that his last appetite is to fight as he does—half-heartedly. All these actions are equally voluntary, and the whole weight of explaining the differences between them rests not on the role of the will, but on the idea of deliberation, understood both as an intellectual calculation and as an alternation of feeling, as an inferential exploration of consequences and a succession of images, associations, and emotions.

To produce plausible Hobbesian interpretations of these three cases, we need to get away from the idea that action marks the end of deliberation. Although Hobbes's claim that people act on the last appetite suggests that, once we act, deliberation is over, we can make better sense of the conflicts that the soldiers in our example undergo if we regard their deliberations as open-ended. The man who decides to fight, we can suppose, makes a decision and is then too busy staying alive to deliberate any further. But the other two act before their deliberations are resolved. The deserter is perhaps plagued as he flees by anticipations of shame and images of a glorious battle, which continue to alternate with his desire to get home and his conviction that his comrades are even now being massacred. His case prompts us to ask what makes people act before a deliberation is concluded, and draws our attention to Hobbes's remark that we deliberate 'till the action be either done, or some accident come between to make it impossible'.[45] Deliberation about a particular action, we are here

---

[45] *Elements of Law*, 61.

reminded, does not occur in isolation; it is surrounded by and interconnects with other deliberations and events which may overtake it. In our example, battle is about to begin, and the soldier acts on the appetite he has so far arrived at and runs away. But since he has not reached a settled judgement about what to do, his deliberation goes on, merging perhaps into a related internal debate about what he should say when he gets home.

The third soldier is also still deliberating when battle is joined and, acting on the appetite he has so far arrived at, stays to fight. But he remains afraid, and his fear affects his performance. Deliberation, as Hobbes presents it, is thus a sequence of oscillating passions which ends when we reach a stable emotional attitude. Because he is still deliberating, the soldier has not arrived at a settled emotional mood of boldness or fear and is subject to swings of feeling which interfere with his ability to attack the enemy. This last case helps us to see what is unusual and counter-intuitive about Hobbes's account of volition. As it is traditionally understood, the will gives us some power to control the actions deriving from our passions. Moreover, because it is allied to the understanding, this power partly consists in various intellectual abilities such as assenting to or dissenting from judgements. Hobbes, however, reverses both these traditional expectations. On the one hand, the volitions that prompt us to act are judgements that are also passions; Hobbes describes them both as last judgements of the appetite and as last appetites. On the other hand, the deliberation that gives rise to a volition is not just an intellectual process of judging, assessing, and so forth; it is a sequence of judgements that are passions. So when we deliberate, we feel this way and that about a course of action, and the sequence of our feelings need not be one over which we always have full critical control. We may not be fully aware, for example, that one image is associated with another, or that an idea of a particular person is allied to a feeling of envy. Nevertheless, this sort of sequence issues in action which, according to Hobbes, is voluntary. What feels odd here is the dissociation of voluntariness from critical control. The feelings of the half-hearted soldier just before the battle are still alternating and unsettled, and he is not in a good position to reflect on them, so that there is a sense in which they are going on in spite of him. But whereas Descartes would take this as evidence that his action in joining the battle is the result of a struggle between voluntary and involuntary forces, Hobbes regards it as evidence of voluntary action. In his view, we exert various degrees and kinds of control over our deliberations. A theory of action needs to explore the diverse patterns of deliberation from which actions can arise, but the differences between these do not bear on the question of whether or not an action is voluntary.

Why is Hobbes so determined to expand the range of actions that are counted as voluntary? Part of his motivation is connected, perhaps, with the aftermath of the English revolution, and the experience of watching those who

had lost the war pleading and squirming before their conquerors, protesting
that they were not politically obliged to the new government.[46] In Hobbes's
view conquest is compatible with free consent, so the fact that they have been
conquered does not necessarily lessen their obligation. However, as we have
begun to see, he also has a more narrowly philosophical reason for resisting
the view that some actions are more free than others, since he belongs to a
diverse group of philosophers who are all keen to overturn the view that the
mind contains two distinct and potentially conflicting powers, passions and
volitions. Hobbes holds that the only way to produce a unified conception of
the mind is to get rid of this division completely by identifying what had previously been classed as volitions with passions. The result is a picture in which
there is no will. There is just passion. However, Hobbes also wants to avoid
the objection that actions caused by passions are involuntary, since to allow
this would be to allow the unacceptable consequence that there is no difference between humans and tennis balls. What, then, are his options? He can
say that some actions caused by passions are voluntary and some are not. But
this would require him to explain the difference between actions of the two
kinds, and would probably lead him back to the very distinction between desires
and volitions he is trying to escape. So he takes another way out and claims
that all actions prompted by passions are voluntary. How, then, can he account
for the various kinds of conflict that are usually characterized by appeal to the
interplay of passions and volitions? He proposes to do this via his notion of
deliberation, and concludes that while actions arise from various types of deliberation, they are all free.

The Case for Volitions

Despite the power of the Hobbesian view, there remains in seventeenth-
century philosophy a more-or-less pressing sense that, because deliberation is
a causal process, the agents portrayed by Hobbes or Spinoza have lost control
over their actions. At the same time, accounts of action inspired by Stoicism
are held to do less than justice to mental conflict, so that Hobbes's conception
of action as the last appetite, for example, does not satisfactorily explain how
people can act against their desires. A further attempt to deal with these problems was made by Locke, who aims for a compromise, reintroducing a fissure
between passion and volition and modifying Hobbes's analysis of what it is to
act voluntarily. As we have seen, Locke distinguishes two antecedents of action:
desires and volitions. The first of these, desire or uneasiness, is rooted in our

---

[46] See Q. Skinner, 'Thomas Hobbes on the Proper Signification of Liberty', *Transactions of the Royal
Historical Society*, 40 (1990), 121–51.

natural disposition to pursue happiness, which takes different forms in different individuals. People's experiences of uneasiness or desire presuppose judgements that certain things or states will make them happy, and because humans are naturally inclined to seek happiness, they are naturally inclined to make judgements of this kind. Volitions, on the other hand, are our power to begin or end actions. At some points in his discussion of this topic Locke claims that the will is determined by uneasiness or desire—'but that which immediately determines the will . . . to every voluntary action, is the uneasiness of desire fixed on some absent good'.[47] He thereby appears to place desire in the position occupied by Hobbes's last appetite, as the final term in a causal sequence resulting in action. However, Locke introduces a modification into this account. Even when we desire something, we can always will ourselves not to act on our desire. This is because volitions, the last item in the causal sequence preceding action, possess a special power to hold up the action in question. 'For the mind having . . . in most cases a power to suspend the execution and satisfaction of any of its desires . . . is at liberty to consider the objects of them; examine them on all sides, and weigh them with others.'[48] Locke's interpretation of volitions here diverges from the Hobbesian account of the will, and reintroduces some elements of the conflict model that Hobbes and Spinoza reject. First, volitions are quite different from desires; the will's capacity to hold up action is not itself a desire but a separate kind of thought. Moreover, it is the capacity to suspend the prosecution of a desire that makes us free. 'This seems to me the source of all liberty; in this seems to consist that which is (as I think improperly) called free will.'[49] Whereas Hobbes had argued that freedom consists in the ability to act on the last appetite of a deliberation, Locke holds that it consists in the ability to act on or refrain from acting on our desires. Hobbes would retort that Locke's volitions are simply one stage in the alternation of appetites and aversions that occur when we deliberate. But Locke denies this, partly, it seems, because he is anxious to capture a phenomenological sense of conflict that is lost in Hobbes's account. More importantly, Locke is reintroducing an element into the chain of antecedents of action which cannot be explained as an effect of the earlier elements, thereby reinstating the agent's control over the connection between desire and action.

By insisting that people have a distinct power to refrain from acting on their desires, Locke echoes Hobbes's plea against excuses. 'And how much this is in every one's power, every one by making resolutions to himself such as he may keep, is easy for everyone to try. Nor let anyone say, he cannot govern his passions, or hinder them from breaking out and carrying him into action; for what he can do before a prince or a great man, he can do alone, or in the presence of God, if he will.' In elaborating this view, however, he uncovers a

---

[47] *Essay*, II. xxi. 33.   [48] Ibid. 47.   [49] Ibid.

tension within his own position about the scope and power of the will, and thus of voluntary action. As we have seen, voluntariness was initially defined as our capacity to refrain from acting on our desires. But suspending action is not an end in itself; the point of it is to make way for further deliberation so that we can act more prudently. We are free 'to hold our wills undetermined, till we have examined the good and evil of what we desire'.[50] What, though, enables us to make proper use of the breathing space created by the will? Locke seems to assume that a natural tendency to pursue happiness manifests itself as a disposition to deliberate about whether the objects of our desires will really make us happy. 'For the inclination and tendency of their nature and happiness is an obligation, and motive, to them, to take care not to mistake, or miss it; and so necessarily puts them upon caution, deliberation and wariness, in the direction of their particular actions, which are the means to attain it.'[51] However, this conclusion seems both stipulative and over-optimistic in the light of his other claims. On the one hand, we only deliberate if uneasiness creates in us the desire to do so. On the other hand, our power to suspend action makes space for deliberation, and a man who chooses too hastily 'has vitiated his own palate and must be answerable to himself for the sickness and death that follow from it. . . . He had a power to suspend his determination: it was given to him that he might examine and take care of his own happiness, and look that he were not deceived.' If he failed to make proper use of this power, the consequences 'must be imputed to his own election'.[52] Locke here seems to move from the relatively modest view that our liberty consists in the capacity to suspend action, so that it is always in our power to create a space in which we may, if we are able, deliberate, and the view that we are free to deliberate, so that it is our own fault if we fail to take care of our happiness. As his vindictive tone suggests, he is anxious to establish the latter claim; but it is easier to reconcile his overall argument with the former. Because we are often free to refrain from acting immediately, we are often free to prevent ourselves from implementing our uneasinesses or passions. But this is not to say that we are always free to deliberate further about what to do, let alone deliberate effectively. Whether we can manage this depends on the passions and habits we already possess. Nor are we always free to act on the fruits of our deliberation, and our minimal power to suspend action may be little use in a situation where, if we act at all, we will act badly.

Locke's exploration of the relations between judgement, passion, and action places his analysis of volition under considerable strain. People only exercise their power to suspend action if they already see some reason to do so or, as Locke puts it, are already uneasy about performing the action in question. Ignorance or carelessness will often lead us to act in ways that undermine our

---

[50] *Essay*, II. xxi. 52.   [51] Ibid.   [52] Ibid. 56.

happiness,[53] as will the familiar disposition to give greater weight to the present than the future. 'Objects near our view are apt to be thought greater than those of a larger size, that are more remote: and so it is with pleasures and pains, the present is apt to carry it, and those at a distance have the disadvantage in the comparison.'[54] In both situations, our responsibility for the consequences rests on the fact that, although we saw no reason to exercise it, we had the power to refrain from acting. There are also cases where people believe they should suspend action, but are unable to do so. This happens, Locke observes, when great physical pain operates forcibly on the will[55] and creates an uneasiness which drives out all other thoughts, or when a vehement passion has the same effect. 'But if any extreme disturbance . . . possesses our whole mind . . . as when an impetuous uneasiness, as of love or anger or any other violent passion, running away with us, allows us not the liberty of thought, and we are not masters enough of our own minds to consider thoroughly and examine fairly; God, who knows our frailty, pities our weakness.'[56] Here Locke reinstates a conflict model in which passions and volitions appear as competing forces: strong passions can overturn the normal sovereignty of the will so that it is powerless to resist them, and we go ahead and act. Moreover, in such cases we are not free. We are, therefore, back at the view that free actions have volitions among their causes, whereas unfree ones are the effects of passion. Finally, there are people like Medea, 'that unhappy complainer',[57] who know what they should do but not how to do it. Medea lacks the capacity to strengthen the uneasiness that will enable her to act dutifully, and it is doubtful whether suspending action will make much difference. She is, in Locke's view, free to refrain from helping Jason, and consequently responsible for what she does. But since she is unable to alter her passions, her freedom to suspend action has little bearing on her problem. She is like a drunkard who 'sees and acknowledges [the greater good], and in the intervals of his drinking hours will take resolution to pursue [it]; but when the uneasiness to miss his accustomed delights returns, the greater acknowledged good loses its hold, and the present uneasiness determines the will to the accustomed action'.[58] Despite his efforts to transcend its limitations, Locke's emphasis on an alternating sequence of passions which determine action implicitly reverts at this point to the Hobbesian conception of the will as the last appetite.

Locke's analysis offers a blend of the divergent accounts of the explanation of action we found in the work of Descartes and Hobbes, a blend, one could say, of the legacies of Aristotelianism and Stoicism. He is sufficiently persuaded by Hobbes's view that we act on our passions to argue that the volitions that are the immediate causes of action are themselves caused by desires. But at

---

[53] Ibid. 67.   [54] Ibid. 63.   [55] Ibid. 57.   [56] Ibid. 53.   [57] Ibid. 35.
[58] Ibid.

the same time he stands back from the aspects of Hobbes's view which under-pin this claim. Instead of identifying will with appetite, as Hobbes does, Locke distinguishes desires from volitions, and reintroduces the possibility of conflict between these two kinds of thought. Instead of claiming that actions result from a sequence of causes, as Hobbes does, Locke introduces a conception of volition as the capacity to refrain from acting on our desires, re-establishing the idea that we have a kind of control over our actions which does not derive from our passions. Claiming that we are only free when we possess the power to refrain from action, Locke reintroduces, almost in spite of himself, the ques-tion of what can interfere with the working of the will. And instead of inter-preting passions as judgements in the manner of Hobbes, he argues that desires and judgements can diverge, so that we are capable of judging that it would be good to do something without feeling in the least uneasy about it.

These modifications undermine the overall coherence of Locke's position which remains torn between the view that we are free to act or refrain from acting on our desires and the view that our desires determine our wills and thus our actions. But at the same time they contribute to his attempt to arrive at, and perhaps also to resuscitate, a theory of action which is phenomeno-logically satisfying. A division between desires and volitions serves, in Cartesian vein, to explain familiar kinds of mental conflict.[59] The reintroduction of volitions returns to the agent control over his or her actions. The claim that actions are only free when we can will either to act or refrain from acting re-establishes the view that liberty has something to do with voluntariness. And the division between judgements and desires provides the material for an account of an important kind of dislocation: the inability to act on a considered judge-ment. The attempt to deal with these issues by reorganizing them within the framework of a determinist theory of action and an integrated conception of the mind did not immediately prevail, and Locke's work helped his contem-poraries to identify what they, like him, regarded as its limitations.

The Decline of Active and Passive Thoughts

The shifting theories traced in this and the preceding chapter carry the marks of the end of an era, the signs of an altered understanding of the passions and their relation to action. Embedded in the transitions we have discussed are pro-found changes, which were later put together to form the basis of the influential orthodoxy that actions are explained by beliefs and desires. Among these changes are a new understanding of the active and passive aspects of the mind; a new interpretation of desire and its relation to action; and finally the ingredients,

---

[59] *Essay*, II. xxi. 41.

so to speak, of a distinction between beliefs and desires. To elucidate the character and implications of the work we have discussed, it will be helpful to end by drawing together what it contributes to these three themes.

As we have seen, the distinction between volitions and passions was habitually allied to the view that the mind is capable of acting and being acted on. When we will, we ourselves initiate thoughts and actions, whereas our emotions are the effects of other things upon us. Philosophers who deny the existence of volitions as a distinct and self-generating kind of thought therefore challenge a deeply rooted understanding of the mind's creative power, of its ability to go its own way independently of the world around it. In fact, however, some of them embrace this implication of their attack on the will more cheerfully than others. Spinoza starts by making the bold claim that what we call volitions are simply a subset of the ideas that constitute our strivings to persevere in our being,[60] and, like all our other ideas, are caused. There is consequently no sense in which willing is an especially active kind of thinking. Nevertheless, because it is important to Spinoza to retain a distinction between active and passive thought-processes, he attaches this difference not to kinds of thought but to the character of the judgements that constitute our thinking: when we think with inadequate or partial ideas we are acted on, but in so far as our ideas are adequate we act. Certain characteristics traditionally ascribed to the will and used to qualify it as active are here transferred to adequate ideas. Most importantly, its generative power is recast in the claim that the completeness of an adequate idea enables further adequate ideas to be inferred from it alone; the character of the idea ensures that anyone who possesses it can in principle pursue certain chains of thought by working through its implications, generating further thoughts out of the thoughts they already have. This analogy between willing and active thinking is complemented, in Spinoza's philosophy, by two significant disanalogies. First, whereas willing is, at least in some of its guises, the epitome of self-expression—the independent power of the mind to think what it likes—the Spinozist conception of activity as thinking with adequate ideas is constrained by the truth. We act only in so far as our ideas really are complete and undistorted, and active thinking involves submitting oneself to the discipline of working out what they truly imply. Secondly, while volitions are understood as antecedents of both thoughts and bodily movements, Spinoza allies activity with thinking. It is, to be sure, the kind of thinking that provides us with the best possible reasons for acting in certain ways, and the ideas that contribute to it are also, according to Spinoza, states of our bodies. All the same, we understand activity not by considering actions in the ordinary sense of the word, but by focusing on the judgements of which actions are the expression.

---

[60] *Ethics*, III. P 9s.

By reworking a traditional interpretation of the opposition between action and passion, Spinoza is able to abandon the will while retaining a distinction between the actions and passions of the mind. Hobbes, by contrast, follows out the implications of his view that the will is the last appetite, and implicitly allows that, if there are no volitions, there is then no remaining sense in which some kinds of thinking are more active than others. Any thought can be described as an action when it is the cause of some further thought or motion; and any thought can be described as a passion when it is an effect. From this position, one can arrive at the implication that the categories of activity and passivity have no place in discussions of the philosophy of mind and action, and should be replaced by talk of causes and effects. While this radical view was later to become an orthodoxy, it would not of course have recommended itself to most of Hobbes's contemporaries, who read him as claiming not that thought is neither active nor passive, but that it is entirely passive. Hobbes, it seemed to them, had not transcended the opposition between action and passion, but had rather attacked the will, the active ingredient of thinking, leaving behind only passions, and it was the idea that all human thought is passive that astounded and exasperated critics such as Bramhall. To abandon the idea that there is something uniquely active about human thinking would, as we have seen, be to give up some of the central tenets of the Christian order, including the superiority of humans to animals and the affinity between humanity and an active God. Humans would be swept from their place in the Great Chain of Being, relieved of their authority, and absorbed into the natural realm.

Hobbes's analysis of action and passion, together with its implications, consequently remained unacceptable to most—perhaps all—seventeenth-century philosophers. The seeds of doubt had, however, been sown, and because writers who disagreed with so challenging a figure felt bound to give their reasons, his view remained current, like a shadow lying behind the print on the pages of a wide range of texts. Moreover, its consistency and clean lines made it attractive, so that Hobbes's most insightful critics found themselves torn between acknowledging the strengths of his arguments and rescuing a conception of the difference between active and passive antecedents of action. Locke, as we have seen, embarked on this struggle, conceding that the will is often determined by passion, yet insisting that it is nevertheless an independent power which enables us to act and refrain from acting. It is therefore hardly surprising that he was thrown back on a traditional understanding of the difference between action and passion, which he expresses in terms of powers. When a motion or thought is the result of an impression received from some external agent, he tells us, the power to move or think 'is not properly an active power, but a mere passive capacity in the subject'. However, '[s]ometimes the substance or agent puts itself into action by its own power, and this is properly active power'.

The active power of motion is, therefore, 'in no substance which cannot begin motion in itself'; and in thinking, 'to be able to bring into view ideas out of sight, at one's own choice, and to compare which of them one thinks fit, this is an active power'.[61] Thus, 'when I turn my eyes another way, or remove my body out of the sunbeams, I am properly active; because of my own choice, by a power within myself, I put myself into that motion'.[62] Although Locke here holds to the Aristotelian line, his reiteration of a long-accepted distinction between action and passion does not help to resolve the tensions that run through his theory of action. The problems raised by Hobbes conspire to make his response look more question-begging than constructive, and draw attention to the intractability of the problems he faces as a metaphysical foundation which has sustained a series of interpretations of the passions unexpectedly subsides. Locke steps in valiantly to shore it up. But the scale of his repairs suggests that they will not last for long.

Alongside the increasing precariousness of the fundamental categories of activity and passivity, we find in seventeenth-century theories of action a new conception of desire, which emerges as two established views are challenged. The view that actions are caused by sequences of passions culminating in desires begins to give way to the view that desires are the principal passionate antecedents of action. And the view that actions arise from a conflict between volition and passion starts to collapse as volitions get absorbed into desires. Instead of a single, comparatively specialized passion, desire comes to be conceived as the central appetitive force which enables us to stay alive and governs all our actions. It absorbs the tasks previously allotted to other passions such as hatred and love and the work previously ascribed to the will. This reconceptualization is, as we have seen, part of a more comprehensive urge to unify the mind, which is itself an endorsement of an aspect of Stoicism. In place of the divided, Aristotelian soul, it posits an integrated mind within which there are no competing powers. At the same time, this approach elbows aside an Augustinian interpretation of the soul and the passions within it. It eclipses Augustine's conviction (shared, as we have seen, by Malebranche) that volitions are the active ingredient in all our actions and in all our judgements, practical and theoretical, leaving no space for Malebranche's conception of the will as a kind of inexhaustible truffle hound, equipped by God to search out truth and falsehood as well as good and evil. Instead, desire, embedded in a web of natural causal relations, becomes the force that spurs us on. Simultaneously, desire takes over some of the all-encompassing quality that Augustine had attributed to love. Since his analysis of the various passions as modifications of a central drive—love—had been widely regarded as unduly reductionist, it is interesting that a more modest, Scholastic understanding of love as one passion among

---

[61] *Essay*, II. xxi. 72.　　[62] Ibid.

others gave way to an almost equally reductionist interpretation of the passions as varieties of desire.

The emergence of this position represents the consolidation of some traditions and the marginalizing of others, a realignment of the complex and intertwining treatments of the passions we have discussed into a new view. As with most realignments of this sort, however, its achievements are bought at some cost. On the one hand, an increasingly generic conception of desire paves the way for the modern orthodoxy that beliefs and desires are the antecedents of action. On the other hand, explanations of actions grounded on the view that the passions only move us to act in so far as they are kinds of desire, or are mixed with desire, are often comparatively blank. Taken generically, desires lack the inflections that would make them explanatory. Once we begin to expand them, we are drawn back into the intricate and sometimes baffling territory of the passions. The tension between these two stances is perhaps most obvious in analyses of psychological indecision and dislocation, where philosophers like Locke strongly wish to retain a theory of conflicting kinds of thought. In these contexts, the resources of the Aristotelian divided soul are not easily matched by theories which posit desires as the principal affective antecedents of action. A Stoic insistence on the integrity of the mind, albeit one which can oscillate from judgement to judgement, seems to miss something out. In our own time, psychoanalytic theories of the conscious and subconscious, and of unconscious fantasy, aim to recoup this loss, and in doing so Freud and his successors rework some of the themes and mechanisms explored by early-modern theorists of the passions.

From our present perspective, one of the strangest features of the theories of action discussed in these chapters is their failure to distinguish desires from beliefs, or to analyse the respective roles played by these kinds of thought in bringing about action. Instead, they appeal to passions that are ideas— complex interpretations of an agent's experience in which several elements are usually incorporated. Orpheus' desire to rescue Eurydice, for example, contains a number of interrelated ingredients, including a representation of an object, an evaluation of it, some sort of grounds for the evaluation and the emotion of hope. These elements may be differently balanced: Descartes distinguishes ideas with a minimal evaluative content that have no impact on the will from those that bear on our good and evil and move us to action;[63] and at the other end of the spectrum there are ideas that are predominantly evaluative, such as a generalized anger that has no determinate object. But these diverse elements all belong within a single idea.

The multi-faceted character of our passions ensures that our affects change with our representations and vice versa. For instance, once we come to believe

---

[63] *Passions of the Soul*, in *The Philosophical Writings of Descartes*, ed. J. Cottingham *et al.* (Cambridge, 1984–91), i. 47.

that a future state is impossible we usually give up hoping for it—as Descartes reminds Huygens in another of his steely letters of condolence.[64] Equally, our perceptions of people alter as we come to love or hate them. This internal complexity of our passions captures the fact that humans are by nature interpreting creatures who understand themselves and their environment in a highly articulated manner. In addition, it captures something about our own experience of thinking—the fact that we do not usually separate out the various elements of our ideas but interpret the world in chunks. In doing so we make mistakes. But a theory which tried to break ideas down into discrete components would lose its grip on a basic feature of our experience, which can be simultaneously reflexive, cognitive, evaluative, and unreliable.

The fact that early-modern theorists are content to treat passions as ideas does not mean that they are unaware of their complex character, or that they are completely uninterested in dissecting them. It is striking, however, that this interest does not surface in explanatory contexts, so that there is little trace in their work of the view that one could arrive at stronger or more incisive explanations of action by analysing passions into their representational and affective components. Hobbes, for example, distinguishes the motions in the brain that are ideas or conceptions from those in the heart that are passions, thereby laying the physical ground for a distinction between non-appetitive and appetitive ideas. But when he comes to discuss the relation between passions and actions he does not make anything of this; on the contrary, he treats passions as unified ideas that encompass both representations and emotions. The context in which the separation of these elements is discussed is not in fact explanatory but therapeutic. As we have already seen, Descartes takes up the idea that we can modify our unwelcome responses to the world by separating an emotion from its object and attaching it to different feelings, as when we try to replace a fear of public spaces with a zest for civic life, or a loathing for beetroot with comparative indifference. In describing this technique, Descartes speaks of separating one component of an idea from another, as though emotions could float free of their objects and come to rest somewhere else. He seems to have in mind here a relatively mechanical type of conditioning, distinct from the kind of case where an agent does not so much aim to separate the components of a passion as to alter the passion by altering its components. People who school themselves to enjoy beetroot by playing soothing music every time they eat it seem to fit Descartes's bill better than people who try to conquer their fear of public spaces by modifying their habitual representations of council chambers or lecture rooms. In relation to either case, however, the central point is that we resort to the dissection of our ideas in order to manipulate them when they are in some way pathological or unsatisfactory. And there remains a gap

[64] Letter to Huygens, 20 May 1637, in *Philosophical Writings*, ed. Cottingham *et al.*, iii. *Correspondence*, 54. See also *Passions of the Soul*, 145.

between this approach and the view that such dissection is relevant to the explanation of action in general. We can disassemble our affections, Descartes implies, when something goes wrong. But as long as they are functioning reasonably well, the richest explanations of action mirror our experience, and deal in the fragile, multi-faceted ideas that are our passions. This approach to action is therefore shaped by an interest in the line between the normal and pathological, the functional and dysfunctional. Only when this concern dwindles is there a demand for comprehensive theories that can be applied to actions of all kinds, such as the view that they are explained by beliefs and desires.

This book has focused on the rejection of the Schools and their Aristotelian authorities, and on the many and varied conceptions of the passions that stemmed from this central feature of early-modern philosophy. As we have seen, these diverse analyses helped to shape a variety of complex interpretations of the mind. However, as the simplifying view that one affection—desire—is the motor of all action came to be accepted, the pictures with which we have been concerned began to dissolve and fade. They were replaced by a set of views that are far more familiar, but which carry philosophy decisively beyond the traditions of thinking examined in this book.

Bibliography

Primary Sources

AQUINAS, *Summa Theologiae*, ed. and trans. the Dominican Fathers, 30 vols. (London, 1964–80).

ARISTOTLE, *The Complete Works of Aristotle*, ed. J. Barnes, 2 vols. (Princeton, 1984).

—— *Metaphysics*, in *Complete Works*, ed. Barnes, ii.

—— *Nicomachean Ethics*, in *Complete Works*, ed. Barnes, ii.

—— *On Dreams*, in *Complete Works*, ed. Barnes, i.

—— *On Generation and Corruption*, in *Complete Works*, ed. Barnes, i.

—— *On Memory*, in *Complete Works*, ed. Barnes, i.

—— *On the Heavens*, in *Complete Works*, ed. Barnes, i.

—— *On the Parts of Animals*, in *Complete Works*, ed. Barnes, i.

—— *On the Soul*, in *Complete Works*, ed. Barnes, i.

—— *On the Universe*, in *Complete Works*, ed. Barnes, i.

—— *Physics*, in *Complete Works*, ed. Barnes, i.

—— *Problems*, in *Complete Works*, ed. Barnes, ii.

—— *Rhetoric*, in *Complete Works*, ed. Barnes, ii.

—— *Sophistical Refutations*, in *Complete Works*, ed. Barnes, i.

ARNAULD, ANTOINE, *Vraies et fausses idées*, in *Œuvres*, ed. G. du Parc de Bellegards and F. Hautefagel (Brussels, 1965–7), xxxviii.

—— and NICOLE, PIERRE, *La Logique ou l'art de penser*, ed. P. Clair and F. Girbal (Paris, 1981).

—— —— *Logic or the Art of Thinking*, trans. and ed. Jill Vance Buroker (Cambridge, 1996).

AUGUSTINE, *City of God*, ed. D. Knowles (Harmondsworth, 1972).

—— *Confessions*, trans. R. S. Pine-Coffin (Harmondsworth, 1961).

BACON, FRANCIS, *Translation of the Novum Organum*, in *Works*, ed. J. Spedding, R. Ellis, and D. D. Heath, 14 vols. (London, 1857–61), iv.

—— *The Philosophy of the Ancients*, in *Works*, ed. J. Spedding, R. Ellis, and D. D. Heath, 14 vols. (London, 1857–61), vi.

—— *Sylvana Sylvanum or a Natural History in Ten Centuries*, in *Works*, ed. J. Spedding, R. Ellis, and D. D. Heath, 14 vols. (London, 1857–61), ii.

—— *The Advancement of Learning*, ed. G. W. Kitchin (London, 1973).

—— *The Great Instauration: Plan of the Work*, in *Works*, ed. J. Spedding, R. Ellis, and D. D. Heath, 14 vols. (London, 1857–61), vi.

BOYLE, ROBERT, *The Origin of Forms and Qualities according to the Corpuscular Philosophy, Illustrated by Considerations and Experiments* (Oxford, 1666).

—— *A Free Inquiry into the Vulgarly Received Notion of Nature*, in *The Works*, ed. T. Birch, 6 vols. (London, 1772), v.

—— *The General History of Air*, in *The Works*, ed. T. Birch, 6 vols. (London, 1772), v.

BOYLE, ROBERT, *Some Considerations about the Reconcileableness of Reason and Religion*, in *The Works*, ed. T. Birch, 6 vols. (London, 1772), iii.

BRAMHALL, JOHN, *A Defence of True Liberty from Antecedent and Extrinsicall Necessity: Being an Answer to a Late Book of Mr Thomas Hobbes of Malmesbury entitled 'A Treatise of Liberty and Necessity'* (London, 1655).

BRIGHT, TIMOTHY, *A Treatise of Melancholy* (New York, 1940).

BURTON, ROBERT, *The Anatomy of Melancholy*, ed. T. C. Faulkner, N. K. Kiessling, and R. L. Blair (Oxford, 1989–94), vol. i. Text.

CAMUS, JEAN PIERRE, *Traité des passions de l'âme*, in *Diversitez*, 10 vols. (Paris, 1609–14), viii.

CHARLETON, WALTER, *A Brief Discourse Concerning the Different Wits of Men* (London, 1669).

—— *A Natural History of the Passions* (London, 1674).

—— *Physiologia Epicuro-Gassendo-Charltoniana: Or a Fabric of Science Natural upon the Hypothesis of Atoms* (London, 1654).

—— *The Darkness of Atheism Dispelled by the Light of Nature: A Physico-Theological Treatise* (London, 1652).

CHARRON, PIERRE, *Of Wisdome*, trans. S. Lennard (London, 1608).

CICERO, *Tusculan Disputations*, trans. J. E. King, Loeb Classical Library (Cambridge, Mass., 1927).

—— *De Oratore*, trans. E. W. Sutton and H. Rackham, 2 vols., Loeb Classical Library (Cambridge, Mass., 1942).

COEFFETEAU, NICHOLAS, *Tableau des passions humaines, de leurs causes et leurs effets* (Paris, 1630).

CUDWORTH, RALPH, *A Sermon Preached before the House of Commons*, in *The Cambridge Platonists*, ed. C. A. Patrides (Cambridge, 1969).

—— *A Treatise concerning Eternal and Immutable Morality with A Treatise of Freewill*, ed. Sarah Hutton (Cambridge, 1996).

CUREAU DE LA CHAMBRE, MARIN, *The Characters of the Passions*, trans. J. Holden (London, 1650).

DE LA FORGE, LOUIS, *Traité de l'esprit de l'homme*, in *Œuvres philosophiques*, ed. P. Clair (Paris, 1974), 69–349.

DESCARTES, RENÉ, *The Philosophical Writings of Descartes*, vols. i. and ii, ed. J. Cottingham, R. Stoothoff, and D. Murdoch (Cambridge, 1984); vol. iii. *Correspondence*, ed. J. Cottingham, R. Stoothoff, D. Murdoch, and A. Kenny (Cambridge, 1991).

—— *Comments on a Certain Broadsheet*, in *Philosophical Writings*, ed. Cottingham *et al.*, i.

—— *Description of the Human Body*, in *Philosophical Writings*, ed. Cottingham, *et al.*, i.

—— *Discourse on the Method of Rightly Conducting one's Reason and Seeking the Truth in the Sciences*, in *Philosophical Writings*, ed. Cottingham *et al.*, i.

—— *Meditations on First Philosophy*, in *Philosophical Writings*, ed. Cottingham *et al.*, ii.

—— *Œuvres de Descartes*, ed. C. Adam et P. Tannery, 11 vols. (Paris, 1964–74).

—— *Optics*, in *Philosophical Writings*, ed. Cottingham *et al.*, i.

—— *Les Passions de l'âme*, ed. G. Rodis Lewis (Paris, 1988).

—— *The Passions of the Soul*, in *Philosophical Writings*, ed. Cottingham *et al.*, i.

—— *The Principles of Philosophy*, in *Philosophical Writings*, ed. Cottingham *et al.*, i.

—— *Rules for the Direction of the Mind*, in *Philosophical Writings*, ed. Cottingham *et al.*, i.

—— *The Treatise on Man*, in *Philosophical Writings*, ed. Cottingham *et al.*, i.

—— *The World*, in *Philosophical Writings*, ed. Cottingham *et al.*, i.

DONNE, JOHN, *The Sermons of John Donne*, ed. E. M. Simpson and G. R. Potter, 10 vols. (Berkeley and Los Angeles, 1953–62).

HOBBES, THOMAS, *Elements of Philosophy: The First Section, Concerning Body*, in *The English Works of Thomas Hobbes*, ed. Sir William Molesworth, 11 vols. (London, 1839–45), i.

—— *Leviathan*, ed. R. Tuck (Cambridge, 1991).

—— *On Liberty and Necessity*, in *The English Works of Thomas Hobbes*, ed. Sir William Molesworth, 11 vols. (London, 1839–45), iv.

—— *The Elements of Law*, ed. F. Tönnies (2nd edn, London, 1969).

—— *A Minute or First Draft of the Optics*, in *The English Works of Thomas Hobbes*, ed. Sir William Molesworth, 11 vols. (London, 1839–45), vii.

HOOKE, ROBERT, *Micrographia . . . Or Some Physiological Descriptions of Minute Bodies made by Magnifying Glasses, with Observations and Enquiries thereupon* (London, 1665).

HOOKER, RICHARD, *The Works of Mr. Richard Hooker*, ed. J. Keeble, 3 vols. (7th edn, Oxford, 1888; repr. New York, 1970).

JUNIUS, FRANCISCUS THE YOUNGER, *The Painting of the Ancients* (Farnborough, 1972).

LA MOTHE LE VAYER, FRANÇOIS, *De l'instruction de Monseigneur le Dauphin*, in *Œuvres* (2nd edn), 2 vols. (Paris, 1656), i.

—— *La Morale du Prince*, in *Œuvres* (2nd edn), 2 vols. (Paris, 1656), i.

LAMY, BERNARD, *Entretien sur le science* (1684), ed. François Girbal and Pierre Clair (Paris, 1966).

LE BRUN, CHARLES, *Conférence sur l'expression générale et particulière*, in *The Expression of the Passions*, ed. J. Montagu (New Haven, 1994).

LE GRAND, ANTOINE, *Man without Passion: Or the Wise Stoic according to the Sentiments of Seneca*, trans. G. R. (London, 1675).

LOCKE, JOHN, *An Essay Concerning Human Understanding*, ed. P. H. Nidditch (Oxford, 1975).

LONG, A. A., and SEDLEY, D. D., *The Hellenistic Philosophers* (Cambridge, 1987).

MALEBRANCHE, NICHOLAS, *De la recherche de la vérité*, ed. G. Rodis Lewis, 3 vols., in *Œuvres complètes*, ed. A. Robinet (2nd edn, Paris, 1972), i–iii.

—— *The Search after Truth*, trans. T. M. Lennon and P. J. Olscamp (Columbus, Oh., 1980).

MERSENNE, MARIN, *Les Préludes de l'harmonie universelle*, 8 vols. (Paris, 1634).

MILTON, JOHN, *Il Penseroso*, in *John Milton: A Critical Edition of the Major Works*, ed. S. Orgel and J. Goldberg (Oxford, 1991).

—— *Paradise Lost*, in *John Milton: A Critical Edition of the Major Works*, ed. S. Orgel and J. Goldberg (Oxford, 1991).

MORE, HENRY, *An Account of Virtue or Dr. More's Abridgment of Morals put into English*, trans. and abridged E. Southwell (London, 1690).

—— 'Cupid's Conflict', in *Cupid's Conflict annexed to Democritus Platonnisans*, ed. P. G. Stanwood (Berkeley and Los Angeles, 1968).

MORE, HENRY, *Enthusiasmus Triumphatus*, ed. M. V. De Porte (Berkeley and Los Angeles, 1966).

—— *The Immortality of the Soul*, ed. A. Jacob (Dordrecht, 1987).

NEWTON, ISAAC, *Opticks, Based on the Fourth Edition* (New York, 1979).

NICOLE, PIERRE, *De l'éducation d'un prince* (Paris, 1670).

—— *Essais de morale*, 4 vols. (Paris, 1672).

OVID, *Metamorphoses*, trans. M. M. Innes (Harmondsworth, 1955).

PASCAL, BLAISE, *Pensées*, trans. A. J. Krailsheimer (Harmondsworth, 1966).

—— *Entretien avec M. de Saci*, in *Œuvres complètes*, ed. L. Lafuma (Paris, 1963), 291–7.

PERKINS, WILLIAM, *The Art of Prophesying*, in *The Workes of that Famous and Worthie Minister of Christ, in the University of Cambridge, Mr. William Perkins*, 3 vols. (Cambridge, 1609), ii.

PLUTARCH, 'De Virtute Morali', in *Moralia*, trans. W. C. Helmbold, 16 vols., Loeb Classical Library (Cambridge, Mass., 1962), vi.

POUSSIN, NICOLAS, *Nicolas Poussin: Lettres et propos sur l'art*, ed. A. Blunt (Paris, 1964).

—— *Actes*, ed. André Chastel (Paris, 1960).

QUINTILIAN, *Institutio Oratoria*, 4 vols., trans. H. E. Butler, Loeb Classical Library (Cambridge, Mass., 1920).

REYNOLDS, EDWARD, *A Treatise of the Passions and Faculties of the Soul of Man* (London, 1640).

SENAULT, JEAN FRANÇOIS, *The Use of the Passions*, trans. Henry Earl of Monmouth (London, 1649).

SENECA, *Medea*, in *Tragedies*, trans. Frank Justus Miller, 3 vols., Loeb Classical Library (Cambridge, Mass, 1917), i.

SHAKESPEARE, WILLIAM, *Hamlet*, in *The Complete Works*, ed. S. Wells and G. Taylor (Oxford, 1988).

—— *Othello*, in *The Complete Works*, ed. S. Wells and G. Taylor (Oxford, 1988).

SIDNEY, PHILIP, *The Defense of Poesie*, in *The Prose Works*, ed. A. Feuillerat, 4 vols. (Cambridge, 1962), iii.

SMITH, JOHN, *The True Way or Method of Attaining to Divine Knowledge*, in *The Cambridge Platonists*, ed. C. A. Patrides (Cambridge, 1969).

—— *The Excellence and Nobleness of True Religion*, in *The Cambridge Platonists*, ed. C. A. Patrides (Cambridge, 1969).

SPINOZA, BARUCH, *Ethics*, in *The Collected Works of Spinoza*, ed. E. Curley, 2 vols. (Princeton, 1985), i.

WHICHCOTE, BENJAMIN, *The Use of Reason in Matters of Religion*, in *The Cambridge Platonists*, ed. C. A. Patrides (Cambridge, 1969).

WILKINS, JOHN, *Sermons Preached upon Several Occasions* (London, 1682).

WRIGHT, THOMAS, *The Passions of the Mind in General* (2nd edn, 1604), ed. W. Webster Newbold (New York, 1986).

Secondary Sources

ACKRILL, J. L., 'Aristotle's Definition of Psûche' in J. Barnes, Malcolm Schofield, and Richard Sorabji (eds.), *Articles on Aristotle*, iv. *Psychology and Aesthetics* (London, 1979), 65–75.

ADAM, MICHEL, 'L'Horizon philosophique de Pierre Charron', *Revue philosophique de la France et de l'Étranger*, 181 (1991), 273–93.
—— *Études sur Pierre Charron* (Bordeaux, 1991).
AIRAKSINEN, TIMO, 'Hobbes on the Passions and Powerlessness', *Hobbes Studies*, 6 (1993), 80–104.
ALANEN, LILLI, 'Reconsidering Descartes' Notion of the Mind–Body Union', *Synthese*, 106 (1996), 3–20.
ALLISON, HENRY E., *Benedict de Spinoza: An Introduction* (New Haven, 1987).
ARIEW, ROGER, 'Descartes and Scholasticism: The Intellectual Background to Descartes' Thought', in J. Cottingham (ed.), *The Cambridge Companion to Descartes* (Cambridge, 1992), 3–20.
—— 'Descartes and the Tree of Knowledge', *Synthese*, 92 (1992), 101–16.
ARMON JONES, CLAIRE, *Varieties of Affect* (London, 1991).
ATHERTON, MARGARET, 'Cartesian Reason and Gendered Reason', in Louise M. Antony and Charlotte Witt (eds.), *A Mind of One's Own: Feminist Essays on Reason and Objectivity* (Boulder, Colo., 1993), 19–34.
AYER, A. J., The *Problem of Knowledge* (Harmondsworth, 1956).
AYERS, MICHAEL, *Locke*, 2 vols. (London, 1991).
BAIER, ANNETTE, 'Cartesian Persons', in *Postures of the Mind* (London, 1985), 74–92.
BALDWIN, ANNA, and HUTTON, SARAH (eds.), *Platonism and the English Imagination* (Cambridge, 1994).
BARNOUW, JEFFREY, 'Passion as "Confused" Perception or Thought in Descartes, Malebranche and Hutcheson', *Journal of the History of Ideas*, 53 (1992), 397–424.
BEAVERS, ANTHONY F., 'Desire and Love in Descartes' Late Philosophy', *History of Philosophy Quarterly*, 6 (1989), 279–94.
BENHABIB, SEYLA, *Situating the Self: Gender, Community and Postmodernism in Contemporary Ethics* (Cambridge, 1992).
BENJAMIN, JESSICA, *The Bonds of Love* (London, 1990).
BENNETT, JONATHAN, *A Study of Spinoza's 'Ethics'* (Cambridge, 1984).
BEYSSADE, J.-M., 'L'Émotion intérieure/l'affect actif', in E. Curley and P.-F. Moreau (eds.), *Spinoza: Issues and Directions* (Leiden, 1990), 176–90.
BITBOL-HESPÉRIÈS, ANNIE, 'Le Principe de vie dans *Les Passions de l'âme*', *Revue philosophique de la France et de l'Étranger*, 178 (1988), 416–31.
BLUMENBERG, HANS, *The Legitimacy of the Modern Age*, trans. Robert M. Wallace (Cambridge, Mass., 1983).
BOAS, MARIE, *The Scientific Renaissance 1450–1630* (London, 1962).
BORDO, SUSAN, 'The Cartesian Masculinisation of Thought', in Sandra Harding and Jean O'Barr (eds.), *Sex and Scientific Enquiry* (Chicago, 1987), 247–64.
—— *The Flight to Objectivity: Essays on Cartesianism and Culture* (Albany, NY, 1987).
BRANDT, FRITHIOF, *Thomas Hobbes' Mechanical Conception of Nature* (London, 1928).
BRENNAN, TERESA, *History after Lacan* (London, 1993).
BRIGGS, JOHN C., *Francis Bacon and the Rhetoric of Nature* (Cambridge, Mass., 1989).
BROCKLISS, LAWRENCE W. B., *French Higher Education in the Seventeenth and Eighteenth Centuries: A Cultural History* (Oxford, 1987).
BRUNDELL, BARRY, *Pierre Gassendi: From Aristotelianism to a New Natural Philosophy* (Dordrecht, 1987).

CARR, THOMAS, *Descartes and the Resilience of Rhetoric* (Carbondale, Ill., 1990).

CASSIRER, ERNST, *The Platonic Renaissance in England* (London, 1953).

CHAPPELL, VERE, 'Locke on Freedom of the Will', in G. A. J. Rogers (ed.), *Locke's Philosophy* (Oxford, 1994), 101–21.

—— 'Locke on the Intellectual Basis of Sin', *Journal of the History of Philosophy*, 32 (1994), 197–208.

CHESNAU, C., 'Le Stoïcisme en France dans la première moitié du XVIIᵉ siècle: Les Origines', *Études franciscaines*, 2 (1951), 384–410.

CHEW, AUDREY, *Stoicism in Renaissance English Literature* (New York, 1988).

CLARKE, DESMOND M., *Descartes' Philosophy of Science* (Manchester, 1982).

—— *Occult Powers and Hypotheses: Cartesian Natural Philosophy under Louis XIV* (Oxford, 1989).

COCKING, J. M., *Imagination: A Study in the History of Ideas* (London, 1991).

COLMAN, JOHN, *Locke's Moral Philosophy* (Edinburgh, 1983).

COPENHAVER, BRIAN C., and SCHMITT, CHARLES B., *Renaissance Philosophy* (Oxford, 1992).

COTTINGHAM, JOHN, *Descartes* (Oxford, 1986).

—— 'The Intellect, the Will and the Passions: Spinoza's Critique of Descartes', *Journal of the History of Philosophy*, 26 (1988), 239–57.

—— 'Cartesian Dualism: Theological, Metaphysical and Scientific', in id. (ed.), *The Cambridge Companion to Descartes* (Cambridge, 1992), 236–57.

—— 'Cartesian Ethics: Reason and the Passions', *Revue internationale de philosophie*, 50 (1996), 193–216.

CRAIG, EDWARD, *The Mind of God and the Works of Man* (Oxford, 1987).

CROCKER, 'Mysticism and Enthusiasm in Henry More', in S. Hutton (ed.), *Henry More (1614–1687): Tercentenary Studies* (Dordrecht, 1990), 137–55.

CURLEY, EDWIN, *Behind the Geometrical Method* (Princeton, 1988).

DAINVILLE, FRANÇOIS DE, *L'Éducation des Jésuites* (Paris, 1978).

DARMON, A., *Le Corps immatériels: Esprits et images dans l'œuvre de Marin Cureau de la Chambre* (Paris, 1985).

DARWALL, STEPHEN, *The British Moralists and the Internal 'Ought', 1640–1740* (Cambridge, 1995).

DEBUS, ALLEN G., *The English Paracelsians* (London, 1965).

DELAHUNTY, R. J., *Spinoza* (London, 1985).

DELEUZE, GILLES, *Spinoza et le problème de l'expression* (Paris, 1968).

DELLA ROCCA, MICHAEL, 'Spinoza's Metaphysical Psychology', in Don Garrett (ed.), *The Cambridge Companion to Spinoza* (Cambridge, 1996).

DEPRUN, JEAN, 'Qu'est ce qu'une passion de l'âme?', *Revue philosophique de la France et de l'Étranger*, 178 (1988), 407–13.

DICKER, GEORGE, *Descartes: An Analytical and Historical Introduction* (Oxford, 1993).

DIHLE, ALBRECHT, *The Theory of the Will in Classical Antiquity* (Berkeley and Los Angeles, 1982).

DONAGAN, ALAN, *Spinoza* (Hemel Hempstead, 1988).

DUNCAN, DAVID ALLEN, 'Mersenne and Modern Learning: The Debate over Music', in Sorell (ed.), *Rise of Modern Philosophy*, 89–106.

DUNN, J. M., ' "Bright enough for all our purposes": John Locke's Conception of a Civilised Society', *Notes and Records of the Royal Society of London*, 43 (1989), 133–53.

ELSTER, JON (ed.), *Rational Choice* (Oxford, 1986).

FERREYROLLES, GERARD, 'L'Imagination en procès', *XVIIe Siècle*, 177 (1992), 468–79.

FLAX, JANE, 'Political Philosophy and the Patriarchal Unconscious: A Psychoanalytic Perspective on Epistemology and Metaphysics', in Nancy Tuana and Rosemary Tong (eds.), *Feminism and Philosophy* (Boulder, Colo., 1995), 227–9.

FOTI, VÉRONIQUE M., 'The Cartesian Imagination', *Philosophy and Phenomenological Research*, 46 (1986), 631–42.

FOUCAULT, MICHEL, *Madness and Civilisation: A History of Insanity in the Age of Reason*, trans. Richard Howard (London, 1967).

FOX KELLER, EVELYN, *Reflections on Gender and Science* (New Haven, 1985).

—— 'From Secrets of Life to Secrets of Death', in *Secrets of Life: Essays on Language, Gender and Science* (London, 1992).

FRANCE, PETER, *Rhetoric and Truth in France: Descartes to Diderot* (Oxford, 1972).

FRANKEL, LOIS, 'Hows and Whys: Causation Unlocked', *History of Philosophy Quarterly*, 7 (1990), 409–29.

FRANKFURT, HARRY G., *Demons, Dreamers and Madmen* (Indianapolis, 1970).

FUMAROLI, MARC, *L'Âge d'éloquence* (Geneva, 1980).

GABBEY, ALAN, 'Force and Inertia in the Seventeenth Century: Descartes and Newton', in Stephen Gaukroger (ed.), *Descartes: Philosophy, Mathematics and Physics* (Sussex, 1980), 230–320.

—— 'The Mechanical Philosophy and its Problems: Mechanical Explanations, Impenetrability and Perpetual Motion', in J. C. Pitt (ed.), *Change and Progress in Modern Science* (Dordrecht, 1985), 9–84.

GALLAGHER, DAVID, 'Thomas Aquinas on the Will as Rational Appetite', *Journal of the History of Philosophy*, 29 (1991), 559–84.

GARBER, DANIEL, 'Descartes and Occasionalism', in Nadler (ed.), *Causation in Early-Modern Philosophy*, 9–26.

GASCOIGNE, JOHN, *Cambridge in the Age of the Enlightenment: Science and Religion from the Restoration to the French Revolution* (Cambridge, 1989).

GATENS, MOIRA, 'Power, Ethics and Sexual Imaginaries', in *Imaginary Bodies* (London, 1996), 125–45.

—— 'Spinoza, Law and Responsibility', in *Imaginary Bodies* (London, 1996), 108–24.

GAUKROGER, STEPHEN, *Cartesian Logic: An Essay on Descartes' Conception of Inference* (Oxford, 1989).

—— (ed.), *The Uses of Antiquity* (Dordrecht, 1991).

—— *Descartes: An Intellectual Biography* (Oxford, 1995).

GETTIER, E., 'Is justified true belief knowledge?', in A. Phillips Griffiths (ed.), *Knowledge and Belief* (Oxford, 1967), 144–6.

GIBSON, JAMES, *Locke's Theory of Knowledge* (Cambridge, 1917).

GIGLIONI, GUIDO, 'Automata Compared: Boyle, Leibniz and the Debate on the Notion of Life and Mind', *British Journal for the History of Philosophy*, 3 (1995), 249–78.

GILSON, ÉTIENNE, *Introduction a l'étude de St. Augustin* (Paris, 1929).

GOMBAY, ANDRÉ, 'L'Amour et jugement chez Descartes', *Revue philosophique de la France et de l'Étranger*, 178 (1988), 447–55.

GORDON, ROBERT M., 'The Passivity of Emotions', *Philosophical Review*, 95 (1986), 371–92.

GREEN, LAWRENCE A., 'Aristotle's *Rhetoric* and Renaissance Views of the Emotions', in P. Mack (ed.), *Renaissance Rhetoric* (Basingstoke, 1994), 1–26.

GREENBLATT, STEPHEN, *Renaissance Self-Fashioning from More to Shakespeare* (Chicago, 1980).

GREENSPAN, PATRICIA, *Emotions and Reasons: An Inquiry into Emotional Justification* (London, 1988).

GRENE, R. A., 'Whichcote, the Candle of the Lord and Synderesis', *Journal of the History of Ideas*, 52 (1991), 617–44.

GROSZ, ELIZABETH, *Volatile Bodies* (Bloomington, Ind., 1994).

GUEROULT, MARTIAL, *Malebranche*, 3 vols. (Paris, 1955).

—— 'The Metaphysics and Physics of Force in Descartes', in Stephen Gaukroger (ed.), *Descartes: Philosophy, Mathematics and Physics* (Sussex, 1980), 169–229.

—— *Descartes' Philosophy Interpreted according to the Order of Reasons*, trans. Roger Ariew (Minneapolis, 1985).

GUILLAUME, JEAN, 'Cleopatra Nova Pandora', *Gazette des Beaux-Arts*, 80 (1972), 185–94.

GUTTENPLAN, SAMUEL (ed.), *A Companion to the Philosophy of Mind* (Oxford, 1994).

HANSON, DONALD W., 'Science, Prudence and Folly in Hobbes' Political Philosophy', *Political Theory*, 21 (1993), 634–64.

—— 'The Meaning of "Demonstration" in Hobbes' Science', *History of Political Thought*, 11 (1990), 587–626.

HARRINGTON, THOMAS MORE, 'Pascal et la philosophie', in Jean Mesnard, Thérèse Goyet, Philippe Sellier, and Dominique Descotes (eds.), *Actes du colloque tenn à Clermont-Ferrand 1976* (Paris, 1979), 36–43.

HARRISON, PETER, 'Descartes on Animals', *Philosophical Quarterly*, 42 (1992), 219–27.

—— 'Animal Souls, Metempsychosis and Theodicy in Seventeenth-Century English Thought', *Journal of the History of Philosophy*, 31 (1993), 519–44.

HATFIELD, GARY, 'The Senses and the Fleshless Eye: The *Meditations* as Cognitive Exercises', in A. Oksenberg Rorty (ed.), *Essays on Descartes' Meditations* (Berkeley and Los Angeles, 1986), 45–79.

—— 'Descartes' Physiology and its relation to his Psychology', in John Cottingham (ed.), *The Cambridge Companion to Descartes* (Cambridge, 1992), 335–70.

HENRY, JOHN, 'Occult Qualities and the Experimental Philosophy: Active Principles in Pre-Newtonian Matter Theory', *History of Science*, 24 (1986), 335–81.

—— 'Medicine and Pneumatology: Henry More, Richard Baxter and Francis Glisson's *Treatise on the Energetic Nature of Substance*', *Medical History*, 31 (1987), 15–40.

HERBERT, GARY B., *Thomas Hobbes: The Unity of Science and Moral Wisdom* (Vancouver, 1989).

HEYD, MICHAEL, 'Enthusiasm in the Seventeenth Century', *Journal of Modern History*, 53 (1981), 258–80.

HIRSCHMAN, ALBERT O., *The Passions and the Interests: Political Arguments for Capitalism before its Triumph* (Princeton, 1977).

HOLLIS, MARTIN, *Models of Man* (Cambridge, 1977).

HOOPES, R., *Right Reason in the English Renaissance* (Cambridge, Mass., 1962).

HUNDERT, E. J., 'Augustine and the Divided Self', *Political Theory*, 20 (1992), 86–103.

HURLEY, PAUL, 'The Appetites of Thomas Hobbes', *History of Philosophy Quarterly*, 7 (1990), 391–407.

HUTCHISON, KEITH, 'What Happened to Occult Qualities in the Scientific Revolution?', *Isis*, 73 (1982), 233–53.

—— 'Supernaturalism and the Mechanical Philosophy', *History of Science*, 21 (1983), 297–333.

HUTTON, SARAH, 'Lord Herbert of Cherbury and the Cambridge Platonists', in S. Brown (ed.), *The Routledge History of Philosophy*, v. *British Philosophy and the Age of Enlightenment* (London, 1996), 20–42.

IRIGARAY, LUCE, *An Ethics of Sexual Difference*, trans. C. Burke and G. C. Gill (London, 1993).

JACKSON, FRANK, 'Mental Causation', *Mind*, 105 (1996), 377–409.

JACQUOT, JEAN, and JONES, HAROLD WHITMORE, Introduction to *Thomas Hobbes: Critique du 'De Mundo' de Thomas White* (Paris, 1973), 9–102.

JAGGER, ALISON, 'Love and Knowledge: Emotion in Feminist Epistemology', in Ann Garry and Marilyn Pearsall (eds.), *Women, Knowledge and Reality* (Boston, 1989), 129–56.

JAMES, E. D., *Pierre Nicole, Jansenist and Humanist: A Study of his Thought* (The Hague, 1972).

JAMES, SUSAN, 'Spinoza the Stoic', in Sorell (ed.), *Rise of Modern Philosophy*, 289–316.

—— 'Internal and External in the Work of Descartes', in J. Tully (ed.), *Philosophy in an Age of Pluralism* (Cambridge, 1994), 7–19.

—— 'Power and Difference: Spinoza's Conception of Freedom', *Journal of Political Philosophy*, 4 (1996), 207–28.

—— 'Ethics as the Control of the Passions', in M. Ayers and D. Garber (eds.), *The Cambridge History of Seventeenth-Century Philosophy* (Cambridge, 1997), vii 5.

JAMES, WILLIAM, *The Principles of Psychology* (Cambridge, Mass., 1983).

JOHNSTON, DAVID, *The Rhetoric of Leviathan: Thomas Hobbes and the Politics of Cultural Transformation* (Princeton, 1986).

JOLLEY, NICHOLAS, 'Descartes and the Action of Body on Mind', *Studia Leibnitiana*, 19 (1987), 41–53.

JOY, LYNN SUMIDA, *Gassendi the Atomist* (Cambridge, 1987).

JUDOWITZ, DALIA, 'Vision, Representation, and Technology in Descartes', in David Michael Levin (ed.), *Modernity and the Hegemony of Vision* (Berkeley and Los Angeles, 1993), 63–86.

KAHN, CHARLES, 'The Discovery of the Will: From Aristotle to Augustine', in J. M. Dillon and A. A. Long (eds.), *The Question of Eclecticism* (Berkeley and Los Angeles, 1989), 234–59.

KAINZ, HOWARD P., *Active and Passive in Thomist Angelology* (The Hague, 1972).

KAMBOUCHNER, DENIS, *L'Homme des passions: Commentaires sur Descartes*, 2 vols. (Paris, 1996).

KENNY, NEIL, '"Curiosité" and Philosophical Poetry in the French Renaissance', *Renaissance Studies*, 5 (1991), 263–76.

KESSLER, ECKHARD, 'The Transformation of Aristotelianism during the Renaissance', in Sarah Hutton and John Henry (eds.), *New Perspectives on Renaissance Thought: Essays in the History of Science, Education and Philosophy; In Memory of Charles B. Schmitt* (London, 1990), 137–47.

KESSLER, WARREN, 'A Note on Spinoza's Conception of an Attribute', in Maurice Mandelbaum and Eugene Freeman (eds.), *Spinoza: Essays in Interpretation* (La Salle, Ill., 1975), 191–4.

KRAYE, JILL, 'The Philosophy of the Italian Renaissance', in G. Parkinson (ed.), *Routledge History of Philosophy*, iv. *The Renaissance and Seventeenth-Century Rationalism* (London, 1993), 16–69.

KRETZMANN, NORMAN, 'Philosophy of Mind', in id. and Eleanor Stump (eds.), *The Cambridge Companion to Aquinas* (Cambridge, 1993), 128–59.

KRISTELLER, PAUL O., 'Stoic and Neo-Stoic Sources of Spinoza's *Ethics*', *History of European Ideas*, 5 (1984), 1–15.

KRISTEVA, JULIA, 'Motherhood according to Giovanni Bellini', in *Desire and Language* (New York, 1980).

KUKLICK, BRUCE, 'Seven Thinkers and How They Grew' in Richard Rorty, J. B. Schneewind, and Q. Skinner (eds.), *Philosophy in History* (Cambridge, 1984), 125–39.

LA PORTE, JEAN, *Le Cœur et la raison selon Pascal* (Paris, 1957).

LAZZERI, CHRISTIAN, *Force et justice dans la politique de Pascal* (Paris, 1993).

LENNON, THOMAS M., 'Occasionalism and the Cartesian Metaphysic of Motion', *Canadian Journal of Philosophy*, suppl. vol. 1 (1974), 29–40.

LEVI, ANTHONY, *French Moralists: The Theory of the Passions 1585–1649* (Oxford, 1964).

LLOYD, GENEVIEVE, *The Man of Reason: 'Male' and 'Female' in Western Philosophy* (London, 1984).

—— 'Maleness, Metaphor and the "Crisis" of Reason', in L. M. Antony and C. Witt (eds.), *A Mind of One's Own: Feminist Essays on Reason and Objectivity* (Boulder, Colo., 1993), 69–83.

—— *Part of Nature: Self-Knowledge in Spinoza's 'Ethics'* (Ithaca, NY, 1994).

—— *Spinoza and the 'Ethics'* (London, 1996).

LOEB, LOUIS E., *From Descartes to Hume: Continental Metaphysics and the Development of Modern Philosophy* (Ithaca, NY, 1981).

—— 'The Priority of Reason in Descartes', *Philosophical Review*, 99 (1990), 3–43.

LOSEE, JOHN, *A Historical Introduction to the Philosophy of Science* (Oxford, 1980).

LOSONSKY, MICHAEL, 'John Locke on Passion, Will and Belief', *British Journal for the History of Philosophy*, 4 (1996), 267–83.

LYONS, BRIDGET C., *Voices of Melancholy: Studies in Literary Treatments of Melancholy in Renaissance England* (London, 1971).

McCULLOCH, GREGORY, *The Mind and its World* (London, 1995).

MACDONALD ROSS, GEORGE, 'Occultism and Philosophy in the Seventeenth Century', in A. J. Holland (ed.), *Philosophy, its History and Historiography* (Dordrecht, 1983), 95–115.

MacINTOSH, J. J., 'St. Thomas on Angelic Time and Motion', *Thomist*, 59 (1995), 547–76.

McKENNA, ANTONY, 'Pascal et le corps humain', XVIIᵉ *Siècle*, 177 (1992), 481–94.

McLAUGHLIN, PETER, 'Descartes on Mind–Body Interaction and the Conservation of Motion', *Philosophical Review*, 102 (1993), 155–82.

MANDELBAUM, MAURICE, *Philosophy, Science and Sense Perception* (Baltimore, 1964).

MARIN, LOUIS, 'Mimesis et description: Ou la curiosité à la méthode de l'âge de Montaigne à celui de Descartes', in E. Copper, G. Perini, F. Solinas (eds.), *Documentary Culture: Florence and Rome from Grand Duke Ferdinand I to Pope Alexander VII . . . Papers from a colloquium held at the Villa Spelman, Florence, 1990* (Villa Spelman Colloquia, 3; Baltimore, 1992), 23–47.

MARION, JEAN-LUC, 'L'Obscure évidence de la volonté: Pascal au-delà de la "Regula Generalis" de Descartes', *XVIIᵉ Siècle*, 46 (1994), 639–56.

MATHERON, ALEXANDRE, 'Spinoza et le pouvoir', *Nouvelle critique*, 109 (1977), 45–51.

—— 'Amour, digestion et puissance selon Descartes', *Revue philosophique de la France et de l'Étranger*, 178 (1988), 407–13.

—— 'Spinoza and Euclidean Arithmetic: The Example of the Fourth Proportional', trans. David Lachterman, in Marjorie Grene and Debra Nails (eds.), *Spinoza and the Sciences* (Boston Studies in the Philosophy of Science, 90; Dordrecht, 1986), 125–50.

MAURER, A., 'Descartes and Aquinas on the Unity of a Human Being: Revisited', *American Catholic Philosophical Quarterly*, 67 (1993), 497–511.

MERCER, CHRISTIA, 'The Vitality and Importance of Early-Modern Aristotelianism', in Sorell (ed.), *Rise of Modern Philosophy*, 33–67.

MERCHANT, CAROLYN, *The Death of Nature: Women, Ecology and the Scientific Revolution* (San Francisco, 1980).

MERLAN, PHILIP, *From Platonism to Neo-Platonism* (The Hague, 1968).

MERLEAU-PONTY, MAURICE, 'The Eye and the Mind', in James M. Edie (ed.), *The Primacy of Perception* (Evanston, Ill., 1964), 159–90.

MEYER, MICHEL, *Le Philosophe et les passions* (Paris, 1991).

MICHAEL, EMILY and FRED S., 'Two Early-Modern Concepts of Mind: Reflecting Substance and Thinking Substance', *Journal of the History of Philosophy*, 27 (1989), 29–48.

MONSARRAT, GILLES D., *Light from the Porch: Stoicism and English Renaissance Literature* (Paris, 1984).

MORFORD, MARK, *Stoics and Neo-stoics: Rubens and the Circle of Lipsius* (Princeton, 1991).

MORGAN, J., *Godly Learning: Puritan Attitudes towards Reason, Learning and Education, 1560–1640* (Cambridge, 1986).

MULLIGAN, LOTTE, ' "Reason", "Right Reason" and "Revelation" in Mid-Seventeenth Century England', in Brian Vickers (ed.), *Occult and Scientific Mentalities in the Renaissance* (Cambridge, 1984), 357–401.

NADLER, STEVEN, 'Malebranche and the Vision in God: A Note on *The Search after Truth*, III. 2. iii', *Journal of the History of Ideas*, 52 (1991), 309–14.

—— (ed.), *Causation in Early-Modern Philosophy* (Pennsylvania, 1993).

NATOLI, CHARLES M., 'Proof in Pascal's Pensées: Reason as Rhetoric', in David Wetsel (ed.), *Meaning, Structure and History in the Pensées of Pascal* (Paris, 1990), 19–34.

NEUBERG, MARC, 'Le Traité des passions de L'âme de Descartes et les théories modernes de l'émotion', *Archives de philosophie*, 53 (1990), 479–508.

NEWHAUSER, RICHARD, 'Towards a History of Human Curiosity: A Prolegomenon to its Medieval Phase', *Deutsche Vierteljahrsschrift für Literaturwissenschaft und Geistesgeschichte*, 56 (1982), 559–75.

NOURRISSON, JEAN FÉLIX, *La Philosophie de St. Augustin*, 2 vols. (Paris, 1865).

NOZICK, ROBERT, *Philosophical Explanations* (Oxford, 1981).

NUSSBAUM, MARTHA, *The Therapy of Desire: Theory and Practice in Hellenistic Ethics* (Princeton, 1994).

O'DALY, GERARD, *Augustine's Philosophy of Mind* (Berkeley and Los Angeles, 1987).

O'NEILL, EILEEN, 'Mind–Body Interactionism and Metaphysical Consistency: A Defence of Descartes', *Journal of the History of Philosophy*, 25 (1987), 227–45.

OAKLEY, JUSTIN, *Morality and the Emotions* (London, 1992).

—— 'Varieties of Virtue Ethics', *Ratio*, 9 (1996), 128–52.

OESTREICH, GERHARD, *Neostoicism and the Early-Modern State* (Cambridge, 1982).

OSLER, MARGARET J. (ed.), *Atoms,* Pneuma *and Tranquillity: Epicurean and Stoic Themes in European Thought* (Cambridge, 1991).

—— *Divine Will and the Mechanical Philosophy* (Cambridge, 1994).

PACCHI, ARRIGO, 'Hobbes and the Passions', *Topoi*, 6 (1987), 111–19.

PADEL, RUTH, *In and Out of the Mind: Greek Images of the Tragic Self* (Princeton, 1992).

PANOFSKY, DORA and ERWIN, *Pandora's Box: The Changing Aspects of a Mythical Symbol* (2nd edn, New York, 1965).

PANOFSKY, ERWIN, *The Life and Art of Albrecht Dürer* (Princeton, 1955).

PARK, KATHERINE, 'The Organic Soul', in Schmitt and Skinner (eds.), *Cambridge History of Renaissance Philosophy*, 464–84.

PARKER, PHILIPPE, 'Définir la passion: Corrélation et dynamique', *Seventeenth-Century French Studies*, 18 (1996), 49–58.

PASSMORE, JOHN, 'Locke and the Ethics of Belief', in A. Kenny (ed.), *Rationalism, Empiricism and Idealism* (Oxford, 1986).

PETTIT, PHILIP, *The Common Mind* (Oxford, 1993).

PIPPIN, ROBERT B., *Modernity as a Philosophical Problem: On the Dissatisfactions of European High Culture* (Oxford, 1991).

POPKIN, RICHARD, *The History of Scepticism from Erasmus to Spinoza* (Berkeley and Los Angeles, 1979).

—— *The Third Force in Seventeenth-Century Thought* (Leiden, 1992).

POTTS, D. C., 'The Concept of Right Reason in Seventeenth-Century Thought', *Newsletter of the Society for Seventeenth-Century French Studies*, 5 (1983), 134–41.

RHODES, NEIL, *The Power of Eloquence in English Renaissance Literature* (Hemel Hempstead, 1992).

RICHARDSON, R. C., 'The "Scandal" of Cartesian Interactionism', *Mind*, 91 (1982), 20–37.

RILEY, PATRICK, 'Divine and Human Will in the Philosophy of Malebranche', in S. Brown (ed.), *Nicolas Malebranche, his Philosophical Critics and Successors* (Assen, 1991), 49–80.

ROBERTS, ROBERT C., 'What an Emotion Is: A Sketch', *Philosophical Review*, 97 (1988), 183–209.

RODIS LEWIS, GENEVIÈVE, *Le Problème de l'inconscient et le cartésianisme* (Paris, 1950).

—— 'Malebranche "moraliste"', *XVIIᵉ Siècle*, 159 (1988), 175–90.

—— 'La Domaine propre de l'homme chez les cartésians', in *L'Anthropologie cartésienne* (Paris, 1990), 39–99.

—— 'Augustinisme et cartésianisme', in *L'Anthropologie cartésienne* (Paris, 1990), 101–25.

RORTY, AMELIE OKSENBERG, 'From Passions to Emotions and Sentiments', *Philosophy*, 57 (1982), 159–72.

—— 'Cartesian Passions and the Union of Mind and Body', in *Essays on Descartes' 'Meditations'* (Berkeley and Los Angeles, 1986), 513–34.

—— 'Spinoza on the Pathos of Idolatrous Love and the Hilarity of True Love', in Robert C. Solomon and Kathleen M. Higgins (eds.), *The Philosophy of (Erotic) Love* (Lawrence, Kan., 1991), 352–71.

—— 'Descartes on Thinking with the Body', in John Cottingham (ed.), *The Cambridge Companion to Descartes* (Cambridge, 1992), 371–92.

ROZEMOND, MARLEEN, 'The Role of the Intellect in Descartes' Case for the Incorporeity of the Mind', in S. Voss (ed.), *Essays in the Philosophy and Science of René Descartes* (Oxford, 1993), 97–114.

RUDOLPH, R., 'Conflict, Egoism and Power in Hobbes', *History of Political Thought*, 7 (1986), 73–88.

RYLE, GILBERT, *The Concept of Mind* (London, 1949).

SAUNDERS, JASON L., *Justus Lipsius: The Philosophy of Renaissance Stoicism* (New York, 1955).

SCHAFFER, SIMON, 'Occultism and Reason', in A. J. Holland (ed.), *Philosophy, its History and Historiography* (Dordrecht, 1983), 117–43.

SCHEMAN, NAOMI, 'Though this be method yet there is madness in it: Paranoia and Liberal Epistemology', in Louise M. Anthony and Charlotte Witt (eds.), *A Mind of One's Own: Feminist Essays on Reason and Objectivity* (Boulder, Colo., 1993), 145–70.

SCHMALTZ, TAD M., 'Descartes and Malebranche on Mind and Mind–Body Union', *Philosophical Review*, 101 (1992), 281–325.

—— 'Human Freedom and Divine Creation in Malebranche, Descartes and the Cartesians', *British Journal for the History of Philosophy*, 2 (1994), 35–42.

—— 'Malebranche's Cartesian and Lockean Colours', *History of Philosophy Quarterly*, 12 (1995), 387–403.

SCHMITT, CHARLES B., *Aristotle and the Renaissance* (Cambridge, Mass., 1983).

—— and Skinner, Quentin (eds.), *The Cambridge History of Renaissance Philosophy* (Cambridge, 1988).

SCHOULS, PETER A., *Descartes and the Enlightenment* (Montreal, 1989).

—— *Reasoned Freedom: John Locke and the Enlightenment* (Ithaca, NY, 1992).

—— 'John Locke: Optimist or Pessimist ?', *British Journal for the History of Philosophy*, 2 (1994), 51–73.

SCRUTON, ROGER, *From Descartes to Wittgenstein* (London, 1981).

SELLIER, PHILIPPE, *Pascal et St. Augustin* (Paris, 1970).

—— 'Le cœur chez Pascal', *Cahiers de l'association internationale des études françaises*, 40 (1988), 285–95.

—— 'Sur les fleuves de Babylone', in David Wetsel (ed.), *Meaning, Structure and History in the Pensées of Pascal* (Paris, 1990), 33–44.

SEPPER, DENNIS L., 'Hobbes, Descartes and Imagination', *Monist*, 71 (1988), 526–42.

—— 'Descartes and the Eclipse of Imagination', *Journal of the History of Philosophy*, 32 (1994), 573–603.

SHAPIN, STEPHEN, *A Social History of Truth: Civility and Science in Seventeenth Century England* (Chicago, 1994).

SHAPIRO, BARBARA, *Probability and Certainty in Seventeenth-Century England* (Princeton, 1983).

SHEA, WILLIAM R., *The Magic of Numbers and Motion* (Canton, Mass., 1991).

SHUGER, DEBRA K., *Sacred Rhetoric: The Christian Grand Style in the English Renaissance* (Princeton, 1988).

—— *Habits of Thought in the English Renaissance: Religion, Politics and the Dominant Culture* (Berkeley and Los Angeles, 1990).

SKINNER, QUENTIN, 'Thomas Hobbes on the Proper Signification of Liberty', *Transactions of the Royal Historical Society*, 40 (1990), 121–51.

—— *Reason and Rhetoric in the Philosophy of Hobbes* (Cambridge, 1996).

SMITH, PETER, and JONES, O. R., *The Philosophy of Mind: An Introduction* (Cambridge, 1986).

SOLOMON, JULIE ROBIN, 'From Species to Speculation: Naming the Animals with Calvin and Bacon', in Elizabeth D. Harvey and Kathleen Okruhlik (eds.), *Women and Reason* (Ann Arbor, 1992), 77–162.

SOLOMON, ROBERT C., *The Passions* (Notre Dame, Ind., 1983).

SORELL, TOM, *Hobbes* (London, 1986).

—— *Descartes* (Oxford, 1987).

—— (ed.), *The Rise of Modern Philosophy* (Oxford, 1993).

SPELMAN, W. M., *John Locke and the Problem of Depravity* (Oxford, 1988).

SPRAGENS, THOMAS A. Jun., *The Politics of Motion: The World of Thomas Hobbes* (London, 1973).

STOCKER, MICHAEL, 'Intellectual Desire, Emotion and Action', in A. Oksenberg Rorty (ed.), *Explaining Emotions* (Berkeley and Los Angeles, 1980), 323–38.

STRAUSS, LEO, *The Political Philosophy of Hobbes: Its Basis and Its Genesis*, trans. Elsa M. Sinclair (Chicago, 1963).

TAYLOR, CHARLES, *Sources of the Self* (Cambridge, 1989).

TIMMERMANS, B., 'Descartes et Spinoza: De l'admiration au désir', *Revue internationale de philosophie*, 48 (1994), 275–86.

TOPLISS, PATRICIA, *The Rhetoric of Pascal* (Leicester, 1966).

TOULMIN, STEPHEN, *Cosmopolis: The Hidden Agenda of Modernity* (New York, 1990).

TUANA, NANCY, *The Less Noble Sex: Scientific, Religious and Philosophical Conceptions of Women's Nature* (Bloomington, Ind., 1993).

TUCK, RICHARD, 'Hobbes' Moral Philosophy', in T. Sorell (ed.), *The Cambridge Companion to Hobbes* (Cambridge, 1996), 175–207.

TULLY, JAMES, 'Governing Conduct: Locke on the Reform of Thought and Behaviour', in *An Approach to Political Philosophy: Locke in Contexts* (Cambridge, 1993), 179–241.

VAILATI, EZIO, 'Leibniz on Locke on Weakness of Will', *Journal of the History of Philosophy*, 28 (1990), 213–28.

VAN DELFT, LOUIS, *Le Moraliste classique: Essai de définition et de typologie* (Geneva, 1982).

—— *Littérature et anthropologie: Nature humaine et caractère à l'âge classique* (Paris, 1993).

VAN DER PITTE, FREDERICK, 'Intuition and Judgment in Descartes' Theory of Truth', *Journal of the History of Philosophy*, 26 (1988), 453–70.

VICARI, E. PATRICIA, *The View from Minerva's Tower: Learning and Imagination in The Anatomy of Melancholy* (Toronto, 1989).

VICKERS, BRIAN, 'The Power of Persuasion: Images of the Orator, Elyot to Shakespeare', in James M. Murphy (ed.), *Renaissance Eloquence: Studies in the Theory of Renaissance Rhetoric* (Berkeley and Los Angeles, 1983), 411–35.

—— 'Rhetoric and Poetics', in Schmitt and Skinner (eds.), *Cambridge History of Renaissance Philosophy*, 715–45.

—— (ed.), *Occult and Scientific Mentalities in the Renaissance* (Cambridge, 1984).

VON LEYDEN, W. (ed.) *John Locke: Essays on the Law of Nature* (Oxford, 1954).

WALKER, DANIEL P., *The Ancient Theology: Studies in Christian Platonism from the Fifteenth to the Eighteenth Centuries* (London, 1972).

WALLACH, JOHN R., 'Contemporary Aristotelianism', *Political Theory*, 20 (1992), 613–41.

WARNER, MARTIN, *Philosophical Finesse: Studies in the Art of Rational Persuasion* (Oxford, 1989).

WATSON, R. A., 'Malebranche, Models and Causation', in Nadler (ed.), *Causation in Early-Modern Philosophy*, 75–91.

WETSEL, DAVID, *L'Écriture et le Reste: The Pensées of Pascal in the Exegetical Tradition of Port Royal* (Columbus, Oh., 1981).

WETZEL, MARC, 'Action et passion', *Revue internationale de philosophie*, 48 (1994), 303–26.

WILSON, MARGARET DAULER, *Descartes* (London, 1978).

—— 'Superadded Properties: The Limits of Mechanism in Locke', *American Philosophical Quarterly*, 16 (1979), 143–50.

WOOLHOUSE, ROGER S., *Descartes, Spinoza, Leibniz: The Concept of Substance in Seventeenth-Century Thought* (London, 1993).

XANTA, LEONTINE, *La Renaissance du Stoïcisme au XVIe siècle* (Paris, 1914).

YHAP, JENNIFER, *The Rehabilitation of the Body as a Means of Knowing in Pascal's Philosophy of Experience* (Lewiston, NY, 1991).

YOLTON, JOHN W., *Locke and the Compass of Human Understanding* (Cambridge, 1970).

—— *Thinking Matter: Materialism in Eighteenth-Century Britain* (Oxford, 1983).

—— *Locke: An Introduction* (Oxford, 1985).

Index